THE ANTI-OEDIPUS COMPLEX

The Anti-Oedipus Complex critically explores the post-'68 dramatic developments in Freudo-Lacanian psychoanalysis and cultural theory. Beginning with the decline of patriarchy and the master, exemplified by Freud's paean for the Father, the revolutionary path was blown wide open by anti-psychiatry, schizoanalysis and radical politics, the complex antinomies of which are traced here in detail with the help of philosophers, such as Nietzsche, Baudrillard, Levinas, Steiner, Žižek, Badiou, Derrida and Girard, as well as theologians, analysts, writers, musicians and film makers.

In this book, Rob Weatherill, starting from the clinic, considers the end of hierarchies, the loss of the Other, new subjectivities, so-called 'creative destruction', the power of negative thinking, revolutionary action, divine violence and new forms of extreme control. Where does this leave the psychoanalytic clinic – adrift in postmodern indifference? Does the engagement of the Radical Orthodoxy movement offer some hope? Or should we re-situate psychoanalysis within a 'genealogy of responsibility' (Patočka/Derrida) as it emerges out of the sacred demonic, via Plato and Christianity?

The Anti-Oedipus Complex will be of interest to psychoanalysts, psychotherapists, counsellors, social workers and scholars in critical theory, philosophy, cultural theory, literary theory and theology.

Rob Weatherill is a practising and supervisory psychoanalyst in private practice in Dublin. He has been a lecturer on psychoanalysis and taught psychoanalytic theory and practice in University College Dublin, Trinity College Dublin and the Milltown Institute of Philosophy and Theology. He has written several books and over thirty papers and articles in journals and other media, in Ireland and abroad.

THE ANTI-OEDIPUS COMPLEX

Lacan, Critical Theory and Postmodernism

Rob Weatherill

Routledge
Taylor & Francis Group
LONDON AND NEW YORK

First published 2017
by Routledge
2 Park Square, Milton Park, Abingdon, Oxon OX14 4RN

and by Routledge
711 Third Avenue, New York, NY 10017

Routledge is an imprint of the Taylor & Francis Group, an informa business

British Library Cataloguing in Publication Data
A catalogue record for this book is available from the British Library

Library of Congress Cataloguing in Publication Data
Names: Weatherill, Rob, author. Title: The anti-Oedipus complex: Lacan, critical theory and postmodernism / Rob Weatherill. Description: 1 Edition. | New York: Routledge, 2017. | Includes bibliographical references and index. Identifiers: LCCN 2016033707 | ISBN 9781138692343 (hardback) | ISBN 9781138692350 (pbk.) | ISBN 9781315532493 (ebook) Subjects: LCSH: Oedipus complex. | Psychoanalysis. | Critical theory. | Lacan, Jacques, 1901-1981. Classification: LCC BF175.5.O33 W43 2017 | DDC 150.19/5—dc23LC record available at https://lccn.loc.gov/2016033707

ISBN: 978-1-138-69234-3 (hbk)
ISBN: 978-1-138-69235-0 (pbk)
ISBN: 978-1-315-53249-3 (ebk)

Typeset in Bembo
by Out of House Publishing

The subject, Descartes' *cogito*, Kant's transcendental subject, now lies exposed to the drive *per se*; to affects – potentially, raw anxiety, panic and horror. As suggested, all "human" suffering rests in this void of the pure subject. In this gap between the pre-Symbolic Real of the biological machinery of emotion and the Symbolised feelings of the autobiographical self lie everything that must be defended in this work: the sense of the tragic, the melancholic, and so on, followed by the critical necessity for the elaboration of language (the treasure house of signifiers) *qua* containing and subjectivising of affect, the telling of dreams, stories, narratives, etc. All the contemporary "emancipatory" signs point in the *reverse* direction, towards core unmediated machinic "experience" – paroxysms of sex, convulsions of violence and the death drive.

CONTENTS

PREFACE

These are strange times. If you are on the Left you believe that ecological catastrophe is already upon us. If you are on the Right, you understand the world as threatened by religious warriors, Jihadists, like those that greeted the new century with their "spectacular" on the World Trade Center, in which they killed 3,000 people, but openly admit that they would have preferred a multiple of that.[1] Levels of catastrophic anxiety are high. In 1915 the late Italian self-styled seismologist Raffaele Bendandi predicted that an earthquake, "the big one," would strike Rome on 11 May 2011. As the date neared, panic spread across social media. Many Italians fled Rome amid fears of a catastrophe despite reassurances from seismologists and political leaders. Ironically, an earthquake struck Spain instead.

Strange times and apocalyptic times on many levels – ecological, financial, social, techno-digital, racial and so on. We are more than ready to believe in and anticipate catastrophic events, all part of the chaos and non-linearity of postmodernity. Apocalyptic time was preceded by the linear time of modernity, where one advance leads to another, or one breakthrough leads to another, until now, the zero-point of break-down, flux and fibrillation. Prior to modernity and progress, there was cyclical time reflecting the rhythms of nature and the seasons when nothing much changed over time.

Psychoanalysis was central to modernity, and with modernity's passing, the end of psychoanalysis has been signalled many times, by the usual suspects.[2] In France, there was *The Black Book of Psychoanalysis*,[3] which asks: Did Freud lie? Does psychoanalysis cure? Is psychoanalysis the best way to understand who we are? What should we think of other therapies? This was followed a year later by *The Anti-Black Book of Psychoanalysis*.[4] The *Black Book* itself had been preceded by *The Black Book of Communism*,[5] which describes a history of political and civilian repression by Communist countries, including genocides, extrajudicial executions, deportations and artificial famines.

Although psychoanalysis was quite unlike Marxism, which in the guise of Communism has been responsible for crimes against humanity, *both* have been overtaken by postmodernist mixing, levelling and neutralisation. Big ideas now have constantly to reinvent themselves. As far as psychoanalysis is concerned, we must commend Lacan and the Lacanians in this respect.

Still interesting and evolving are the varied theoretical approaches within psychoanalysis, representing a sophisticated theory of human subjectivity, offering a practical philosophy to facilitate reflection and orientation. It stands as the only real alternative to reductionist psychiatric biological approaches to human suffering *that take no account of the Real of human subjectivity*. The alarming thing now is that people have no time for critical self-reflection and see no point in it. We are losing this way of understanding ourselves.

Freud pointed to three key narcissistic conceits: 1) We are (not) the centre of the universe (Copernicus); 2) We are (not) superior beings (Darwin) set apart from animals; 3) We are (not) masters of ourselves because of the unconscious (Freud).[6] Our self-mastery is further undermined in a number of ways. We are the product of historical forces and economic determinism (Marx). The product of an impersonal will to power (Nietzsche). We are passive vehicles for "selfish gene" propagation (Dawkins). At the bio-genetic level, the mind and cognitive processes function like a complex computer (Moravec, Kurzweil). Self-consciousness is exposed as "user illusion" (Nørretranders). Structuralism implies that language has no need of us (Saussure). Extreme pleasure, *jouissance*, rules (later Lacan). The notion of "emergent properties," self-organisation, autopoeisis (Maturana) relegates the subject to contingency and ephemerality. Thus, with each turn of the modernist screw, the one-time nobility and dignity of the human subject approaches zero.

Famously, Leibniz asked, 'Why is there something rather than nothing?'[7] Today, as Baudrillard suggests, we should turn the question around: *Why is there nothing rather than something*?[8] As Lyotard says, 'With the megalopolis what the West realises and diffuses is its nihilism. It is called development. The question it asks of the philosopher is: what remains that is worthwhile when the presentation of every object is stamped with the unreality of its passage?'[9]

The sense of the unreal, which some still people feel keenly, signals that that reality has crashed, but life goes on. The "crash of reality" may be just another weary cliché, but if you take the crash seriously and your palate is not so jaded, you will feel the insane desperation of Nietzsche's madman screaming in the square, not about God being dead, but reality itself. The effects of the crash are everywhere. What passes for "reality" now is nevertheless shadowed by this loss – loss of values, loss of truth, of objectivity, of solid ground, of orientation and so on. This will become apparent on every page that follows.

Anti-genesis.
In the beginning *We* created heaven and earth
And the earth was full and bright
And We said, "let there be darkness."
And We joined the light with the darkness

We saw that it was good.
And We said the earth brings forth grass, the herb yielding seed and
 the trees with fruit
According to natural selection.
And We saw that that was good.
We saw that the great whales and every creature that moveth
As well as cattle and creeping insects and every animal, possessed DNA.
We made men and women, parents and children, equal.
We said go forth and make others like yourselves.
And We said unto them go forth and enjoy without limit
And We saw everything and used every animal that gave us pleasure
And saw that it was good.
We claimed that from star-dust We are made
And unto stars We shall return and We said
Eat of the tree of knowledge and live forever.

And the Lord said, I will destroy man whom I have created
From the face of the earth.
Both man and beast and the creeping thing, and the fowls of the air,
The clones, the genetically modified, the cyborgs, the freaks,
 the aliens, the psychotics;
For it repenteth me that I have made them.
The earth also was corrupt before God,
And the earth was filled with violence.

And again We said unto them go forth and enjoy without limit.
We say – go forth and enjoy without limit.
Without limit!

Journalist Peter Hitchens[10] recalls a moment in Dallas at the City's Museum of Art, seeing Thomas Hart Benton's painting of the Prodigal Son (1939). Unlike the errant son in the New Testament story (Luke 15) returning home exhausted materially and morally to be greeted with love and welcome, Benton's Prodigal Son has arrived home *too late*. Nobody has seen him from afar; no one has run to greet and anoint him. There is no forgiveness, no music or dancing. Nothing. Instead, he is gaping with his hand to his mouth, at the ruin of his family home outlined ominously against the cold sky. Instead of the fatted calf, there is an animal skeleton lying on unkempt grass with a dead tree at his feet. The landscape is dead. He is alone.

To complete the triad of sons, consider the fate of the rebellious son in the Old Testament, Deuteronomy 21:19: *If a father has a rebellious son … then shall his father and mother lay hold on him and bring him unto the elders of the city, and they shall say unto the elders of his city, "Our son is rebellious, he will not obey our voice; he is a glutton and a drunkard." And all the men of the city shall stone the son until he die.* Thus the Christian Prodigal Son, forever loved and cherished, is opposed to the archaic son, who is punished to death by the elders. Key to what we will elaborate here is the postmodern Benton son, alone and isolated. He gets *no* welcome or punishment. *He is alone.*

***

If psychoanalysis allows itself to be duped by a narcissistic culture then the project is doomed, not because of a *Black Book*, not because it is untrue, or out of date, or fails to cure, and so on, but because it itself has become unethical and thus unreal. What follows here is an attempt to rethink psychoanalysis without giving ground to narcissistic forces. Freud commented upon 'what makes it necessary at all for our mental life to pass *beyond the limits of narcissism* and to attach the libido to objects', by saying, 'we must begin to love in order not to fall ill, and we are bound to fall ill if, in consequence of frustration, we are unable to love'.[11] Our ability 'to love and to work' is attributed to Freud by Erik Erikson, but what Freud said in the *Civilisation* book was, 'The communal life of human beings had, therefore, a two-fold foundation: the compulsion to work, which was created by external necessity, and the power of love …'.[12] Freud also characterised psychoanalysis as 'a cure through love'.[13] The founder of psychoanalysis in Ireland, Hanaghan, was very clear that the neurotic and the psychotic subject remains caught in the web of incestuous love-hate relationships and a certain unwillingness to resolve them. For Hanaghan, 'All these sicknesses are due to our spiritual retreat from life. We do not love and we are not loved'.[14] The desert blooms.

This work attempts to square up fully to this complex challenge of desire *with* responsibility. This question was central in *Forgetting Freud?*[15] Here, however, we must be prepared to follow desire to the end, without indifference, without retreat, to establish the new coordinates in the aftermath of '68.

If the Oedipus complex signifies our ongoing fraught entanglements with the ambivalent relationships of childhood, the *Anti*-Oedipus complex signifies a *false* freedom. If a true freedom/resolution of Oedipus is ever possible, Anti-Oedipus is not it. Anticipating what will follow, we will outline some key themes of the Anti-Oedipus complex: 1) Excess of hate over love often turned against the self. 2) Retreat from Otherness of the other sex and the other generation, in favour of the self and the Same. 3) Rejection of and hatred for authority of any kind. 4) Predisposition to pre-Oedipal aims, infantile, demanding, "relating" to part objects. 5) The imaginary and the virtual displace the Symbolic register. 6) Implied by the notion of "complex," a certain pseudo-stability, even an intense resistance to change. 7) Disavowal of reality, leading to borderline phenomena. 8) The replacement of the Ego Ideal and social values in favour of the tyrannical and narcissistic Ideal Ego on the one hand and archaic superego on the other. 9) Failure to initiate and/or maintain relationships and the social bond. 10) Indifference to these developments.

The question must also be posed: *Is it possible to live and thrive outside the Oedipal frame altogether?*

Towards the end of *Totem and Taboo*, Freud summarises his thinking thus: 'The beginning of religion, morals, society and art all converge in the Oedipus complex'.[16] Notwithstanding that post-Freudian psychoanalysis has moved away from this bold assertion from Freud's middle period, we can properly ask now where indeed have religion, morals, society and art gone? *Totem and Taboo* was published just a year before the Great War and the beginning of the long emptying. Freud's words were prophetic.

Notes

1 www.thereligionofpeace.com/ documents daily the numbers of people, mostly Muslims, who are killed in the global jihad. It subtitles itself, "one body at a time." It tells us there have been more than 26,000 deadly terror attacks since 9/11.
2 Grunbaum, A., 1984, Crews, F., 1993, Webster, R., 1995.
3 Mayer, C., Borch-Jacobsen, M., Cottraux, M.J., and Pleux, D., 2005.
4 Miller, J.-A., 2006.
5 Courtois, S., 1997.
6 Freud, S., 1916–1917: 285. See also Weatherill, R., 1998: 1.
7 Leibniz, G.W., 1714: 4.
8 Baudrillard, J., 1995: 2.
9 Lyotard, J.-F., 1993: 22.
10 Hitchens, P., 2010: 78ff.
11 Freud, S., 1914b: 85, italics added.
12 Freud, S., 1930 (1929), 101.
13 Freud, S., in a letter to Jung quoted in Bettelheim, B., 1983: iv.
14 Hanaghan, J., 1957: 160. Hanaghan was the founder of psychoanalysis in Ireland in the 1930s. He was analysed by Douglas Bryan (a founding member of the British Psychoanalytic Association, analysed by Freud). He created the Irish Psychoanalytic Association in 1942, which exists to this day. He wanted to bring to Freudian psychoanalysis a radical Christian perspective.
15 See also Weatherill, R., 2011.
16 Freud, S., 1913: 165.

ACKNOWLEDGEMENTS

Extracts taken from *Anti-Oedipus: Capitalism and Schizophrenia* and *A Thousand Plateaus: Capitalism and Schizophrenia*, © Gilles Deleuze and Felix Guattari, translated by Brian Massumi, 2000, The Athlone Press, used by permission of Bloomsbury Publishing Plc. Also, extracts from *Anti-Oedipus: Capitalism and Schizophrenia* and *A Thousand Plateaus: Capitalism and Schizophrenia* by Gilles Deleuze and Felix Guattari, translated by Robert Hurley, Mark Seem and Helen R. Lane, translation copyright © 1977 by Viking Penguin Inc. Used by permission of Viking Books, an imprint of Penguin Publishing Group, a division of Penguin Random House LLC. Lastly, I want to acknowledge permission to quote from *A Thousand Plateaus: Capitalism and Schizophrenia* by Gilles Deleuze and Felix Guattari, translated by Brian Massumi. Copyright © 1987 by the University of Minnesota Press. Originally published in French as *Mille Plateaux*, volume 2 of *Capitalisme et Schizophrenie*, 1980 by Editions de Minuit, Paris.

Some of the ten chapters that follow have formed part of presentations in conferences, workshops, seminars and periodicals over recent years in Ireland and aboard. Chapter 1 was part of an informal presentation to the Lacan Study Group in Dublin in the fall of 2012. Chapter 5 is an extended and modified version of an article published online in *The International Journal of Žižekian Studies*: 'Žižek: silence and the real desert' www.Žižekstudies.org/index.php/ijzs/article/view/162/256. Chapter 6 is an extended version of a talk given in Cambridge University to the Centre for Research in the Arts, Social Sciences and Humanities (CRAASH): 'Analysis against therapy; speaking out' (March 2011). Chapter 7 is based on a paper presented for trainee analysts in London at the Site for Contemporary Psychoanalysis in 2011. Chapter 8 is a modified and lengthened version of a paper 'New subjectivities in the virtual world', given to IFPP in September 2011, and subsequently published in *Lacunae* (APPI International Journal for Lacanian Psychoanalysis) Issue 10, 10 May 2015, pp. 103–26. Chapter 9 is a modified version of 'Psychoanalysis and the Inhuman', the key presentation in a day-long seminar in University College Dublin, 'Psychoanalysis in Culture, Society & Politics: Critical Reading of Rob Weatherill's *Forgetting Freud: Is Psychoanalysis in Retreat*?' under the auspices of The(e)ories: Critical Theory & Sexuality Studies: UCD Humanities. Part of the Afterword is in preparation for an article in *Lacunae* (Issue 13 Autumn 2016) entitled 'Turning Right: Part 2'.

1

LACAN AND THE FATHER

Wanted – dead or alive

My colleagues and I are discussing Lacan's *Seminar 17* in a Dublin Lacanian reading group in 2012. I am a reluctant participant. Most are young students, fresh from college steeped in Lacanian psychoanalysis and cultural theory. I am old and my orientation is not automatically left-ideological or strictly Lacanian.

My formation was in biological science. During the 1970s, I studied the psychoanalysis of Freud at first, then Melanie Klein and Bion. I read widely on my own and with others in a study group, and towards the end of that decade I like many others became interested in anti-psychiatry, gestalt, Zen and various "active" therapeutic approaches. In the 1980s, Lacan was introduced to Ireland by Dr Cormac Gallagher[1] and Lacan's work became increasingly influential in Irish psychoanalysis thereafter. I undertook two long analyses during this early time totalling about 15 years of between *two* and at one time *four* sessions a week. While I continue to understand Lacan to be an exceptional thinker, I became wary of his equally exceptional hold over people's theory and practice of psychoanalysis and try to make this clear at every opportunity. Furthermore, my days in the front-line service of secondary teaching led me increasingly to immerse myself in writings concerned with the developing crisis in the social.

It is my turn to present some aspect of this important *Seminar 17* (1969–70) on the Four Discourses,[2] which is Lacan's response to *les événements de mai* (Lacan, 1968). As is well known, Lacan's response to the students was quite sceptical, telling them that as hysterics they want a new master and they will surely get one! 'The revolutionary aspiration has only a single possible outcome – as ending up as the master discourse' (207). This iconic warning of Lacan's echoes both forwards and backwards through all the contemporary revolutionary "springtimes."

This seminar was a turning point in Lacanian theory. Instead of *one* symbolic register with its set of societal rules guaranteeing social cohesion based on the Oedipus complex, there have arisen a number of discourses. Lacan takes particular note of the shift from the Master discourse to the University discourse – the discourse of knowledge based in the universities, with student demonstrations erupting across the Western world.

This seminar was only three years before Lacan's famous *Seminar 20* (Lacan, 1972–1973).[3] By this point, Lacan has situated himself within the postmodern libidinal economy of "sexual non-rapport" in which stable forms of social cohesion have begun to disintegrate and the free-wheeling individualistic modes of pleasure become legitimised over and against the basic matrix of marriage and family. For my colleagues in the study group, inhabiting a post-Oedipal world, this is entirely natural and unproblematic. If you have been steeped in one ideology of cultural studies and you are convinced that it is the *only* progressive position to take, and everyone else agrees, you will be non-judgemental and value all things equally and indifferently. With *one* exception: where the ideology of cultural relativism itself is questioned, where personal "freedom" itself seems threatened. At that point you will be very judgemental, as we shall see. Therefore "concern" about the social crisis, about cultural collapse,[4] or relativism *per se*, is a *non sequitur*.

Jouissance

What does the Oedipus complex prohibit or allow? This is an old question for psychoanalysis. Lacan plunges straight in![5] It is a question of surplus *jouissance*, the *jouissance* that we believe brings happiness, which is for that reason excluded. For Lacan, this is the entire meaning of the Oedipus complex.

The concept of surplus *jouissance* (French '*plus-de-jouir*') was inspired by Marx's concept of surplus value.[6] The *objet petit a*[7] is the excess of pleasure which has no use value, and which persists for the sake of *jouissance*, a pleasure for the sake of pleasure, as a "substance" in and of itself. This excess is what is barred by the Oedipus complex, so as to retain and maintain the essential Oedipal link between pleasure *and value* which is culturally desirable. Beyond Oedipus or without Oedipus, value evaporates into value-less pointless and excess pleasure. Use value becomes exchange value, pure exchangeability – fluidity without anchorage or referent, a kind of pure excess unto death. Lacan follows Freud, beginning with the pleasure principle, the principle of least tension or homeostasis that must be maintained for life to subsist. For Lacan, however, *jouissance* overruns the pleasure principle. Lacan emphasises, 'it is explicitly around masochism, conceived only in the dimension of the search for this ruinous *jouissance*, that Freud's entire text revolves' (46). And like Freud, he links *jouissance* with the death drive.

We are creatures with material needs, but we are also beings that have a *surplus jouissance*, as a result of our being language animals. This also works the other way: *language uses us*. Language employs and enjoys us! He links this enjoyment to the existence of God: 'He – with a capital H – enjoys that he is *jouissance*' (66). Thus, from Lacan's structuralist point of view, once one has laid 'this apparatus of signifiers [language] over the physical world' (49), thus constraining things, entropy starts, wasting starts, *jouissance* starts, by way of compensation.

I break off breathlessly from Lacan's mystifying text for a moment, thinking about *jouissance*, wasting, entropy and excess – enjoyment unto death. I am reminded that the outgoing governor, John Lonergan, of the ironically named Mountjoy prison in Dublin asked the rhetorical question – *have you ever seen a smiling or a happy addict*? He was alluding to the discovery of widespread drug addiction within the prison system in Ireland. Maybe, also, he had in mind the lobby that advocates the liberalisation of the drug laws. 'But what did Lonergan mean?' ask two of my colleagues suddenly and more or less together. 'What right does Lonergan or anyone else have to talk about another's *jouissance*? We do not know what brings the other enjoyment. We must not assume that addicts cannot enjoy'. There is no point in my appealing to the ruinous state of areas of greater Dublin, or other towns and cities around Ireland, laid waste by drug addiction and the crime and degradation that follow. Your *jouissance* is your business. Period.

What I have encroached upon and offended is the Lacanian understanding of the human subject as a singularity, a once-off assemblage, unique, with her own destiny and absolute freedom to be, to exist, to conduct her life, use her body *in any way she chooses*, including a "ruinous" wasting, entropic way. From this perspective, analogous to God's regard for each one of us absolutely, no *jouissance* can be judged pathological *per se*. Does this assertion of the subject's singularity preclude any intervention or any criticism on the part of the analyst or observer?

My colleagues' exclamations raise the question as to *what precisely is jouissance*? It is a term that can encompass everything! It can represent the most sublime experience, the most extreme pleasure and the direst distress. From a limited worldly viewpoint it cannot be understood. From our position of relative ignorance of how the other enjoys, *jouissance* must not be interfered with, appraised or judged. Analogous to the Catholic view that joy and suffering are incomprehensible to finite beings – beyond human understanding – not so for God; Lacan equates *jouissance* and God.

It is *the Word* that divides, while *jouissance* is *one*. The Word negates the infinite harmony of, for instance, the lilies of the field. Lacan cites Luke 12:27: those lilies with their whole body given over to *jouissance*! He continues, 'It is perhaps infinitely painful to be a plant – each stage of its growth, identical to a formless sensation' (77). Heidegger described animals as poor in the world. He spoke of pain and suffering permeating the whole animal realm. Schelling spoke of the infinite melancholy of living nature. Romans 8:22: *The whole creation groaneth and travaileth in pain together until now*, until the arrival of the Word, the arrival of the Symbolic. So when Jesus says *I am the way the truth and the life* is he is speaking about his speechless pain, his infinite melancholy, his infinite *jouissance*? Lacan refers to de Sade and his appeal to allow nature its murderous operation to create new forms. 'What is he doing', asks Lacan, 'if not displaying his impotence to be anything other than the instrument of divine *jouissance*' (66).

My colleagues defend the addict's enjoyment, akin to this *divine jouissance*, at the most extreme end of our hedonistic culture of enjoyment. The addict has had the "courage" to go to this ultimate point and therefore what right does the fearful Lonergan or anyone else have to make comment on or judgement about this. *Jouissance*, according to Lacan, is the 'sister of truth', likewise hidden from us, situated within discourse, which by its *re*-presentative nature cannot include everything, all at once. By converse: within *jouissance*, *everything* (*is nothing*).

With the title of the seminar, *The Other Side of Psychoanalysis*, Lacan stresses *l'envers*, the other side, the lining (as in lining of a jacket), and *endriot*, the outside: 'the lining doesn't explain the outside', and, '*envers* is assonant with *verité*, truth' (54). Analogously, *wunsch zu schlafen* – the wish to continue sleeping – is the key to the dream's operation. Or, as Lacan says, a dream wakes you just as 'it might let drop the truth, so that the only reason one wakes up is so as to continue dreaming' (57), to continue in the hallucinatory state, on the outside, or dreaming – hallucinating while awake as Bion emphasises. We wake before the horror of the Real, the *other* side, the truth, the *jouissance* of the story-dream. The truth and its sister *jouissance* are incendiary.[8] Thus, truths remain stubbornly hidden.

Lacan points out that Freud's theorising always remains close to *jouissance* and its sister truth. Once on the path of *jouissance*, there is no knowing where it will lead.[9] Lacan likens *jouissance* to the jar of the Danaïdes: 'It begins with a tickle and ends in a blaze of petrol' (72). Incendiary! The Danaïdes were the fifty daughters of Danaus, who were forced to marry their cousins, the fifty sons of Danaus's twin brother Aegyptus, the mythical king of Egypt. All but one stabbed their husbands to death on the wedding night with daggers their father had provided. They were punished in the Underworld by having to fill leaky jars with water for ever. They represent, like Sisyphus, the deathly futility of a repetitive task that can never be completed.

Lacan, unlike Freud, wanted to distance psychoanalysis from biology. In particular, he stressed that *jouissance* has nothing to do with biology as such. Thinking of sex and *secare*, to cut, he says 'the entire game revolves around the phallus' (75). And speaking of the privileged organ itself, he says that its *jouissance* is isolated. He emphasises its local and exceptional quality. Under the prevailing conditions of phallogocentrism – the logic of male power in patriarchy – it may be 'infinitely painful' to be a woman. He says, 'woman lends herself to *jouissance* by daring the mask of repetition. She presents herself here as what she is, as the institution of masquerade'.[10] Lacan refers to the specifically feminine *jouissance* which is a surplus, 'because she … plunges her roots, like a flower, down into *jouissance* itself' (78). Here is the "earth mother" or maybe Freud's "elemental woman" with her rootedness in the Real, possibilities for repetition and wild pleasure beyond any phallic logic!

As the theory goes, the little man will renounce the (feminine) *jouissance*, i.e. renounce the mother, via castration and the Oedipus complex. Thus the woman is produced as a sexual object precisely by not being what *he* is.

Therefore, sexuation is vastly asymmetric requiring the male subject to distance himself from this "foreign *jouissance*," this Other side. From the translator's notes we glean "Other" can also mean obscene, the bad side, evil and so on, of psychoanalysis. The woman distances herself too, but with her roots in *jouissance* as well. Thus hysterics implicitly know 'that language runs off the rails (in respect of) the magnitude of what she is capable of revealing concerning *jouissance*' (34).[11]

Axiomatically for Lacan, the speaking subject is structured by a set of formal relations, referred to as a discourse; "beyond" is *jouissance*. Although Lacan also suggests that discourse and *jouissance* are said to be *woven together* like a Möbius strip. Thinking maybe of political passions running high, Lacan proposes that the '*only* discourse there is, and not just analytic discourse, is *the discourse of jouissance*, at least when one is hoping for the work of truth from it' (78, emphasis added). Therefore: 1) *jouissance* is on the other side of discourse; 2) *jouissance* is seamlessly woven into discourse; 3) revolutionary political discourse aiming at truth is (the half-sister of) *jouissance*.

Recall the story about the Tsars' punishment of their opponent involving ramming a long spike through the anus and then staking them out in the snow with a fur coat so that they would die slowly. More recently, Ben Judah (Standpoint May 16th, 2010), a journalist reporting on his travels in the Central Asian republics, formerly in the USSR, now "liberated" with their economies contracting by half in the last 20 years, their drug trade increasing, witnessed young men just smashing shops, schools and bus stations, and so on – the (political) discourse of *jouissance*?

Like Freud with his notion of organic repression, Lacan suggests that *jouissance* might be limited by "natural processes," but he rejects this notion as too comforting, rather like the "mollycoddling" of our 'nice sexual ambiance' (176–7). What is really key for Lacan, as opposed to non-Lacanian analysts, is that *jouissance* has little to do with natural biological processes and everything to do with 'the very origin of the signifier's coming into play' (177). With animals there is no gap between the body and *jouissance* in the absence of the signifier; *jouissance* is coincident upon the arrival, or the appearance of what he terms the 'unary' trait.[12]

Following 'the play of inscriptions', the mortification of the body (in Catholic terms), *jouissance* switches to the Other side. The word is the murder of the Thing-*jouissance*. Against all the integrationist rhetoric, joining hearts and minds, uniting thought and feeling, Lacan emphasises the cut, the rupture, the lack. And we will have cause to return to this trope again and again. For now, it is the signifier and *jouissance* that appear together.

In its "blazing" the subject is voided by *jouissance*. If you do away with the ego and rely only on the fading subject what chance have you *against jouissance*? Anyway, should we be "against" *jouissance*? In this seminar, Lacan notes with his usual sarcasm that the *International Journal of Psycho-Analysis* is celebrating the so-called "autonomous ego." Lacan insists this is a departure from the real Freud. This is quite misleading, because Freud came to understand that without the ego in its later subtle complexity and important agency, so many capacities become lost. Thus Freud spoke of the three impossible professions – education, governance and lastly analysis.[13] Without the ego you cannot make judgements, you have no reason, no morality and no defence. Without the ego's always threatened mastery, there can be no differentiation. The subject is quite literally too sub-*ject*, too cast-down, to make any choices worth the name, and therefore Lacan's joke about analytic "goodness" is well made, because, without the ego, there is indifference between "good" and "bad." Therefore his claim to "return to Freud" is disingenuous, as he regards the later Freud as quite un-Freudian. The indifference between good and bad, underscored by the absence of the more or less precisely judging ego, leads precisely to the confusion about whether or not the addict's *jouissance* can be criticised or even called into question, indeed whether it can be *analysed* at all. This is the effect of Lacan's reversal of Freud and indeed his imperilling of psychoanalysis. *We cannot, are not permitted to make a judgement about jouissance. The study group students are correct*!

Oedipus

The Oedipus complex is the knot/not which determines the subject's dividedness as normal/neurotic, paranoid or psychotic and/or as perverse. In the "discourse of the analyst,"[14] elaborated by Lacan, the analyst herself as "agent" occupies the zero position: the silent enigmatic analyst. She addresses the divided subject of the analysand (S-barred), who will in time produce S1, the master signifier(s), that shore up the neurosis, i.e. the subject's private belief systems. In the fourth position in the formula, in the place of *truth*, is S2, meaning precisely *knowledge* – an enigmatic knowledge, most likely a truth so important that it is an *ontological* truth that the mother, *qua* Oedipal mother, is *the* obstacle to desire *par excellence*.

David Blake Knox's short film, *A Mother's Love's a Blessing*,[15] beautifully illustrated this 'mother as obstacle' theme. The mother, played by the late Joan O'Hara, blocks the ever more pathetic attempts by her adult son, played by Pat Kinevan, to get a woman of his own. He ends up trying to shoot the mother but hits a dog, a bitch, instead. With *this* mother's love, the son becomes deranged, psychotic, and perverse.

Freud emphasises the importance of the father, which Lacan as a Catholic links immediately to an *all loving father*. The first thing to be loved in this world is the father. Freud claims in *Civilisation and its Discontents*, 'I cannot think of any need in childhood as strong as the need for a father's protection'.[16]

However, Lacan now describes this love of the father as a "myth" (99, 101), which is *Freud's defensive idealisation of the father* because now in contemporary political reality the father is castrated, he is a spent force, his rule is over. Lacan believes that it should have been his hysterical patients, Anna, Emma, and Dora, that should have guided him rather than the Oedipus complex, as he would have seen that everything regarding the father would then have been put in question.

At the site of "truth" in the "discourse of the Master" is the *divided* subject. What is repressed, i.e. below the bar, is that the master is in truth divided and fading; *the father is castrated*. This is Lacan's wish, in this time of Cultural Revolution, to underline the father's essential weakness.

Freud's "use" of the Oedipus myth, according to Lacan, makes the mythographers laugh. He goes on to say that anglophone psychoanalysts, who are not real psychoanalysts at all, are increasingly interested in the *nurturing* mother. However, the mother's desire *qua desiring* (as opposed to nurturing) is not something that is bearable – 'It will always wreak havoc. A huge crocadile in whose jaws you are – that's the mother. One never knows what might suddenly come over her and make her shut her trap' (112). You can be spared only by the phallus – 'It's the roller that shelters you, if, all of a sudden she closes it' (112). He is referring here to the phallic mother's desire, so commonly met with in analysis, who exerts complete control (with her weapon), 'for your own good', and knows you better than you know yourself. She frequently escapes detection because she is a mother! But she may be the criminal *par excellence*, in the disguise of love.[17] She uses the classic double bind: 'if you loved me you would obey me'. Or as Theodore Lidz has it: 'A mother imposes herself upon a child, hounds him so persistently that he can't make sense of what he does or see clearly how he can break loose from her'.[18]

Lacan says that the only way *he* has spoken about the Oedipus complex is in terms of the abstract notion of the "paternal metaphor." For Freud, Sophocles' play reveals that you kill your father and sleep with your mother, and the fact that Oedipus does not know that he has committed either crime is for Lacan 'a fine example of the unconscious' (114). Oedipus's unconscious? No! Not for Lacan, it is *Freud's* unconscious, that is on the side of the father and the Law, against the little criminal. Lacan laughs about the myth of primal father killed off by the sons who then discover their "brotherhood" in their shared guilt. It points to the opposite result from the Oedipus crime, namely, that the killing of this father leads *not to unfettered jouissance* (with the mother/women) but to the instantiation of the Law – another of Freud's wishes!

Freud or Lacan, notwithstanding, Oedipus brings about his tragic end because *he* wants to know the truth. Along with murder and *jouissance*, there is a third dimension, the analytic truth-telling one, that brings Oedipus to his sticky end. For Baudrillard, the Oedipus myth is not so much about the father and the mother, 'but the circular operation of and revelation and detection of crime'. By his detective work, Oedipus discovers himself to be the criminal. This truth-searching, Baudrillard calls 'the transpiration, the showing through, or the transparency of Evil'.[19] This tallies with our current political preoccupations: *all* masters/fathers are not only castrated, but criminals covering up the truth? Just as Oedipus, genuinely searching for the truth, uncovers a "criminal" in the end, who has (unconsciously) concealed that he is a criminal. For Baudrillard paradoxically, the virtual hyper-perfecting (of the world) via a similar unsparing transparency is the *uber*-crime itself – *the perfect crime*[20] – a crime without a criminal, without a victim and without a motive. Were it not for transpirations, for the little cracks, the failures, the sins – Oedipus, the father, the Master – perfection via transparency would achieve the final solution, the terrifying prospect of *total Law*. This is for later.

Returning to Lacan's revisionism, what Oedipus, Moses and the primal father have in common is that they are part of Freud's dream. Lacan believes: 'what we propose is to analyse the Oedipus complex as being Freud's dream' (117). 'The father's death. In effect, everyone knows that this appears to be the key to … what psychoanalysis is about' (119). Confusingly, his death might signal total freedom, on the one hand, or the instantiation of the Law on the other. For the radicals of that time and today no less, the father defeated, castrated, divided, exposed, etc., *frees us from the law*. Fat chance, declares Lacan, emphasising that this is what he means by the *other* side of psychoanalysis. Now, The 'other side' indicates a conservative side, because as he suggests, following Nietzsche and the news that God is dead, it 'does not seem to me to be the kind [of news] to liberate us, far from it'. Freud was linking the death of the father with the Law and religion in a political and repressive sense, i.e. 'it is the father who is recognized as *deserving of love*' (119, emphasis added), and that, as Lacan concedes, psychoanalysis maintains the field of religion. Far from a radical abolition of the law, it consolidates it. True, old father Karamazov said, if God is dead then everything is permitted, but Lacan rejoins, 'God is dead means *nothing is permitted anymore*' (120). In other words, the father's death establishes the prohibition of *jouissance* (out of love, guilt, reverence and respect), even more strongly than if God were still alive. "Nothing" in the strong sense: i.e. if God is dead, *nothing* – literally nothing – is permitted in a fundamentalist clampdown on anything. And this may yet be our geo-political fate during the twenty-first century. The aforementioned virtual utopia (Baudrillard) with its transparency will "see" all, surveil all, condemn all. Recall the Islamist banning of dancing, music, education for girls, and so on.

It is not just the father's death that counts, but specifically his *murder*. This is the manifest content of the dream – Freud's latent wish being that if the father is killed the law will be established. However, if father Laius had not been killed, then there would not have been any *jouissance* with Jocasta! Either way the father wins, which fulfils Freud's latent wish. Oedipus solves the riddle of sphinx (his first trial of truth) and thereby anticipates his own drama, having access to Jocasta and his fall into the second trap of truth. Upon realisation, the scales fall from his eyes or rather, as Lacan says, the *eyes fall from him* as he becomes the object of castration itself. And as Oedipus himself discovers the truth, he becomes the master by completing his own discourse – the master *who is castrated*, thus confirming the secret truth about the master that he is, in the place of truth, a divided subject (S-barred) i.e. castrated. This is the fate of every master – to be compromised, levelled, found out, rendered guilty in the end.

If we stay with the original myth, Oedipus did not murder his father in order to sleep with his mother. He believed his father was Polybus, i.e. 'The father is he who acknowledges us'. In Lacanian psychoanalytic theory, however, the father is reduced to a pure symbolic function independently of any real agent. As Lacan says in the *Ethics* seminar, 'in our theory, the sole function of the father is to be a myth, to be always only the name-of-the-father, or in other words the dead father'.[21] Thus, for Lacan, hedging his bets with the radicals within his midst, *father is worth more dead than alive*. Or, *the only good father is a dead one*. Thus ambiguity remains: the dead father *qua* dead is no threat to my permissiveness therefore I am free; and/or the dead father is *more* of a threat because he is dead and must be loved, atoned for, idealised and obeyed without end.

Freud's key volume, *The Interpretation of Dreams*, emerged from his own father's death. As he says, 'For this book has a further subjective significance for me personally – a significance which I grasped after I had completed it. It was, I found, a portion of my own self-analysis, my reaction to my own father's death – that is to say, to the most important event, the most poignant loss, of a man's life'.[22] Thus Lacan concludes, 'Freud thus wished to be guilty for his father's death … or the mark of something more hidden … a wish for his father to be immortal' (122). However, against Lacan, Freud might insist that his father's death was a *real* death and a *real* loss. Some things *are* real (even if they have a fantastical overlay)! There is some irony in the fact that Freud in the key text of psychoanalysis, in its introduction no less, is talking about real loss, something that cannot be exchanged, analysed or interpreted, something that really stands out as heart-felt, despite Lacan's best efforts. And this is a position Freud will maintain for the rest of his life.

Then in a further twist, Lacan adds, 'the fact that the dead father [*Urvater*] *is jouissance* presents itself to us as the sign of the impossible itself' (123). The dead father as *jouissance* places the impossible (myth) at the centre of Freud's work *Totem and Taboo*. This has nothing to do with the *psychology* of the primal father which provokes some derision – he who enjoys *all* the women was impossible for Lacan to imagine. Maybe – Lacan jokes one woman is normally enough. Freud's primal myth draws an equivalence between the Father and *jouissance*, i.e. the *Urvater* guards *jouissance* for himself alone. Žižek has cited the primal father's return to *life* in the figure of the paedophile. Disgraced Irish priest Father Brendan Smith leers into the cameras defiantly as he is carried off in disgrace to prison – disgrace to himself, to men and to the church in Ireland; his is the lecherous laughter of *jouissance* – the father as horrific who enjoys too much, not just women but little children as well.

While Lacan *et al.* laughed at Freud's mythic invention of the originary *jouisseur*, we know better now. Consider Žižek's recent account, as he recalls somewhat shamefully meeting some "ethnic cleansers" in Belgrade during the 1990s, when Milošević was still in power. They told him how nationalist fundamentalism works. 'We experience your Western European world as over-regulated. You are all the time bombarded by messages: be politically correct, don't be racist, don't be sexist, be careful what you eat, discipline yourself, no this, no that, no the other, etc., etc.'. And they countered, 'But, I want to smoke! I want to eat what I want, I want to beat women, rape them and so on … So becoming a nationalist, doing some ethnic cleansing, gives me this terrifying freedom'. Žižek extrapolates, 'when I think of Syria, Iraq, the area controlled by ISIS, there is not just religious fundamentalism, but also gang rapes, tortures, free-lance killings, extortions, etc.'. He concludes, 'With religious fundamentalism, it not just that there is no freedom, but what comes as well is this terrifying explosion of obscene freedom'.[23]

For Lacan unlike Freud, the father does not exist: 'the real father is nothing other than an effect of language' (127). This post-structural theorising could not be further from lived empirical reality. Worse still, sounding like a contemporary reproductive technician, Lacan states, 'There is only one real father which is the spermatozoon' (127). Further, the father is reduced to an agency of the symbolic structure – that of castration.

Gone over the intervening decades is Lacan's earlier extolling of the father, in *La Famille*, as the one who 'gives to reality a life-like density', or who facilitates 'the moment of sublimation which in man opens up dimensions of reality that extend beyond self-interest'.[24] And, 'the very structure of the Oedipal drama designates the father to give the function of sublimation its purest and therefore most eminent form'.[25] Here too Lacan underlines the central point: 'the death of the father at no matter what stage of development it occurs and according to the level of the Oedipus complex that has been achieved, *tends similarly to fixate the progress of reality and bring it to a halt*'.[26] Every bit as much as Freud, Lacan was suggesting that, 'whatever its future, this decline [of the paternal imago] constitutes a psychological crisis. It may even be that the emergence of psychoanalysis itself is linked to this very crisis'.[27]

Lacan recognised that the Oedipus complex as constituted was fragile because *within one and the same figure*, there would have to be repression *and* sublimation, resulting in the crystallisation of superego and the ego ideal, respectively. Possibilities for failure and neurosis/psychosis were legion, as were possibilities for creative (or uncreative) subversion of authority. Cultural advance could proceed on the basis of a repression that was in a kind of creative tension, or "dialectical crisis" between authority and subversion. Freud discovered Oedipus in old Europe, Vienna – the melting pot of the most diverse forms of family – when the Oedipal function was already bound to fail.

In primitive societies, the two paternal functions are not united in the one person: the son's aggressive erotic meets, encounters the radical otherness/mystery of the initiatory function of the totem, separately from the real father. Freud, on the other hand, wrestled with the double function in the one person: the father to be both idealised and followed on the one hand and fought against as a rival on the other.

Lacan "separates" the two functions with his understanding of the Imaginary father as rival (sometimes excessively idealised and/or denigrated) and the Symbolic father, the Name-of-the-father, the dead father, who signifies the Law and normativity in a culture. The neurotic/normative "solution" for the "Freudian" Oedipus complex is for the son to identify with the real father, whereas in the Lacanian formulation, the son will come to desire what the father possesses (the phallus) by accepting *not to be* the phallus for the mother – not to be her "little thing" – and, *not to have* the phallus either, but to desire its (ideal) promise into the future. *Not to be* (i.e. not to be identified with), but simply to be *nothing* in order to desire into the future; *Oedipus at Colonus*, who tears out his eyes – *rather not to be*. This represents the negation of the subject at the behest of the signifying chain, his disappearance under the signifier. Thus negated, the subject revives the fight with and against the Imaginary/real father as a defence against the Symbolic already dead father, because the former provides, what Lacan refers to as, 'the narrow footbridge thanks to which the subject does not feel directly invaded, directly swallowed up by the yawning chasm that opens up as pure and simple confrontation with the anguish of death'.[28]

The well known versions of the Oedipal drama, formulated by Lacanian psychoanalysis, can be summarised. The hysteric 'emphasises the Other, making herself into the object of the Other's desire so as to master it ... the hysteric orchestrates things in such a way as to ensure the Other's desire remains unsatisfied'.[29] The obsessional, forever controlling, 'seeks to neutralise or annihilate the Other'.[30] While the phobic feels the anxious need to 'shore-up a crucial element in the Other (this element being the Name-of-the-father), which although not altogether lacking, has a precarious status'.[31] In all three categories of neurosis, the paternal metaphor is more or less securely instantiated, whereas in perversion there is a refusal to give-up *jouissance* (in the Name-of-the-father), a refusal of the sacrifice of castration, but instead the perverse subject wants 'to make himself the instrument of the Other's *jouissance*',[32] while at the same time, 'perversion involves an attempt to prop up the law [to make the Other exist] so that limits can be set to *jouissance*'.[33] In psychosis, there is a complete foreclosure of the Name-of-the-father.

In *Seminar 3*, Lacan outlines *three* functions of the father. First, Freud's statement that Oedipal realisation is brought about by *aggression* between father and son. In other words it's by way of an imaginary conflict that symbolic integration takes place. His second point, taken from ethnological experience involving the phenomenon of the *couvade:* 'an imaginary realisation here takes place by the symbolic putting into play of conduct ... the hysterical pregnancy'. According to Masoni *et al.*, the *couvades* should be considered as the psychosomatic equivalent of primitive rituals of initiation into paternity.[34] The third point concerns the part played by the father in 'the begetting of soul, the begetting of mind'.[35] These are three *substantial* points that Lacan makes which when expanded underline Lacan's early commitment to the father, which for our purposes cannot be emphasised strongly enough, in stark contrast to the later theorising.

The first point, lost these days with our soft strategies, is that the father–son encounter is one of aggressive rivalry. After all, who could imagine that symbolic castration could occur without crisis? Freud said as much in his 1924 article "The dissolution of the Oedipus complex." Ferenczi objected to the use of the term "dissolution" (*Untergang*), whereas Freud himself had used an even stronger word, *Zertrümmerung* (demolition). What should we make of this, dissolution, demolition, shattering of the complex? Clearly, it signals the fear of punishment at the hands of the father. Freud writes about, 'the authority of the father or the parents is introjected into the ego, and therefore form[ing] the nucleus of the superego, which takes over the severity of the father and perpetuates his prohibition against incest'.[36] But Freud underlines, 'the process we have described is *more* than a repression. It is equivalent, if it is ideally carried out, to a destruction and abolition of the complex'. Freud justifies the use of the word "destruction" in relation to castration due to the collision of two opposite forces: of phallic ascendency of the libido (Lacan's imaginary phallic agency), on the one hand, and the fear or terror of retaliatory punishment from the father's superego on the other. Even the hated term "castration" is entirely appropriate for the violent shock involved.

Second, with regard to the *couvade*, and the usual simplistic interpretation of the phenomenon as testifying to men's envy of the woman's fecundity, this 'putting into play of conduct', this 'hysterical identification', should indeed be seen as an attempt to assume symbolic power, an initiation by proxy, equivalent to the paternal function.

And Lacan's third point takes the paternal project forward into future generations. Paternity goes beyond mere genetic continuity, but extends its spiritual reach into the future. 'From the presence of the male body, something is transmitted to the "I" that makes the child blossom', claims Cardinal Paul Josef Cordes. 'Whoever as an individual has never been generated or raised in the way by his father will have a limited self-esteem'.[37] *The begetting of soul, the begetting of mind* – we are back with Lacan's 'tender virile identification'. With the loss of fathers, the whole ecology of the social landscape changes. This "something" that is transmitted to the child from the father is ultimately indefinable. Without it, whatever it is, as Freud warned, a plague descends.

Lacan laughs a few decades later when someone says you know castration is only a fantasy. Not so says Lacan, 'castration is a real operation and it is introduced by the incidence of the signifier, no matter which, into the sexual relation'. He goes on, 'it is now a question of knowing what is meant by this castration, which is not a fantasy, and the result of which is that the only cause of desire is produced by this operation and that fantasy dominates the entire reality of desire, that is to say, the law' (129). Law, castration, loss and desire are the basic coordinates of human subjectivity as understood by psychoanalysis.

However, as we have seen the later Lacan reduces the Oedipus complex to a *dream* of Freud. Lacan refers to 'this residue of myth regulating the life of men'. And Patricia McCarthy, following Lacan, has suggested that the latent content of Freud's dream is the mythification of the real of enjoyment and unconscious knowledge, both of which being outside of language and asocial can *only* be symbolised via myth. As McCarthy summarises, 'This can be further imaged as unconscious knowledge [truth] and enjoyment [*jouissance*] forming the flipside or the other side of mythification'.[38] She suggests also, 'The problem with the Oedipal myth is that it is pressed into service in the manner of an all-purpose truth, covering up the [impossible] interface between discourse and enjoyment'.[39] Further, Cormac Gallagher queries, 'why did Freud leave the solid ground of experience [with Anna, Emmy, Dora …] and lead his followers onto a path that has proved to be ultimately sterile. It is not in the supposed knowledge of the myth of Oedipus that analysts can find their bearings but in the authentic knowledge that hysterical patients possess [pure gold] and are willing to reveal to those that have ears to hear'.[40] Jean Clavreul prefers the *ethic of the subject*, as opposed to the Oedipal discourse of the Master, who represses the truth. As we would say today, it is the hysteric who speaks truth to power. For Lacan, what the hysteric was saying in effect was: 'I want a man who knows how to make love' (204).

Lacan was drifting with the times? As he says, 'the Oedipal show cannot run indefinitely in forms of society that are losing the sense of tragedy to an ever greater extent'.[41] Should this not concern us? The father discredited. Everyone can freely hate the father without opposition. Žižek, a generation later, says: 'The Oedipal matrix of socialisation is no longer operative'.[42] With the father's symbolic role now discredited, the way is wide open for the return of the primal father – predatory, anal and perverse – on the look-out for his *jouissance* wherever he can get it, reversing the *Totem and Taboo* myth. He is back with a vengeance and can hardly believe his luck.

Lacanians are equivocal about the father, in spite of the role of the paternal name and its key function in the prevention of mental illness. Fink, for instance, takes all the panic about the father with a grain of salt. He then lists *all* the reasons why we *should* be so concerned! The rising percentage of single-parent families. Changes in ideology and discourse regarding sexual roles, thus 'the importance of men in families and of their symbolic roles as fathers is ever more widely contested'. More and more single women having children, rejecting the importance of Oedipal triangulation. More and more lesbian couples are raising children. There is an increase in divorce, with children being raised solely by their mothers. Feminist discourses are encouraging an anti-authoritarian attitude among men towards children. He concludes: 'the paternal function seems to be in danger of extinction in certain social milieus'.[43] But he draws no conclusion from this observation.

In a similar vein, Paul Verhaeghe speaks of the widespread cynicism and distrust of *any* symbolic function: 'this confronts us with the reversal of the primal myth, and thus with the loss of protection against *jouissance* and consequently a return to original chaos. The original myth installed binary gender differentiation; therefore, its reversal must have serious effect on this differentiation'.[44] He also noted the backlash in terms of predatory male *jouissance*, the growth of patriarchal fundamentalisms and new fascisms, and is aware too of the problems of young men who remain immature and anxious in the absence of fathers with which to identify, they are afraid of sexually desiring women, maybe choosing children instead as their sexual objects. Some men become perfect "mothers." In spite of acknowledging that 'Every social bond is heir to the Oedipal structure',[45] he contradicts himself by insisting that the real father is "superfluous"! J-A. Miller goes further, pronouncing 'we are in the exit phase in the age of the Father … we must leave the reign of the father'. Then remarkably, he refers to the Father as 'this plague',[46] thus precisely *reversing* the original Freudian insight about the Oedipal crime.

To summarise the reactions of psychoanalysts to the contemporary crisis of the father: 1) Carry on as usual; act as if nothing has really changed. The unconscious remains more or less as Freud described it. 2) Acknowledge the realities of borderline and narcissistic personality disorders and modify technique accordingly without referring to the Oedipus complex and the loss of the father. 3) "Update" psychoanalysis via the neurosciences and neuro-psychoanalysis. 4) Seek a rapprochement with Jung, New Age holism, Zen practices and counselling in general. 5) Assert that the "Names-of-the-father" are an adequate stand-in/linkage to prevent psychosis. 6) Normalise psychosis itself – it is just another interesting take on reality – and call it "ordinary psychosis."[47]

Levinas and paternity

In the main body of his work Lacan was referring to the paternal *function*, the "name" within the Symbolic, not the actual father. Lacanians tirelessly insist that it is not the *actual* father who installs this Symbolic function. Later, Lacan pluralises the concept to the Names-of-the-father:[48] i.e. whatever it takes to knit the Symbolic, Imaginary and Real together, whatever mythic function can make life liveable, a "regulating fiction," or in the 1970s Lacan will refer to a "tool" to stabilise *jouissance*.

In empirical reality, it is normally the actual father who wants/desires to be this "narrow footbridge" to the Symbolic universe for his child. Quite possibly no one else will have this commitment so strongly, which unites both ethics with desire. To reduce this quality of desiring-giving to a de-substantialised "Name" and then to a "fiction" and so on, shows just how tied to the structuralist ideology Lacanian psychoanalysis became.

Levinas amplifies the nature of the footbridge that the father provides. His key question for us: 'How can the ego become other to itself?' His answer: 'This can only happen in *one* way: *through paternity*'; by becoming a father.

Levinas outlines the paradoxes of paternity. It is the relation with a stranger, one entirely other to me, yet it is 'the relationship of the ego with a myself who is nonetheless a stranger to me'. Beyond any thought of ownership or creation as such, like a poem or an artefact, for instance, 'I do not *have* my child; I *am* in some way my child'. However, this "I am" implies, not an identification, not "he is just like me!" but on the contrary, a multiplicity of possibilities of transcendence contained within the verb "to exist."

Levinas stresses that the father does not have power over the child, nor does he merely empathise with him. He does not live *through* him or *for* him, nor is the son his alter ego. For Levinas, as always, it is a question of openness and a non-totalising, *for-the-other*: 'It is through being, not through sympathy, that I am my son'. This is brought about by 'the perspective of the future opened up by Eros [desire]'. Time itself is structured by fecundity. By becoming a father we are freed from ourselves, 'not according to the category of cause, but according to the category of father that freedom comes about and time is accomplished'.[49] Paternity is a renewal of the father in the son, but also the father's exteriority, what Levinas calls a plural existing – 'the coexistence of several freedoms in a multiplicity that leaves the unity of each in tact … Existing itself becomes double'.[50] He quotes Isaiah 49: *My child is a stranger*.

Thus, "the me," the ego is rescued from itself, its narcissism and its repetition compulsion. It means that, 'In fecundity the personal I has its place [which] indicates the end of its terrors whereby the transcendence of the sacred, inhuman, anonymous, and neuter, menaces persons with nothingness or with ecstasy'. For Levinas, what menaces the subject in the Real – nothingness or ecstasy – *jouissance* – is transcended via paternity. What overcomes *jouissance* is the going beyond the self: 'transcendence transcends towards him who transcends – this is the true adventure of paternity'.[51] 'The I is divested of its tragic egoity'.[52] 'In this "I am," being is no longer an Eliatic unity. In existing itself there is a multiplicity and a transcendence'.[53]

Levinas continues, 'The I breaks free from itself in paternity without therefore ceasing to be an I, for the I is its son. The converse of paternity, filiality, the father-son relationship designates a relation of rupture and a recourse at the same time'. Paternity *releases* the son into the world and relieves the father of the "burden" of his narcissism as he goes out to the other being that transcends him. With filiality, however, there is a breakdown and a return to the other, *not* the future. Ultimately, 'the I owes its unicity to the paternal *Eros*'.[54] The son is a unique, inexchangeable son through being chosen, through election: 'each son of the father is the unique son, the chosen son'.[55]

Generalising, Levinas states that 'Every love must approach paternal love'. But this relation of love is not just "added" to an already constituted "I" as good fortune, as it were; 'his I *qua* filial commences not in enjoyment [*jouissance*] but in election. He is unique for himself, because he is unique for his father'. This election will form the basis of the son's self-esteem throughout life. And furthermore, because of this election, Levinas continues, 'he can be brought up, be commanded, and can obey, and the strange conjuncture of the family is possible'. Paternity is thus bound to the time of the future. The elected one together with other elected ones form a "fraternity," where, 'the I as I hence remains turned ethically to the face of the other … as a privilege and a subordination'.[56]

This Levinasian statement about fecundity and paternity and the father's *Eros* is one of the high points of theorisation *beyond* Oedipus. The Levinasian father is not a metaphor or a name, a Real, Imaginary or Symbolic father, but beyond all that, an ethical being *without* an Oedipus complex. The Oedipus complex is the pathological form, where desire and the Law battle it out. With Levinas, the father is called out and beyond himself to the other who is a stranger, who paradoxically is also myself, out of myself – my life into the future.

Jouissance for Levinas is *life enjoying its life*! Immediate pleasure sensation, 'before any reflection, any return upon oneself'. Enjoyment is the enjoyment of enjoyment, 'the singularisation of the ego in its coiling back upon itself. Winding of a skein, it is the very movement of egotism'.[57] However, in its complacency and non-sense and its 'supreme passivity of sensibility', Levinas invokes a sudden twist: 'in its *vulnerability as an exposure to the other*' (italics added), there may occur 'a tearing from oneself despite oneself', being torn from one's enjoying. '[T]he for-the-other, is the tearing away of the mouthful of bread from the mouth that tastes in full enjoyment … an attack made immediately on the plenitude of the complacency in oneself'.[58] *Sharing your bread with the famished … welcoming of the wretched into your house* (Isaiah 58).

Here, *jouissance* – enjoyment/suffering becomes ethical. However, this is not the familiar Oedipal morality that denies enjoyment or parcels it out according to the law and the regulatory pleasure principle; quite the reverse, only the subject who is capable of enjoyment in this immediate sense of life enjoying life senselessly, also *gives* senselessly without reserve. Whereas, Oedipal pathology is the opposite: a defence against life itself, the giving and counting the cost of the bread in a guarded, watchful fashion.

Levinas' notion of *first philosophy as ethics* takes us beyond the subject *qua* subject divided of Oedipal psychoanalysis and indeed ordinary living. When I am held hostage by the naked face of the other, I am nothing except pure proximity, pure giving, pure hospitality. Such extreme and senseless election ruptures my Oedipal perseverance, my on-going-being, my *conatus*. Such enjoyment-suffering-*jouissance*-ethics and bread taking destroys *my* life! This is the explosive (non) power of *agape*, which we will take up again later.

The son has been chosen. Thus, in his being he is unique because he has been chosen and he will 'accept commandment and can obey'. This is the most favourable outcome of the Oedipus complex. He has that great spirit of enjoyment bestowed by the father into the future.

Notes

1 Dr Cormac Gallagher introduced Lacan to Ireland in the early 1980s. He is a Jesuit scholar who was analysed by Lacan and went on to translate Lacan's seminars and disseminate them to Lacanians in Ireland and abroad.
2 Lacan, J., 1969–1970. Page numbers in parentheses refer to this seminar.
3 Lacan, J., 1972–1973.
4 Weatherill, R., 1994.
5 Lacan's somewhat impenetrable style will be unavoidably repeated here. We are also reading this work at this point as a naive reader, leaving out the secondary texts that have appeared on this work for the time being.
6 Surplus value means the *new* value created by workers in excess of their own labour cost, which represents profit for the owner.
7 *Objet petit a* stands for the just unattainable object of desire that arises as a result of our insertion into language and culture. It is the always lost object to which we (unconsciously) orient our passions.
8 Biff Loman says in Miller's *Death of a Salesman*, despairing of his family's and his father's lies and illusions born of the American dream, 'We never told the truth in the house for ten minutes'.
9 Baudrillard refers to Mauss's well known notion of the potlatch, which it seems is analogous to the nomadic entropic of *jouissance* – 'a certain type of circulation of goods operates, exonerated from the idea of value, a type of circulation which includes prodigality and the squandering of things, but must never stop. Exchange must never have an end, it must always increase in intensity, possibly continuing until death'. (Baudrillard, J., 2000, [2003]: 16). And now we talk about the widespread "failure of regulation" in the economic sphere after our economic potlatch, in which the Euro might fail.
10 He is referring to Riviere, J., 1929.
11 Lacan is alluding to his famous formulae of sexuation. See, for instance, Wright, E., 2000.
12 Lacan introduces this term in Lacan 1966–1967. It is the single stroke of the painter's brush that marks the beginning of the untangling of the original chaos. Likewise the infant's initial symbolisations with the *fort/da* game that similarly inscribes a trace. It is the initial signification, the S1 that sets things going.

13 See Freud, S., 1937a: 248.
14 The schema for the *four* discourses that Lacan outlines can be found in the seminar under discussion. For instance, pp. 31, 79, 169 and so on.
15 David Blake Knox's film of "A Mother's Love's a Blessing" won a Torc at the 1994 Celtic Film Festival.
16 Freud, S., 1930: 72.
17 Irish comedian Brendan Grace on the phallic mother: "I brought you into the world and I can take you out again."
18 Lidz cited in Boyers, R., 1971: 136.
19 Baudrillard, J., 1990.
20 Baudrillard, J., 1995. For Baudrillard, long after Freud, what is criminal is the virtual perfection of the world brought about through scientism, psychoanalysis and the perfection of the Real, which nevertheless continues to "transpire" with all its ugly imperfections and evil – at least this is how it now appears from the post-criminal insistence on absolute techno-perfection.
21 Lacan, J., 1959–1960: 309.
22 Freud, S., 1900: xxvi.
23 Žižek, S., 2014.
24 Lacan, J., 1938: 34.
25 Ibid.: 38.
26 Ibid.: 39, emphasis added.
27 Ibid.: 45. It is amazing to think now that Lacan backed away from that diagnosis as if the fate of Western culture was a matter of indifference.
28 Lacan, J., 1958–1959. Session of 7 January 1959.
29 Fink, B., 1997: 123.
30 Ibid.: 119.
31 Ibid.: 163.
32 Lacan, J., 1970: 697/823.
33 Fink, B., 1997: 165.
34 Masoni, S., Maio, A., Trimarchi, G., de Punzio, C., and Fioretti, P., 1994.
35 The reference here is from Lacan, J., 1955–1956: 212–13.
36 Freud, S., 1924: 176–7.
37 See http://newsinfo.inquirer.net/inquirerheadlines/nation/view/20090124-185270/Feminism-blamed-for-erosion-of-manhood.
38 McCarthy, P., 2002: 123.
39 Ibid.: 118.
40 Gallagher, C., 2002: 20–1.
41 Lacan, J., 1970: 813/688.
42 Žižek, S., 2001: 33.
43 Fink, B., 1997: 110.
44 Verhaeghe, P., 1999: 18–31.
45 Ibid.: 141.
46 Cited in Castenet, H., 2015: 43.
47 Brousse, M.-H., 2009.
48 Lacan, J., 2013.
49 Levinas, E., 1947: 91.
50 Ibid.: 92.
51 Levinas, E., 1961: 269.
52 Ibid.: 273.
53 Ibid.: 277. "Eliatic" refers to the figure and archetype of the prophet Elias/Elijah/Ilyas in Judaism, Christianity and Islam. Elias exemplifies the esoteric pole of religion. He ascended directly to Heaven while remaining perpetually alive to guide seekers on the spiritual path.

54 Ibid.: 278.
55 Ibid.: 279.
56 Ibid.: 279.
57 Levinas, E., 1981: 73.
58 Ibid.: 74.

2

THE ANTI-OEDIPEANS

By the time of Lacan's *Seminar 17*, with *les événements* just past, the father, tradition, and the family are under renewed attack as never before. The Beat Generation of poets and writers like Kerouac and Ginsberg of the early 1960s, celebrated, alternative living, enviromental awareness, "dropping-out," sharing, decentralised politics and so on. *Sergeant Pepper*, released in 1967, the "Summer of Love," typified the soft counterculture ambience of the first total "youth culture," which rejected bland pop and commercial music. *All You Need is Love* was an epoch-making broadcast on 25 June by the BBC to 400 million people. This simple message went global – love is all you need. The Stones, inspired by rhythm and blues, promoted a darker erotic image. Rock 'n' roll became rock. San Francisco became the centre of psychedelic rock. In the summer of 1967, as many as 100,000 converged in the Haight-Ashbury district of San Francisco, with bands like Jefferson Airplane, the Grateful Dead, the latter leading the transition from urban folk to folk rock to acid rock, and Janis Joplin, the most successful white blues singer of the 1960s. The Doors' *Light My Fire* had a big impact. Santana fused Cuban salsa, rock and jazz; Hendrix, Clapton added intensity and passion, and so on. Without doubt, a blaze of *jouissance* was exploding onto the scene in a Dionysian carnival of body, mind and mind alteration. The cultural revolution was underway which would turn thinking inside-out, create a radical break with the past – a "before" and an "after," turn grey into colour, austerity into hedonism, hate into love, love into peace, reality into acid fantasies, offer flowers to policemen, wear flowers in your hair, be sexually generous and promiscuous (with the first oral contraceptive pills becoming widely available). All this in the dark shadow of the greatest *jouissance* of all: 'We're on the eve of destruction ...'

European Fascism, defeated in 1945, had allegedly morphed into a softer version and diffused widely but also *inter-personally*. From the love perspective, any figure of authority was *de facto* a fascist. The perceived sheer *intimacy* of fascist control led to the assertion from second wave feminism that *the personal is political*.[1] The libidinal revolution was underway.

New Left ideas were igniting a new generation of students with time on their hands, cooped up on campuses, radicalised and horrified by the Vietnam war, the first televisual war seen every night on TV news, reading Marcuse on the *Military Industrial Complex*, *One-Dimensional Man* and Mao's *Little Red Book*, second only to the Bible in the number of copies sold, was published by the Chinese government in 1966. It owed its immense popularity to the Chinese Cultural Revolution of the 1960s and 1970s. In China, not carrying, reading and quoting the book was a sign of divergence from Mao's way, which could lead to ostracism or even death.[2] Militancy was ablaze. However in China it was all over after barely a decade, whereas in Europe and the West it is still ongoing.

Radical therapist-activist David Cooper coined the term "anti-psychiatry" and the bourgeois family was its key target: 'The social functioning of the family is as an ideological conditioning device'.[3] Breaking the family was key. The family as the basic unit of society must be destroyed. '"Bringing-up" a child is in practice more like bringing down a person. Education similarly is leading a person out of himself and away from himself'.[4] Recall Lacan's notion of alienation, following Hegel, Marx and Sartre, locating desire to be the *other's* desire; we want to be what the other wants us to be. With added emphasis, we are forced ideologically to be what the fascist-educating parents want (desire) us to be. This "other" is masculinist, phallic and global: 'Men in first-world countries persecute the third world as well as minorities within the first world, including the major "minority" called women'.[5]

Herbert Marcuse called his talk "Liberation from the Affluent Society" at the *Dialectics of Liberation* congress in London at the Roundhouse in Chalk Farm, London, in July 1967. In his opening remarks, he says how pleased he is to see so many "flowers," but warns that flowers have no power by themselves against aggression and destruction. The irony is, he says, 'today we have to be liberated from a relatively well-functioning, rich, powerful society … a society which to use a slogan, delivers the goods to an ever larger part of the population'.[6] Just 10 years earlier, British Prime Minister Harold Macmillan told a Conservative rally in Bedford that 'we have never had it so good'.

The "flowers" were the most affluent generation on the planet, with the greatest and brightest futures! Born post WW2, they had not known the horrors of war, famine or suffering of the parental generation. Marcuse pointed to the fatal paradox of late capitalism: 'namely, the apparently inseparable unity – inseparable for the system – of productivity and destruction, of satisfaction of needs and repression, of liberty within a system of servitude – that is to say, the subjugation of man to the apparatus'.[7] Need is suppressed by the satisfaction of needs (the flowers are so well fed and looked after, they will be passive) and by a 'massive scientific manipulation and administration of needs – that is, by a systematic social control not only of consciousness, but also of the unconscious of man'. Marcuse blames what he calls 'the greatest liberating sciences of our time', such as psychology, psychoanalysis and psychiatry, which he asserts have become 'the most effective agents of suppression'.[8] What is most liberating becomes a form of biopolitical control.

In the introduction to her recent book, *Philosophy in Turbulent Times*, Roudinesco celebrates this 'freedom of the self', fought for during the previous century. But after four decades, we have 'solitude, the use of mind-altering drugs, boredom, fatigue, dieting, obesity, the medicalisation of every second of existence'. Freedom, she complains, has turned back into 'a demand for puritanical restraint … a little everyday fascism [which] slips inside each individual without his realising it'.[9]

Sartre, Foucault, Althusser, Deleuze, Derrida and so on, generally agree, rather hysterically perhaps, that the 'great fascist enemy' is 'the project to normalise the human being – a project that, in its most experimental version, is no more than an ideology of submission in the service of barbarity'.[10] Žižek defines Fascism, lumping in New Age followers for good measure, as the Pagan desire for harmony, balance and order. All those who long for order are crypto-fascists. Thus, in this way of thinking, normalisation leads inexorably along a line to carpet bombing Vietnam. Maybe, fear of banal normalisation led my colleagues to defend the *jouissance* of the addict no matter the consequences. Terms from the enlightenment – reason, consensus, normality, and so on – now strike terror as they are suffused with violence. In the same way one will be told that striking a child leads down the line to child murder.

In his introduction to *Anti-Oedipus*, Foucault asks: 'How do we rid our speech and our acts, our hearts and our pleasures, of fascism?'[11] Just five years after 'the summer of love', the very influential *Anti-Oedipus* is to be regarded as an introduction to the non-Fascist way of life. We will see.

Machinic

Rupture, detonation, destruction. It had to come, the complete break from the old logic of repressive desire based on Oedipus. The nuclear complex of psychoanalysis is 'daddy-mommy-me', stressing its so-called infantilising and domesticating aim. Remain with Oedipus and confine yourself, "to the playpen" with daddy and mommy in charge. What endangers the subject, they argue, is located *externally*, with Oedipus as the local representative of the totalising repressive System of capitalism as a whole – Father, Family, Church, School, Party, Nation State and so on. Theirs is a massive sweep; Freud's carefully balanced and nuanced view of the psyche is entirely blown out of the water.[12]

Foucault says that the dream, that cast its spell between the wars over the radical Europe, of Reich and the surrealists has returned in *Anti-Oedipus* and set fire to reality itself: 'Marx and Freud in the same incandescent light' (xiii). Mark Seem adds an important caveat in his opening comments on the text, 'The experience however is no longer that of man, but of what is *inhuman* in man … a politics of desire directed against all that is egoic – *and heroic* – in man' (xxi, emphasis added). We are sick of ourselves!

Recalling earlier mass convulsions of modernity: from Robespierre's Reign of Terror, whose motto was, Hannah Arendt tells us, '*par amour pour l'humanité, soyez inhumain*', to the Fascist call '*Viva la muerta!*'; from Dostoevsky's nihilist Kirillov to Warhol's 'I'm painting this way because I want to be a machine'; from Karl Kraus's prediction that gloves would be made of human skin, and Russian poet Mayakovski's use of the human skulls for an ashtrays, we will stay close to *this* great anti-Oedipal polemic, its relentless declaration of war on all reactionary fronts, a paean to (in)humanity and the primordial earth, 'a magnificent vision of madness' as Cooper celebrated it, the roar of being itself, terrorising the safe and secure, all in the name of Nietzschean *becoming*.

Everywhere, the language of *the machine*. 'Everything is a machine' (2). Nothing new here: Ezra Pound saw words as machines; modern architects saw houses as machines for living in; the industrial revolution had created bureaucratic machine states and the fascists ran their trains (with their human cargoes) like clockwork. Machines displaced slave labour. The modern world was built on mechanical power. Now there are intelligent machines and more displacement.

Slavery had been condemned as inhuman and degrading. Christian awareness that humans are made in the image of God ordained that humans are *not* machines and must not be treated as such. The soul incarnated in the flesh is not part of any machine. The soul stands between us and the monstrous cold, deaf and blind mathematic infinity of the universe *qua* machine. The soul is always *a beyond* of the body-machine to be glimpsed, to be re-collected in responsibility. However, for the contemporary radical materialist position, remove any veil of consoling illusion: *we always were and we are machines. Nothing else*! Long ago we gave up any belief in transcendence.

As if to polemicise this assertion, the adjective used to describe the machine process is not "mechanical" but "machinic,"[13] to underscore the automaticity of desiring phenomena. The machines are not metaphors *but real*, to drive home the immediacy of *non*-familial, *non*-mommy-daddy, the *unheimliche* character of the new ideology. The effect should be unfailingly chilling and terroristic. They describe a universe of desiring machines, all connected to one another: 'There are no desiring-machines that exist outside the social machines that they form on a large scale' (373).

Gone is the traditional notion of *desire based on lack* (from Plato to Lacan), which places desire under the category of the "negative" – together with law, limit, castration, differentiation, lacuna, etc. Instead, Deleuze and Guattari understand desire as a positive, productive force without lack! Here Nietzsche and Spinoza are key. On this basis, 'desire is a machine, and the object of desire is another machine' (28).

Organs are machines and man is a 'vertebro-machinate mammal', indeed 'aphid parasite' *of* machines. In consequence, 'the machine passes to the heart of desire … with *the residual subject off to the side*' (314, emphasis added). The subject can be discerned on the recording surface of the body: 'a strange subject however, with no fixed identity, wandering about over the body without organs,[14] always peripheral to the desiring machines, garnering here, there … a reward in the form of a becoming or an avatar …' (17). The subject is thus, 'a residuum alongside the machine, as an appendix, a spare part' (21).

The demotion-elimination of the subject by the ubiquitous machinery of drives and counter-drives is reminiscent of borderline conditions or psychosis. For our authors this is a cause for celebration. In the later volume of their work,[15] they refer to the "mechanosphere," the machinic sphere around the earth analogous to the atmosphere, biosphere, hydrosphere, etc.

The traditional distinction, vital/mechanical, no longer holds. No longer affronted by the breast machine, the mouth machine, the talking machine, organ machines plugged into energy source machines, and so on, we envisage in general terms desiring machines opposing the paranoiac machine, as the desiring machines try to break into the Body with Organs (BwO) – an instance of the return of the primarily repressed.[16] With the threatened return of the repressed machines, their attraction reverses the primal repulsion of the paranoiac machine (counter-cathexis) and miraculating machines are produced. Celibate machines appear to be akin to *jouissance* itself – 'a schizophrenic experience of intensive quantities in their pure state, to a point that is almost unbearable – celibate misery and celibate glory experienced to the fullest … naked intensity stripped of all shape and form' (20).[17]

Machinic language creates total rupture of all things tragic, representative, divided and formerly regarded as "civilised." Desiring machines are akin to Kleinian "partial objects" in the paranoid-schizoid world, but our authors complain that Klein does not go on to exploit their explosive potential as desiring machines to 'blow up all of Oedipus and totally demolish its ridiculous claim to represent the unconscious', failing indeed 'to shatter the iron collar of Oedipus' (48).

The unconscious is no longer structural, personal or symbolic, it *engineers*; it produces; it is a factory or a workshop; it is Real. Whereas, our authors assert that in traditional psychoanalytic theory, the unconscious 'is crushed, subjected to the requirements of representation' (61). The psychoanalyst is reduced to being 'a director of a private theatre' (62) rather than an engineer or mechanic who sets up units of production. The new unconscious knows nothing of castration or Oedipus, just as it knows nothing of parents, gods, the law and lack.

Repeatedly, the authors refer to the unconscious as "orphan" (*orbus* – bereaved). Dispensing with and escaping from the care of the family ("care" is *nowhere* in the text!), the unconscious is "set free," gloriously abandoned. No time for the orphanage and no time for sorrow! Instead, the unconscious produces itself in a 'cyclical orphan movement' (319). They cite Artaud, *I got no papamummy*. The Cartesian subject 'has no parents', is not 'boxed-up' in the Oedipus complex; the unconscious is *auto*-produced. Instead of 'the dirty little family [Oedipal] secret … [there is] the fantastic factory of Nature and Production' (53).

The subject/child is allegedly "blackmailed" by the Oedipal threat: if you don't follow the lines of differentiation laid down – Daddy//Mummy//Child – 'you will fall into the black night of the undifferentiated'. And overcoming or resolving Oedipus is no better: 'everybody knows what psychoanalysis means by resolving Oedipus: internalising it so as to better rediscover it on the outside, in social authority, where it will be made to proliferate and be passed on to the children' (87). There is only the old choice: undifferentiated, incestuous and psychotic, or weak, castrated and neurotic. Our authors insist that Oedipus is a ligature that cuts off all desiring production.

Schizoanalysis however will free the unconscious as orphan, without the law, transforming the old analytic machine into a revolutionary new machine. Schizoanalysis is the "curettage" of the unconscious – 'the splendid affirmation of the orphan-and-producer unconscious; the exaltation of the process as a schizophrenic process of deterritorialisation that must produce a new earth' (329). It will break through representational theatre-drama, bodying forth a new world. The 'molecular unconscious' produces multiple break-flows, makes connections and non-exclusive disjunctions, nomadic conjunctions, microscopic transsexualities, *n* sexes, and so on, forever. 'Desiring machines are the nonhuman sex' (324).

Disappointment with the later Freud is everywhere in evidence as it had been from Reich onwards: against the Freud who linked sexuality with procreation and genital primacy; who subsumed sexuality into (the healing) Eros in the final drive theory; who re-theorised anxiety as the cause of sexual repression, rather than the result of sexual repression.

Just as Marx admired capitalism, our authors celebrate the mad energy of the capitalist megamachine (Mumford, 1971) – its so-called deterritorialisations and *re*-territorialisations, decoding flows of desiring production, all paradoxically to *further* capitalist ideology itself! Capitalism loves crisis, like the epochal failure of Communism in 1989 leading to *global* capitalism.

The global dynamic consists of opposed tectonic forces now written on the earth itself. Psychoanalysis has always been astride the middle ground of this dynamic, between decoding (of language) and recoding, with Lacan tending towards the former. But for our authors, psychoanalysis is part of the abhorred, faintly Christian, always enfeebling castrating machine, that is, 'the machine for putting lack into desire' (391).

For schizoanalysis, molecular formations oppose molar formations; desiring machines oppose social machines; the schizophrenic 'dispersed lines of escape' and deterritorialisations oppose the paranoiac machines or perverse reterritorisations; nomadic, polyvocal, revolutionary tendencies oppose sedentary, biunivocal, reactionary-fascist tendencies; subject groups oppose subjugated groups; molecular multiple singularities breach the "coded wall," the structural wall of language, the territorialised limit, and so on. *Anti*-Oedipus 'gives the revolutionary the right to say, "Oedipus? Never heard of it"' (401).

What is the fate of the schizoanalysand?[18] Either to break through the wall of the signifier and escape to continue the "voyage" by becoming; or bounce off the wall of the signifier to fall back into 'the most miserably arranged territorialities of the modern world as simulacra' (311), i.e. asylum versions of paranoia and schizophrenia *qua* clinical entities. The task of schizoanalysis is to support the great flows of deterritorialisation in the arts and sciences. Do whatever it takes not to leave the schizo alone to fall back into the trap of "madness." Escape enables other escapes by linking revolutionary machines, artistic machines, science machines and schizo machines, causing to flow all together.

The schizoanalyst is not an interpreter but a mechanic who undoes all totalisations, creating dispersions and the return to partial objects and "anarchic multiplicities." The schizoanalyst's task is to learn 'what a subject's desiring machines are, how they work, with what syntheses, what bursts of energy in the machines, what misfires, with what constituent flows, what chains, what becomings in each case' (371). The schizoanalyst is not interpreter, archaeologist or excavator, but a micro-mechanic, who discovers what immobilises, silences, traps, sabotages, holds down and silences the desiring machines. "Escape" signifies *courage* to flee from 'false refuges … values, morals, homelands, religions and these private certitudes that our vanity and our complacency bestow generously on us' (375).

Schizoanalysis attains 'non-figurative, non-symbolic unconscious … flow-schizzes or real desire apprehended below the minimum conditions of identity' (385). Schizoanalysis is 'the constant destructive task of disintegrating the normal ego' (396). Egos must be constantly taken apart to liberate their knots, vibrations and singularities. Schizoanalysis is a gigantic process of undoing: 'violent, brutal, defamiliarising, de-Oedipalising, de-castrating, undoing theatre, dream fantasy …' (417). Schizoanalysis is destruction, nothing less!

Lacan is largely spared by our authors. Deleuze was his analysand at one time. However, psychoanalysis remains an obstacle to schizoanalysis. It is regarded as no more than a puny thing seeking shelter in the familiar, familiarising family. No opportunity is spared to ridicule the whole discipline. 'Psychoanalysis is an immense perversion, a drug, a radical break with reality … a narcissism, a monstrous autism' (344).[19] Psychoanalysis is portrayed as belittling, judging, mortifying, abjecting – 'Leave your desiring machines at the door, give up your orphan and celibate machines, your tape-recorder and your little bike, enter and allow yourself to be Oedipalised … flows of speech in exchange for flows of money' (63).

Everything about psychoanalysis is allegedly repressive: 'commit incest and you'll be a zombie and a hermaphrodite' (83). Instead, you must take a woman *other than your sister-mother* and you'll create a new triangle with a child at its vertex, 'which is called surmounting Oedipus, but reproducing it as well, transmitting it, *rather than dying all alone, incestuous, homosexual, and a zombie*' (79, emphasis added). An accurate summary! Whereas, the schizo multiplicity releases so many spores as singularities that it is 'closest to the beating heart of reality' (96). However, they do concede that if indeed you 'bounce off the wall', you could end up with 'a paucity of reality', becoming autistic, athymic … a growing desert, 'a solitary machine [that] hums on the beach, an atomic factory' (95).

We contend that the father is at the heart of the Oedipal structuring of subjectivity. Our authors, following Nietzsche, stress the *orphan* unconscious: 'the question of the father, the question of God is what has become impossible; a matter of indifference, so true is it [that] to affirm or deny such a being amounts to the same thing, or to live it or kill it: one and the same misconception …' (118). Better to be an orphan than a child of a father and mother.

They hate the "analyst-priest," the "pious" analyst who preaches lack, Law and signifier – in order to crush the desiring machines. The earth is dead, the desert is growing and analysands are alone with their bad faith and false consciences. Instead of 'the song of castration', psychoanalysis ought to be 'a song of life' (364), not mere 'snivelling desire … A maudlin crying to be loved …' (367).

They negate the fear of incestuous desire itself: 'desire does not threaten a society because it is a desire to sleep with the mother, *but because it is revolutionary*' (127, emphasis added). Because desire can be linked with incest, they claim that desire *per se* is thereby displaced, shamed and feared. 'This terrible mother, the sphinx; her non-differentiation is merely the reverse of the exclusive differentiations created by Oedipus' (343).

Lacan suggested that we live 'between two deaths';[20] well, our authors go further, suggesting we "live" between two *abortions*: the incestuous mother and the aseptic clinic waiting to treat our mental illness.

Of flowers and weeds

With psychoanalysis now overwhelmed by therapy culture, our authors' attack was farseeing. A lachrymose philosophy around victimhood, the allegedly traumatic nature of ordinary life, the "fragile child," the "loving" mother, the regressive infantilisation of language, and so on, have become commonplace since *Anti-Oedipus*. However, has schizoanalysis fostered this regression, while aggressively asserting the opposite?

The "flowers" were told that they had *no* power against the fascist System. They were traumatised by excess! No wonder the mass of ordinary working people at the time failed to understand and sympathise with their hysterical protesting! The paranoid logic machine deployed through books, TV, lectures, sit-ins, workshops, etc., convinced and seduced many into believing that the "military industrial complex of the West" was at work everywhere; the silent masses were complicit, as fascistic as the war-planners in Washington or Moscow. They were told and believed that they had been alienated, colonised, violated and conditioned into fascistic "normality;" and with this ideology the engine of narcissism and hurt was set going demanding a whole therapeutic culture to put things right.[21] They were tuning in and dropping out like flies. The baby-boomers had the biggest tantrum in history.

Born into an unprecedented age of prosperity after WW2, protected by the welfare state, educated beyond what any former generation could ever have hoped for, pampered with consumer goods, and *they* are the ones to complain! They felt guilty about war, about violence (televised from anywhere in the world for the first time in real-time), about wealth, about living. They succumbed to *ressentiment*, as activated anti-Oedipal force or desire is turned around against itself, 'pushed back and repressed, incarcerated within and finally able to discharge and vent itself only on itself' (Nietzsche cited: 234). Baudrillard referred to this self-hatred or backlash as the last stage in the liberation of the species, a paradoxical turning around against the self at the advanced stage of rationality and civilisation. 'There is no need to posit a death drive at work, a biological nostalgia for a state prior to individuation and sex',[22] just a reflexive mortification as we glimpse the degree to which the soul has lost its grandeur.

Two post-psychoanalytic strands took shape during the past half century. First, the non-erotic infantile logic based in hurt and trauma; second, the "nonhuman erotic" spirited on by neo-Reichians and anti-Oedipeans with their desiring machines and molecular rhizomal energies. Both strands claim a psychoanalytic heritage; both have polemicised an aspect of Freud to the detriment of his whole opus. And now it is probably too late to rescue that *whole* thing.

Sloterdijk noted that psychoanalysis lacked thymos and thymotic potential, what he called a "bank of rage." Instead of mobilising prideful rage, honour and ambition, we domesticated rage, turning it into hurt, while becoming preoccupied with sex as an end in itself. In short, we went crazy about both love and humility, creating 'subcultures in which beautiful souls sent one another messages of love'.[23] The interruption of pride for the sake of a libidinal politics entirely suits contemporary capitalist consumerism, buying off the *dignity* of human beings with gadgets as concessions. Pride, dignity and honour are not part of the psychoanalytic lexicon. Instead they have become pathologised by 'the thymos-forgetting therapeutic culture … in the tradition of Christian moralists'.[24]

The rage generated in the pages of *Anti-Oedipus* against familial domestication in all its forms is a great burst of freedom, a mass break-out and escape-release of great thymotic potential. Why in practice does it fall back to earth in narcissistic ruins, a failed project easily reterritorialised by the capitalist machine? In the last chapter of *Rage and Time*, called "The Dispersal of Rage in the Era of the Centre," Sloterdijk points to this diffusion of desire where 'every individual is turned into a consumption citizen, who unless uplifted by family, cultural and cooperative counter-forces, is increasingly fixed to a poisoned loneliness with a doomed irritation of desire'.[25]

Desire *per se*, destined for total liberation by anti-Oedipeans, forever free and untrammelled, becomes *just an irritation*. Enzenberger, seeming to echo *Anti-Oedipus*, refers to "molecular civil wars." 'The reality is that civil war has long since moved into the metropolis'. As Enzensberger[26] says, 'The beginning is bloodless, the evidence circumstantial. Molecular civil war starts unnoticed; there is no general mobilization'. Rubbish accumulates, syringes and broken bottles appear in the park, graffiti is daubed on the walls. In schools and colleges, classroom furniture is smashed. These are 'muted declarations of war which any experienced city-dweller can interpret'. Then, tyres are slashed, cars set on fire. In one incident after another, rage is vented, hate turns on anything that works, and forms an insoluble amalgam with self-hate'. He concludes, 'its only message [is] one of autism'.[27]

Not *dispersal* of rage, but a free-floating random affair, a lone-gunman syndrome – molecular, atomistic, homicidal-suicidal. The desiring machines exact their revenge for their wholesale failure to break through and break out by turning themselves into rage machines. Add self-radicalisation here as Islamism is a ready conduit for rage.

The flowers are turned into weeds, dominated not by Oedipus and daddy, but by mommy *alone*, or indeed by no one at all. *Be orphan. Be nomad. Be free.* Go viral: 'Make rhizomes, not roots, never plant! Don't sow, grow offshoots! Don't be one, be multiple, be multiplicities!'[28] Free – to be bereaved, homeless, rootless, aimless "singularities" with "enjoyments," left absolutely alone with 'the unconscious that produces itself in a cyclical orphan movement' (319). The wreck of psychoanalysis is to be found at these two extremes: at the weedy end with mommy, safe but fragile; or with mommy and daddy slaughtered long ago as part of the libidinised, schizo killing machines – 'knowing nothing of persons … nothing of the ego' (392) – in total indifference creating a level killing field and a race to the bottom-anus-shit.

If you take schizoanalysis seriously you seem bound to end as a speck on a pseudopodium of the erotic (Foucault), or a green-fly parasite consumer sucking on the erotic juices of Capitalism. No effective thymotic, no bank of rage, no balls, just generalised neurasthenia and stress. Every bridge back (to civilisation) has been burned by the scorched earth deterritorialisations of capitalism and schizoanalysis, with no way of deciding about these mass "enjoyments," daring not even to venture a judgement.

Sloterdijk shares our disillusion with a reference to Lacan. 'In its pretension to co-form a revolutionary subject, politicised psychoanalysis failed miserably'. So, as a half-way house to revolution, 'the new purists [Lacanians] mark themselves off from everything to do with sense-giving, interpretation, construction, life-projects, because this would once again put into play the need to explain people normatively, to develop positive ideas of culture [civilisation], and introduce creative processes'.[29]

By retaining notions such as castration, the Law, the Symbolic, they are still part of the kill-joy processes, while pretending to be otherwise. As our authors say, psychoanalysis spans a mixed semiotic. On the one hand, 'a despotic regime of significance and interpretation', and on the other, 'an authoritarian regime of subjectification and prophetism'. Between the fetishised authority of the unconscious and the aura of the silent analyst: '[T]he worst, most underhanded of powers are founded on it' (138).

For its part, however, romanticised schizoanalysis has been influential. Like Zarathustra, these romantics know incredible sufferings and sicknesses. Fifty or more years on are they still remarkable? 'They must reinvent each gesture. But such a man produces himself as a free man, irresponsible, solitary and joyous, finally able to say and do something in his own name, without asking permission; a desire lacking nothing …' (142).

A thousand rhizomes

Just as bricks (concepts) can be used to build the rational State, the "courthouse of reason," bricks can also be thrown through windows. Throw enough bricks and you level the courthouse of reason. This is deemed "progress" in our inverse-universe.

Rhizomes are preferred to trees with their phallocratic power, hierarchies of side branches and complex differentiated organisation. Rhizomes are more primitive than trees. Monocotyledons (e.g. grasses that spread by rhizomes) are less evolved than the dicotyledons (e.g. trees). Similarly, flatworms cut up can regenerate the missing parts. Protista, á la Weissmann and Freud, can divide and divide forever. Rhizomes, flatworms and protista proliferate *a*-sexually – they create more of the *same*, with identical genetics and zero variation.

Regression is progress; getting *away* from trees, to getting down below ground, away from the light (of judgement)! The "rhizosphere" is liberation *from* the old regimen of sexual difference, binarism and genital ascendency. Don't build; ramify. We are tired of the arborescent culture, i.e. the tree of man, preferring guerrilla culture, deforestation, immanence not transcendence, East not West, the smooth BwO rather than the striated (i.e. organ-*ised*) organism.

The Thousand Plateaus themselves are rhizomic and nomadic: wandering, drifting, budding, breaking, reforming, dissolving, coalescing, segmenting, micro-segmenting, etc. Plateaus are imagined as smooth elevations of continuously vibrating intensities, *qua* a non-Western libidinal economy (described by Gregory Bateson), without orientation or phallic-orgasmic end points. Bateson had observed these plateaus of extended enjoyments in Balinese culture.

However, eight years after *Anti-Oedipus*, our authors are more thoughtful and meditative. Nevertheless, the same rhetoric can be discerned: multiplicity, heterogeneity (in spite of multiplication of the same), a-signifying rupture, cartography and decalcomania, random dendritic fractal forms, machinic networks of finite automata.

The geology of the earth itself is co-opted for ideology and counter-ideology. The earth has its ideologies. For instance, strata are lines of resistance; sediments are rock-solid, imprisoning intensities, locking in singularities. 'The strata are the judgements of God (Artaud) … but the earth, or the BwO, constantly eludes that judgement, flees and becomes destratified, decoded, deterritorialised' (45). Thinking must seek ever wider open spaces to break through the Oedipal strata and the fossil-thinking of psychoanalysis, to find ever new "passional lines," 'carrying desire to such a point of excess and unloosening that it must either annihilate itself in a black hole or change planes altogether'. De-stratify! 'Open up to a new function … let consciousness cease to be its own double … make passion a field of continuous intensities … abolish subjectification …' (148). The poetry of anarchic desire.

The schizo's BwO faces *three* principal strata of aggregated, consolidated mass resistance: 1) the organism itself with its pre-ordained hierarchy of organ systems; 2) signification and the wall of language; and 3) subjectification occurring during Oedipus. Our authors issue a word of caution about the dangers of too-violent schizo *de*-stratifications; they can go wrong, leading to, for instance, a cancerous BwO, or indeed a fascistic one. A BwO can form on the strata themselves, augmenting the strata. Or an empty BwO may result – the addict, the paranoiac and the hypochondriac. It can go wrong for a whole country. Artaud cites America (of course!) as a cancerous BwO – the body of war and money.

However, what cannot be acknowledged by this polemic is that these ancient stratifications contain the highest wisdom! Taking each one: the gift of the organism itself developed during eons of evolution; the encounter with the otherness of language and its limitless "treasury of signifiers," its inexhaustible texts;[30] and subjectification itself with its call to responsibility and ethical living, *for the other* and the escape from narcissism. No need to mention mommy-daddy, although undoubtedly they start things off. Everything is already there; everything is already given. *It just needs the love of the father who elects us.*

No one is listening. The Symbolic space that at one time tolerated/celebrated(?) a conservative view of the earth's stratifications has been wiped out, but maybe returning this time *with vengeance and the judgements of a ferocious God under the sign of Islamism.* Meantime, double-consciousness has become *un*-consciousness with un-reflection and undifferentiated desire.

Perinatal potentialities

The proper BwO is not necessarily some abyssal state of regression and retreat but a *contemporary* experimental potentiality, like the Dogon twin who takes a piece of the placenta with him. Bion had something similar in mind with his notion of the caesura. Vestiges of intrauterine life persist as pre-mental potential, maybe causing a possible breakdown/breakthrough at some point in postnatal existence. Biologically, each cell remains totipotent as it differentiates and becomes self-limiting during development and growth. It retains the *total* DNA of the organism, suggestive of latent potential – metamorphoses, doppelgangers, doubles, mirror people, clones and so on. You leave behind your twin at birth.

Along similar lines, the "matrixial" is the term Bracha L. Ettinger uses to propose another mode of human (a)subjectivity linked to archaic traces of intra-uterine life in which the maternal and the as yet unknown other coexist. For Ettinger, like our authors, the *separate* subject is a fiction. Instead, 'We are matrixially transconnected in trans-sensitive psychic affective hidden levels in the Real, with those with whom we traversed a pregnant duration'.[31] Beyond the Freudo-Lacanian phallic universe, Ettinger deciphers an intersubjective or even telepathic paradigm, like the Winnicottian mother and the newborn. Ettinger associates herself within the field of the "later Lacan." Ettinger understands subjectivity as originating in 'an encounter between "I" and un-cognized yet intimate "non-I" neither rejected nor assimilated'. There are traces or links, "matrixial strings" or vibrations, "webbing links," beyond the loss-filled separated consciousnesses of the subject.

"Metramorphosis" is the term she invents to describe the potentially transformative non-psychotic, beyond-the-phallus, web of links, ignored by contemporary psychoanalysis. Everything joins up. The matrixial designates "woman" not as the Other but as co-emerging self with m/Other, a "*link a*" rather than "*object a*" not as lack or absence/presence but as a '*border-linking* figure of *differentiation in co-emergence* of "I" and "non-I"'. The paradox of the matrixial is 'Relations-without-relating and distance-in-proximity preserve the co-emerging Other as both a subject and an object without turning the Other into an object only'.[32]

Forget essence, forget biology, social construct, gender and so on, and think instead of feminine as "interlaced." Maybe, forget organ-ism, think BwO, but Ettinger is not as nomadic and dispersed as our authors in their endless multiplicities and orphaned singularities. Ettinger is pre-Oedipal rather than anti-Oedipal; Edenic not psychoanalytic or madly schizoanalytic. With the notions of primary compassion and proximity, there is reference again to Levinas.[33]

The feminine transgresses boundaries, enabling co-poeisis. As well as citing Bion's concept of "alpha function," which metabolises and detoxifies preverbal postnatal communication, Ettinger adds trans-subjective attunement, jointness-in-difference. The matrixial can be transformative throughout life, as an always evolving originary position of potential, unless entirely foreclosed by the phallic universe. Ettinger claims that metramorphosis calls for rethinking empathy, intuition, even initiation; what she calls 'this invisible unconscious trans-subjective aspect that is not yet recognized as a part of the psychoanalytic process'.[34] The limited, immature nature of the schizoid "I" can open itself toward Being in aesthetic modes (Ettinger is a distinguished artist), via "self-fragilisation" as well as compassionate hospitality and wit(h)nessing. This recalls the opening of the self towards the unrepressed unconscious and the so-called "oceanic feeling"[35] that Freud himself felt unable to reach.

There are clearly important clinical imperatives that follow from Ettinger's approach and her privileging of the compassion hospitality of the womb, or "holy place." For instance, Ettinger warns, if the analyst expresses hate toward the patient's mother, the "chaos" that follows is like 'an "instruction" to un-birth herself'.[36] The analyst's hatred of the patient's mother severs the matrixial string, turning what might have been matrixial Eros towards Thanatos, and the now foreclosed time of *non-life becoming into life* thus joins the only form of non-life we recognise: death or psychosis, especially in the vulnerable female subject.

In other words, in the absence of this matrixial eros, there can be no compassionate counterbalancing of the paranoid-schizoid phenomena of infancy. Links are severed. An anorexic adolescent, for example, often hates her past and present mother, 'who is already located in a virtual *future* self'. If the analyst also succumbs to hating the mother, the analyst in effect 'rejects major partial-selves, I(s) and non-I(s) that compose potential future selves'.[37] Thus, the patient may hate her mother with full force, but the analyst *must not join in*. If the analyst believes 'that the mother gives poisoned milk, yet the daughter is still alive, the patient becomes in her nightmares a potential future poisonous mother'.[38]

However bad the mother was, the daughter *is alive* as a consequence of the archaic matrixial time of maternal compassion – the daughter's ongoing life, her bare survival to this point, proves that. The analyst's task, therefore, is to be open to the faintest echoes or vibrations of this primordial matrixial time. The other alternative, that many analysts (and schizoanalysts presumably) fall into, is "symbolic orphanisation." They create not just atomised subjects but orphans.

The principle of the talion,[39] the mechanism of "identification with the aggressor,"[40] whereby you become like the one you most hate, leaves the door open to suicide, as Ettinger illustrates by reference to Sylvia Plath and Alejandra Pizarnik. If you, the analyst, cut the link with the patient's mother by joining in with the patient's hatred of her own mother, then the daughter must become the same hateful and hated mother in her turn, without links and without love.

Ettinger's work, like the "later Lacan," follows current trends in the wider culture. Note that the father has long since gone! In her introduction to her presentation in Dublin, Ettinger stressed that she wants to make a contribution to modernising and actualising psychoanalysis theoretically and clinically in the new century, so that psychoanalysis will *not* disappear but continue to become the historical adventure from the twentieth century, particularly 'in the areas having to do with the feminine, motherhood, maternal subjectivity, queer subjectivity, trans-subjectivity, connectedness, and so on'. While not going as far as our authors in their Dionysian shaking of psychoanalysis, Ettinger belongs firmly in the feminisation of the movement and the infilling of the Real which is conciliatory, beyond psychoanalysis á la Freud–early Lacan.

However, Ettinger has a word of caution about our generalised transconnectedness via the internet and new media. 'It is important to emphasise', she says, 'that in the matrixial I talk neither of Self-identity nor endless webbing, but about webs of "severalities" – the few with whom affective ties are woven'.[41]

Can we count on the "webs" being more than a wish-fulfilling fantasy? At the level of the Real the matrixial *must* be there somewhere in the hinterland of some unconscious, because of the primacy and the duration of pregnancy and that endometrial/placental interpenetration with a vast surface area the size of a tennis court.[42]

The thesis began with Freud's "dream" of the father's love. Levinas goes beyond psychoanalysis, with the father leading the son/daughter out of narcissism beyond Oedipus; leading the father out of his narcissism via paternity – the mystical non-totalising, *for-the-other*, through being, not through sympathy – *that I am my son*. But the schizo-account has arrived here with no mention of the father! In between, *any* notion of parental care (mother or father) is murdered ecstatically by the anti-Oedipal impulse. For any other time or culture this would be a crime.

Notes

1 Hanisch, C., 1969.
2 We will return to Mao in Chapter 9.
3 Cooper, D., 1971: 5.
4 Ibid.: 15. The "being led out of oneself," *qua* Levinas above, is now *reversed*.
5 Ibid.: 147.
6 Marcuse, H., 1969: 176.
7 Ibid.: 180.

8 Ibid.: 182.
9 Roudinesco, E., 2008: xi.
10 Ibid.: xii.
11 Deleuze, G., and Guattari, F., 1972: xv. All page numbers in parentheses in the text refer to this work.
12 Any analysts who subscribed to the more nuanced view of the later Freud, such as Paris section IPA members Bela Grunberger, Jannine Chesseguet Smirgil and others like them, were accused of supporting the *repressive Oedipus*, the asylum and the police state.
13 A word that does not exist! Although "machinism" exists – preoccupation or dependence on machines, as in politics or economics – *Webster.*
14 A "Body with Organs" (BwO) is the high intensity but smooth unity of the desiring body, but a whole that is not totalising. It is the immanent substance of desiring continuous with natural forces, creating a molecular chain of desiring that traverses it. Fragmented and not organ-ised, but not depleted. The whole is greater than the parts.
15 Deleuze, G., and Guattari, F., 1980.
16 See p. 10 and p. 180 in *Anti-Oedipus* for a fuller explanation of the anti-Oedipal significance of this break-out of primary repression.
17 The celibacy of *jouissance* seems consistent with our earlier discussion. At this extreme notions of subjectivity, gender, eros and desire based on lack have been swept away – "trans" everything as we will see.
18 A term not used by the authors.
19 It is a measure of the Deleuzian extremism that this derogatory statement about psychoanalysis could be precisely turned around against schizoanalysis!
20 "Between two deaths." Our "Symbolic" death occurs through, for instance, breakdown, bereavement, social ostracism, or dying while still alive, ahead of our biological death. Lacan's example is Antigone.
21 See, for instance, Weatherill, R., 2004.
22 See Baudrillard, J., 1976: 46–7.
23 Sloterdijk, P., 1947: 16.
24 Ibid.: 17.
25 Ibid.: 209.
26 Hans Magnus Enzensberger, German author, poet, essayist. His writing was shaped by first-hand experience of the Third Reich. His work has been translated into more than 40 languages.
27 This is an adaptation from a book by Enzensberger, H. M., 1995, which appeared in *New Perspectives Quarterly (12:1).*
28 Deleuze, G., and Guattari, F., 1980: 27. With the exception of the first two, from here page numbers in the text refer to this volume, the second in the *Capitalism and Schizophrenia* work.
29 Sloterdijk, P., with Heinrichs, H.-J., 2001: 277.
30 See discussion in Chapter 7.
31 Taken from Ettinger's opening remarks to a Dublin Seminar dedicated to her work in March 2012.
32 Ettinger, B. L., 2006: 218. The complex language that Ettinger uses matrixialises itself in its compounding and merging of boundaries, inter-weaving, and so on.
33 See Levinas, E., 2006a.
34 Ibid.: 221.
35 See Freud, S., 1930: 64–5.
36 Ettinger, B. L., 2012.
37 Ibid.: 3.
38 Ibid.: 7.
39 Lex talionis. Matthew 5:38–42. Also the basis for the primitive retaliatory mechanism in Kleinian theory.
40 See Freud, A., 1936.

41 Ettinger, B. L., 2012: 7

42 I have in mind those electron-micrograph sections that show the villi of the placenta invading the endometrium of the womb generously prepared for during the menstrual cycle by progesterone. This complex placental–endometrial junction represents, clearer than any theorising, the *biological* evidence for Levinasian hospitality – the womb's unconditional welcome. However, Ettinger seems to reject any biological "essentialism," while at the same time falling back on the irrefutable point that even the most allegedly devouring, abandoning, frustrating mother *did carry the baby alive to biological birth.*

3

BECOMING VERSUS BEING

Žižek believes that the genius of Deleuze resides in his "transcendental empiricism," where the impersonal machinic flow of pure becoming teems infinitely more richly than the dullness of perceived being. The genius of the real philosopher is that his thinking enlivens ordinary reality. You can see the stratifications and segmentations of political opinion that resist any deterritorialisations: people remain in their defensive molar aggregations, locking in intensities, repelling with their paranoid machines. You can trace the molecular developments of youthful enquiry, the lines of flight, the singularities, before they are bounced off the solid wall of language and reabsorbed into the existing sediments. You can sense the spinning in the black hole of the empty BwO of the addict.

Deleuze "sees" the quantum level *before* the collapse of wave forms. He imagines the infinite possibilities of fluid open multiplicities, before they precipitate out as concrete actualities. Deleuze's ultimate reference, following Nietzsche, is "pure becoming," against the dull opacity of Being. The assertion of continuous movement, flight, break-flows, escapes, fluxes, etc., is the pure hidden potential of the virtual, not to be misunderstood as the "before" and "after" of any historicism, but pure becoming – *no* stratigraphy or evolution, *no* development or progress, *no* context, *no* reference to real events. Deleuze was the key interpreter of Nietzsche in France. Nietzsche pointed out that nothing important is ever free from a "non-historical cloud." This leads to the paradox that something really new can only emerge via repetition out of the cloud, the repetition of the past "failure" to realise itself properly. Žižek cites Walter Benjamin's example of the October Revolution's repetition of the French Revolution, "redeeming" the latter's alleged failure. What is repeated is the transcendental-non-historical-cloud that was betrayed, missed, not fully realised at the time. The Spirit (Becoming) has been betrayed by the Letter (Being).

It is tempting to add that schizoanalysis, as the true *Spirit* of human freedom, has been betrayed by the (repressive) *Letter* of psychoanalysis. Schizoanalysis might redeem the failure of psychoanalysis: the "betrayal" by the later Freud of the originality of the early Freud. Schizoanalysis is more (early) Freudian, closer to the Freudian spirit, than all the subsequent Freudians – more Freud than Freud himself! Stick to the Letter and you betray the Spirit – always *becoming* – fluid-multiple-molecular-singular. Schizoanalysis is the truly new version of psychoanalysis, redeeming its potential vitality, its failure to aspire to full liberation. This is the lesson to be learnt from our authors.

Against the thrust of the previous chapter, Žižek asserts that, 'What Deleuze calls "desiring machines" concerns something *wholly different* from the mechanical'.[1] Against dull machinic repetition of the same, what emerges is the miraculous new, on the lines of Chesterton's Christian ontology.[2] For instance, there is nothing "mechanical" in the sun's rising every morning; on the contrary, it reveals the miracle of God's creativity! Therefore, *our* negative assertion, that "machinic" refers to an inhuman banality, emphasising *not* the miraculously new but quite the reverse, the totally repetitive – the emerging post-human, the ticking atomic clock, should *not* be conceded here but held in suspense.[3]

While the schizo may celebrate this miraculous "becoming machine" of everything, the neurotic fears the increasing reductionism and automation of human experience, the translation of the most sublime experiences into pure "functioning" and the inherent violence of such thinking. The more human capacities are handed over to prosthetics, the more we emerge as de-substantialised (parasitic) subjects controlled by the machanosphere and artificial intelligence.[4]

The proximity of miraculating machines can terrify. After he had settled, a man described his ordeal on the main thoroughfare of the capital city. He had had a sudden *real*-isation. Reality had decomposed. He heard the grinding mechanics, gears, bearings, pistons, explosions in the engines of passing lorries and buses *without any mediation or imaginary filter*, as in a nightmare, and he had collapsed in shock. A woman described the horror she felt when she saw the bony skeletal articulations of people and the skulls like an X-ray machine. Anorexics can describe in minute detail the machinations of food in their digestive machines. A man says he will only sleep in a room that contains hundreds of ticking alarm clocks all timed to go off at the same hour. Another says, all I can tell you is that we are fluid luminous beings made of contracting and relaxing fibres. Another man says, 'I am a block of ice'. In this, he has all the frozen smoothness of a BwO. The schizos and our authors "see" machinic assemblages everywhere and these monstrosities approach the Real in the Lacanian sense, or Hegel's "Objective Spirit."

Žižek points to a crack in the edifice of the simple opposition between molar and molecular, between being and becoming, the Symbolic and the Real. These opposed registers are *not* equal and opposite. Representation (Symbolic) cannot be opposed to production (Real). With Deleuze, 'The virtual field is (re)interpreted as that of generative, productive forces, opposed to the space of representations'. And for Žižek, the proper site of production cannot be the virtual space as such, which is the "empty" Lacanian Real, but, rather, the passage from it to constituted representational reality. Žižek therefore questions the *duality* of Deleuzian thinking – becoming versus being; the nomadic versus the State; the molecular versus the molar; the schizo versus the paranoiac. He concludes, 'This duality is ultimately over-determined as "the Good versus the Bad"'.[5]

To pursue Žižek's ontological "crack," the first step is to question this simple duality with similar duality, that of Badiou's Being and Event, emphasising their ultimate incompatibility. Event(s) cannot be simply mapped onto the field of becoming which generates the order of being. Event(s) are only be posited *retrospectively*. Only later can we "believe" that *this* was indeed "*an Event,*" standing out from the multitude – an Event to which to remain politically faithful in a *militant* way, as opposed to the ephemeral indiscriminate spontaneous way of the "*anarcho-désirants*."

Žižek suggests that our authors are doing no more than re-heating the old humanist-ideal: regressing from the "reified" and reduced result *in the world*, to its abundant productive becoming. It is the old story of vitalism, the elevation of life to a new "becoming." Whereas, Žižek believes that Badiou's "mathematics" is the *only* adequate ontology: 'the meaningless Real of the pure multitude, the vast infinite coldness of the Void'; i.e. the indifference of truth to the chaotic flow of the world. While Deleuze asserts *life* in its multiple singularities, for Badiou there is only the Hegelian from 'nothing to nothing'.[6]

Žižek creates another reversal. Against the notion of BwO and its high-intensity prolonged pleasure/joy, the pure body of immanent desire, he pits "*organs without a body*" (OwB). The latter might be, for instance, the lonely masochist staging his sterile rituals for futile pleasure – maybe one of those failed, empty or cancerous BwOs.

Žižek complains that *Anti-Oedipus* is the worst book Deleuze ever wrote, citing the political ideological "bad influence" of Guattari. He concludes that our authors, despite protestations to the contrary, end up as 'the ideologist[s] of late capitalism'.

For Éric Alliez, however, Deleuze and Badiou typify the *polarity* of French philosophy. For Badiou, Deleuze's work and politics lacks coherent theoretical *autonomy*, being imbued with Romantic mystical pretensions. Badiou sees mercantile possibilities in communities demanding their singular recognitions – women, gays, transsexuals, ethnic groups, etc., although clearly *not* what our authors had in mind with their revolutionary explosive field of immanence. As Alliez says,

> The BwO is to be considered as the very body of desire, as its purest expression, so absolutely coincident inseparate from what it can do that it relates back to an *unliveable power*, a power which is as such the pre-condition of every real experience of desire, driven by the necessity of [machinic] constructions that cut [striate] the BwO *in itself*.[7]

Thus, *Anti-Oedipus* confronts structuralism head-on by establishing beyond any doubt the biopolitical *primacy* of desire. In other words, the deterritorialising lines of flight, etc., come *first* and are therefore not *reactive* to established biopolitical structures. The schizo is not a revolutionary subject (or indeed a "subject" at all), but merely the site of interruption, mutation, rupture, the potential for revolution, schizzing effects – undercutting state, party and even utopian communitarian projects. Inevitably, desire becomes exile, the unconscious is orphan. What Alliez concludes is that we should not oppose the Badiou–Žižek–Lacanian–structuralist axis with a shallow post-structural, 'making room for a spontaneous democracy of desire and its pop-philosophical flights of fancy', but oppose it much more vibrantly, 'with a Biopolitics of Multitudes whose socially constitutive character is the ontological fact that sustains the constructivism of desire'.[8]

Inhuman excess

Baudrillard pours cold water on the whole schizo project. He describes the rhizomal and the molecular as 'very poetic', but as far as the multiplication to infinity and deterritorialisations, etc. are concerned, our authors were 'simply ratifying the future state of things'.

He deploys his well-known triptych: *illusion*; *realisation*; *simulation*. First, the conceptual moment, the exciting intuition and hypothesis, the moment of magic – illusion and appearance, the first exciting approximations, prior to any realisation, the other still being other and strange. Second, the slow becoming real (actual), spoiling the illusion through increasing scientific investigation and discovery (realisation). Third, the plateau of total technological operationalism. With this final stage in mind, we are in the anti-Oedipal utopia of limitless functioning desiring machines – desire in its most virtualised, optimised form, *with no one present*. Baudrillard emphasised that the postmodern era was, as he put it, 'After the orgy' (of *Anti-Oedipus*), an indifferent dull time of repetitions and simulations of what was once real and exciting, multiple bachelor machines humming in the desert, the sexual and emotional equivalent of factory farming, *jouissance* on an industrial scale.[9]

At the simulation stage, we are stuck with the hell of the Same, as the Other of sex or the erotic has been thoroughly reworked as pornography. The beautiful intuition or hypothesis of the erotic has given way to the radical indifference of desire *qua* machinic pulsation.

Take for example, *Crash*, by J. G. Ballard.[10] The narrator, also James Ballard, smashes his car by skidding on a motorway slip-road and colliding with another, setting off a whole pathological erotics of trauma.[11] Ballard's crash, in which he kills a doctor and injures the doctor's wife and himself, forms the traumatic nucleus for a sacrificial logic that will equate sex and death: eroticising the hard chromium edges of windshields, dashboard switches and vinyl interiors, on the one hand, and technologising sex – the desiring machines of pulsating orifices and orgasmic ejections – on the other. The fascination is the conjunction of hard technology with soft orifice, a blend of 'semen and engine coolant'. 'The deformed body of the crippled young woman, like the deformed bodies of crashed automobiles, revealed the possibilities of an entirely new sexuality'.[12] Freud quipped that dreaming about sex in a motor car signified auto-eroticism.[13] Fictional Ballard, recovering from his accident, complains that since the crash, he can only have sex with his wife in a motor car! The story is set in the depersonalised mobile landscape of motorways and flyovers between London and Heathrow.

According to author Ballard, a man in a motor car, driving along a concrete highway to some unknown destination, depicts the old century: 'Here, we see all too clearly the speed and violence of our age, its strange love affair with the machine, and conceivably, with its own death and destruction'.[14] In this surreal story, machinic sex is not only Deleuzian but also recalls Bataille's "passion for the Real." The trauma of the crash resets the co-ordinates of the narrator's life. As Martin Amis observed, this story is like a case of chronic shock, welcomed by the sufferer. Fictional Ballard relives the crash by having an affair with the wife of the man he killed. He comes under the influence of Vaughan, a former TV scientist, who films crash scenes and collects crash victims who, like Ballard, are caught in the same loop of the repetition compulsion. Vaughan craves the ultimate crash scene: 'In our wounds we celebrated the re-birth of the traffic slain dead, the deaths and injuries of those we had seen dying by the roadside and the imaginary wounds and postures of the millions yet to die'. At one point Vaughan produces a piece of blood-stained leather cut from the seat of a car in which a woman died. For Vaughan, this is a 'saintly relic [which] contained all the special magic and healing powers of a modern martyr of the super-highways'.[15]

War machines

Carried along by the sheer exhilaration of the prose, celebrating the schizoanalysts of liberation and freedom, the drift towards fascism, via the war machines, is inevitable at some point, when freed-up schizo lines of flight might suddenly condense into '*a cold line of abolition*'.[16] The desire to become free of fascisms and the "micro-fascisms" of everyday life, with which we started – to pursue, to flush out the slightest traces of fascism in the body – can become fascistic in its own right, so-called Left fascism.[17]

The totalitarian State does its best to seal in all the lines of flight, but when fascism comes into play, the State army is taken over by a war machine which is not just totalitarian but also *suicidal*. Instead of being content to seal off lines of flight, fascism is predicated upon an intense line of flight all of its own, 'which transforms into a line of pure destruction and abolition' (254). The war machine appropriates the State and channels its machines towards total war. Hitler wanted death through the death of others: 'A war machine that no longer had anything but war as its object and would rather annihilate its own servants than stop the destruction' (255).

The war machine was originally the invention of the nomad to create and preserve the smooth (unstriated/unorganised) space of the desert or the steppe, the wild open spaces. However, the nomad war machine inevitably collides with states, cities, striated formations, and then, in this secondary phase, the state becomes its enemy. War is neither the condition nor the primary object of the nomad war machine, but a supplement or consequence of this urbanisation with which it collides and which it then must destroy.[18] From then on the war machine has the State as its enemy.

Thus the war machine becomes war. Attila, for instance, was one of the most feared enemies of the Western and Eastern Roman Empires in the fifth century. Genghis Khan came to power by uniting many of the nomadic tribes of northeast Asia. After founding the Mongol Empire, he started the Mongol invasions that resulted in the conquest of most of Eurasia in the early thirteenth century. These campaigns were often accompanied by wholesale massacres of the civilian populations. Moses, leading the Israelites, leaves the Egyptian State behind and launches forth into the desert. Taking inspiration from the nomadic past of the Hebrews, he creates a war machine, the war machine of the Just, but one that does not yet have war as its object. However, Moses realises that war itself will be a necessary supplement to the war machine, because it will encounter cities and States. Joshua became the leader of the Israelites after the death of Moses, when he led the Israelite tribes in the conquest of Canaan, and allocated land to the tribes.

The State appropriates the war machine, changing its nature and turning it against all nomadic forms or State destroyers. The State builds and strengthens its war machine with the resources generated by Capitalism which enables it to grow and grow. Our authors overturn the well-known Clausewitzian formula that asserts the primacy of policy over warfare, i.e. war is a means for a pre-determined political purpose. Instead, war becomes the continuation of politics by other means. War becomes a total phenomenon, with a global reach. War grows stronger and stronger with "unspecified enemies," requiring the taking of 'a line of destruction prolongable to the limits of the universe' (466). That is one pole. The second pole of warfare attempts 'a creative line of flight, a smooth space of displacement', advanced through various revolutionary means to make war not as a primary object, but as a supplementary object, i.e. to be creative in a new way.

However, as the State monopolises the war machine, sometimes going as far as fascist destructiveness by developing a pure cold line of annihilation, it creates what the controversial German philosopher and cultural critic Peter Sloterdijk terms a "megathymotic," a massive bank of rage. Recall Hitler's *telegram 71* 'If the war is lost, let the nation perish'. Hitler resolved to join with his enemies to exterminate his own people.

Breaking eggs

How far does the Foucault–Deleuze–Guattari axis tend toward the very fascism it abhors, becoming 'a pure line of destructiveness', a nomadic-urban war machine to overturn or fatally weaken the bourgeois State, or significant groups, institutions or classes within the State? How far is anti-fascist destructiveness *creatively* destructive along the developmental lines of flight – necessarily breaking eggs to make omelettes? Recall, "breaking eggs" might well lead to breaking *heads*, as the human skull apparently has about the same fragility as the shell of an uncooked egg. There is in Left fascism a similar 'let the nation perish' extremism and glorification/

purification through violence. Further breaking eggs might lead to *no* omelettes, just broken eggs. Recall also that an egg is an achievement. It is itself the start of new potential life. It approximates to a totality of the differentiated organism as opposed to the BwO.

Many of the Left had former fascist sympathies. The best known are Paul de Man, deemed a "collaborationist" and "anti-Semite" after his death,[19] Frantz Fanon, a follower at least in part of George Sorel, whom Mussolini claimed as his master,[20] and Carl Schmitt, the crown jurist of the Third Reich, who resisted de-nazification after the war but was nevertheless hugely influential on the Left. His notion of "the state of exception" and the eruption of concrete life, *qua* Badiou's Event, into the democratic rule of law was attractive to radicals of both the Left and the Right. Mouffe, Laclau, Agamban thus rubbed shoulders with authoritarian counter-revolutionaries.[21] Heidegger is reserved a special place as he never recanted his support for Nazism even after the death camps were revealed in all their spectral horror. And many of the *contemporary* Left have Islamo-fascist sympathies, not least Foucault who, for a time at least, controversially backed the Iranian Revolution in 1979.

The term "deconstruction" was linked originally to Nazism. *Dekonstruktion* was first used in a Nazi psychiatry journal edited by the cousin of Hermann Göring. Logocentrism (*Logozentrismus*) was coined in a critical way in the 1920s by the protofascist thinker Ludwig Klages.[22] Key terms for the French Left had their origins in Nazism. Humanistic enlightenment Euro-centric ideas, following on the calamities of the Holocaust, Hiroshima, French collaboration, Dien Bien Phu, the Algerian war, and so on, seemed utterly to discredit reason, humanism and enlightenment ideas in toto. To the post-war generation of the 1970s, 'reason equalled violence'. Hence the radical Left's reheating of the old fascist terminology, which in its day also served to uproot Jewish cosmopolitan reason, logocentrism, Bolshevism, in favour of blood and soil. Thus Derridean deconstruction and anti-logocentrism created a sense of cognitive collapse and impossibility, all to confound reason and truth – anti-foundationalism, a breaking eggs phenomenon par excellence with no hope of an omelette. Reason was thus shattered twice over: first by the fascist radicals alarmed by communism, decadence and humiliation inflicted by the Axis powers at Versailles, second by leftist radicals horrified by the West's legacy of domination. The extreme Right and the extreme Left have their violent hatred of reason and enlightenment in common – *les extrêmes se touchent*.

Jeffery Mehlman refers to 'a phenomenon so glaring and so unacknowledged', that he feels tempted to fantasise about the "passion" of deconstruction, with Derrida on the Cross flanked by Blanchot crucified under the sign of *Combat* on one side and de Man on the other crucified under the sign of *Le Soir*. And the "Father" who has forsaken them all is Heidegger from whom Derrida took the term deconstruction.[23] Mehlman goes on to point out how Derrida conspicuously avoids commenting upon Blanchot's fascist articles for *Combat*.

In fact, according to Wolin, Blanchot in the 1930s was very enthusiastic about the far Right, writing for a wide range of journals, all of which shared an 'undying hatred of French Republicanism',[24] civil liberties, the rights of man, and so on. Blanchot and the apostles of the French *Jeune Droite* shared the belief that liberalism had been an economic and political disaster, blaming the Jews for the "evils" of capitalism, Bolshevism and cosmopolitanism, and advocating redemptive revolutionary violence, borrowing Robespierre's rhetoric of terror and virtue. They viewed the defeat of France by the Nazis in June 1940 as a "divine surprise," promising a "spiritual revolution" – the "new order" that 'would be authoritarian, hierachical, nativist and corporatist'.[25] Contrary to popular myth, Blanchot did not recoil from his extreme Rightist views in the late 1930s and join the resistance. In a letter to Mehlman in 1979, Blanchot defends his dubious wartime activities by claiming that by collaborating with Vichy he had really 'allowed himself to be coopted by Vichy *all the better to combat Vichy from within*'.[26] Quite untrue: "integral nationalism" was to be the Nazi-inspired 'wave of the future' that Blanchot *et al.* had tirelessly supported for over a decade. And French support for fascism freed up manpower for the Wehrmacht and SS to continue their genocidal policies. Worst of all, Jewish de-emancipation in France in October 1940 was an autonomous French act, *not* carried out at the behest of the Nazis. It opened the floodgates to anti-Semitism. In 1942, the round up of Jews from the Unoccupied Zone sent 76,000 Jews to their death – the only case of Jews being deported from a region *not* under Nazi administration.[27]

Blanchot illustrates the shift from the pre-war radical Right to a deconstructive mode after the war, a kind of Left fascism, that *similarly* attacks head-on reason and meaning, this time around in literature. Blanchot followed Heidegger with the "abyss," the *Ab-Grund*, the without ground, without reason – nothing – asserting, '*silence and nothing are the essence of literature*'.[28] Literature exists within the being of language rather than things in the world, defying any (enlightened) social utility or truth – the essence of post-structualism.

Although writing about his "incomparable friend" de Man *before* specific knowledge of the *Le Soir* articles, Mehlman wonders how Derrida could have bypassed such a key element of de Man's fascist sympathies. Likewise with Heidegger, Derrida seems to argue that Heidegger was "temporarily" caught up in a racist biologism (Nazism) and a racist humanism, i.e. a metaphysics of the subject, a metaphysics of presence, will to power, etc., thus racist and nihilist by default. For Derrida, Nazi racism could *not* be opposed to humanist racism, and therefore Heidegger the philosopher of Being, of deconstruction no less, was guilty for a time at least of the "crime" of humanism! Thereafter, from the revisionist viewpoint of the French Left, Heidegger became the real *anti*-Nazi! Whereas all those other naive humanists who opposed fascism and racism in the name of the enlightenment were still really fascists at heart!

In reality, Heidegger, in three decades after World War 2, could never bring himself to condemn Auschwitz. Undoubtedly, the world's greatest twentieth century philosopher of "the forgetting of Being" was a Nazi. Heidegger's blanket hostility to modernity, technology and humanism was all of a piece with his commitment to the "national revolution" in Germany. According to Lucien Aychenwald,

'He likened the Shoah to industrialised agriculture. He claimed that America was equivalent essentially to Bolshevism'.[29]

What might we conclude? Surely not that Heidegger's philosophy as a whole should be in question. However, as Jean-Michel Salankis points out, 'the French left should now recognise that there is nothing in Heidegger that has anything whatsoever to do with the "promise of freedom and equality"'.[30]

Early on Lacan was allied with the xenophobic wing of the SPP (Société Psychanalytique de Paris), especially Edouard Pichon, the avowedly anti-Semitic militant psychoanalyst, supporter of pro-fascist Action Françoise. Pichon proposes a number of French terms for a French psychoanalysis, "scotomisation," for example, being closely linked to the preferred term "*foreclusion*," the key trigger for psychosis.[31] Apparently, Lacan liked the 'radicalism and elitism'[32] of the collaborationist group. Pichon managed to 'strong-arm' Lacan into the SPP as a training analyst in 1938.[33]

Many new Left preoccupations have distinctly old fascist roots. Eugenics, the application of science to the improvement of the human population, was enthusiastically taken up by the Nazis with their State policy of "racial hygiene" – a pure line of destructiveness leading to sterilisations and extermination of the *Untermenschen*. Eugenics was also favoured by progressives under the headings of social planning, family planning, responsible parenthood and world population control. Key British socialists, such as H. G. Wells, Sidney and Beatrice Webb, George Bernard Shaw, Harold Laski, Havelock Ellis, Aldous Huxley, John Meynard Keynes, were enthusiastic eugenicists. But the Holocaust clearly discredited this utopian movement. Notwithstanding, eugenics persists under various guises today, such as pregnancy screening techniques, the selection of embryos, gender selection, genetic selection, all of which are *de rigueur* for the Left and Left feminism. Reproductive technologies bring eugenics to undreamt-of heights. More and more alleged genetic markers for diseases can be identified, leading to terminations and the prospect of genetic editing. Here "breaking eggs" (zygotes) has deeply sinister implications. The *only* decisive opposition to such technological machinics comes from the Catholic Right.

Other Left-wing tropes betray fascist origins and thus represent a kind of Left fascism. Take, for instance, race pride or identity pride. Recall the Nazi mythology about the lost glory of the Aryan past. The Nation of Islam, the Back to Africa Movement, the Black Panthers, likewise assume the racial superiority of ancient African civilisation. It is not a question of achievement. Far from it, it is merely *because* you are black, *because* you are a woman, or gay or transgendered, etc., that you must feel pride. Such "pride" can be justified on the basis of identity plus a historic claim to victimhood and inequality, creating a tidal wave of emotion – "We shall overcome" – to bring about a change of attitude and policy largely *in the absence of real debate*. The fascist trick was/is to hit those unenlightened few who question these forceful and emotive narratives of prideful righteousness and entitlement, and then *shame* them publicly. Unity is key. No dissent. *Gleichschaltung*, meaning coordination or alignment, an early fascist word, captures precisely this wave of emotion and sentiment to trump reason.

With serious thinking forbidden because it is likely to offend, cause conflict, trigger warnings, very rapid social change becomes possible and passes largely unchallenged, spurred by key social activists and a younger anti-Oedipal generation on social media who cannot believe their luck as they find themselves pushing at an open door. Change that used to take a generation or two can now come about within a decade. Change now changes exponentially.

Put simply, the challenge here is to try to fathom the anti-fascist-fascist war machine ripping through culture, scorching it, burning it, tearing its fabric, dismantling it brick by brick, to break any impediments to pure rhizomal equality. This is Nietzschean becoming versus being: anything that simply "is" must change radically.

In 1967, the German student movement leader Rudi Dutschke reformulated Gramsci's theory of "cultural hegemony"[34] with the phrase "der lange Marsch durch die Institutionen," denoting the rhizomal war of *position*, an obvious reference to the Long March (1934–5) of the Communist Chinese People's Liberation Army. If there is a cultural equivalent of anti-matter, it may be *der lange Marsch*. The aim was to seize and radicalise every institution from within, in an allegedly non-sectarian way, using the resources of civil society – cinema, theatre, entertainment generally, the family, schools, universities, the Church, newspapers, magazines, radio, television, and then laws, civic organisations and the courts, as well as literature, science and history. Get everyone on-side. Absolutely no part of culture and language and no part of people's thinking could be exempt from cultural cleansing. This quiet march is now well advanced on every front.

The old style communist/fascist war machine had ended in disaster for the Left, creating huge resistance and eventual implosion. By contrast the New Left will capture the hearts and minds of young people in advanced democracies, repelled by the crude Communist excesses, the last of which was the crushing of the Prague Spring in 1968. As older Left causes like trades unionism and nationalisation faded with the coming of welfarism, workplace health and safety laws and the minimum wage for worker protection, cultural, ethnic and sexual egalitarianism – libidinal politics – came to the fore, post-'68, overturning everything: sexual mores, artistic freedom, lifestyle, drug experimentation, all of which slowly became mainstream and increasingly unproblematic. For the new Left and gradually for nearly everyone in recent times came an entirely "benign" development based around feminism, environmentalism, peace activism, anti-racism and gay rights.

Add to this mix the revolution coming from the neo-liberal Right, globalisation and capitalism, and the schizo dream gathers to complete itself. The two revolutions came together in the 1980s in Britain with "New Labour," which managed to be radical Left on social, moral, cultural, educational, sexual and international matters, while Thatcherite Right in the economic sphere. With neo-liberalism, the historical Left–Right polarity was solved! Unlimited entitlement in every sphere won out against any form of constraint. The new enemies are the conservatives: of the old Right, hopelessly "last century," mired in traditional values and parochialism, and the old Left with its class war. At the head of *der lange Marsch* are university academics, technocrats, entrepreneurs, mainstream media anchors, white-collar bureaucrats and NGO activists, and the educated middle class, changing, advocating and regulating global policy from within. In spite of their post-materialist, anti-capitalist ideological bent, they are generally very well paid, so they worry constantly about "equality," having secured their own elite positions.

The CEOs of global brands now preach *anti*-capitalism! Business promotes "revolution" and "social mission" as a by-product of making money. The new language of *business* is openness, connectedness, equality, inclusion. They are anti-capital capitalists, egalitarian elitists, proud subversives. They are hackers in jeans and T-shirts, nomadic worker/players, collaborator/competitors, capitalists who are good for the planet. They become rich by giving everything away, bless the poor with outsourcing and tax sequestration, seek deep spirituality with deep wealth, are team players who love to break the rules. They break every mould. They are always ahead of the curve and thus they empower by pacifying – consumers no longer necessarily know what they want! You have to show them what they want! Steve Jobs is deemed the CEO of beauty, also of art, taste, soul and life.[35] At Apple, work is play; work areas are play areas. These multiple double binds make up the joyous frenetic schizo process. As one of the Google slogans has it: 'Even great is not good enough'. Incidentally, that little formula for excess informs every extreme of mental suffering. True, there are still a few old-style external rules, but the relaxed atmosphere of "play" belies the *internal* "passion" for excellence – *work never done, worthiness never achieved*. Even great is not good enough – perfection beyond perfection *without limit*. Fascist ideology at its purest: *Arbeit macht frei*.

The old paternal conservative superego pales into insignificance beside the potentially unlimited severity/excellence/transparency of the ego ideal everywhere enjoined. To be an "entrepreneur of the self," to invest in oneself – as a sexual being, as an economic being. From Weber's "iron cage" (*stahlhartes Gehäuse*)[36] of rational technological efficiency to the modern "glass cage" of the open-plan office space, with no barriers to work and cooperation. Or the "glass ceiling" that denies advancement, thus inviting yet harder striving and competition. From the medieval church bell, to the factory whistle of the industrial revolution, to the beeping of postmodern 24/7 connectedness. These are all part of the gradual ramping-up process. Such is the success of the schizo scrambling heads process that we fear humans being taken over by robots, when all along have we not been welcoming our subjection in the mechanosphere?

> Obedience to God,
> becomes obedience to man,
> becomes obedience to the machine,
> becomes obedience to the code.
> "Code wins arguments."

Bernard Steigler, student of Baudrillard, speaks of "proletarianisation" – education for consumption.[37] In modernity, craft skills gave way to automation by machines manned by newly de-skilled labour – the industrial proletariat. In postmodernity, information technology de-skills whole swathes of white-collar workers. First manual then intellectual work is proletarianised. At the same time comes the proletarianisation of consumption with the emphasis shifting from desire (Symbolic register) to the drive (Real register). Consume, enjoy – now! Steigler distinguishes between the slow "long circuits" of education (and psychoanalysis) and reflection and the "short circuits" demanded by the drive: consumable/disposable knowledge. 'The result', says Steigler, 'is a psychological and social disorder whose overriding consequence is the liquidation of our cognitive faculty itself, and its replacement by informational dexterity'.[38] Short circuits create sparks, explosions and fires – the new proletarians and their *jouissance*. Short circuits create destruction and creation. Zuckerberg speaks of "rewiring" no less, creating this manic short-circuiting effect. Against the civilising notion of patience, he refers to 'the foolish wait', as he calls it in the "Hacker Way" – 'an approach to building that involves continuous improvement and iteration'. This is surely the way to stop thinking. The rewiring will stop real thinking. The 'liquidation of the cognitive' is an *anti*-thinking approaching zero. Iterate, reiterate, like a child's rapid movements to disperse anxiety. As Zuckerberg ordains, 'Move fast and break things'.[39]

Transience is key. Nothing must last. Contingency is all. The schizo process is defined by its ultimate lack of solidarity and loneliness. Bauman confirms that 'consumption is a lonely activity, endemically and irredeemably lonely, even at such moments as it is conducted in company with others'. He adds, 'cooperation is not only unnecessary, but downright superfluous'.[40] Old enlightenment notions such as commitment, thinking and trust must yield to schizzing effects, which Bauman refers to as a "liquefaction."

George Soros is an exemplary culture warrior, financial speculator-cum-social benefactor, the "hit-and-run" capitalist who gives money to cannabis and drugs legalisation and money to social activists in Ferguson and elsewhere, to the anti-market Occupy Wall Street movement for example, through his "Open Society Institute." He funds other grass roots causes like MoveOn.org and Media Matters to fight left-wing causes and buy liberal politicians, journalists and liberal media generally to undermine the very forces who defend his position of extreme wealth, privilege and asset speculation. As a Hungarian Jew at 14, watching his fellow Jews being transported to the camps, he narrowly avoided the same fate through the protection of his "godfather," a non-Jewish official at the agriculture ministry, bribed by George's father into claiming that young George was his Christian godson. While Hungarian Jews were being shipped off to the death camps, George accompanied his "godfather" on his rounds confiscating property from the Jews. Much later in 1998, when asked in a CBS interview[41] how he felt about this confiscation, he said that he had no regrets, no guilt as he had no part in the confiscation. He acknowledged that it was a character-forming experience, but that he himself had to look to the future. It reminded him of market acquisition; if *he* doesn't do it (asset strip), someone else will. The property was going to be taken away by someone. Thus, by extension, ruthless impoverishing financial speculation on a global scale is compatible today with charitable donation and the inclusion of all humanity. In 1992, he speculated against sterling, causing it to crash, devastating the retirement savings for millions of Britons and making an estimated $1bn in a day. Soros also played a part in triggering the East Asian financial crisis in 1997, and problems for the Yen in 2013.[42]

Maybe, Soros proves that anyone can become a socialist. Bertie Ahern, recent Irish Prime Minister, while presiding over a disastrous property boom that greatly enriched his cronies and the banking elites, claimed he was really a socialist at heart! The Communist party of China justifies its authoritarianism as the best protection for Chinese capitalism. New Labour in Britain presided over increasing inequality, being 'intensely relaxed about people getting filthy rich'.

No wonder that Sloterdijk concludes that 'the world-soul project' has failed and as a consequence he recommends 'death by exposure', a long hard cold look at the dissolution of meanings and what he calls, 'the riven bonds of life'.[43] After the long march, the militant, machinic march, there are multiple lines of flight released that criss-cross the face of the earth, like aircraft vapour trails. Schizo lines of flight, but also pervo, narco, necro lines of flight, imagined and celebrated by our anti-Oedipal authors. The result: those bonds of life that were once termed Oedipal bonds that might have been worked through (*durcharbeiten*) to some kind of accommodation with the other are now uprooted and flung away in the name of freedom.

Trans-forms

The Symbionese Liberation Front was an urban militant group formed around the time of *Anti-Oedipus*. Part of their manifesto stated: 'The name "Symbionese" is taken from the word "symbiosis" and we define its meaning as a body of dissimilar bodies and organisms living in deep and loving harmony and partnership in the best interest of all within the body'. Harmony implies a plateau of intensity, a BwO. They went on to commit two murders and numerous other acts of violence before disappearing in 1975.

In *A Thousand Plateaus*, our authors celebrate all manner of exotic symbiotic assemblages, strange contiguities, trans-forms, transversals and metamorphoses, becoming-animal, peopling by contagion, unnatural participations, and so on. Becoming-whale – Ahab chooses Moby-Dick, the becoming-dog of Penthesilea, the becoming-woman of Achilles. Imagine all manner of illicit unions: wild-men; leopard-men, haecceities, fugitive beings, Lolito – eater of bottles and bicycles (half-animal, half-man), Hitchcock's birds that do not sing but produce eerie electronic vibrations. Even musical fragments like intermezzos or refrains that stick to us: 'a child in the dark, gripped with fear, comforts himself by singing under his breath' (343). Likewise, the *Fort–Da* game of Freud's grandson will be rethought as the child's first accompanying refrain to himself. Musical becomings, like birds' territorial songs, ethnic songs, women's songs, folk, blues refrains, or the songs of the deep sea creatures – part of our creaturely being. Musical notes need each other, just as symbionts as different as the spider and the orchid need each other.

These *becomings* are not to be confused with imitating, identifying, progressing/regressing, which operate rationally on the plane-of-*organisation*. Becomings are assemblages, packs, swarms, anomalies, borderline states forming on planes-of-*intensity*. These individuations are *not* subjectifications, but rather *de*-subjectifications, which transect and transgress diagonally *against* the psychoanalytic reductive regimen with its *repression* of the imaginary, hallucinatory, mad and seductive planes. Here, following Baudrillard, *everything is seduction*. What is celebrated on the plane-of-immanence is Kerouac's dream of 'saturating every atom', forsaking all resemblance, analogy and comparison, without memory or desire. *Being present at the dawn of the world* (309).

More prosaically, symbionts discovered in nature are every bit as common, yet as strange and exotic as our examples above. The familiar lichen is composed of unlikely symbionts, an alga (plant) and a fungus. Many plants live symbiotically with fungi: the plants fix carbon from the air, and the mychorrizae extract minerals from the substrate. Nitrogen "fixers" are bacteria that grow inside the cells of plant root nodules of the Leguminosae, the pea family. Bacilli in the guts of ruminants make possible the digestion of plant cellulose. Combinations of animals and plants exist. Corals contain photosynthetic bacteria that live within the coral's tissues. Sea anemones associate with clownfish, which are protected from predator fish by the stinging tentacles of the anemone. The goby fish uses the shrimp's burrow for protection; the tube worms (of hydrothermal vents) are reliant on bacteria for food. Hermit crabs in gastropod shells. Flowering plants and pollinating insects – the insects are "paid" in nectar.

In addition to the systematic plane-of-organisation discovered by Darwin, biologist Lynn Margulis believes that symbiosis, *not just* competition for survival, is a key driver of evolution, based on co-operation, interaction and mutual dependence among *radically different* organisms. According to Margulis and Sagan, 'Life did not take over the globe by combat, but by networking'.[44] Even in biology, everything is seduction.

The ultimate bizarre symbiosis, or biological haecceity, is the living cell itself, the fundamental unit of all life. The cell is an assemblage, a cobbling together of strange "organelles" networking in and for the overall cell structure. Mitochondria from ancient bacteria were incorporated into the cell at the dawn of life to provide for the energy needs of every eukaryotic cell on the planet. Plant cells went further, incorporating photosynthetic bacteria which became chloroplasts, the *universal food machines of photosynthesis upon which the whole of life on earth depends*.[45] The whole biosphere is fundamentally dependent upon these strange symbionts.

Not content with natural symbiotic combinations and assemblages, mankind had to go further. The first "recombinant bacteria" were created in 1973, the beginning of the new schizo-biology to run in parallel with the new schizo-psychology. New plant and animal varieties have always been "created" by artificial selection, where the (genetic) *integrity* of the organisms involved was never in question. With genetic modification that integrity was breached, allowing new unimaginable combination-machines, *abolishing the primal distinction between natural and artificial.* This is a breach that has passed largely unnoticed.

New realisations: fish that glow in the dark; weeds that self-destruct; bacterial machines that produce insulin; man–mouse cell assemblages; bacteria that eat plastics; rice that produces beta-carotene for vitamin A production; triple stack corn, which resists herbicides and insect attacks; cows that produce human breast milk; the "enviropig" that excretes less phosphorus in manure; transgenic goats that make a spider-like protein that can be polymerised into "biosteel" fibre; salmon that grow at three times the normal rate; mice with ears on their backs. The revolution in biology represents the "the long march" through the species.

Some natural assemblages created lines of abolition and destruction, such as pathogenic bacteria and viruses. Viruses could opportunistically jump hosts – the AIDS virus, for instance, that jumped from monkeys to man and set in train a killing line of flight, a viral war machine that weakens or kills its unwilling hosts from *within* their BwOs.[46] This particular line of destruction created a pandemic.

However much we might benefit from exotic schizo-species, promising increased food supplies, pharmacological products, and new cancer treatments and so on, the problem with *artificial* trans-genesis is fundamentally an ethical one. The promiscuity involved in inserting foreign genes into integral species, or creating artificial life forms (synthetic biology), entirely in line with anti-Oedipal imaginings, oversteps an ethical line, creating "species" that are cosmic jokes. The commandment to 'have dominion over the fish of the sea and over the birds of the heavens and over the livestock and over all the earth and over every creeping thing that creeps on the earth' (Genesis 1:26) becomes with trans-genesis the *humiliation* of species in their *genetic* integrity. Species are "created" that are entirely unnatural and bizarre: *a crime against life itself.*

No negation

Negative assemblages rarely merit a mention because the new paradigm knows *no negation*. Like the unconscious, 'the plane of consistency is also the plane of non-contradiction … It is thus a plane of proliferation, peopling contagion' (294). Becoming opposes being. However, there are some cautionary words from our authors. Not only are forms continuously scrambled, with particles spinning off strata, and so on, but our authors ask: 'is it necessary to retain a minimum of strata, a minimum of forms and functions, a minimal subject from which to extract materials, affects and assemblages?' (298). Also, 'The fact that there is no deterritorialisation without a special reterritorialisation should prompt us to rethink the abiding correlation between the molar and the molecular' (334).

The molecular *requires* the molar, as a river requires its banks. Becoming must after all be tempered by being. There is an implicit acknowledgement of strata of repression and of at least some molar organisation. They ask, 'How could unformed matter, anorganic life, non-human becoming be anything but chaos pure and simple?' They advise (unspecified) rules and strict caution because, as they warn, 'too sudden destratification may be suicidal, [or, may sometimes] end in chaos, the void and destruction'. They warn, chaos may 'lock us back into the strata which become *more rigid still*' (554, emphasis added).

The explosion of promiscuous imaginings that tears through the once solid stratifications generally was a premonition of what is to come. The cultural storm uprooted trees and blew off the branches of old hierarchies to replace them with underground rhizomics that cared nothing for the storms that they had whipped up and the destruction wreaked. The beauty of the tree is replaced by the banality of the rhizome. Those intellectuals, who had gained most from the old arborescent systems, used their intellectual superiority to destroy and flatten. They used the richness of the old language to destroy the old language. They owe an immense debt to transcendence while denying its existence.

Our authors called for passions of a *collective* nature. What happened instead was increasing molecularisation and atomisation. In the introduction to *Anti-Oedipus* we learn that man connected and in tune with his desires ceases to worry about the behaviour of his fellow men, about right and wrong, justice and so on, 'he will float on the surface like a lotus and he will blossom and give forth fruit'.[47]

We have observed how virtual "ideas" become mainstream, affirming nomadic schizophrenic thinking, a + b + c + x + y … collecting a multiplicity, creating a smooth space, with no external vantage points. No judgement can be made unless one returns to old philosophies of negation, x = x *not* y.

We argue that in the (schizophrenic) absence of the negative, the refusal/disavowal of the negative, leads to a *burgeoning* of the negative "underneath" the virtual rhizomic affirmative celebratory universe. Indeed, this "negativity" is deployed most clearly in Chapter 12 of *A Thousand Plateaus*, 'Treatise on Nomadology. The War Machine' (387–467), to which we have already made reference. Now, however, we want to emphasise the *ubiquity* of the war machine *per se*, i.e. the ubiquity of the negative!

The progressive view seeks to claim intensely and repeatedly that the war machine was *all on one side*, the side of the all-powerful phallic, stratifying, elitist, negating State, which would crush the nomadic flowers, the lotus blossoms with affluence and war. However, in this Chapter 12, we learn that the war machine *is primary*. Our authors are clear. 'The war machine in itself … seems to be *irreducible* to the state apparatus, to be *outside* its sovereignty and *prior* to its law … In every respect, the war machine is of another species, another nature, another origin than the State apparatus' (388–9, emphasis added).

In the next move, as we have indicated, the State fights the nomad war machine and the nomad war machine resists, and/or the State appropriates the war machine and augments it, uses it for its conquering purposes. Only at this point of the State's appropriation of the nomad's weapon, progressive anti-Oedipals scream "negativity:" *Can you not see how negative the State is? Can you not see how cancerous America/the West/Israel is?* Negativity resurfaces, it is *out there* in the State apparatus, justifying the uprooting, the long nomadic march through the institutions, brick by brick, concept by concept, value by value, molarity by molarity. Set fire to reality! The blaze of *jouissance*!

A series of three programmes by Adam Curtis with the Deleuzian title, *All Watched Over by Machines of Loving Grace*,[48] documents the failure and disappointment of the dream of liberation through machines. Growing excitement around the networking technologies created the utopian belief in the 1970s and 1980s that all would be connected and empowered to be heroic and equal individuals, creating a society where hierarchical forms of political control would be unnecessary and where animal and humans would be cybernetically linked into a rhizomic "web of total harmony." No need for the nomadic war machine at all.

In the last two decades this dream of connectivity was realised in three broad areas: through an understanding of ecological systems; through social networking; through global financial systems. Communes were the prototypes of these self-organising systems. Connected as nodes in a system, we could negotiate without being allowed to form coalitions or power blocs. However, Curtis demonstrated that power relations did *not* disappear, because people themselves are intrinsically different and unequal. Power and inequality inevitable reassert themselves. The phallic economy returns. In the twenty-first century, "machines of loving grace" watch over us but in maybe sinister new ways creating unimagined perfect surveillance systems implying perfect power and perfect control.

Whatever deterritorialised freedoms briefly appear, they are quickly re-territorialised (negated) by powerful vested interests that arise from within (or without). The revolution may be started on social networks and everyone comes together, but then sinister phallic molarities take over, often *in a more virulent form*, as every revolution since the Jacobin terror testifies.

The guillotine was called the "National Razor," the symbol of the revolutionary cause, the people's avenger, the return of the phallic castrating machine. The nomadic war machine, the creator of smooth revolutionary spaces, becomes the nomadic hyper-castrating machine. As our authors note, the *nomos* 'has a rigour and cruelty all of its own (get rid of what cannot be transported, the old, the children …)' (542) … the authors themselves fail to complete this sentence. Where have we heard this "transporting" theme before?

The nomads' material is metal: 'metal is everywhere. Metal is the conductor of all matter … Metal is neither a thing nor an organism but a BwO' (454). 'Metalworking was the "barbarian," or nomad art par excellence' (442). They created tools, but more significantly weapons – the lance, the sword, knife, dagger, pike, all of which imply pure speed, flux, turbulence, the pure cut, 'a way of making violence durable, even unlimited' (437). This is where the long march will ineluctably end: 'a machine [with] a set of cutting edges that insert themselves into the assemblage [institution, tradition, life form, Being] undergoing deterritorialisation …' (367). Thus each is cut from within, like an abortion, a dilation and curettage cleansing mechanism. Not surprising therefore that the cover picture on the Continuum edition of *Anti-Oedipus* is a close-up image of an auger with its spiral cutting edge.

Mimesis

In the absence of landmarks – the Law, Oedipus, the Symbolic register and civilisation itself, there is nothing for it but to collapse backwards into imaginary rivalry and the escalating violence of the war machines.[49] It is only the Law and the thin seam or stratum of civilisation that stands guard over and against the (violent) *jouissance* of the BwO, and all the desiccated and de-structured remains of the molecularised aborted institutions, the bricks on the ground, the bodies strewn about, the fires still burning. And for those who correctly point out that the Law itself is founded on violence and maintained by violence, let them compare this "violence of normality" with Mogadishu (1993), Sarajevo (1992), Rwanda (1994), Phnom Penh (17 April 1975), Srebrenica (1995), Grozny (1999–2000), Darfur (2003–), Baghdad (2003–11), Misrata (April 2011), Homs (2012), all in the hellish non-striated grip of their various war machines which show no pity and that is in just the last quarter century.

At this point, we will turn our attention to a theorist of war, René Girard. From his early work on literary theory and criticism, Girard turned his attention to anthropology and the primitive mythological origins of violence and the means of its cessation. In his key text, *Violence and the Sacred*,[50] written coincidentally in the same year as *Anti-Oedipus*, Girard underlines the ubiquity of violence in primitive societies, like our authors' theorising of the nomadic war machines. Girard, however, draws attention specifically to the *mimetic* character of violence.

Envy is the response to ontological lack; jealousy and resentment of what the other has. Girard is unnecessarily critical of psychoanalysis when much of his theorising amplifies both what Freud emphasised about the ubiquity of the death drive and Lacan's Hegelian-Kojévian theory of desire. Girard's explication sounds Lacanian: 'he [the subject] desires being, something he himself lacks and which some other person seems to possess. The subject thus looks to that other person to inform him of what he should desire in order to acquire that being' (155). We desire what the other desires because they desire it, not because we need it, but because they have it and we want it. Very quickly, *many* people will desire the *same* thing, because it seems desirable. Desire *mimes* the other's desire; we want the same as the other.

Two key points emerge: first, desire manifests as a *social* phenomenon, not just biologically rooted in the drive; and second, desire (as in the "mirror stage") quickly becomes aggressive and rivalrous, in which case it becomes a *fight* for what the other possesses, with the potential for escalation. Girard likens this extremism to an infection or pollution, or the spilling of blood. Our perceiving evil in the other and the violent measures taken to combat it, inevitably converge sowing chaos and destruction. So-called "mimetic violence" will only be controlled, not by counter-violence, but by religion, i.e. by sacred rituals involving the killing of a scapegoat – an unimportant third party who can "safely" be sacrificed to defuse the crisis which is tearing apart the social fabric. The scapegoat must be foreign, an enemy or "other," designated by the warring factions as sufficiently different so that his death does not lead to more killings within the society. The sacrifice is a sacred duty, a perfect cover for the violence of the act, the true logic of which must never be disclosed to the participants.

The so-called "bad" violence of the warring factions will be countered only by the "good" violence of a sacrifice that will end the chain reactions of violent reprisals. As if taking his cue from psychoanalyst Matte Blanco, Girard demonstrates again and again how violence becomes symmetrical, reciprocal, eliminating difference as the combatants become mirror images of each other, "monstrous doubles," with their tit-for-tat killings, spreading throughout the community. For instance, Oedipus, Creon, Laius, Tiresias, taking their cue from the oracle, each seek the other's downfall. Each becomes similarly and symmetrically violent. *Oedipus* is selected as the sacrificial victim, because he alone is regarded as guilty of patricide and incest. He is the monstrous exception. Oedipus becomes the repository of all the community's ills, to be done away with in order for peace to return.[51] Likewise here, the anti-Oedipals unite in their hatred of Oedipus, who therefore must be sacrificed. Oedipus is scapegoated because he wasn't sufficiently anti-Oedipal, thus remaining a tragic divided figure.

The list of potential sacrificial victims is varied: prisoners of war, slaves, adolescents, children, the handicapped, anyone sufficiently *different*, sufficiently *other* from Pharmakós to King, might be selected for sacrifice. Twins are regarded as impure and demonic especially if identical. Other potential victims include a warrior steeped in blood, an incestuous couple, menstruating women, and so on. Recalling our argument, the erotic eliminates difference, celebrates confusion, because it allows for the "return of the repressed" and thus provokes counter-cathectic violence against such "evil." This recalls Laplanche's "sexual death drive" theory,[52] and George Bataille's erotic.[53] As Girard says, 'naked or pure sexuality is directly connected to violence. It is the final veil shielding violence from sight' (122).

Violence once started creates an orgy of destruction. Violence is con-fusion, difference is eliminated: between god and non-god; between man and woman; parent and child – 'a hallucinatory state that is not a synthesis of elements, but a formless and grotesque mixture of things that are normally separate' (169). This is *anti*-Oedipus, everything is reduced via mixing to the sameness of shit! Violence has this eviscerating effect. Our authors, averse to *key* Oedipal differentiations (mother, father. child, brother, sister, etc.), celebrate contagion. Differentiation, on the other hand, establishes culture, peace with the "violence of normality," where the scapegoated "monsters" are marginalised and some stability is assured provided the paranoid machines continue to function in the background, with their counter-cathexes.

However, ambiguities should not to be passed over too lightly. The so-called differentiations within civilised culture, from the exorcised, excluded, violated position of the scapegoat, are clearly *stigmatised* differences; differences that threaten the civilised repressive edifice. The apparent peace and stability of the civilised culture depends on these exclusions. In other words, the differentiating and thus civilising process is a violent process. Whereas the anti-Oedipal utopian vision is inclusive: the promiscuous and multiple "becomings" are multiply differentiated singularities, molecularities, apparently without *any* exceptions, antagonisms or rejected scapegoats.

The anti-Oedipal "successes" are celebrated by the number of formerly excluded "others" that have been brought back from the outside: women, children, the disabled, gays, transsexuals, ethnic groups, those with mental illness, and so on. All part of a massive ongoing programme of *de*-stigmatisation promoted by powerful lobby groups, NGOs and protected by new human rights legislation underwritten by supra-national bodies such as the EU and the UN. The new "tolerance" believes in its own utopia; it has done away with the scapegoating, stigmatising mechanism.

The era of scapegoating is *not* over. In the late 1930s, George Orwell went to Spain to fight in the civil war. Surprised and heartened by a new spirit of subversive equality, he observed that:

> I had dropped more or less by chance into the only community of any size in Western Europe where political consciousness and disbelief in capitalism were more normal than their opposites. Up here in Aragón one was among tens of thousands of people … *all living on the same level and mingling on terms of equality.*

This was a foretaste of real socialism, no snobbishness, no money grubbing, no class divisions or fear of the boss, no one on the make, genuine camaraderie. Orwell noted that it lasted long enough for those who experienced it to feel that they had been in contact with something very memorable. But Orwell concluded that such a state of affairs could not last. It was simply a temporary and local phase in 'an enormous game that was being played out over the whole surface of the earth'.[54] Violence returned with re-differentiations, reterritorialisations by Stalinist Left fascism and the creation of new scapegoats. Orwell himself was accused of being a Fascist, by the resurgent Stalinists, who declared the dissident Communist POUM[55] to be in the pay of Hitler and Franco.

Only the Bible and Christianity – Girard's key insight – offer *the* potential turning point for a violent world. Christianity unveils the victim mechanism, exposing the scapegoating myth and *takes the side of the victim*. In the wonderfully named *Things Hidden Since the Foundation of the World*, Girard discusses the role of Christianity.[56] In the prototypical story of Cain and Abel, Cain murders his brother and God makes him a wanderer on the earth. However, God puts a mark on him to protect him from vengeance for the suffering that he inflicted on Abel. In Judaism, the mark is not a scapegoating punishment but *a sign of God's mercy*. Cain builds the first city and this is the beginning of a civilisation capable of both judgement *and* mercy.

However Christianity, by exposing the scapegoating myth via the crucifixion, also risks plunging us *back* into sacrificial crisis and the potential for retaliatory violence – unless, that is, we acknowledge Christianity is *the* religion that exposes the dire plight of the victim-excluded and thus shows mercy. However, since Christianity does not bring peace *but truth*, it is not clear how it can actually make a difference, because violence is always *violence against truth*. And the greatest truth, that the scapegoat should be shown mercy, requires (violent) repression. This truth is too violent to be spoken.

Christianity is a religion that brings division because it deprives warring factions of their sacrificial death machine. As Girard says, 'People will escalate violence in reaction to the Revelation because they will be increasingly unable to find an outlet for their mimetic struggles'.[57]

Violence today is indeed increasing across the world. Western secularism refutes this. As Girard says, 'Western rationalism operates like a myth: we always work harder to avoid seeing the catastrophe' (213). It is quite shameful how the radical Left has been tacitly supporting militant Islam during this century.[58] For Girard, we are back in the medieval village facing the Vikings. Girard advocates 'apocalyptic reasoning' (120), which takes account of the divine, by taking account of the radical *absence* of the divine, and the danger of a return to the mimetic war machines. Thus, he claims, 'it is up to each one of us to hold back the worst; *this is what being in an eschatological time means*' (131, italics added).

The anti-Oedipeans have given us privileged access and insight into apocalyptic reasoning and the massive destructive potential capable of being unleashed at the end of times, after all the "long marches" breaking up civilising strata, molar assemblages, power structures and powerless structures, biological organisms, genetic codes, and so on.

Hölderlin was a key influence on Girard. Hölderlin was deeply Christian and suffered his own private form of mimetic tension; he was bipolar. Hölderlin withdrew into interior exile or "mystical quietism." For Girard, the poet's great silence represented in some way 'the absence of God, an imitation of his withdrawal' (125). In order to avoid mimetism, 'We have to rise to the nobility of this silence' (121).

In spite of 'the implacable Law of mimetism', exemplified by the Napoleonic era, and Clausewitz's analysis of the inexorable trend towards extremes with France and Germany eyeing each other as an obstacle to be eliminated, Girard insists that beyond mimetism lies the Kingdom.

As Pascal observed, 'All nations were given up to unbelief and concupiscence'. The Kingdom corresponds to what Pascal believed was the order of the spirit, the necessary passage towards the order of charity. Furthermore, 'The infinite distance between body and mind symbolises the infinitely more infinite distance between mind and charity, for charity is supernatural'.[59] Charity may be powerless to change the course of events, but it alone makes it possible to understand them. This order of charity is linked to space for reflection beyond the mimetic law, creating a critical distance. Pascal suggested the precise distance to be from a painting in order to see it properly. Too close, you will empathise too much, you will be too attracted with the danger of being sucked into violent reciprocity; too far, you may become indifferent to the other. The solution lies in identification: I am the other, I become the other through a non-possessive, non-totalising, non-mimetic openness for-the-other.[60]

Christianity is the paradoxical religion of peace and of war. Girard concludes: 'I have always been utterly convinced that violence belongs to a form of corrupted sacred, *intensified* by Christ's action when he placed himself at the heart of the sacrificial system' (217, emphasis added). Christ exploded the safety mechanism, whereby the sacred violence could be hidden. Was Christ himself anti-Oedipal? He had to be put to death, as a massive act of negation. And likewise, Christianity itself will be sacrificed. With Nietzsche this appalling realisation is made explicit. *What was holiest and mightiest of all that the world has yet owned has bled to death under our knives. What were we doing when we unchained this earth from its sun?*[61]

For Girard, violence is all. Original sin is vengeance, never-ending vengeance: 'we have to imagine that for these very reasons the first human groups self-destructed' (19). Hinting at the radical autonomy of the death drive *per se*, its "machinic" self-propulsion, Girard says, 'Violence is the divine force that everyone tries to use for his own purposes and that ends up *by using everyone for its own*'.[62] He quotes Heraclitus: violence is the father and king of all.

With the mechanosphere, the subject, the human agency *par excellence*, has become the scapegoat! The whole import of our argument is contained in this paradox; this immense backfiring of the "liberation" process, or the great (unintended or strongly intended) consequence of the whole anti-Oedipal revolutionary struggle.

The need for the scapegoat mechanism has only *apparently* ceased, and ceased temporarily and necessarily, in the more stable democracies of the world, with the invention of the Law, the basis of every power structure today in liberal democracies. This something we have called, "the violence of normality." As Girard says, 'the judicial system and the institution of sacrifice share the same function, but the judicial system has been infinitely more effective in creating civilisation. However it can only exist in conjunction with a firmly established political power' (23). This power rarely shows its hand directly, allowing us to believe the necessary lie that civilisation is essentially non-violent. Therefore, just as Christianity exposed the truth of the scapegoat mechanism, the anti-Oedipeans have exposed the lie that liberal democracies are peaceful by showing that the Law and reason itself is violent and sacrificial.

Has not our little psychoanalysis itself become a scapegoat, caught between scientific psychological approaches, neuroscience on the one hand, and radical anti-Oedipal analytic enthusiasts on the other?

The question of Moses

The memory at least lives on. Freud has survived his murder! In anticipation of his demise, Freud made Moses the substance of his final message. Freud was aligning and reorienting psychoanalysis towards Judeo-Christian civilisation, just as Europe was about to implode into mimetic violence for the *second* time in a generation.

In *Moses and Monotheism*, Freud contradicts the Biblical story of Moses with his own retelling of events. Moses was not a Hebrew but an Egyptian priest born into Ancient Egyptian nobility, maybe a follower of Akhenaten, who had abandoned traditional Egyptian polytheism and introduced worship centred on *monotheistic*

Atenism. According to Freud, far from being chosen by the Jewish people as their leader, Moses *chose* the Jewish people to be *his* followers. The origins of monotheism are to be discovered in the transposition of the Egyptian religion of Aten via Moses to the Jews. The Jews, hating the harsh commandments of this monotheistic religion, murdered Moses. However, the guilt about this primordial murder lived on. The rebels regretted their crime, and in its place created the myth of the Messiah, the hope for the return of Moses as the saviour.

Freud wondered why monotheism had made such a deep impression on the Jewish people. He suggested that fate had led the Jewish people to repeat the primal murder this time on the figure of Moses, 'an outstanding father-figure' – a case of "acting-out" rather than remembering. Freud's construction is thus: 'remorse for the murder of Moses provided the stimulus for the wishful phantasy of the Messiah, who was to return and lead his people to redemption and the promised world-domination. If Moses was this first Messiah, Christ became his substitute and successor'.[63] Thus Paul could exclaim with some historical justification that the Messiah had really come. Freud's Moses myth is a precise reversal of the one described in *Totem and Taboo*. In *Moses and Monotheism*, the primordial father who is killed is not the old *jouisseur*, but *already the bearer of the Law*, and he is killed by the primitive "volcano" god, Yahweh, who is described as 'violent and blood thirsty'. Clearly Freud approves of the "permanent imprint" of monotheism on the Jewish character: 'its rejection of magic and mysticism, its invitation to advances in intellectuality (*Geistigkeit*) and the encouragement of sublimations … the possession of the truth … stress on what was moral … consciousness of being chosen'.[64]

Why did Freud need Moses? According to Jacques-Alain Miller, Freud, in keeping with the ominous decade in which he wrote the Moses book, was looking for the "signifier one," the master signifier, the great leader.[65] As Miller stresses, the logic of the "great man" is already fully apparent earlier in Freud's *The Future of an Illusion*. His fundamental thesis in *Civilisation and its Discontents* is that every culture worth the name is built on constraint and the renunciation of the drives, i.e. built on a sacrifice of *jouissance*. This sublimation of *jouissance* requires exemplary individuals, with which we can identify.

However, Freud believed in the power of reason and science to educate the drives, not least the analytic cure itself. Freud's enlightenment faith in the inevitable progress of science was countered by Lacan's anti-enlightenment ideology. Lacan, following Heidegger, linked science with the death drive, cut off from tradition, cut off from life, in which the subject of science as subject of the signifier *is already dead* (already sacrificed). Lacan saw that the domain of the Real is extended by means of science. Miller echoes our own concerns here when he states that psychoanalysis is not common-sense, 'It has to accommodate the Real, the new Real, the Real which is the production of the discourse of science'. Indeed Miller also follows Heidegger by proposing that the analyst should be 'the shepherd of the Real'.[66]

The notion of the shepherd is quite at odds with our authors, who will sense a gross paternal metaphor at work, the shepherd with his sheep. However, Miller adds that 'psychoanalysis should be ironic … the Lacanian preference is for "unreaderbility" and the 'half-telling (*mi-dire*) of truth'.[67] Does this still qualify the analyst as the shepherd of the Real – a sophisticated shepherd, no doubt, that is both engaged and stands back ironically?

For Miller, *Moses and Monotheism* is Freud's effort to save the Father and he concludes that it is therefore a 'strange, extravagant book'. As we have noted, the later Lacanians see no need to save the father. They refer to Freud's discourse as a "suspended" discourse,[68] where the Father and S1 are only a "preamble." Whereas, in at least three key texts, across the later part of his working life, *Totem and Taboo* (1913), *The Future of an Illusion* (1927a), *Moses and Monotheism* (1939), Freud comes to the master signifier through the father; he wanted the father to be real, i.e. not an illusion.

In *The Future of an Illusion*, Freud disingenuously trivialises religion as an illusion while implicitly affirming God through the father. For Freud, mankind is caught between two constraints: culture and religion on the one side, and raw nature on the other. Religion is *the* defence against nature; whereas the defence against traditional constraints is the place Freud appeared to reserve for the work of psychoanalysis. However, while clearly not a believer, Freud does want to stress the social, psychological and political roles of religion as productive of social cohesion and control, to counter the drive. For Freud, Moses is the father imago, while Jesus is relegated to only a repetition of the Mosaic prototype. Freud believes that Judaism stands for the father.

Freud's stress on the father and his prohibitive role is compensated for by the love coming from his internal representative, the superego. The harshness of the superego with religion in the background forbids *jouissance*, but the reward is the love of the father. This is the "promise" of submitting to castration. Thus Lacan accuses Freud, in *Seminar 17*, of defensively including religion, by promising the conciliatory notion of an all-loving father. According to Miller, some analysts hoped that Lacan like Freud would push psychoanalysis toward the Judaic tradition. They wrote in a recent book: 'We hoped that Lacan would push psychoanalysis toward Judaism in order to take its place in Christian speech'.[69] 'Ah well, they are confused', concluded Miller, 'it was Freud who did that. *And everything Lacan did led to exactly the opposite*' (emphasis added).

True to form, Miller asserts that 'the path of a psychoanalysis in the permission-to-*jouir* era, in the era when the prohibition was not at the top of the list … is not sheltered any more behind the father'. For Lacanians, there is no need of the father and his prohibition, because allegedly 'the structure of *jouissance* itself conveys a gap or a hole and thus finds *its own limits* in the traumatic effects of the repetition compulsion'. Thus, we can reject the nostalgia for the Father as so much "phantasmagoria"!

No need, it appears, for 'a shepherd of the Real'; the Real and the subject are able to shepherd themselves! Thus Miller concludes, 'Freud, establishing the genealogy of God, stopped at the Name-of-the-Father'. Lacan went further, as we have seen, to the desire of the mother and the other *jouissance*. Thus, Miller establishes his true radical credentials by suggesting that analysis is no longer constrained 'by a monocentric ideal where Freud held it captive to the end'. And as for the father, Miller hopes that analysts will not follow any church. He stresses, 'They are not the children of the father, but each one has his own path, appropriate for only him ... in the post-paternal era. And it is, as Lacan indicated, the path of his escapade'.

Thus, the Lacanians and in particular the Millerians have caught up with our schizoanalytic authors and all agree passionately about the "permission-to-*jouir*" era, which began in earnest in the late 1960s. More than four decades later, capitalists and psycho-schizo-analysts are largely of one mind in their permission-to-*jouir*. Molecularisations, singularisations and de-molarisations are in play, fighting without limit in the global market. Tensions are reduced and phallic differences flattened and un-striated. Who can stop us now?

However, returning to the 'mind of the moralist',[70] Freud's position was nuanced. True: 'Men cannot remain children forever'.[71] Freud, like Lacan *et al.*, derided religious belief as childhood dependence, immaturity and fear of authority and so on. Freud says he fears, not for the "educated people" – 'such people are to a large extent themselves vehicles for civilisation', but for the masses no longer held in check by traditional religious beliefs, who will accept all too easily the liberation of scientific rationality, 'without the change having taken place in them which scientific thinking brings about in people'.[72] Is there not a danger that,

> if men are taught there is no almighty and all-just God, no divine world order and no future life, they will feel exempt from all obligation to obey the precepts of civilisation? Everyone will, without inhibition or fear, follow his asocial, egoistic instincts and seek to exercise his power. Chaos, which we have banished ... will come again.[73]

His Girardian conclusion is that, 'when you learn that there is no God and that you need not fear His punishment, you will certainly kill your neighbour without hesitation'.[74]

However, Freud's view of monotheism as authoritarian, stratifying, consolatory and protective for the masses needs an extra twist. His chosen example of Moses as a father, a bearer of the Law, is at the same time a figure of defiance. Moses was *subversive* of the old pagan order. Consider also the Old Testament prophets, who reproach unjust leaders, defending the rights of the poor against the rich and powerful. Jesus, preceded by St Paul, was the most subversive of all bringing the new religion into prominence: 'I did not come to bring peace but a sword' (Matthew 10: 35). 'If any man come to me and hate not his father and mother and wife and children, and brethren and sisters, yea, and his own life also, he cannot be my disciple' (Luke 14: 26). Far from being stabilising and normalising, the paradox of the Judeo-Christian religion as we have seen with Girard is precisely its subversive character. It is the most revolutionary of all.

Kierkegaard is exemplary in this subversive sense. In his praise for Abraham, who by being willing to sacrifice his son Isaac for his faith in and absolute duty to God 'suspends the universal Hegelian ethical' as a paradoxical exception, risks everything in loneliness, isolation, terror. Thus Kierkegaard challenges the bourgeois religious of all time. He says, 'So let us either forget all about Abraham or learn how to be horrified at the monstrous paradox which is the significance of his life, so that we can understand that our time like any other can be glad if it has faith'.[75] Being willing to sacrifice his son in obedience to God is a truly Kierkegaardian "Either/Or," that cannot be supported by reason, but faith alone. And Faith, for Kierkegaard, is the highest passion. He says, 'Many in every generation may not come that far, but none comes further'. As if to make a riposte to Freud, Lacan and atheists in general, he insists: 'I can refer to my own experience, that of one who makes no secret of the fact that he has far to go, yet without therefore wishing to deceive either himself or what is great by reducing *this latter* [faith] *to a triviality, to a children's disease* which one must get over as soon as possible'.[76]

Atheists are disingenuous with their blind confidence concerning the non-existence of God. As Lacan observed, 'The true formula of atheism is not God is dead – even by basing the origin of the function of the father upon his murder, Freud protects the father – the true formula of atheism is *God is unconscious*'.[77]

Finally, to answer our question as to why Freud needed Moses, we have Freud's own answer. Referring to the marble statue of Moses by Michelangelo in the church of S. Pietro in Vincoli in Rome, Freud says, 'no piece of statuary has ever made a stronger impression on me than this. How often have I mounted the steep steps from the unlovely Corso Cavour to the lonely piazza where the deserted church stands'. Freud considers his guilt: 'the angry storm of the hero's glance', and the thought that 'I myself belonged to the mob upon which his eye is turned – *the mob which can hold fast to no conviction, which has neither faith nor patience and which rejoices when it has regained its illusory idols*'.[78] Freud marvels: 'Michelangelo has chosen this last moment of hesitation, of calm before the storm, for his representation. In the next instant Moses will spring to his feet – his left foot is already raised from the ground – dash the Tablets [with the Decalogue] to the earth and let loose his rage upon his faithless people'.[79] What impresses Freud here is Moses' moment of self-control. Instead of letting go his rage upon the mob he *restrains* himself. Therefore, what Michelangelo has created 'is not an historical figure, but a character-type, embodying the inexhaustible inner force which tames the recalcitrant world';[80] what Freud refers to as 'the highest mental achievement that is possible in a man, that of struggling successfully against an inward passion for the sake of a cause to which he has devoted himself'.[81]

Notes

1 See Žižek, S., 2008.
2 See, for instance, Chesterton, G. K., 1908b.
3 These opposed perspectives on "machinic," as miraculous new versus old undead repetition, are an example of parallax, explored in Žižek, S., 2006. See also Chapter 5 below.
4 See *Time* (10 February 2011). 'We are fast approaching the moment when human and machines merge. Welcome to the Singularity movement.

5 Žižek, S., 2008.
6 Ibid.
7 Alliez, E., 2004.
8 Ibid.
9 *The Sunday Times* (15 January 2012) carried a report by Christopher Goodwin about Berlin, the so-called club capital of Europe, where each weekend an estimated 20,000 clubbers arrive from Britain and other European countries. Every extreme sexual, narcotic and musical preference is catered for in the myriad of venues. The scene is disturbingly reminiscent of the Weimar Berlin during the inter-war years, depicted in films like *The Blue Angel* (1930) with Marlene Dietrich and *Cabaret* (1972) with Lisa Minnelli. The Kitkat, named after the club in *Cabaret*, is the most flamboyant while Insomnia offers 'erotic games in an atmosphere of Babylonian diversity'. In Weimar times, there were 16 different types of prostitutes in the city including child prostitutes. After 1989, and the fall of the Wall, huge empty factory spaces became available in the East Berlin, which enterprising hippies and anarchists turned into industrial-sized clubs. The basement of one club (Berghain) is referred to as 'the laboratory, the dungeon, the torture chamber'. It has all the necessary instruments of *jouissance* – machines, chains and bars. Even the reporter becomes 'deeply unnerved' by what he has seen, with 'insistent images of writhing naked bodies playing through my head. I watched thousands of drugged-up clubbers dancing in their own dreamscapes and saw hundreds of anonymous bodies desperately clutching for flesh in dark sex rooms'. All this in the capital that should, but currently refuses, to hold the key to the European financial crisis. 'A profound depression washed over me as I took a taxi home'. He glimpses the morning newspapers about a neo-Nazi cell that has been murdering Turks for the last 10 years with impunity.
10 Ballard, J. G., 1973.
11 Three years after this book was published, Baudrillard referred to car crashes as the modern form of sacrifice in an otherwise de-sacralised world (Baudrillard, J., 1976).
12 Ballard, J. G., 1973: 81.
13 Freud, S., 1900: 408–9.
14 Ballard, J. G., 1973 PS p. 14, at the end of this volume.
15 Ibid.: 155.
16 Deleuze, G., and Guattari, F., 1980: 253. (Page numbers in brackets refer to this volume.)
17 See, for instance, Goldberg, J., 2007.
18 This view is contradicted below.
19 Barish, E., 2014.
20 Antliff, M., 2011.
21 Critchley, S., 2012: 105–6.
22 Goldner, L., 1998.
23 Mehlman, J., 2006: 124.
24 Wolin, R., 2004: 191.
25 Ibid.: 201.
26 Ibid.: 207.
27 Ibid.: 205.
28 Ibid., Blanchot cited on p. 214.
29 Comment by Lucien Aychenwald in Derbyshire, J., 2013.
30 Ibid. We return to Heidegger and the question of Nazism in Chapter 6.
31 See Macey, D., 1988: 34–8.
32 Roudinesco, E., 1993: 16.
33 Ibid.: 86.
34 Gramsci was an Italian Marxist, political philosopher and linguist of the early twentieth century. He was founder of the Italian Communist Party. He is best known for his concept of "cultural hegemony;" the notion that power is maintained via culture itself, invisibly, by the ruling ideology affecting our whole world-view – beliefs, explanations, perceptions, values, mores, etc., as a means of maintaining the capitalist status quo. He was imprisoned by Mussolini's Fascist regime.

35 See "The Soul of Apple" by Kevin Kelly http://qideas.org/articles/the-soul-of-apple/.
36 Weber, M., 1905 (1930).
37 Steigler, B., 2010: 27.
38 Steigler, B., 2008: 183.
39 Mark Zuckerberg's letter to investors: www.wired.com/2012/02/zuck-letter/.
40 Bauman, Z., 2000: 161.
41 See here: www.youtube.com/watch?v=CW8ENFOCeBs
42 Wilson, J., 2014.
43 Sloterdijk, P., 2011: 216.
44 Sagan, D., and Margulis, L., 1986.
45 As an undergraduate in the biological sciences (Southampton) in 1968, part of my research involved separating out chloroplasts from plant cells and showing that they could live independently of the host cells in a test tube, providing evidence that they once had lived outside cells.
46 At about the same time a *psychical* immuno-deficiency spread throughout the West and the Third World requiring the development of a massive therapy culture to cope with the "stress" involved.
47 Deleuze, G and Guattari, F. 1972: p. xxv.
48 A BBC documentary series in 2011, by Adam Curtis. The title is taken from poet Richard Brautigan's 1967 "hippie manifesto." The manifesto was Brautigan's fifth poetry publication and all 1,500 copies were distributed free on the streets of San Francisco. The title poem looks forward to a world where cybernetics has advanced to the point where we could return to a balance and harmony with nature. Adam Curtis's earlier series, *Century of the Self* (2002), showed how Freud's discoveries led to Edward Bernays's development of public relations – the use of unconscious desire for status as a means of achieving economic growth and even political control of populations.
49 In the Oedipal drama, the father who fails to instil the Law will be thrown back into imaginary rivalry with his sons. Not infrequently, the police (the Law) have to intervene to separate fathers from sons, and brother from brothers.
50 Girard, R., 1972.
51 A modern example of the scapegoat mechanism, acquainted with the Girardian thesis, is the recent publication in English of Henri-Levi, B. and Houellebecq, M. 2011. 'You can bring all the legal actions you wanted and you'd still only be a nauseating matricidal killer, a racist and an Islamophobe … [while] I am a bourgeois bastard who knows nothing about social questions …': 197. The authors discuss their destroyed reputations as writers marginalised by the scapegoat mechanism: punished for writing novels, in Houellebecq's case, about 'the absolute irreversibility of all processes of decay once they have begun … In my novels there is no forgiveness, no way back, no second chance … it is like a universal law …': 111.
52 Laplanche, J., 1999.
53 Bataille, G., 1962.
54 See Orwell, G., 1938, pp. 83–86.
55 Catalan: *Partit Obrer d'Unificació Marxista.* The far-left Workers' Party of Marxist Unification was a Spanish communist party formed during the Second Republic and mainly active around the time of the Spanish Civil War.
56 Girard, R., 1978.
57 Girard, R., 2010: 118. Page numbers in parentheses refer to this volume.
58 See, for instance, Cohen, N., 2007; also Phillips, M., 2006. See also Kopping, W., 2008, a documentary on radical Islam in the United States, narrated by Muslim American Dr M. Zuhdi Jasser, arguing that there are two types of jihad being waged in the United States, these being violent jihad and cultural jihad. The argument for cultural jihad is that Islamic groups are using the laws and rights they are given to work against society and overthrow it. A religious version of the Long March.
59 See Pascal, B., 1670: 123–4.

60 This critical distance of the right proportion is precisely analogous to the analyst's position vis-à-vis the analysand. Not too empathetic but not too indifferent, being-for-the-other. This non-orthodox "positioning" of the analyst will be discussed at greater length in subsequent chapters.
61 Nietzsche, F., 1882: Aphorism 125.
62 Girard, R., 1972: 153, emphasis added.
63 Freud, S., 1939: 89.
64 Ibid.: 85–6.
65 Miller, J.-A., 2003.
66 The reference to Heidegger: 'Man is the shepherd of being. It is in this direction alone that *Being and Time* is thinking when ecstatic existence is experienced as "care"' (Heidegger, M., 1978: 234). This link with Heidegger, if we are to follow it, places the analyst in the position of "care," the way *Dasein* is involved with the other, is concerned for the other through existential anxiety, by literally *being-there*. It is a 'standing in' in the sphere of Being. It consists in *Dasein*'s openness to Being. Maybe Miller envisages a larger role for the analyst than our current fetish – the repressed unconscious. Winnicott distinguished between Being and Doing, with Being being linked to liveliness and spontaneity, for him the outcome of an analysis. Roustang spoke of "life" – the symptom being an important bit of dead-life that was trapped (encysted) by consciousness, causing anxiety, requiring more representation (through analysis) before it could rejoin the stream of life, of the Real. A shepherd on the other hand minds sheep, protecting the flock from predators and has a link back through history six millennia.
67 Ibid.
68 Page 429 of "Radiophonie."
69 I have not been able to trace this book.
70 The title of a key book, Reiff, P., 1959.
71 Freud, S., 1927a: 49.
72 Ibid.: 39. These days, the "educated people" are vehicles for civilisation because they have a stake (a house and a job) in its remaining stable, whereas this may increasingly not be the case for "the masses." Here we see Freud's touching liberal belief in scientific rationality that in time will educate all, so that there will be no need for religion. We see the same today with people demanding more education to control unwanted pregnancies, drug abuse, criminal behaviour, etc. Freud is undermining his own argument that the drives require something more than "education." Even some Lacanians acknowledge that some "shepherding" is required!
73 Ibid.: 34.
74 Ibid.: 39.
75 Kierkegaard, S., 1843: 81.
76 Ibid.: 146, emphasis added.
77 Lacan, J., 1964: 59, emphasis added.
78 Freud, S., 1914a: 213, emphasis added.
79 Ibid.: 216.
80 Ibid.: 221.
81 Ibid.: 233.

4

EVEN YOUR DREAMS ARE POLICE RECORDS

> Culture is the great help out of our present difficulties; culture being a pursuit of our total perfection by getting to know … the best that has been thought and said in the world.[1]

Student protests in France start in late March 1968. On 13 May over one million people marched in Paris and larger French towns. The French Labour movement and the Communist Party supported the student revolt. High-school students joined in, younger workers, contemporaries of the students, began striking and taking over factories all over France. Wildcat strikes followed. By the following week, 10 million workers were on strike, two-thirds of the French workforce. In the meantime the students had occupied the Sorbonne, the Odéon theatre and the School of Fine Arts. Red flags and posters of Marx and Chairman Mao covered the walls. Slogans like *It is Forbidden to Forbid* were posted all over the Latin Quarter. Calls for the end of the de Gaulle regime and a government of the people issued from all quarters.

De Gaulle, however, sought and got the backing of the army. On 30 May there was a massive counter-demonstration. Significant minimum wage and salary increases were made and the students rescinded. De Gaulle dissolved the government and came back with an increased majority for the Right in elections on 23 June. Was that a revolution? Blink and you might have missed it. For Baudrillard it marked the starting point for the virtual and the postmodern.

In Germany, the new generation of students realised that the obscene German chapter of Fascism was *not* closed. Many former Nazis were still in place in government or at the universities, as teachers, judges and so on. The mix of the historical calamity of starting and losing two catastrophic wars, political radicalism, the drug culture and the new music created the apocalyptic zero-hour (*Stunde Null*), the attempt at the severest break with the past that could possibly be imagined.

Between 1968 and 1977 bands like Neu, Can, Faust, Amon Düül II, Kraftwerk and others ditched the Anglo-American rock, blues and folk mould to create a new music *ex nihilo*, against the banal backdrop of the post-war folksy sentimental *schlager* music.

'*There must be some way out of here*' (Bob Dylan, Jimi Hendrix, 1968)! The way out was to create a *blitzkrieg* all of their own, a lightning war, an all-out attack on the old music. As Nietzsche said, 'It is not enough for me that lightning no longer does any harm. I do not wish to conduct it away: *it shall learn to work for me*'.[2] At the time of the album *Phallus Dei*, for instance, with its guitars, abstract percussion, strange chants or screams, Amon Düül II, the offshoot of Amon Düül, a revolutionary musical and political commune of German intellectuals, artists, musicians, radical activists of the late 1960s, formed the Munich commune, which was the locus of a radical Left libidinal politics that inspired, *beyond* music, a "passion for the Real," an anti-imperialist urban guerrilla warfare, Baader-Meinhof, the Red Army Faction, which became the most wanted terrorist group in Europe.

By tweaking the new electronic machines at random – oscillators, synthesisers – pure technological sounds, sine waves, multiple wave forms can be combined into immensely complex noise. The birth of electronic music by "musicians" created a virulent anti-music with haunting trance-like random free-form nihilistic sound. Stockhausen at the electronic music studio in Köln was a central influence. His interests – science, technology, religion, cosmology, mysticism – included using mathematical structures, such as the Fibonacci series, to dictate pitches, rhythms, articulations, and so on.

Oftentimes, one chord was sufficient to create the "break" from melody, from any kind of musical narrative or meaning. Monotony and repetition were key. Repetition became the repetition compulsion. Jaki Liebezeit's drumming, for instance, drove Can's compelling sound. He had been Germany's top jazz drummer, until he had an "epiphany." Someone told him to make his drumming monotonous, which he did to great acclaim! Faust, formed in 1971, used, among other items, a cement mixer and the sound of a brush being swept over concrete. There was a cartoon at the time: learn how to play a Faust song on guitar. Step one: learn the first riff. Step two: repeat the first riff for six minutes. Kraftwerk went fully electronic and robotic, together with smart suits and handmade shoes, an ironic return to the clean boys who sang *schlager*. Their aim: 'no separation between humans and technology; for us they belong together as a unity'. Machinics. Repetition. Monotony.

***

On 7 December 1970, West German Chancellor Willy Brandt travelled to Warsaw, Poland and dropped to his knees before the monument to the Warsaw Ghetto uprising of 1943.

***

In Britain, between the 1973 oil crisis and the winter of discontent, 1978–9, punk was the music of radical disaffection, as the anti-Oedipal moment of the late 1960s turned from love to hate. A rage space was created. As one fan quipped: punk means some guy in prison who got fucked up the arse! Recall the infamous *Today with Bill Grundy* (1976) – a mainstream ITV show. Grundy talks condescendingly to his guests, the Sex Pistols and their fans, referring to them as 'our heroes', but not like our nice clean Rolling Stones. Grundy observed provocatively that it is classical music that turns most people on, but not them! John Lydon rejoined, 'that's their tough shit'. Grundy made him repeat the offensive word, turning to the girls nearby for support, and when Siouxsie Sioux replied in a friendly fashion, Grundy suggests meeting later. Steve Jones responded calling Grundy a dirty sod, a dirty old man. Then, nothing to lose, Grundy goads Jones:

- Say something outrageous.
- You dirty bastard.
- Go on, again.
- You dirty *fucker* (more emphasis).
- What a clever boy!
- What a fucking rotter.

As the show ended and the credits rolled, the lads can be heard laughing as they begin to cavort about in the studio. The tabloid press next day reacted angrily: TV FURY AT ROCK AND ROLL FILTH.

'God save the queen; the fascist regime'. Talent was nothing, it was down to whether or not you had the balls to get up and do it. With bands such as The Damned, The Buzzcocks, Slaughter and the Dogs, X-Ray Spex and The Raincoats, punk as a grassroots movement spreading worldwide in the mid-1970s. Emerging from early forms of hard rock, such as garage rock, punk developed a frenetic, hard edged, anti-establishment, high intensity sound. A mix of hate, poverty, solidarity between musicians and fans, it was self-regarding aggression, a study in ugliness. With a DIY ethic of basement self-sufficiency, it bypassed the music industry, created a mass appeal – anyone now could create music – a precursor to the internet and uploads to YouTube.

'So let's all grab and let's all enjoy' (Sham 69). 'The rebels were waltzing on air'. It was anti-corporate, underground, rhizomic and anyone could form a band, there was no need to learn an instrument, no need to tune your guitar. But the Left oriented Clash signed up for CBS for £100,000 in January 1977 for their first album and were promptly accused of selling out. In the tradition of Romanticism, punk quickly succumbed to revolution fatigue.

> But you're not *into* music! You can't even play?
> So what!

Torn clothes, safety pins, paint-spattered T-shirts, offensive slogans, swastikas (the New York Dolls), bin liners, clothes as collage, rags held together, falling off – determined nihilism! But the shock index is falling. Capitalism that had already absorbed rock and hippie styles, would soon hoover-up punk by incorporating and commodifying it. As music critic Paul Morley indicated, punk was so successful that the corporate world stamped on it quickly. The genre far outlived the music and went mainstream, fashion, design, art and aesthetics, promoted by a whole new line of niche market retailers, reproducing punk's quirky obscenities as fashion, art and adornment. Punk rock's outright hostility to the straight world was collapsing. Bands like Green Day and Nirvana even made it into the mainstream by the early 1990s. *Fuck Authority* (Pennywise) was even played on the radio! Your mum took you to get your ears pierced and let the kids dye their hair.

So what are you rebelling against?, Brando was asked. I don't know. What have you got? I am an antichrist/And I am an anarchist/Don't know what I want/But I know how to get it.

★★★

1968 was a momentous year for America. The Vietnam War was raging. President Johnson faced a challenge from within his own Democratic Party from the anti-war candidate Eugene McCarthy. In April, Martin Luther King Jr. was assassinated leading to rioting in cities across America. Bobby Kennedy was killed after winning the California primary in June. In August, Republicans met in Miami choosing Richard Nixon as their candidate. In September, Democrats in Chicago backed Vice President Hubert Humphrey. Anti-war protesters filled the streets of Chicago with police running amok, attacking and arresting demonstrators and delegates alike. Norman Mailer was there to capture the anti-Oedipal bedlam.[3] 'The reporter' – Mailer refers to himself in the third person – was a Kennedy man but respectful of McCarthy.

It was meant to be "a Festival of life," according to the Yippie organisers. 'A clock can be wound too tight', said Tom Hayden of the New Left, referring to the Chicago police authorities readying for the fight with American radicalised youth. The "Yippie Manifesto" (25 August) demanded an immediate end to the war in Vietnam, legalisation of all drugs, the abolition of money, the promotion of "full *un*-employment" ending the drudgery of work, abortions when desired. 'We believe people should fuck all the time', they declared.

The Yippies were the militant wing of the hippies who, the reporter believed, revealed an American schizophrenia. Yippies naively believed that people should live without hurting each other. 'They had yet to learn', says Mailer, 'that society is built on many people hurting many people' (131). Mailer at 46, 'knew they were a generation which lived in *the sound of destruction of all order*' (emphasis added), issuing through the music. The reporter himself admitted he could not bear the, 'nihilisms … encountered in such musical storm … flesh plus hate, and blood plus hate' (133).

The attack when it came was ferocious. Newsmen were singled out. Phil Ochs captures a key *counter*-Oedipal theme. 'It's always the old who lead us to war; it's always the young who fall'.[4] In the tumult, Allen Ginsberg was chanting the ancient Sanskrit word "om" in a hoarse voice clearly damaged by tear gas. Suddenly tear gas canisters explode everywhere. Police were clubbing the protesters, people were running, fleeing for their lives, choking, vomiting.

Next day, Mailer watched from the 19th floor of the Hilton the attack on demonstrators in Michigan Avenue in front of the hotel; the imagery threatens castration: 'like a chainsaw cutting into wood ..., like a scythe through grass ... like a razor cutting a channel through a head of hair' (159). The reporter interprets and no doubt exaggerates the pent-up mood of the authorities: 'let them ... mock us, defy us, resist. There are more millions behind us than behind them, more millions who wish to weed out, poison, gas and obliterate every flower ...' (163).

Doesn't Mailer speak for most radicals, who in reality are reluctant to lose the America they had had? It had allowed him to live a good life and now the yippies might yet be disruptive enough to serve as a pretext to bring about 'totalitarian phalanxes of law and order ... the plague he had written about for years ...' (177). Mailer, the "Left-conservative," is alive to the concerns that we are addressing here. 'Society was held together by bonds no more powerful proportionately than spider's silk' (165). Yet he was proud of the youth, the "troops," as he called them, 'they had the courage to live at war for four days in a city which was run by a beast' (184).

> The bad cops, US marshals, generals, executives, rednecks, insane black militants ... [even] his own side [who] made jokes about putting LSD in drinking water ... believed in drugs and he did not ... burning money – he thought it was the last sanity for a Romantic ... taking the pill and going bare-ass in the park ... The children were crazy [but] they had vision not void of beauty; the other side ... only the nightmare of smashing a brain with a brick. (204)

On his last night in Grant Park, the reporter comes across a group he describes in religious terms: 'Fifty communicants sat on the grass, mountaineers, varlets, knaves, Hindu saints, musketeers, tank men, and wanly beautiful Yippie girls, while a priest in a violet satin chasuble recited Mass over their bloody heads and an acolyte held the cross' (212–13).

***

In the background always, the radiation of the *uber*-crime of the Holocaust and total war. How is it possible to represent these monstrosities? What desperate and demonic music can ever convey such things? The chaotic ferment of the Cultural Revolution, 'the flesh plus hate, and blood plus hate', has boiled away leaving a residual anti-traditionalist linguistic order, which for the younger generation of students today is *the* world order. The older versions of the Left, revolutionary Bolshevist, the self-improvement Left of the unions, co-ops and churches, have ceded ground to Cultural Marxism and the divisive wholesale policing of language. Cultural Studies departments and their tiny elites have become the place to do politics and sustain the soft Revolution, the key success of the post-'68 Left. Language, "the house of being," is purged of its patriachal, hierarchical, colonialist, Eurocentric, conservative Christian traditions. As Baudrillard asserts, 'We are afraid of language since we have been told about the signifier and all that. The signifier has introduced *terror* into language. "The unconscious is structured like a language" – nothing has wreaked such havoc as that kind of proposition'.[5]

The social doctrine of the Catholic Church[6] expresses serious concern about the "dictatorship of relativism" and "the culture of death." The Church stands alone in this. The colonisation of human nature, via the global mobilisation of the mass media, this *second* wave of colonialisation by the West – the decisive wave is a veritable tsunami: fragmentation of social bonds, disincarnated individualism (BwOs) – choose your gender, choose your sexual orientation, float free, float virtual. Pope John Paul warned about not just "the death of God," but about the *death of man.*

***

In 1967 Timothy Leary spoke at the "Human Be-In," a gathering of 30,000 young people in Golden Gate Park in San Francisco. He compared drug experimentation to a "great religion," in which, as he says, 'we seek to find the divinity within and to express this revelation in a life of glorification and the worship of God … – *turn on, tune in, drop out*'.[7] The bitter fruits of the libidinal revolution: four decades later, more than one person a day in Ireland dies of a drugs overdose. The figure has exceeded the number killed in car accidents. Drug deaths and car deaths, contemporary pagan sacrifice.

***

Four decades after the libidinal-feminist revolution, the moral panic about men as sadists and the moral panic about women as victims of "rape culture," is in full swing. No doubt, increased freedoms and atomisation has made women much more vulnerable and has tempted men into more predation and general misogyny. It has come to this. From *Homo sapiens* to *Homo rapiens* (John Gray). Women in Britain regularly report being afraid to walk alone on the streets after dark. Some report being seriously stalked, so much so that they have to move job, move house or apartment. Maybe the feminist-libidinists have it all wrong, but they will never see it. All this chasing down of power, the absolute grab for power off men, with men in the background plotting … an undreamt of violent reaction …

***

– Oh yes, (the questioner has a look between irony and contempt, head on one side) remind me again (inaudible sigh) why do you so nostalgically continue to emphasise the father?

- Because clinically we note again and again the father is so important for mental health.
- But there are many families are there not *without* fathers and they are doing just as well.
- No. There are half a million families without fathers now in the UK and this is, let us say, a quiet catastrophe, a catastrophe in the making.
- You are stigmatising single mother headed families. This is nothing to do with "no father" it is because of lack of resources. It is because we live in such an unequal society. This is elementary.
- No! Families without fathers are poorer financially because there is only one breadwinner. Family breakdown leads to poverty every bit as much as poverty leading to family breakdown. Families without fathers lack that special 'X' that only fathers can bring.
- Look, it is perhaps understandable that as we have been living during the era of patriarchy, now coming to an end, we have tended to think of the father as special. Now thankfully, this special father thing is being rethought and renegotiated. Even in early Lacan the father is a "Name-of" only. Now, he's nothing.
- Yes. Maybe you can hold with that if you have *no* real connection with the loss of a father and how devastating that can be. If you lose your father to divorce, early death, drug addiction, alcoholism and so on, its leaves a devastating hole in the real.
- Oh, but that is *only because of patriarchy* with its special privileging of the father. End patriarchy and there is nothing special about the father. We'll manage things without him. He's not coming back, thankfully.
- Your metallic reasoning destroys the father (and the mother and the child!). Welcome to the new era of barbarism! The family is destroyed!

[She has already walked off …]

***

- Yeah, I have a two-year-old.
- Do you see him much?
- Nah. I did for a while, but there were problems. So I left it all up to her. It's better that way. She's better with 'em. She prefers it. It's not fair to them to keep coming and going.
- Yeah, you're right. Leave them at it.

***

Following Charles Maurras and devout Catholic Paul Claudel, Lacan in his early period from 1938 to 1950 was not afraid to call on religious and political "Fathers" to counter the alleged paternal humiliation that founds psychoanalysis. This was Lacan's "Durkheimian period" defining the contraction of the family, the decline of the paternal imago, the degradation of the Oedipus complex and the genesis of neurosis and psychoanalysis. Markos Zafiropoulos refers to this "infantile theory," based on Durkeim's "invention" in 1892 at the age of 34, as quite obsolete. He explains that 'the theory of the decline of the father is itself a myth … [I]t is precicely those who experience it most intensely – or who believe in it most sincerely – who are least able to take stock of it as a myth'.[8] Zafiropoulos cannot go along with "de-symbolisation" either and our sense of desertion by the Other. And had Lacan been able to give his 1964 seminar on the *Names-of-the Father*, he would have been able to analyse Freud's desire for the Father and 'go back to the origin … to put analysis on its feet'.[9]

- Okay, so now you see this passion for the father was always a myth! (a little laugh!)
- I see. So the Lord's Prayer is a myth?
- Religious stuff!
- A two-millenial myth!
- Yes! It has taken that long … Look, patriarchy is finished. The truth is that recent generations are not having enough children. Patriarchy is dying. It's done for.

***

Just think of the many achievements to be notched up for feminism. 42 per cent of marriages in the UK end in divorce, mostly initiated by courageous, intelligent women, who are then free to live lives of sexual freedom again. But the long overdue collapse of marriage has created new poverty concentrated among single-parent families, headed mainly by women, and the male-dominated State bureaucracies are reluctant to step up to the plate financially. At least in these male-free zones, the children can grow up free from the authoritarian control of their fathers. Comedian Harry Enfield ran a sketch with a young child screaming at his parents and demanding – why weren't they separated like all his friends' parents?

***

We have a pixelation problem here. Our cultural picture is being interfered with and much of it is being lost, or broken up, fragmented. We've no idea what's going on. Can we get the picture back please? The picture? We want it back. No answer; you're "on hold."

***

Detroit has the highest murder rate of all US cities. You should buy a gun to protect yourself and learn how to use it. Are you prepared to shoot a 12-year-old boy? No? Well, you have to be if he is about to shoot, threaten or rob *you*. Teachers are getting guns too to protect themselves and the pupils.

***

Single vehicle crashes. An epidemic of single-vehicle crashes. Some night I'll go out and fuckin' drive into a wall and it will look like a fucking accident. Remember Willie Loman. Don't do it Willie. Don't do it Willie. [There is the sound of a car driving off].

***

"The submissive void"[10] of the liberal, educated bourgeoisie. Over-exposed and naively understanding of all, anyone should feel free to hate us. Walk right in: to our computer systems and crash them; to a public space with a bomb (my right to bomb you); to your religion and secularise it; to your secular liberal culture and islamicise it; to your family and take away the father and mother; to your politics and neutralise it; to your free speech and impose a *fatwa*. Even at the level of the body: walk right in and rape it; into your immune system and take out your T-lymphocytes and with them the capacity to resist even low-grade infections. The West is criminal openness and relativity, paralysed by multiplicity and indifference with no resistance offered.

And their children – all they want is ME. The triumphal end point of the libidinal revolution: *ME*! The submissive void is linked to the new libidinal digital bondage of the platform. "Person of the Year: YOU."[11] From the "mirror stage" to the "selfie," submission willingly engaged in. Queuing to be digital slaves.

***

Žižek concludes, unproblematically, we live in times of "generalised perversion."[12] Perversion is the new normal. In modernity, transgression was solicited; in postmodernity transgression is ordained, libidinally and financially: transgress! Perversion: to be at the centre of enjoyment; go as far as it's possible to go 'along the path of *jouissance*'.[13] Lacan speaks of the pervert being a crusader for a new religion, an educator no less. Everyone must to go there (to *jouissance*) in their own molecular atomised way.

The title of Žižek's 2006 film, *The Pervert's Guide to the Cinema*, and the follow-up film in 2012, *The Pervert's Guide to Ideology*, assume provocatively that nowadays, no big deal, we are *all* perverts and that we go to the cinema, as it were ideologically, literally to get ideas as to how to desire in the absence of the old morality, in the absence of the big Other. Desiring these days seems unproblematic, in whatever way you choose, or in whatever way you are educated ideologically: there is no limit to polymorphous desiring and pleasuring. But the catch is: in the absence of meaning, it is *your* responsibility (yours alone) to find a fetishistic screen, a dream, that will work to cover the gaping void of the Real.

Nothing less than *n* "sexualities" must be brought into play. Thus, 'Queer means to fuck with gender'.[14] It is gender that is fucked, i.e. identities that are screwed by becoming polymorphous, while the fucking continues. The pervert stays close to the desiring machines in the same way that the rich man stays close to the money machines. Both reject commitment in favour of "contract-ment," while faking inclusion and openness. Both turn away, turn wrongly (Latin – *pervertĕre*). Now the genders turn away from each other.

Between 1974 and 1983 the Paedophile Information Exchange (PIE) was a pro-paedophile activist group which was affiliated to the National Council for Civil Liberties (NCCL) in the UK. PIE originated in Scotland, then developed links to the Gay Liberation Front (GLF) in south London. Like radicals generally, they rejected the bourgeois family as the basis of an economic, social and sexual system and certain sections of GLF favoured the abolition of the age of consent. In 1976, the argument put forward by the NCCL itself, in a submission to the Criminal Law Revision Committee, stressed 'childhood sexual experiences, willingly engaged in, with an adult result in no identifiable damage'.[15] The oldest Oedipal dream?[16] However, since the 1980s, a line has been drawn in the sand of generally shattered social bonds, to *hyper*-exclude, stigmatise, denigrate paedophiles specifically; better to be a murderer than a paedophile. As Chris Jenks has indicated, the paedophile breaks the 'remaining embodied vestige of the social bond ... The shrill cry of "abuse" is a cry of our own collective pain at the loss of our social identity'.[17] The paedophile is a step too far in the forbidden Oedipal direction that *finally* makes our perverse constellations crystal clear. The paedophile is the last word in the long sentence that spells out perversion. And with that last word, a sense of shock and realisation, all now displaced and condensed onto the paedophile – the modern sacrificial victim par excellence.

The paedophile "loves" the loveless child that he once was in the absence of a loving mother and father, in the absence of an Oedipus complex. As he is too immature to love an adult, he is driven to "love"/abuse a child along the same lines as he was "loved"/abused himself, with all the dire obscene consequences of "proving" how unlovable he was. Thus the paedophile is the detritus of the anti-Oedipal culture. The paedophile is also an opportunist without scruples in the burgeoning sexual marketplace created by the cultural revolution plus globalisation, where abandoned children, children un-linked from families, are a vast vulnerable migrating resource.

★★★

Policing people. Paradoxically, liberation/transgression has spawned multiple policings, liberating undreamt of surveillance and controls: 1) control of what we say and think. 2) The policing of the *social* body via the growth of biopolitical controls of diet, health, life-style, family life. 3) *Self*-policing and trainings, coaching of body and mind, according to various performance parameters. 4) The massive growth of the State administrative bureaucracies and regulatory agencies of all sorts. 5) The growth of surveillance of public spaces, workplaces, computers, phones, crèches, homes, cars, etc. 6) Online security protocols, passwords and encryptions. 7) Risk-reducing automated control systems in cars, transport systems, buildings, hospitals, industrial plants, etc. 7) New laws regulating human intimacy. 8) Neuro-imagery to anticipate "inappropriate" violent or sexual behaviours. 9) Genetic testing to predict/screen in advance for maladaptive behaviours or mental illness. 10) Algorithms to predict crime.

Total analysis will open you up, peel you back and reveal everything on-screen with no intervention, no prevention allowed from the subject. At the beginning, of course, you can override the control systems and return to manual, but that is only at the start to smooth transition. All systems imply: *you* shall be marginalised.

Let us be clear, *men* are the least compliant and the most resistant to change, therefore men must be controlled first. First God is destroyed, then we came for the Masters and then we came for the Fathers. Now we come for the men and boys.

Recall *The Hunt.*[18] Lucas (Mads Mikkelsen) is going about his temporary job at a small nursery school in rural Denmark, having lost his teaching post as a result of economic measures. Fighting a battle with his ex-wife over the custody of their teenage son, he lives with a woman from Eastern Europe doing domestic work locally. Unhappy Klara, young daughter of Lucas's best friend Theo, misconstrues Lucas's refusal of a kiss on the lips and seeks a little revenge, using a sexual idea she had overheard from her older brother. When prompted, Klara nods agreement with Grethe, the school administrator, when asked if Lucas exposed himself to her. Grethe, trained in such things, calls in a child psychologist, who involves the police. The parents and even Lucas's son who could be in need of protection are notified. Lucas becomes an object of hate, a threat to the community. Shops refuse him service. A butcher provokes a fight with him. A shot is fired through his window. His beloved dog is mysteriously killed. He withdraws into himself. Only his son and the boy's godfather stand beside him. For Klara things have gone beyond her control. Tearfully, she tries to tell her parents that Lucas did nothing, but they think she is just frightened. The climax is reached during the Christmas Eve service in the local church, where the whole community is confronted by Lucas with the true meaning of Christian charity. Reconciliation eventually follows, and Lucas returns to hunting with his friends, a manly pastime he initiates his own son into. In the last scene in a woodland, a shot rings out from somewhere. No one is injured. Lucas is safe. But the Hunt is not over! Far from it, it is just beginning.

In his introduction to Jonathan Raban's *Surveillance*,[19] Gaston Bachelard anticipates surveillance of surveillance, surveillance squared, then the surveillance of these systems, surveillance cubed. In the story, Tad Zachary asserts: 'We're all spooks now'. Tad is gay, HIV-positive, grieving his partner, living in the same apartment block in Seattle as Lucy Bengstrom, a journalist, commissioned to write a piece on Augie Vanags, whose Holocaust memoir *Boy 381* has been a bestseller, but may be a fake. Lucy and her young daughter, Alida, travel to interview Augie, hidden by his publisher fearing he will damage his own work by speaking. Tad and Augie are on opposite sides on the security-surveillance question. Tad inhabits the 'counterworld, a community of people hidden behind pseudonyms … post-sexual … disembodied'. He feels a visceral anger at what the Government is doing, 'you think you are living in a democracy, then one morning you wake up and realise it's a fascist police state'. Like many, Tad, 'didn't want to rescue the administration from the folly of its ways: he wanted to see it blown to atomic dust … how dare they so fuck with the world'. Augie warns of the terrible dangers we face: 'Civilisation is just twelve, maybe fifteen hours away from barbarity … less than a day is all it takes to turn a great city into a hell-hole … Yesterday you were living in the world's finest democracy, today its Mogadishu'. However, Lucy is about to expose his book's true origin.

In *The Lives of Others*,[20] all it takes is a word in Communist East Germany and your life could be changed forever. While attending a play by celebrated playwright

Georg Dreyman in 1980s East Germany, Stasi secret agent Wiesler is told by the Minister of Culture that Dreyman does not always toe the party line. Wiesler immediately bugs Dreyman's apartment by occupying the attic of his apartment block. Wiesler pieces together a plot by Dreyman to publish subversive articles outside the country. However, the bureaucratic agent is slowly drawn to the life of Dreyman and his cause. One in seven citizens were co-opted for spying on threat of losing their good name, their job, or damaging the fortunes of a family member, etc. The old KGB joke was that once Communism triumphs there will be no need for the KGB as everyone will automatically report on everyone else.

Gesicht zur Wand (*Face the Wall*)[21] continues the story where *The Lives of Others* left off. We learn that 72,000 people were arrested, interrogated and imprisoned by the East German Stasi, just for trying to leave the country by "illegal" means. Unlike their Nazi counterparts, found, interrogated and shamed, the Stasi feel no guilt and no need to apologise. Five former prisoners tell their stories to German director Stefan Weinert. Currently, the Stasi are spreading disinformation about their former activities. They are paid a state pension, while their former victims struggle to be recognised. As the memory of Communist East Germany fades, there is pessimism among former Stasi victims that their ordeal will be remembered in the history books. 'You don't see the damage', says a school teacher from Chemnitz who recalls in the film her failed escape attempt. 'They destroyed the person I was. There's a stone lying on my soul that will never go away'. For Weinert, *Gesicht zur Wand* was his opposition to Communist revisionism, but the German public broadcaster ARD rejected it. 'These are stations run by the 1968 generation', he says, 'who have either no interest in this topic or who feel they cannot fit it into one of the pre-packaged formats'. Maybe, they were too easily rehabilitated after the war and retained a sense of *Ostalgie* for the old dreams of the Left, continuing on today. They saw only the Nazi wrong.[22] In the "Topology of Terror" museum in Berlin, the story is told *only* of the Nazi prison camps, with virtually no reference to the post-war system, which was a magnitude more in its surveillance capability.

In the 1980s, under Nicolae Ceausescu, Romanians lived in the shadow of his feared secret police force – the Securitate. Carmen Bugan was a village girl whose life was turned upside down when her father, a TV repairman, spoke out against poverty and injustice. He drove around Bucharest throwing anti-Ceausescu leaflets out of his car window. On a day in March 1982, Carmen arrived home from school to find her house occupied by the Securitate, drinking their coffee, smoking their cigarettes, muddying their carpet. Carmen's mother was having a baby in hospital, so Carmen was alone in the house with her grandmother. When her grandfather tried to take her to safety he was threatened – *you'll be found dead in a ditch*. They took the family's food. Bugs were installed in all the rooms and the family were ordered to keep the curtains open at all times day and night. For five years while her father was in prison, every movement, every conversation was taped. She was followed to school by the man in the brown coat. And the children jeered her – *ha! your father's in prison*! Friends brought food, but they too were interrogated. 'Anything could happen. Maybe a black car would speed at me as I crossed the street. My mother became so confused she felt even the trees were staring at her.' In 1988, her father was released. Carmen was 17. But her father was a defeated man. He remained under house arrest, so he couldn't work, and had to report to the Securitate every day. There were death threats on the phone at 2 or 3 am. 'One evening the TV moved suddenly as someone outside yanked the cable. We couldn't shout back, we couldn't speak freely as the house was still wired.'[23]

Three decades on, living abroad, Carmen has seen the Securitate files. 'These contain details of conversations, what we ate, what time we got up, even intimate things too embarrassing to mention. We now know that what we thought were shadows were not shadows, *they have written our lives for us.* They even had a record of our dreams. Even your dreams are police records.'

'Someone must have been telling lies about Joseph K, for without having done anything wrong he was arrested one fine morning'.[24] Kafka foresaw the *jouissance* of the Law. The priest tells K a fable – *Before the Law*. It is about the man from the country who wanted to gain admittance to the Law from an open doorway. The doorkeeper tells the man that he cannot go in, although it is possible to gain entry. The man waits outside for years, bribing the doorkeeper but to no effect. He waits and waits with extraordinary persistence until he is about to die and finally he asks the doorkeeper why no one else has tried to gain admittance to the Law. The doorkeeper answers, 'No one else could ever be admitted here, since this gate was made only for you. I am now going to shut it'. Should the simple country man have seized his chance and just walked through the open door? Or, was he simply in awe of the newly internalised post-Reformation, Protestant Law (the gate made *only for you*). Seized by the Other's transcendence, the Law becomes that nameless, dreadful Thing that awaits and controls us; the Law becomes a symbol of death itself. K anticipates his own death and dies, 'like a dog'. A man observes the execution from an upstairs window overlooking the quarry. For a moment K wonders, was it a friend, a good person, someone who cared? Where was the judge? He raised his hands and spread out his fingers …

***

Former radical André Glucksmann refers to as Europe's "the sleep of reason." As Glucksmann says, 'This is beautifully invoked, for instance, in Chekhov's *The Cherry Orchard*, where the protagonists all live together on an old estate. They know the end is coming but nobody appears to care at all about what might happen, even as they hear the trees falling'.[25]

***

The 13-year-old girl leaves her school to go home. The boys are waiting in the bushes. They want her to do a "blow-job" just as in porn. She will be forced to. Young boys are sending images of their genitalia to girls at school and routinely swapping explicit photographs of themselves. Graphic sexualisation. The consumption of hardcore adult pornography, the sharing of explicit sexual imagery.

A 13-year-old girl fell to her death after begging a boy to delete film footage of her performing a sexual act.[26]

★★★

The liberation of the drives.
The liberation of the gaze.
The liberation of the superego.
An orgy of drives; an orgy of the superego
Jouissance – from a tickle to a blaze.
The sleep of thinking.
The uncaring skies.
No tears shed.

★★★

Greed is good. The fruits of the libidinal revolution. The world's super-rich have taken advantage of tax rules to siphon off at least $21 trillion (possibly as much as $32 trillion) from their home countries and hide it abroad – a sum larger than the entire American economy.[27]

Capitalism (and schizophrenia) produces permanent febrile insecurity that young and young middle-aged academics and media hacks think is cool. We must learn along with them to flourish within the global flux. To be creative about job insecurity, about the impermanent sexual relations, about gross inequalities, about contingency, fraying, precarity and all the rest. Why not live experimentally? Question your serial repetitive attachments. Traverse your structuring fantasies, your personal myths, about what constitutes the good life. Embrace new modes of temporality. As Lauren Berlant suggests, the old trauma theory, with its exceptional and founding Real that shatters the ordinary, is no longer relevant for the analysis of the ways that people adjust once *crisis itself has become ordinary*.[28] Become rootless and cruel; capitalism rejoices!

Impersonal intimacies. Welcome shock and fragmentation. Seek out self-shattering rather than repair. Create new, non-normative stories that escape the dialectics of normativising violence and difference. Barebacking, for instance, involves gay men, "gift givers," who deliberately or habitually engage in unprotected anal sex, risking HIV/AIDS. "Exemplary ethically" in the way it represents unlimited intimacy, a disposition of radical openness to the other.[29]

Forget personal; become impersonal
The self is a covert sanction for violence
Love is a sanction for violence
Become selfless

In *Broken*,[30] Skunk (Eloise Lawrence), the pre-adolescent daughter of Archie (Tim Roth), experiences "continuous crisis" without complaint. Her mother has left Archie. Meantime, Archie is getting closer to the *au pair*, Kasia (Zana Marjanovic), who is splitting from boyfriend Mike (Cillian Murphy), one of Skunk's favourite teachers. They live next to the dysfunctional Oswald family. Mr Oswald (Rory Kinnear) cannot control his rages or his young daughters since his wife's death. The film opens with Oswald violently assaulting Skunk's only friend, Rick (Robert Emms), who has learning difficulties, as Oswald insanely believes that Rick has raped one of his daughters. Rick is terrified and has to be hospitalised. Skunk strikes up a relationship with Jed, whose mother has gone off with her accountant. They meet up in a scrap yard, of broken cars and boats. But the friendship cannot last as Jed has to go and live in Birmingham. She gets bullied by the vicious Oswald daughters in the new school. Her home, neighbourhood and school are broken representing continuous crisis and a complex, broken world fills her future with no right of appeal as there is no big Other.

***

Bedridden people in some NHS hospitals are referred to as "feeders." Relatives found used bandages under the bed, food uneaten and blood stains in the toilets. Some patients were left unwashed for up to a month. Food and drinks were left out of reach. Calls for help to use the toilet were ignored, with the result that patients were left in soiled sheeting or sitting on commodes for hours feeling ashamed and afraid.[31] The softening up process for euthanasia.

In Ireland, a national study of elder abuse has found that more than half of staff in nursing homes have observed neglect of residents. The most frequent forms of physical abuse were restraining a patient unnecessarily and pushing, grabbing, shoving or pinching. Psychological abuse consisted of shouting, insulting or swearing at residents.[32]

In the 1930s, the Third Reich was ahead of the game. They produced very successful short films aimed at health workers and the general public, pleading for the disabled, the mentally ill, the blind, deformed, sick, and elderly to be killed – out of 'pure human kindness'. Aided by pictures of suffering patients, lit from oblique angles, or from below to emphasise long dark shadows, accompanied by eerie animal sounds, moaning, tortured visages and twisted writhing, the female voice-over repeated, *isn't it sheer cruelty to keep these victims alive? Isn't it just cruel and inhuman?*

Ludwig Minelli (Dignitas) says that 'suicide is a marvellous possibility given to a human being'. As commentator A. A. Gill has it, 'Most people in this country die weepingly lonely – cold, starved, and left in no doubt that they have overstayed their welcome. This is the greatest shame and horror of our society and our age'.[33]

Years back, around the time of the smoking ban, there was a cartoon depicting two frail old men bent over walking sticks in a broken-down old peoples' home. One man says to the other, 'Just imagine, if you and I had continued smoking, we'd have missed all this'.

***

From the *Stockholm* syndrome – in thrall to our captor, to the *Stockhausen* syndrome – in thrall to entropy and nothingness. Western subsuicidal guilt meets the murderous bank of rage out there.

***

Bernard Lonergan once observed that 'a civilisation in decline digs its own grave with relentless consistency. It cannot be argued out of its destructive way'.[34]

***

"Death to America"

Hassan Butt, a former British Islamist, recalls 'how we used to laugh in celebration whenever people on TV proclaimed that the sole cause for Islamic acts of terror like 9/11, the Madrid bombings, and 7/7 was Western foreign policy … they also helped draw away any critical examination from the real engine of our violence: Islamic theology'.[35]

DeLillo's "Falling Man," David Janiak, re-enacts the trauma of the people jumping from the Towers. He appears dangling above the street or other public places, upside down. No one knows from where he will "fall" next. He wears a business suit, tie, dress shoes and has one leg bent up, arms at his side, suspended by a crude safety harness. He is characterised as heartless exhibitionist or brave new chronicler of the age of terror. Terror as art, as spectacle, as cruelty.

"Death to Israel"

An Israeli captain on asymmetric warfare. The calculus was simple: 1) launch a rocket from within the civilian population; if you kill Jews *that's a victory*. 2) If the Jews hit back and in so doing kill many civilians, *that's a victory*. 3) If they don't hit back because they're afraid to hit civilians, *that's a victory*. 4) Now repeat the process until you kill so many Jews they have to hit back and in so doing kill more civilians. *That's the ultimate victory*, because they know that in striking just those chords exactly what music the liberal press will play.

There is clarity in the term "genocidal caucus" (a term attributed to liberal *Haaretz* commentator, Bradley Burston), used to describe a movement that has gathered pace in the Western media among liberals and by no means confined to the radical Left, that confidently, proudly and righteously asserts the progressive *de-legitimisation* of Israel. This is barely disguised code for *Holocaust Two*.

You tell people that a new great era will begin if you abolish the ruling class or the bourgeoisie, if you rationalise the means of production, if you use euthanasia on the incurables. To minds so prepared you then propose that the Jews be destroyed. And they make a substantial start. They kill more than half the European Jews … There's no telling which corner it will come from next (an observation attributed to Saul Bellow).[36] We must follow through to the end.

Terror as art as spectacle as cruelty. In a world that has given up on pity, there is no way of measuring cruelty. There is no ethical instrument with which to register degrees of barbarity. How for instance should we calculate the metric between the numbers of virtual crushings of skulls, attacks against women, torture of children, and so on and *real* skulls crushed, women violently raped and children filmed crying and screaming? In the very first episode of *Love Hate*,[37] a man's skull is crushed with a beer keg, a woman is brutally raped. How do we measure the correlation between the fathomless proliferation of violent pollution of the screen and the violent pollution of culture? How can a civilised culture absorb such daily screenings of monstrous barbarity which now passes for art or culture, without succumbing to barbarism itself? Art is the continuation of the culture war by other means.

***

'There is *no* woman [person], *no* blood, *no* war, *no* enemy. Other crises had a name; this thing is nameless; this thing is algorithms'.[38] This evocation of the debt crisis by a Greek poet describes accurately the radically *impersonal* nature of the crisis threatening us. There is graffiti on the metal shutters of all the shops. The city is a slate, people are writing rage now. They are all thieves and burglars! Reality is fragmenting in front of us. Well-off neighbourhoods have turned into ghettoes full of destitute migrants, old shops closed, replaced by gambling dens, brothels and fronts for money laundering.

***

The film *Gomorrah* is based on a book by journalist Roberto Saviano.[39] The title recalls the Biblical reference to Sodom and Gomorrah. The Camorra, the notorious Neapolitan equivalent of the Mafia, has been responsible for more murders – over 4,000 – in the past 30 years than any criminal or terrorist group. Set in and around Naples, *Gomorrah* depicts the unremitting brutality and corruption of the underworld network, known locally as "the System," that holds total violent sway in that region. The film opens in a tanning parlour with four men in the blue light of their cubicles relaxing, then, immediately, shot dead – classic Mafia style murder. Matteo Garrone's so-called "drama" comprises a number of brief storylines. One strand involves a young androgynous boy, Totò (Salvatore Abruzzese), who wants to leave his close friend and join the gang. We see him making this choice in what is the only tragic moment in the movie. Totò passes the initiation, being shot while wearing a bullet-proof vest. 'Now you're a man', the gang leader tells him. Don Ciro (Gianfelice Imparato) is a nervous bagman who hurries to give out cash to families of faithful Camorra members, who never cease complaining. There is Pasquale (Salvatore Cantalupo), an expert tailor on a couture-house shop floor, who gives lessons to a rival Chinese concern. Two pimply youths (Marco Macor, Ciro Petrone) find a cache of guns, tear around firing them, not heeding the warnings, they become a threat to be eliminated. An apparently more respectable face of the System is the linen-suited Franco (Toni Servillo), whose business is the disposal of toxic waste as landfill. The film's most chilling moment comes when an elderly peasant woman gives Franco and his lieutenant a tray of peaches. Once on the road, Franco throws them away: they're toxic. *Imagine a city built by crime. Imagine its people ruled by fear. Imagine a system poisoned by corruption. Nobody is innocent. Nowhere is safe. No one is spared.* Saviano describes Scampia, a suburb north of Naples, as 'the largest open-air drugs marketplace in the world', caught by edgy camera work and the soundtrack from *Massive Attack*.

'I had a huge rage inside', says Saviano in an interview, 'We're all part of this mechanism, just by keeping quiet'.[40] Oppose it and, according to Saviano, the (desiring) machinism will eliminate you in *three* stages: 1) They try to get your money by suing you. Your legal costs escalate. 2) They call you a liar. They have access to the media to defame and denigrate you. With time your popularity falls away, and you may become a *guitto* – denounced and attacked by all sides. 3) Lastly, your family has to move, friends fall away and doubt grows in people's faces; 'yes, the most difficult thing to overcome is the solitude'.

***

Sloterdijk accuses many critics and intellectuals of failing to gauge the "monstrous cold" of the contemporary – isolation, desolation, depression, the withdrawal of meaning and so on. They are like 'the summer guest in his full pension'. He suggests immunisation, but how 'given that the strong forms of solidarity, like those Plato called the Cosmos, and the Christian God, are no longer available to us'?[41] Immunisation? Surely, more than that is needed. We should follow Weil and what she calls "extreme attention" – attention which is so complete and devastated, the "I" disappears.[42]

Steiner refers to the "after-Word," summarising the anti-Oedipal, where 'Today, we stand orphaned but free in the place of the a-Logos'.[43] The loss of the Real began in Europe and Russia between the 1870s and 1930s, with the 'break of the covenant between word and world',[44] the revolution that defines modernity itself, the beginning of the virtualisation of the world and the loss of the Real. The *covenant*, the engagement between God and man (covenant: Old French *con-* together, and *venir*, to come), *comes apart*. Language opens onto abyssal meaning. By the mid-1950s, cultural anthropologists were developing structural linguistics, providing an entirely non-biological but nevertheless scientific basis for the study of culture. In line with their emphasis on the distinction between culture and nature, between humans and animals, they were creating two *autonomous* "worlds." The natural sciences, including biology, could take their inspiration and formation ultimately from physics and chemistry, but socio-cultural studies would look entirely to linguistics for their foundations and methods. Never the twain shall meet. Thus language overwrites everything; *language creates the world*. This follows from Nietzsche's *no facts only interpretations*. There is no Real only shifting meanings and constructions that continuously form and dissolve amounting to nothing in particular. The Real becomes an elusive "X" that haunts the omnipresent textual presence.

***

The strange fruits of the libidinal revolution.

Sex is divorced from love, casual sex.
Sex is divorced from pleasure, pornography.
Pleasure is divorced from joy, desiring machines.
Love is divorced from loving commitment, narcissism.
Sex is divorced from procreation, onanism.
The Other is divorced from Difference, banality.
Parents are divorced from children, children's rights.
The virtual world is divorced from the real world, utopia.

★★★

London, August 2011. From a trickle to a blaze (*jouissance*), burning and looting. Cries went out: Where are the parents of these young children? Will you please find out where your children are? Please check your children for stolen goods. And so on. As one blogger put it, these children are not materially deprived, they still want more! The superego commands: *Consume*! Literally, *Burn*!

★★★

The Left won the culture war, the Right won the economic war and the Centre won the political war. The Left won rights, sexual and ethnic, until they came up against the Real of Islamic violence. The Right won the economic war, until it came up against the Real of greed and economic meltdown. The Centre won the political war until they came up against the Real of the Market.

★★★

Just five years before the Great War, Marinetti's Futurist Manifesto[45] captured a mood of the time, of 'ruinous and incendiary violence', which glorified violence as a purifying cure for the world. 'Let the good incendiaries with charred fingers come!'

The starting point?

When did it start? When did the smashing start, the sheer taste for human cruelty and violence? In Virilio's analysis, by the twentieth century it was well underway in both art and science, which vied with each other to invade, cut up and distort the human form. He refers to the development in the media of the craving for murder, that in art as well as human genetics (as we indicated above) there is a complete absence of human scruples and suppression of human sympathy. So extreme is this anti-humanist violence that Virilio opines, 'You would think the drive to extinguish the suffocating culture of the bourgeoisie consisted specifically in exterminating oneself . . .'.[46]

Where is the *register* of suffering? Where is the fragile space for mercy? It has been replaced by monstrosities. As Virilio points out, 'art remained *demonstrative* right up until the nineteenth century with Impressionism, the art of the twentieth century became "*monstrative*" ... contemporary with the shattering effect of mass societies ... and mass media propaganda'.[47] The space of *re*-presentation, just as the space for *re*-flection, became presentative and monstrous with no time for reflection. Virilio cites Rothko, 'using human representation, for me meant mutilating it'.[48]

In his introduction to *Art and Fear*, John Armitage is critical of Virilio's wholesale attack on the "academy," arguing that he might be overlooking the 'revolutionary questioning' of modern art movements in general. Thus Armitage misses the far more important *connection* that Virilio is making with the signifier "revolutionary" and its free and celebrated deployment through art, aesthetics, politics, science, the media, terrorism of Right and Left. In psychoanalytic terms, Armitage is stressing the manifest content to do with aesthetic experimentation and deconstruction, while Virilio from a Christian perspective points to the largely disavowed latent content, covered by his term "thanatophilia."

"You have to work harder, the graves are not full," urged the voice on the Thousand Hills Radio in April 1994, when the genocide got going in Rwanda.[49]

When did it start? A priest from Rotherham, Michael Sherbrook, whose family had known the great hospitality of the monks of Roche Abbey, wrote, 'all things of price were either spoiled, plucked away, or defaced to the uttermost'.[50] He was referring to the hundreds of monasteries, priories, convents, friaries, wantonly destroyed, their incomes appropriated suddenly and shockingly, during the reign of Henry VIII. The so-called "dissolution of the monasteries" was organised by Thomas Cromwell in the late 1530s. Some monasteries had become corrupt and reforms were too slow.

Cromwell's agents dissolved the smaller monasteries first. Everything was taken, priceless treasures, manuscripts, libraries, the stained-glass windows smashed, even the structure of the buildings dismantled, the lead taken from the roofs. Much of the loot from this revolutionary activity was sold off to fund Henry's military campaigns in the 1540s. The result, the whole medieval system of piety, prayer and devotion, was fundamentally discredited in a very short time. As it was cynically pointed out, *God did not come to the rescue*. The dissolution occurred within the larger context of the violence of the Protestant Reformation in Europe.

A pure line of destruction started from the widespread iconoclastic fury against medieval Catholic art and churches in many parts of Europe by Calvinist mobs in the sixteenth century, with orders even from the governments in Britain and Germany. Lines of destruction radiated from here towards the culture of death, beginning with Descartes' rationalism and reductionism, with the modernist project of clarity, categorisation and exclusion. The material world is left entirely godless and mechanical. The human body, without grace, becomes a machine! The utterly cold universe was a machine three centuries before our authors burst on the scene with the desiring machines and the mechanosphere, converting our humiliation into disappearance – anticipating AI and robotics as unfettered reason continues its destructive trajectory to oblivion. Whatever the contemporary advantages (these are considerable) of the technological realisation of the world, whatever the celebrated *manifest* content of this 400-year-old dream, we cannot escape the *latent* will to destruction involved in the splitting of the atom, the splicing of genes, the humiliation of species, the large hadron collider, embryo experimentation, cloning, reproductive technologies and so on. The only serious critique being offered to these lines of destruction is the still surviving body of two millennia of Catholic thinking. Who is listening?

Kick all the ladders away. Kick all the others away. Kick *the* Other away. The old way of thinking has to be destroyed.

Notes

1 Arnold, M., 1869: vii.
2 Nietzsche, F., 1883–1891: 299.
3 Mailer, N., 1968: page numbers in parentheses.
4 Hanaghan highlighted this death wish of the fathers against the sons, the old men who send the sons to war. Hanaghan, J., 1957.
5 Baudrillard, J., 2005: 95, emphasis added.
6 Rowland, T., 2011.
7 Transcript. *American Experience* documentary on the Summer of Love. PBS and WGBH, 14 March 2007.
8 Zafiropoulos, M., 2010: 7.
9 Lacan, J., 1964: 12.
10 A phrase used by Leni Riefenstahl when asked about her epic films that glorified the Nazis and mesmerised the ordinary German people. The messages in her films came from "above," but depended on the "submissive void" of the German public, which included the liberal elites, indeed everyone!
11 Cover of *Time* 18 December 2006.
12 Žižek, S., 2001: 20.
13 Lacan, J., 1977: 323
14 McIntosh, M., in Bristow, J., and Wilson, A., 1993.
15 See http://en.wikipedia.org/wiki/Paedophile_Information_Exchange.
16 However, in communes where sexual freedom was explicitly advocated, a line was drawn that excluded sex with young children, but only demanded by their mothers.
17 Jenks, C., 1996: 22.
18 *The Hunt*, 2012. Thomas Vinterberg.
19 Raban, J., 2006.
20 *The Lives of Others*. Director: Florian Henckel von Donnersmarck, 2006.
21 *Gesicht zur Wand* (Face the Wall), 2009. Stefan Weinert.
22 A joke was doing the rounds. Hitler and Stalin are in Hell. But why was Hitler up to his neck in boiling oil, while Stalin was only up to his ankles? Ah, but see, says Stalin laughing, I am standing on the shoulders of Lenin.
23 Taken from BBC Radio 4, "Witness: Life in Ceausescu's Romania," 24 March 2013.
24 Kafka, F., 1925.
25 "Bin Laden, Dostoevsky and the reality principle: an interview with André Glucksmann," 2 May 2011. www.opendemocracy.net/faith-iraqwarphiloshophy/article_1111.jsp.
26 A bullied 13-year-old schoolgirl fell 60 ft to her death as she tried to convince one of her tormentors to delete a sex tape of her, a coroner has ruled. Chevonea Kendall-Bryan plunged from her bedroom window on the top floor of Seldon House in Battersea, south-west London, in March 2012. Westminster Coroner's Court heard how the

schoolgirl had been forced into performing sex acts on two boys at a party just a month earlier and had called one of the boys to beg him to delete footage of the incident.

27 See *The Guardian*, 4 April 2013. "Wealth doesn't trickle down – it just floods offshore, research reveals." www.guardian.co.uk/business/2012/jul/21/offshore-wealth-global-economy-tax-havens.
28 See Berlant, L., 2011.
29 Gauthier, D., and Forsyth, C., 1999.
30 *Broken* (2012) directed by Rufus Norris, premiered at the Cannes Film Festival in May 2012. It is based on the 2008 novel by Daniel Clay, inspired by *To Kill A Mockingbird* by Harper Lee.
31 The Mid-Staffordshire NHS hospital scandal. www.theguardian.com/society/2013/feb/06/mid-staffs-hospital-scandal-guide.
32 National Centre for the Protection of Older People at University College Dublin. www.rte.ie/news/2012/1206/357160-elder-abuse-study-ucd/.
33 See A. A. Gill. *The Sunday Times Magazine*, 29 March 2009, p. 36.
34 Morelli, M., and Morelli, E., 1997: 20.
35 See www.theguardian.com/commentisfree/2007/jul/01/comment.religion1.
36 Bellow, S. Source not found.
37 *Love/Hate* is a much acclaimed Irish crime drama from October 2010. The show depicts fictional characters in Dublin's criminal underworld. Since its release, it has grown in popularity. In spite of drawing criticism for its scenes of violence and criminality, series 3 has attracted close to one million viewers on several occasions.
38 Quoted in *Greece: Broken Marble, Broken Future*, Maria Margaronis (Radio 4, 11 December 2011).
39 Saviano, R., 2006.
40 Interview with Roberto Saviano, "Italy: Taking on the Mafia." In *Frontline World*. www.pbs.org/frontlineworld/stories/italy801/interview/saviano.html.
41 Sloterdijk, P., with Heinrichs, H.-J., 2001: 217–19.
42 Weil, S., 1986: 231–7.
43 Steiner, G., 1989: 127.
44 Ibid.: 93.
45 http://vserver1.cscs.lsa.umich.edu/~crshalizi/T4PM/futurist-manifesto.html.
46 Virilio, P., 2000a.
47 Ibid.: 35.
48 Ibid.: 37.
49 See www.crimesofwar.org/a-z-guide/incitement-to-genocide-2/.
50 From "The Dissolution of the Monasteries." www.bbc.co.uk/programmes/b009jtq1#auto.

5

ŽIŽEK – SILENCE AND THE REAL DESERT

Up to this point, we have considered the anti-Oedipal hate of tradition and value, all part of the revolutionary upheavals during the modern period. Transgression has become mainstream, i.e. *post*modern. Psychoanalysis, a modernist invention, has been a casualty. How can you be subversive, when subversion is mainstream? How to be critical when everyone is critical? Here, we begin the rehabilitation, or re-invigoration of psychoanalysis for the twenty-first century. Psychoanalysis has become a sickness in need of cure, or maybe palliative care? Central to this treatment, whatever the nature of it, has undoubtedly been Lacan popularised by Žižek.

Why would anyone read Žižek? Why should Žižek be compulsory reading in the minutes before an analysand arrives for their session? Because he writes in the kind of way that analysts should be able to think, with full dialectical complexity. As he says himself, where there are networks there is also the possibility of short-circuits – cutting across the network to create a spark. Not only can one cross these synapses like a flash, but the reverse, there are pathways in the networking system that are blocked, where there is a parallax situation. What opens up, then, is impossibility, incommensurability.

Žižek explores these in his *magnum opus*, *The Parallax View*.[1] Parallax, put simply, is the apparent shift of an object against the background that is caused by a shift in the observer's position. You are driving along a country road and stop. At this point the tree by the roadside is aligned from this perspective with a church in the background. Drive a little further and look back at the tree and it is aligned now with a farm. Everything has remained the same except your position as observer. The two viewpoints taken alone seem incompatible. The same holds true for Jastrow's duck–rabbit parallax, where one can see just the duck or the rabbit but *not both* at the same time. No mediation or synthesis is possible whereby one can see the duck and the rabbit simultaneously. They are on opposite sides of a Möbius strip and there is no possibility of a short-circuiting. The same problematic holds true for the wave/particle duality in physics. Electromagnetic waves "interfere" with each other very much like water waves creating peaks and troughs. However, with the discovery of the photoelectric effect by Einstein in 1905, light must be understood, not as waves, but as tiny packets or particles of energy called photons.

Against New Age notions of opposites, polarities, *Yin* and *Yang*, that may dance and interact with each other, like some contemporary music to relax with that has no beginning or end, Žižek's work is based on what he admits is 'a strategic politico-philosophical decision', namely, to outline and hold to the 'inherent "tension," gap, noncoincidence of the One with itself' (7). Further on he says, 'What if the actual problem is not to bridge the gap but, to *formulate* it as such, to conceive it properly'? (214). This is Žižek's counterintuitive, provocative Hegelian stance. The "gap" is the *parallax*. Here, Žižek follows Lacan with "the lack" in being, and Freud with the *conflict* model of human desire: life versus death drives; unconscious/conscious and so on – 'the opposites are not reconciled in a "higher synthesis" – rather *their differences are posited "as such"*' (299).

In this work he outlines the parallax view in relation to three key areas: 1) the philosophical; 2) the cognitivist brain sciences; and 3) the political. In each area he will set "cruel traps" for progressivists, whom he refers to as 'the usual gang of democracy-to-come-deconstructionist-postsecular-Levinasian-respect-for-Otherness suspects' (11). Always provocative and ironic, Žižek replicates Oscar Wilde's fear that people will not misunderstand him![2] Thus Žižek, like Lacan his mentor, is the philosopher of the impenetrable Real, the implacable opponent of the political consensus and soft ideological forms. He writes from *within* the catastrophe. He lives the catastrophe.

However, the parallax is more than just a problem with perspective, there is the additional complication of one's subjective conditioning, the prejudices with which we come to the "object." This reaches its apogee with *l'objet petit á*, this ordinary object transformed into a special object-cause-of-desire, the "strange attractor" around which desire and ideology gravitate. Žižek suggests that this is an exemplary parallax problem, of "pure" difference, where this unfathomable X, perceived to be "in" the object, cannot be pinned down to any particular properties of the object itself. As an example of this impossible X, he gives the Laplanchian gloss on Freud's seduction theory. From one perspective, there is the brutal real of adult seduction of the helpless child leading to sometimes severe adult pathologies. From the more nuanced psychoanalytic *other* perspective, there is the whole problematic of the child's sexual *fantasies*. Laplanche points out that seduction cannot be (and never was merely) reduced to infantile *fantasies* by Freud, but always was a traumatic encounter with the X of the Other's "enigmatic message," of unconscious sexual desire. Seduction should therefore never be reduced to a simple event in the subject's life. It is always somewhere "between" these two viewpoints, partly "real," partly "fantasy," always a "shock," always a "too soon," a *Thing* that cannot be wholly integrated into a narrative of meaning.[3]

Basic antagonisms

The *foundational* parallax concerns, on the one hand, the finite, phenomenal, ontic domain, the *not-All*, which parallels, on the other, the infinite, noumenal, ontological domain of Being. We exist in the gap between finite and infinite. In this gap, we experience the seductively Real unknown with its truth which distorts our perceptions of empirical reality. This is what Žižek calls the "parallax Real," which always creates social antagonism, what he calls the 'hard bone of contention which pulverises the sameness into a multitude of appearances' (26). This also explains postmodern relativism, multiple worlds each held by specific language games, 'with no shared terrain, no common language between them' (37). In this chaotic dissensus, there is no Master-Signifier or quilting point, or, in Bion's terminology, "selected fact" that will enable all the "facts" to cohere in a new arrangement. By contrast, Žižek mentions the exemplary Master-Signifier, the Nazi's citing of the "Jewish plot," as the master stroke that puts (infinite) order on defeat, economic crisis and moral degeneracy in pre-War Germany. Anyone outside that particular language game was in great danger.

Similarly, Žižek, via Kierkegaard, stresses the infinite gap between God and man and thus two incompatible notions of love: Christian love that is love that *asks for nothing in return* and human (ambivalent) love, of giving what one doesn't have, of giving *and* counting the cost. This *non*-exchange value of Christian love marks it out from the Symbolic, calculating, cost-benefit form of love – give *and* take. Christian love is *for nothing*, like Abraham's absolute willingness to sacrifice Isaac. 'A man is required to make the greatest possible sacrifice, to dedicate his whole life as a sacrifice – and wherefore?' (80). There is no guarantee, no value, nothing to be gained. Instead, a leap of faith is required, which tears through the Symbolic rationale.

Levinas distrusted psychoanalysis because of its focus on *conatus*. Levinas's key reference was Vassily Grossman's book, *Life and Fate*.[4] Grossman is regarded as the first and the greatest of the dissidents of the post-Stalin era, who emerged *within* Russia. Against progressivism, against scientific reason, Grossman pits human freedom, gratuitous giving, senseless kindness, which is unspoken for the most part, not part of any *system* of goodness and which by and large goes unobserved and unrewarded.[5] It is not part of any Symbolic or Imaginary register, although it might later be taken up by both. Unknown and unheeded, it remains *specifically* and *uniquely* human. Similarly, Žižek follows Kierkegaard in this respect by asking whether or not 'every translation of ethics into some positive universal frame already betrays the fundamental ethical Call, and thus necessarily gets entangled in inconsistencies [ideologies]? Is the only true ethical stance, therefore, the acceptance of this paradox and its challenge'? (87). Fortunately, the religious sensibility (and the analytic sensibility) cannot and will not synthesise this parallax – 'the lack of a common measure, the insurmountable abyss between the finite and the infinite' (103).[6]

Silence

Between the infinite abyss, on the one hand, and finite empirical reality on the other, people often ask of what use is mere speaking? Empty words, empty speech, which will betray the unspeakable. While speaking, free-associating, signifiers inevitably emerge, to do with the process of subjectivisation and maybe the dawning realisation of, and the possibility of, reflection upon one's life. All to the good, but one's life is sub-ject *to the vast silence of the universe*. Lacan stressed that the subject is located *behind* the "wall of language." Thus, we do not possess language as such, but are suspended between the wall of language and the wall of the infinite silence. Recall, Edvard Munch, suspended *over* the abyss by virtue of mental illness, said of his famous 1893 painting, *The Scream*, 'I sensed an infinite scream passing through nature'. He was within earshot of the slaughterhouse and the mental asylum where his sister was incarcerated. 'I painted this picture', he continued, 'painted the clouds as actual blood. The colour shrieked'.[7]

Stories emerged from the "Truth and Reconciliation" process in South Africa. Victims and tormentors were put into a room together and told to talk; implying – just sort things out between you! Reconcile your parallax positions. The logic of equivalence dictates that victims and tormentors – *all are victims*. The same logic was operational in Northern Ireland when all those who had suffered a violent death – bombers, killers and innocent victims – were deemed worthy of equal compensation of £12,000 per person.[8] Killers equal victims; clearly a violent betrayal of radical difference. The real victims are rendered speechless.

Beyond the Symbolic Order lies the *dis*-order of the Real. Take for example the victim who reported her radical disorientation after experiencing the Tōhoku earthquake and tsunami on 11 March 2011, followed by the explosion in the Fukushima nuclear plant the next day. Her symbolic coordinates were shattered, as she lay suspended between her life on 10 March and the fear unleashed by these events on the next day.

Or ponder this famous example recalled by Milan Kundera. Nietzsche sees a horse being savagely beaten with a whip. Suddenly, terribly moved, he puts his arms around the horse's neck and bursts into tears. This was 1889, when Nietzsche was already mentally ill and was withdrawing from people. As Kundera says, 'I feel his gesture has broad implications: Nietzsche was trying to [wordlessly] apologize to the horse for Descartes'.[9] As he withdrew from people, he was identifying with the animal victim, being objectified, caught impossibly between the (brutal) human world and the infinite.

Steiner asserts that the *Urnatur* of language is silence,[10] in three senses: the silence that antedates speech, before speech emerges with the hominid brain; the silence that eerily surrounds all speaking, like the joyless silence of the empty school or the deserted factory, or the tangible silence of the countryside; lastly, the Holocaustal silence of the "Night of the world" – the *No. I can't ever speak of such things.*

Consider *this* silence, described by W. G. Sebald in his book, *On the Natural History of Destruction*, the title of which was taken from an article written by Solly Zuckerman for a journal called *Horizon* after visiting Cologne which had been ravaged by allied bombing. Sebald's question was about the *strange silence* that surrounded the mass destruction of 131 German cities, the death of over 600,000 civilians in the Allied bombings. This was destruction on a scale without historical precedent, which 'seems to have left scarcely a trace of pain behind in the collective consciousness'.[11] It is as if what he calls, 'the true state of material and moral ruin in which the country found itself' became taboo, a 'shameful family secret'.[12] There is a similar silence around the great Irish famine of the 1840s, between the holocaustal events and words to begin to address them.[13] As author Michael Cronin has pointed out, 'more than one hundred and fifty years after the event, not one single psychology department in Ireland has carried out a major study on what is arguably the most traumatic psychological event of the nineteenth century'.[14]

For Žižek however, the primordial void is not silence, waiting to be broken by the divine word, but generalised noise, 'the confused murmur of the Real'. The question then becomes, how a space of silence can open up? As Heidegger claimed, all speech answers the sound of silence, therefore the first creative act is to strike a blow *for* silence to stop the confused murmur of the Real. A ritual frame is needed to open up a "clearing" in which words can be spoken, as Lacan suggested the vase or vaulted Gothic architecture *creates* a central void. Similarly, the potential space or "transitional space" guaranteed by the analyst represents this clearing silence in which words can be spoken, in marked contrast to the generalised "the clamour of being."[15]

Žižek, however, cites the Argentinean writer Alejandra Pizarnik's haunting words – 'Everything makes love with silence'. *This* silence is not some ultimate support, but 'a mirror for our sad reflections … this song of regret, alert, behind my poems … denies me, chokes my voice'. Žižek understands *this* song, the song of silence, unsung as it were, unanswered, failed lovemaking, as the radical defeat of all our efforts, as the terrifying noumenal domain of the Real, 'in which a kind of "objective" truth (or rather, a *totally objectifying knowledge*) about me is inscribed' (155, my emphasis), a truth shorn of *any* narcissistic gloss, without "me," a last indifferent judgement.

For example, consider the parallax difference of perspective between the patient told the objectifying and irrefutable fact that she will die within weeks from a newly discovered cancer, and the oncologist who gives the diagnosis kindly and professionally but hardly pausing before going for his usual round of golf. The oncologist's subtractive words, unanswerably, choke and silence normal speech with a nihilating truth, that strikes one dumb, a 'song of silence'.

Martin Amis's heroine, astrophysicist Jennifer Rockwell,[16] kills herself when she realises through her researches the monstrous enormity of the universe in its glacial empty objectivity. This realisation is overwhelmingly a subtractive realisation that absorbs and nullifies her great achievements in science, what it means to 'make love to silence'.

Julie Vignon de Courcy (Juliette Binoche), in Krzysztof Kieslowski's film *Blue*,[17] is the lone survivor of a car accident that killed outright her husband, a renowned composer, and their young daughter. The fatal crash happened on a country road when the family car smashed into a tree, at the precise moment that the father was telling a joke, without getting his usual chance to repeat the punch line. What we are struck by seconds after the accident is the absolute silence at the scene.

We should not miss the critical parallax here, avoided by Žižek between two versions of the death drive. The one favoured by Freud and Klein that sees the death drive as an extreme of the drive leading to violence, dissolution and the silence and peace of the inorganic, an entirely smooth BwO. The other, favoured by Lacanians, understands the death drive as a violent striking out for freedom, against the noise of the real, clearing a space, the act of creation. As Pizarnik says, 'Like every profoundly subversive act, poetry avoids everything but its own freedom and its own truth'.[18] The death drive as "freedom" is politically congruent for the radical Left. But with a slight shift in parallax, the death drive becomes the foundational basis for mental illness, the evil to be fought against without limit.[19]

On being no one

Žižek follows a number of contemporary authors on the mind-body (parallax) problem. Do we believe there is *someone* there when we look into the eyes, ignoring the brute biological fact that *there is no one* in the brain tissue? As Metzinger puts it: 'You look down into an open head, watching the brain pulsate, watching the surgeon tug and probe, and you understand with absolute conviction that there is nothing more to it. There's no one there' (Metzinger cited on p. 163).

The reduction of the postmodern subject from the high Renaissance estimation of man at the pinnacle of creation is almost complete: through Copernicus, Darwin, Freud, Marx and Nietzsche, to the emergence of the subject as pure immaterial void. Notwithstanding the turn towards appearances with phenomenology (albeit *without* substantial realities "behind" them), notions such as autopoeisis, the "emerging properties" of systems, events e-venting themselves, self-organising phenomena, quantum phenomena and the autonomy of pure flux events, the ontology of pure becoming – these are all part and parcel of the de-substantialised "reality," which barely recovers some last flickers of subjectivity as the not-quite-nothing of contemporary theory.

The brain–machine interface implies devices that can realise Orwellian thought control, surveillance, communication, and so on, the prospect of post-human "undead" virtual entities, the blurring of the distinction between hardware (brain) and software (mind), with the latter being able to detach from the former completely and enter the virtual.

Of particular fascination is the parallax between brain chemistry and consciousness. Everything experienced has neurophysiological correlates. For instance, brain processes accompany intense religious experiences. However, the question of causality remains unresolved. Taking an ecstasy pill creates in the user a feeling of ecstatic love towards the other. How does this short-cut compare to a religious training and spiritual devotion over a lifetime that might produce "naturally" similar experiences? Consider, for instance, the dour father, melancholic most of his life, who, on his deathbed is given morphine to relieve pain and seems cheerful, good-humoured and loving, for the first time in his life! Does the morphine neurophysiologically transform the father on his deathbed into this "loving" man, or does it merely facilitate a very moving loving last gesture ("choice") at the final moment, that was always buried within this depressed man?

Žižek cites Taylor's "skating" analogy of consciousness.[20] Taylor understands consciousness as a relational phenomenon where past memories, representations, emotions are used to fill in and inform present sensory imputs. This triggers a host of related activities endowing the mental process with substantiality, which, at some critical point, "lifts" the original input into a new arena, like the skater who having launched himself onto the ice glides off effortlessly. Thus, consciousness emerges released from the "friction" of the processing stages. Consciousness floats free when a threshold is crossed. Therefore, there is no consciousness without *self*-consciousness. The "I" emerges as the self-relating interaction *between* present input and past. The "self" is this escape into the fluid field of awareness and de-centring, creating the impossibility of the I's immediate self-presence. Consciousness spins off from the substrate that created it. 'A new quasi-object thus emerges' (213), the final states of which involve "attractor nets" which attract initial activity to become similar to their own, but remain insubstantial as they were created, posited and generated by the very substrates which react and interact to them in endless feedback loops. So subject and object (attractor) are *almost* one. The all-important minimal "gap" is also the programmed space for *freedom*.

Thus, there is no subject prior to neural activity; no top-down, only bottom-up effects. Žižek emphasises, 'cognitive scientists repeat again and again how our mind does not possess a centralised control structure which runs top-down … it is rather a bricolage of multiple agents who collaborate bottom-up' (241). The self is its own self-*ing*, unaware[21] of the steps towards its own emerging, for good evolutionary reasons to do with the necessity of rapid autopoietic information processing. So when Žižek concludes that 'as true Freudians, we should reject the notion of "Me" as a substantial background of the ego' (217), he is following Lacan and indeed Winnicott, whose understanding of "aliveness" is a similar process of emergence via relating and "primary illusionment."[22] This is thinking the unthinkable to Western minds – a self-less world, living as being *no one* – forgetting that for two and a half millennia, Buddhist enlightenment has been practising the assumption of non-being.

How do we get from passive primary illusionment, or the assumption of "non-being," to something more active to do with subjectivity? Or how does *self*-consciousness arise amidst and minimally separate from being potentially overwhelmed by billions of neural data? The answer seems to be by some process of *negation* or by some malfunction or fault in the nature of the smooth running of the system, otherwise we would be no more than passive processing machines. Maybe self-consciousness is stumbled upon through an "ontological crack" (242) in "reality" itself, which enables one to say: YES, I AM HERE, over and against being a passive (unconscious) recipient of neuronal impulses. Žižek dramatises this crack by reference to a traumatic excess, through an "error" that creates a measure of freedom.

The Cartesian consciousness of pure reflection that gets caught up in emotion is the price the mind has to pay for being lumbered with a body. Consciousness emerges through the disturbance of the organism's homeostasis. Consciousness *is* the activity of dealing with disturbances. For Damasio, for instance, 'the core *you* is only born as the story is told, *within the very story itself* ... You are the music while the music lasts'.[23] In Lacanian terms, the subject is the 'answer of the Real' (225). The subject has the possibility of answering for the Real. Žižek recalls the joke about the patient in a large hospital ward who complains to the doctor about constant noise and crying from the other patients. The doctor replies that nothing can be done to prevent these suffering people from expressing their despair, since they know they are dying. The patient then asks why they cannot be put in a separate room for the dying. And the doctor replies that this *is* the separate room for the dying.

However, Žižek believes that Damasio leaves out of consideration the 'proper empty core of subjectivity', radically exposed as it is, *not* to mere life experience, but also to affects such as anxiety and horror; 'anxiety as correlative to confronting the Void that forms the core of the subject; horror as the experience of disgusting life at its purest, "undead" life' (227). Here again, Žižek is asserting the Lacanian void. Not life experience as it teems forth with Deleuze and Guattari to blow apart the constraining Symbolic, but more like Badiou's 'from nothing to nothing', the awareness of the raw flesh and blood body.

When the subject is violently attacked, for instance, the emotional response is such that the cortical areas of the brain focus on the stimulus and inhibit interest in sex and food. Such stressors over evolutionary time have acted to accelerate the development of our cognitive and behavioural capacities, not least our acquisition of language, "placed" as it is between these higher capacities and our emotional sub-systems. Žižek emphasises this all-important structural "gap" in connectivity between cognitive systems and language on the one hand, and emotional abilities on the other. This gap, or point of "failure," where emotions lag behind cognition, defines our *humanity*. In the absence of the gap humans would be machines. To be specific and crucial for our argument, *human* emotions (like anxiety) arise when the human animal loses its footing in biological functioning, requiring this loss to be supplemented inadequately 'by the symbolically regulated emotions *qua* man's "second nature"' (228). Or to put it another way: imagine that our emotions and cognitive abilities precisely *coincided*, with *no* lag or gap: was this not our central concern with the desiring machines in their machinic-ness? Rather than being human, *re*-presentational and failing, they seemed inhuman, presentational – perfectly functioning monstrosities, incapable of anxiety and concern, because the subject was reduced to a vestigial parasite of no consequence.

In addition, animals themselves are not machines, because of a similar but narrower gap between their biological instincts and cognitive abilities. The gap indeed may be a measure of our evolutionary ascendancy, with lowly insects, for instance, being more or less indistinguishable from machines, with their robotic creepy-crawliness capable, for that reason, of inspiring fear and anxiety.

This gives a new significance to the gaps or lacks of the analytic session, the space to speak, the creation of silence, punctuation and so on, in order to lessen the machinic automaticity of alienated speech/action, and to increase "human" qualities for reflection which can occur only *in* the division of the subject. It is no exaggeration to say that Freud's invention of the psychoanalytic space therefore is linked to civilisation itself. Without this reflective-gap-pause between the drives and manifest behaviour, there is no civility. As Damasio says, 'Memory, language, and intelligence make the difference, not emotion'.[24]

This subject, Descartes' *cogito*, Kant's transcendental subject, is exposed to the drive *per se*; to affects – potentially, raw anxiety, panic and horror. As suggested, all "human" suffering rests in this void of the pure subject. In this gap between the pre-Symbolic Real of the biological machinery of emotion and the Symbolised feelings of the autobiographical self lie everything that must be defended in this work: the sense of the tragic, the melancholic, the human – pity, empathy and compassion, followed by the critical necessity for the elaboration of language (the treasure house of signifiers) *qua* containing and subjectivising of affect, the telling of dreams, stories, narratives, etc. All the contemporary trends, as we have stressed, point in the *reverse* direction towards the inhuman – core unmediated machinic "experience" – paroxysms of sex, convulsions of violence, pitilessness, autism, *jouissance* and the death drive.

Damasio's rather utilitarian and the Darwinian 'towards cooperation with the other' deserves its full *ethical* import however. Levinas is there – "in the gap." The relative failure of homeostasis and the radical exposure of the pure subject *qua* empty to affect and trauma can be re-stated in terms of the trauma of the 'naked face of the other', which prises open the human *qua* human. Before we close off into "full" subjects, we are opened by the ethics as *first* philosophy, prior to any and every *conatus*. And insofar as the same minimal "gap" separates the hind-brain and the more advanced cortical layers in higher organisms of the animal kingdom and mammals in particular, we discover the same "human" qualities to do with care and concern for offspring as well as for the other of other species, increasing as you ascend the evolutionary tree. Consider the Levinasian temperaments of dogs in total devotion to their owners after 15,000 years of co-existence.[25] In this insignificant gap, this ontological crack that Žižek points to are found the imperilled civilised values.

Music arises here too, in this gap between speech, limited to re-presentations, and the unfathomable "deeper" Real. Music creates its own time, keeps its own time, takes its time. As Schopenhauer believed, music will survive at the end of the world. Žižek suggests that music expresses the 'underlying "noumenal" flux of *jouissance* beyond linguistic meaningfulness ... it is the inaccessible excess which forms the very core of the subject' (229–30). Nietzsche hoped 'for a Dionysian future of music',[26] and declared, 'I do not know how to distinguish between tears and music'.[27] Cioran insists that whoever is not struck by the profundity of this assertion does not know music. 'I know no other music than that of tears. Born out of the loss of paradise, music gives birth to the *symbols* of this loss: tears'.[28] Between the loss of *jouissance* and the inadequacy of the Symbolic order, lies music. For "string theorists," the myriads of sub-atomic particles correspond to vibrating strings each with their own note. Thus physics becomes a world of harmonies, chemistry is a melody of strings and thus the universe a symphony.

No Other

At the level of the (bio-)political, the basic antagonisms have never been clearer. Regulation, bureaucratic totalitarianism, the "administered world," work as an ideological cover for the explosive, contingent, a-teleological nature of late capitalism with its auto-revolutionary effects. So utterly complicated have things become that one no longer tries to overthrow the system, one does one's best just to figure its chaotic complexity and then tries to enjoy it.

For a brief moment, against the flow, Žižek himself suggests that, 'we should … elevate the unfortunate "Oedipus complex" to the dignity of ontology' (405, n16).[29] "Unfortunate," yes! What an understatement, implicitly acknowledging the Lacanian travesty? Nevertheless the general cry goes up: Who would nostalgically *re*-Oedipalise the Symbolic? Žižek duly falls in line with the fashionable injunction, namely, 'to fully assume the *non-existence* of the Other' (296). This Lacanian cliché, first mentioned in 1959,[30] can be read in a number of ways: as a "truth-without truth" (Lacan); no metanarrative (Lyotard); no master signifier; no master discourse; no Father; no pre-ordained hierarchy; no moral compass; no teleology; no *common* good, and so on. For Vattimo,[31] for instance, the death of God means the death of any ultimate structures of value or belief. There is *no* objective foundation of meaning or worth, *no* secular account of the worth of human life. All values are *impromptu* interpretations – the making of meaning from within a particular cultural moment, lacking in any ultimate authority or persistence. The irony is that such notions embrace decentralisation and chaos, the freedom upon which capitalism depends for its fullest unfettering.

"There is no Other" risks slippage to the *no Other* in the Baudrillardian sense *qua* unique inexchangeable singularity – no original – everything is phoney, fake, fraudulent, nothing is real, etc. Further, the *non-existence of the Other* risks being read in a Levinasian way: there is *no* other *qua* neighbour in his absolute non-negotiable, irreducible nakedness. That is, there is *no* debt, nothing owing, no place for him in my (absolutely narcissistic) world. Ultimately, therefore the non-existence of the Other must lead to the *death* of the other, the extermination of the other. With the stripping away of (Christian) values, the way is no longed barred to the Girardian sacrificial logic – anyone can be a victim, anyone *will* be a victim.

Multicultural "inclusiveness" is only a stage *en route* to the elimination of the Other – the other of gender, the other of race. Baudrillard parodies Freud, 'Where the Other was, there has the Same come to be'.[32] One can only imagine the violence that has been done to the other to neutralise its otherness, to level it, to and force it to "come out" into the generalised exchange system of choice, simulation and unreality. Just how can the Other *qua* Other survive in the massive recalibration and deracination machine we call capitalism? In bad faith, we can maintain a tolerant neutrality for any and all neutered others. For Father, for Mother, now read "significant other." For wrong-doing, crime or evil, read "inappropriate" and "disadvantaged." For impossibility read "challenging," for savage spending cuts and reduction in wages read "reform," for killing read "termination," for "group" of atomised, isolated individuals with maybe a single characteristic in common, read "community," and so on.

Consider the neutralisation involved in transposing, recycling the Chinese/Vietnamese/Indian/Bangaladeshi, etc. cuisine from centuries of rural custom to a modern Western metropolis melting pot, where such food becomes a mere consumer choice. Consider the orthodox Catholic/Jew/Muslim, who is now told by the secular authorities that he may practice *his* religion only in a purely private capacity. Religion is *your* choice; keep it to yourself! It is the same with the Muslim veil. If the woman wears the veil out of a free choice, that's okay by us tolerant people, but its function as part of the otherness of the Muslim way of life has no meaning for us.

Rhizomatisation represents the creeping underground mat of the Same. The same consumerisation wherever you go in the world. The global market has realised Virilio's "dromosphere," the sphere of acceleration around the earth, with its cry of *everything right now*, 'where everything crashes together, telescoping endlessly … into this proximity that has nothing concrete about it except its infectious hysteria'.[33]

Thus, the much celebrated (illusion of) difference remains within the sphere of the Same. Otherness, raw Otherness belongs to the enigmatic singularity – unknown, non-existent – until its virtual denatured reincarnation in the metropolis as a choice among mega-choosing, by the masses, no longer people, similarly denatured into mere "consumers," like the tourist ticking her list while she is "doing the sites." Look at how one emerging modern metropolis (like all others) has to advertise itself in the twenty-first century:

> Shanghai's multicultural flair endows the city with a unique glamour. Here, one finds the perfect blend of cultures, the modern and the traditional, and the western and the oriental. New skyscrapers and old Shikumen lanes together draw the skyline of Shanghai. Western customs and Chinese traditions intertwined, form Shanghai's culture, making a visitor's stay truly memorable.

Time and space contraction: all customs and eras are present together simultaneously. The utopian transnational neutralisation of otherness.

The Other doesn't exist after its appropriation by its adulterated, decaffeinated, hystericised form. There is no stopping its promotion, visibility, virality in the dromosphere. Everything begs to be real, to eviscerate itself in a fun-loving way for enjoyment, even *jouissance*, whatever the cost to its integrity. Selling itself. It is appalling to imagine what will be, what already is the Other's imaginings of revenge against all this.

The parallax: from the Other to the Same. Along this pitiful parallel we observe the fashionable shift from the "privileged" heteroerotic parallax, to the homoerotic to the ultimate autoerotic utopia. Queer theorist Tim Dean, for instance, wants to 'thoroughly de-heterosexualise desire,'[34] i.e. to get the Other out of desire – stripping out the ineffability of desire, beauty, nubility, wonder and danger, the fertile non-rapport between men and women, to attain a fantasy of fluid-sex-functioning – playful, contingent, mobile, to have fun. To borrow Terry Eagleton's phrase, thus "effing the ineffable."

The thought that heteronormative discourse is a discourse of power relies upon the infantile fantasy that people should live without hurting each other. So threateningly Other and violently rapacious is the erotic that reason *demands* that it be manacled, shackled in the name of freedom, equality and, above all, safety. Ethical sexuality is fertile ground for dozens of learned journals dedicated to official (de)-sexualisation, sexual policing, technology and re-education conferences plotting strategies of control, as more and more subgroups claim sexual marginalisation, victimisation and sexual poverty.

Sexual materialists are about as far from the erotic *qua* Other as it is possible to be. For them sex is equivalent to money. They demand fair trade in sexuality, where everyone has a right to recreational sex, equally and without stigma, even if it means runaway sexual inflation, devaluation of the whole currency. Indifferently, this fair trade extends to pornography, the most degrading forms of which are not only permitted, but celebrated and enjoyed *provided they are consensual.*

This form of sexual logic is aptly opposed by Levinas. Giving oneself 'pleasure ready made' is opposed to the erotic, where 'the subject enters into relation with what is absolutely other … and is never converted into "mine"'.[35] Secular reason opposes tradition, forcing the Other in the other to demystify and disenchant itself in order to fit the rational, reasonable, risk-averse pleasuring for all equally. Potentially, everything is mine for the choosing, particularly for the taking and consuming.

The post-'68 libidinal political rush to *jouissance* was already leading to the consumption of an endless lonely supply of orgasms, paroxysms and fibrillations together with new products promising *jouissance*, up to and including what Žižek refers to, 'autistic-masturbatory "asocial" *jouissance* whose supreme case is drug addiction … a commodity *par excellence*' (311). The fall-out from this virtual revolution, which amounts to a massive retrenchment, is the *real* desert of the social in several key respects: social breakdown, not just at the margins, with the end of the family; violent rage, terrorism as a response to anomie in men; the turn *inwards* towards pleasuring, mysticism, drug states and virtual reality. What all three represent is mass withdrawal from concrete socio-political engagement, in favour of a short-circuiting immediacy beyond the social.

> *Each. Himself. Herself. Alone.*
> *There is no other.*
> *That's not our concern*
> *Nothing – is our concern*
> *Nothing. Nothing.*

Thus, for Žižek and left-Lacanians generally, the analyst's discourse should stand for 'the emergence of revolutionary-emancipatory subjectivity' (298). Restating the "discourse of the analyst" in revolutionary terms shows how far we have come from the Freudian balance. The analyst becomes a "revolutionary agent," addressing the divided subject at the point(s) of "symptomal torsion," the weak points in the normalising (capitalist) ideological position, literally, where the strain produced by twisting (*tortum*, to twist) to fit into the dominant ideology will create a break or rupture, undermining and eliminating the Master signifier (S1) and overturning a whole life world.

Tentatively, Žižek hints at new quilting points, new Master Signifiers, 'a new naming of our situation', beyond the crazy undermining caused not by revolutionary analysts but by capitalism itself, undermining any lasting ideological-political commitments in favour of the carnival of enjoyment, a carnival of brutality? How can a "subject" so empty, ephemeral, contingent and light, so machinic and residual – within a system that both mirrors and creates it – be committed to anything for long enough to effect any change?

Analysis has yielded to cool seduction. No Father; no Other; no Oedipus; no difference: the Real is hyper-realised on the shifting sands of the wide open desert nomad spaces of the BwO, post-psychoanalysis.

Arguably, the greatest casualty arising from the forced non-existence of the Other is woman. Lacan stressed: *the* woman does not exist.[36] What he meant was that the *essential*, *universal* woman no longer exists. Woman, in modernity, is freed from any "essentialist" "feminine" role, and enters the virtual free space, the greatest achievement of the libidinal revolution: *a woman can be anything she chooses.*

Deracinated by choice, is she not *more prone* to the desire of the Other, *qua* fashion, *qua* liberated woman, qua any contingent whim, and so on? The weakening, blurring or denial of the irreconcilable Otherness of woman to man risks destroying what even Žižek again, in a traditionalist moment, refers to as '*the ultimate difference, the "transcendental" difference that grounds human identity itself*'.[37] Similarly, Levinas suggests that the feminine, *this* difference defines difference as such. He refers to 'an insurmountable duality', and the 'absolutely contrary contrary [*le contraire absolutement contraire*]'.[38] He also makes clear, 'This [feminine] subjection is to an *absolute* order, to the authority par excellence of the Good'.[39] For Levinas, specifically maternity is as close as we get to the ultimate ethical relation, being for the other, love without concupiscence (Levinas is fond of quoting Pascal), the principle of absolute substitution – being a hostage to the other. Pregnancy is exemplary here. The word womb means utter hospitality.

However, such a primal ethical role for the feminine seems to bolster in the most extreme way the sexist idealisation of the feminine, as absence, silence, modesty, that de Beauvoir noted at the time. However, Levinasian ethics is *beyond* sexual politics, the striving of beings and inter-subjectivity *per se*, having instead to do with the Real of ethics, prior to ontological/political considerations. Derrida, paying tribute to Levinas, having spoken of the home and 'the implacable law of hospitality' beyond the Law (of the Symbolic), where 'the dwelling opens itself to itself',[40] points out that 'the pre-original welcome, the welcoming par excellence, *is feminine*; it takes place in a place that cannot be appropriated, in an open "interiority" whose hospitality the master or owner receives before himself then wishing to give it'. And so as not to fall into this implicit sexist trap, Derrida says, this welcoming welcome 'confers the opening of the welcome upon the "feminine being" and not upon the *fact* of empirical women'. It 'belongs to "the dimension of femininity," *beyond* ontology and not necessarily to the empirical presence of a human being of the "feminine sex"'.[41] Therefore, it matters not that a home, a dwelling, a *domos*, does or does not have a woman in it, 'the feminine has been encountered in this analysis as one of the cardinal points of the horizon in which the inner life takes place'.[42] The disjunction between de Beauvoir and Levinas-Derrida is the radical difference between being (*conatus*) and *otherwise*-than-being, or between (sexual) politics and ethics. And while the "feminine" as such is beyond empirical men and women, women are most likely to be nearest that cardinal point and not because they have been put there by men. They have been put there by nature prior to any enculturation.

Such thinking recalls the old psychoanalytic tropes first explored by Deutsche, Horney and Freud, connected with, rooted in, very specifically and inescapably with the feminine: menstruation, defloration, intercourse, pregnancy, infertility, childbirth, lactation, the mother-child relation and menopause. Now, we must add physical and sexual abuse and rape as the vast majority of these crimes are suffered by women. No wonder then that the feminine á la Levinas–Derrida is intimately connected with the Real and the ethical *otherwise*-than-being, with a specifically hidden welcoming suffering *jouissance* connected intimately to the life and death of the other. It is women who suffer birth, women who look after the very young, rear children and who watch over the old and infirm, the sick and the disabled. It is women who exemplify the ethical relation of utter hospitality and the pre-original welcome. Women are closer to the Real of suffering and affliction than men.

Academic feminists transpose these Other phenomena of the erotic, of the utterly hospitable feminine "for-the-other," from the Real to the Symbolic whereby women become politicised, promoted, entitled as never before, all grist to the feminist mill, so that such ancient feminine truths become re-written as male idealisations, polemically hierarchialised allied to the old patronising patriarchal plot to keep women inferior. Serving thus becomes *sub*-servient – beneath service. Sacrifice becomes waste. Caring becomes devalued and menial, maternity becomes the poor and unequal sister of feminism. A new hierarchy is created between the political class of educated feminist activists, who generate a new superego, restricting language use, identifying new forms of harassment, sexism, etc., plus what Žižek refers to as an "obscene superego supplement" (368ff) that consolidates the power of *any* political grouping – feminism no less than any other. Poorer women, unseen women, women who have *no choice* but to continue to serve, women who make sacrifices, remain largely outside the system. Without *them* the system would collapse from its own contradictions and antagonisms.

A tension, in the form of a parallax, arises between the ego ideal of liberated feminism – the advancement of women's rights, freedom, health, protection, life chances, etc., and a Girardian type sacrifice, not just of poor outcast ethnic women worker-slaves, but beyond them, the hidden radically voiceless violence of abortion.[43] The "right to choose" the signifier of modern liberal democratic consumers: what is more reasonable, tolerant and civilised, more than four decades after abortion was legalised in Britain and the scourge of deaths from back-street abortions minimised, that a *woman herself and no one else should determine what happens to her body*?

Currently there are two hundred thousand abortions a year in Britain, up from 5,000 since 1967, a million in France equal to the number of live births, three million a year in Russia double the number of live births, thirteen million a year in China, and so on. All part of the giant abortion machine that creates and maintains the smooth BwO of liberated woman. The abortion issue has always been at the cutting edge – the feminist guillotine razor of the longest revolution. This demand has been widely conceded and its obscene superego effects have gone underground. Abortion up to full term,[44] gender-based abortions, early infanticide widen the sacrificial franchise, all justified politically on the basis of the priority of women's reproductive and mental health. Thus the liberal ethical justification for feminism rests on the unavoidable obscene superego supplement of abortion. This may be the greatest irony of the libidinal revolution: the canonical assertion of the *non-existence of the Other* leads ultimately and logically to the death of the Other, the machinic extermination of the Other, to deprive the other of its own end. The foetus, as literally unseen, has no rights, no voice and represents the ultimate outcast, trash, *otherwise-than-being*, of ferocious being itself.

The gap of wisdom

Žižek explores a "new space," *outside* the totalised hegemony of Being that eliminates, kills the Other. It is the opening up of a place of refusal, where, to quote Mallarmé – 'nothing will have taken place but the place itself' (cited on p. 381). In his paradoxical logic, this gesture is nothing – *no-thing*. It doesn't exist! In impossible Žižekian terms, it is the 'immanent difference, gap, between this [everyday totalised] reality and its own void; that is to discern the void that separates material reality *from itself*, that makes it "non-all"' (383). The analyst's silence emphasises the void behind everyday speaking, the all important void for reflection, anxiety, mourning, etc., that reflects the division in the subject, the gap between emotion and speech, an opening or a crack in Being.

Returning to the *soixante-huitards*, their protests were framed against a background of a world dominated by scientism (Harold Wilson's "the white heat of technology"), the burgeoning discourse of scientific knowledge, the terrifying nuclear option discourse of Mutually Assured Destruction. Alienation was precisely *not to see* that scientism – this universal belief that science has *all* the answers – is fundamentally dislocating – not to see the void created by *this* hard irredeemable reality. The void, as such, did not exist – what are you talking about? Are you mad? But *not* to see the void in the everyday life of burgeoning consumption was to be estranged, cut off from what used to be called wisdom.

It was no coincidence that First World youth were the first to revolt, in the most technologically *advanced* centres with the greatest affluence. Here, for some of the best and the brightest, the *felt* gap was greatest, not among workers or Third World peasants. Maslow's famous hierarchy of needs dictated that the most wealthy, the most affluent and idealistic must rebel, not the poor or the hungry. Scientific knowledge was running way ahead of meaning. The gulf between scientific knowledge and wisdom about life and living was widening, with the astounding success and promise of technological advance. The medieval notion that the cosmos had a unity, purpose, a *telos*, broke apart during the early modern period with Descartes asserting that the search for final causes in physics was over, by the mid-seventeenth century. The cosmos has no purpose and into the abyss where wisdom should have remained, came eventually all the "ghosts of religion" (Octavio Paz)[45] – totalising ideologies and technological advancement of potentially fratricidal proportions.

The students were returning to the Socratic injunction: 'the greatest good of man is daily to converse about virtue', albeit with a new urgent ideological twist, a Marxist inflection: how can one live a good life under late capitalism which itself promises all the answers and more besides?

In Mike Nichols's *The Graduate*, Benjamin (Dustin Hoffmann) is in this desert of alienation. At exactly the point when he surfaces from the family swimming pool where he has been lazing and drifting for far too long after finishing college, Elaine's father leans over and signals to him advice through his misty goggles – just one word: "plastics"! "Plastics, Benjamin" – *the* solution! Go into plastics – that is where the new money will be! For Benjamin, the yawning gap of meaning opens wider.

This empty, alienated subject was illustrated by Stephen Poliakoff's *Caught On A Train*, a 1980 BBC2 play for television, based on an overnight claustrophobic train journey across Europe, following the route of a journey Poliakoff himself had made from London to Vienna. In the play, Peter (Michael Kitchen) is a young professional *en route* to an important book fair. But his train trip is complicated by two women assigned to his compartment. One is an independent American woman (Wendy Raeback) in Europe to discover the roots of Western civilisation only to find herself threatened by the breakdown products of that civilisation – by drunken louts and skinheads on the one hand and authoritarian police on the other. The other woman is Frau Messner (Peggy Ashcroft) – a demanding yet somewhat seductive older European woman, definitely old Europe. She chastises Peter for his smirking, his rudeness and lack of deference. He doesn't care about anyone but himself she declares. He clearly despises what she stands for, her thoroughly discredited neo-fascist nostalgia. But when she asks him *what he stands for*, he cannot answer, *he has nothing to say*. He stands for himself, alone.

Levinas like Heidegger before him was concerned about the *anti*-humanism of the (human) sciences – he included psychoanalysis – for undermining the sovereignty of man and losing sight of the *holiness* of man. Recently, for example, the *New Scientist* had a title page, "The Self. The greatest trick your mind ever played."[46] The autonomous self is an illusion, as neuroscience has demonstrated, and for Levinas too, there is no autarchic self *per se*. However, for Levinas the self is always already *not all* by virtue of being opened up, persecuted by the ethical demand of the other. Levinas thus safeguards a humanism *beyond* humanism. Into the gap *that we cannot close* comes the other. As Levinas says, 'Humanism has to be denounced only because it is not sufficiently human'.[47] However, Levinas acknowledges the paradox that the ethical absolute passivity, persecution, substitution, hostage, etc., to the other, must have some limits otherwise the gap of our humanity will be entirely plugged by the other as persecutor. 'The fact that the other, my neighbour, is also a third party with respect to another, is the birth of thought, consciousness, justice and philosophy'.[48] This is the birth of thought in the gap of wisdom.

Baudrillard invokes the paradisal unity of the cosmos before the break/fall, the unsullied moment prior to the fall into representation and the symbolic. It is the moment of first contact, 'when things have not yet noticed we are there … It is the same with language when it has not yet had time to signify'.[49] It is thus with any new thing, but gone in a trice once *we* appear. We bring along the gap. Against the utopian ideology of "one world" – technological synthesis and the alienated "reconciliation" of all with all – Baudrillard, like Žižek, opts strategically for the dual form, irrevocable divergence [parallax]. Against all striving to reconcile the antagonistic terms: 'maintain *impossible* exchange … play on that tension and dual form, which nothing escapes, but everything opposes',[50] leaving open the possibility of the void-gap that makes you think otherwise.

The Act

For Lacanians and thus for Žižek, release or break-out from enslavement, alienation and estrangement in the Symbolic (technologically advanced) is via the "ethical act,"[51] whereby the anti-Oedipal subject reverses the "forced choice" of the Oedipal era, between Symbolic castration and the potential for psychosis. For Žižek, as already noted, the death drive is not the blind pointless will to self-destruction, but the violent energy required for the (revolutionary) Act-Event to blast a way through the ontological blockage. As Zupančič makes clear, 'After the act I am not the same as before. In the act the subject is annihilated and subsequently reborn (or not)'.[52] The act carries this suicidal risk, beyond the limits of the Symbolico-political community. It could turn out to be good or diabolical evil; either way, it has a shattering effect. These self-designated Acts for freedom, however, will be inevitably taken up and reabsorbed into the Symbolic thus eventually losing their revelatory and revolutionary (counter-)power.

Not content with pondering the gap of wisdom and reflection, the birth of thinking, Žižek chastises Lacanians for losing their 'socio-political critical edge'. Lacan himself was never explicitly political or revolutionary, being first and foremost a psychoanalyst. However, his relentless critique of American ego-psychology is an attack on American imperialism, most notably in the famous 1953 Rome Discourse.[53] What marks out Lacan politically is his radical anti-utopianism. As Stavrakakis quips, 'in true Lacanian style, one could even declare that "the Lacanian left" does not exist!'[54] By which he means, there is no *totality* on the Lacanian Left, but rather, *the politics of lack* – with Lacan at the centre. At varying distances from this centre are, for instance, Butler and Castoriadis at the furthest distance, Laclau and Mouffe, then Badiou. The constant focus on "lack" or "gap" is controversial. Acknowledging that '[i]t [Lacanian theory] has almost invisibly gained a foothold in theoretical literature', Robinson concedes that '[t]his is at least partly due to its radical pretensions', but continues, '[i]t is, however, crucial to challenge it, because its [a-]political effects paralyse "radical" theory. It provides a very weak basis for any kind of politics, and certainly no basis for a radical or transformative agenda'.[55] Everywhere the signifier "impossibility" pops up. Lack operates as a mythical essence, recall the Žižekian 'strategic politico-philosophical decision', giving rise to the foundational inevitability of the parallax contradictions under discussion!

However, the ontological crack offers the possibility of what St. Paul meant when he exhorted us *not to be conformed to this world* (Romans 12:2). Arguably, this not being conformed is the most radical position today, conserving the essentially *human* space: the preserve of civil values, of family, of the silent majority, the site of resistance to contingency and inexorable change. It is that space that the State will infiltrate to regulate as it tries to come between each of us, separating parents from each other and parents and adults from children.

Žižek however is not paralysed by lack; far from it, he argues for a violent transformative agenda. Žižek's Act is to write: to smash by writing; to create short-circuits and strict antinomies. Against progressivism, he favours *inhuman* rights: 'we should directly admit revolutionary violence as a liberating end in itself' (380). However, recall the same strict warning that Lacan gave the aforementioned Paris students. Žižek is aware of the problem, but still follows Badiou favouring the revolutionary violence of, for instance, the exemplary Chinese legalists, the Jacobins, Lenin and Mao, who between them have been responsible for the deaths of countless millions.[56] He favours, 'The community of believers *qua* "uncoupled" outcasts from the social order – with, ideally, authentic psychoanalytic and revolutionary collectives as its two main forms'.[57] In the foreword to *The Fragile Absolute* Žižek suggests: 'the explosive combination of Lacanian psychoanalysis and Marxist tradition detonates a dynamic freedom that enables us to question the very presuppositions of the circuit of Capital'.

The most radical parallax is formulated thus: 'the pacifying God of love is not the opposite of the vengeful Jehovah, but his other face' (280). Never to be resolved, merely posited as such, this antinomy can be summarised thus: 'violence, as the work of love'. *I come not to bring peace, but to bring a sword* (Matthew 10:34), and, on the other side, the apparently senseless utter *passivity* of Christ on the Cross. Irreconcilable.

Violent Acts by "fundamentalists," who have come to *know directly, totally and absolutely*, emerge from the Real, seizing the moment, like the epochal Event of the October Revolution. *Sublime* Acts, but committed by *limited human subjects*, become immediately "pathological" (when "retrieved" in the Symbolic) leading often to the most monstrous abuses, with consequences possibly affecting whole continents for decades to come. What is the difference between "creative" violence and what Žižek himself describes as "Id-evil," skinhead random violence; between *Kristallnacht* (Night of Broken Glass) and Stalingrad? How, for instance, should one evaluate the following? 'A well known Slovene Catholic intellectual, ex-Minister of Culture and ex-Slovenian ambassador to France, recently wrote:

> The only weapon is rebellion and destruction, as the recently deceased apostle Jacques Derrida taught us. Whenever you see a window, throw a brick into it. Where there is a building, there must be a mine. Where there is a high-rise building Bin Laden should come. Where there is any kind of institution, law or link, one should find a falsification, a 'law' of the street or of the underground.[58]

Incidentally, Žižek quips that *Where there is a high rise building Bin Laden should come*, sounds like Freud's *wo Es war soll Ich werden* (421). An "emancipatory" Act, or a sick joke? Žižek pleads context is all; by their fruits, we shall know them: does the Act lead to a fundamental change in the Symbolic coordinates?

Here is an exemplary (radical, revolutionary, Žižekian-ethical) Act, the 'leap of faith' and the *step outside* the global circuit – an incident during the Vietnam war:

> [A]fter the US Army occupied a local village, their doctors vaccinated the children on the left arm in order to demonstrate their humanitarian care; when, the day after, the village was retaken by the Vietcong, they cut off the left arms of all the vaccinated children ... Although it is difficult to sustain as a literal model to follow, this complete rejection of the enemy precisely in its caring 'humanitarian' aspect, no matter what the cost, has to be endorsed in its basic intention.[59]

Although Marchant criticises this example, as 'difficult to sustain for an emancipatory project of the Left', with its absolute rejection of the enemy, and its 'sanitary effort at purification', that might 'serve as a generalizable recommendation ... and, in the last instance extermination[60]', his criticism here is only one of tactics for the Left. There is absolutely no mention or criticism of the barbarity of the Vietcong in their "counter-vaccination" anti-American programme: the Vietcong were acting ethically in their total break with the enemy. Similarly, in Iraq, counter-insurgency "Acts" involving suicide bombings of innocent civilians and children at random, 'although difficult to sustain', would be regarded as ethical nonetheless.

However, as always the margins are interesting! Those little hesitations, doubts ('difficult to sustain') might mark these hesitant intellectual theorists themselves out, why not, for Badiou's *third* moment of "revolutionary justice" – 'egalitarian justice' and its '*immediate brutal imposition*, with *no* understanding of the "complex circumstances"' (379, emphasis added) – maybe the gulag or worse.

How many intellectuals have been in receipt of such *Real* Love/violence – the "obscene stain" of revolutionary power? As Lenin put it succinctly: 'Intellectuals are lackeys of capitalism, who think they are the brains of the nation. They are not the brains of the nation. They're its shit'.[61] 'Could my former comrades', asks Azar Nafisi in relation to the Iranian Revolution, 'have predicted that one day they would be tried in a Revolutionary Court, tortured and killed as traitors and spies? … not in their wildest dreams'.[62] Could Orwell have imagined that the thousands of working class people who went to Spain to fight fascism would be declared 'traitors in the pay of the enemy?'[63]

Žižek's uncompromising 'passion for the Real' clears a space for radical "freedom," violent transgression. Not for him a safe government position in the newly emerging Slovenian state in the early 1990s. He says, 'the notion of serving as a minister of culture, education or science seemed to be utterly ridiculous, not even worth consideration'.[64] The arrogant dismissal of any working *within* the system shows just how indiscriminate is Žižek's nihilation of *any* System *qua* liberal-capitalist system – even the newly emerging Slovenian state, his own people freeing themselves from totalitarianism. Surely Žižek's "Act," to smash by writing from his Marxist-Lacanian position, is no more than his own little *Rumspringa*, running around, jumping around, before he returns to the safety of academia and publishing.

The question remains, however, how can such a de-substantialised postmodern subject commit to anything in the ominous shadow of the Other's absence? And what new horror might transpire when he tries? Welcome to silence and the real desert. Not the silence of our absence, not the silence that subtends speech, but the Holocaustal silence brought about by our monstrous presence, monstrous Acts and the obscene stain of revolutionary power.

Notes

1 Žižek, S., 2006. All subsequent page numbers in parentheses are referring to this work. While this chapter focuses on this volume in particular, it does not constitute a review of the book. It is fair to say that Žižek almost single-handedly has revived psychoanalysis, brought it back from the dead and reclaimed a vibrant place for the discipline at the centre of culture, ethics and indeed religion.

2 Žižek himself is the butt of jokes like Terry Eagleton's spoof: 'The crack between the herring and the side of the can, to put the matter in Hegelese, is actually a crack within the pickled herring itself. It is the way the pickled herring differs minimally from itself ...'.
3 See also an extended discussion in Weatherill, R., 2011: 93–112.
4 Grossman, V., 1980.
5 What stand out for Levinas are 'scenes of goodness in an inhuman world ... *exterior to all system*' (see Levinas, E., 2001: 81), where 'the human [*qua* human] pierces the crust of being' (ibid.: 90), 'where goodness escapes every ideology ... goodness *without* thinking' (ibid.: 217). Grossman is clear. He describes the uniformity of the wooden barrack huts in the Russian camp: 'Everything that lives is unique ... If you attempt to erase the peculiarities and individuality of life by violence, then life itself must suffocate' (Grossman, 1980: 19). Grossman privileges simple human devotion, like Lyudmila's grief for her illegitimate son, Tolya, killed as a boy in the war, at his simple graveside by the rows of wooden crosses, talking to him in a delirium of grief all the cold night. 'Nothing matters to her; there was nothing she needed. All that existed was some agonising force that was crushing her heart' (ibid.: 154).
6 We will return to the ethical question in relation to political action later in this chapter and others. Levinas has been criticised for ignoring the *finite* specificities of ethics. The same criticism could be levelled at Žižek who favours revolutionary love against the finite reformism of the non-revolutionary Left.
7 See http://legomenon.com/meaning-of-the-scream-1893-painting-by-edvard-munch.html.
8 See www.telegraph.co.uk/news/worldnews/europe/ireland/4412809/Its-blood-money-truly-the-wages-of-sin.html.
9 Kundera, M., 1984: 282.
10 Steiner, G., 1998.
11 Sebald, W. G., 2002: 4.
12 Ibid.: 10.
13 I have pointed out similar radical discontinuities in Weatherill, R., 2004: 82–5.
14 Cronin, M., 2016: 22. "From vivid faces to frozen masks? Remembering to forget in latemodern Ireland." *Lacaunae* 12:22.
15 "The clamour of being" is the title of Badiou's critique of Deleuze; Badiou, A., and Burchill, L., 1999.
16 Amis, M., 1997.
17 Krzysztof Kieslowski's film, *Blue*, 1993, the first of the *Three Colours Trilogy*.
18 http://jacket2.org/commentary/alejandra-pizarnik-uncollected-poems-1962–1972.
19 See Weatherill, R., 1998, where I emphasis the "sovereignty" of the drive taken from diverse psychoanalytic viewpoints and other discourses.
20 See Taylor, J., 2001: 37.
21 Just as the eye sees without seeing itself seeing. The transparency of perception belies the opacity of the *means* of perception. What we see, out there, is really opaquely generated by a tiny flickering image, which is a little different on each retina. The inputs are synthesised by the visual cortex and projected back onto external objects with the added bonus of depth vision.
22 See Winnicott, D., 1971. Emergence is what happens in groups as well as neural networks. Recently, I was asked to give a (top-down) talk/lecture on projective identification to a group of postgraduate students studying on a group training course. We duly sat in a circle and I gave my talk in which, at one point, I gave some graphic vignettes of *violent* projective identification. The reaction of some of the students was to question *why* I had used these *violent* examples. The switch was from manifest *content* to latent *process*. So I became absorbed in the emerging *group process of becoming* – to do with affect rather than content.
23 Damasio, A., 2000: 191.
24 Ibid.: 311.

25 The body of Alzheimer's patient Peggy Mangan was found in waste ground in North Dublin on 29 September 2013 after a huge search, since she went missing five days earlier. Her pet King Charles spaniel stayed with her for the five days and died soon after she was discovered.
26 Nietzsche, F., 1967: 252.
27 Ibid.: 274.
28 Cioran, E., 1995: 11.
29 Maybe Žižek secretly still longs for this real and indispensable nodal complex of psychoanalysis when considering the reality of Hölderlin's breakdown.
30 'There is no, I have told you, Other of the Other. There is not in the Other, any signifier which is able on this occasion to answer for what I am'. Lacan, J., 1958–1959: Lesson 16, 16 April 1959: 206.
31 Vattimo, G., 2004.
32 Baudrillard, J., 1990: 125.
33 Virilio, P., 2005: 100.
34 Dean, T., 2000.
35 Levinas, E., 1961: 276.
36 Lacan, J., 1972–1973: 68.
37 Žižek, S., 2009: 28 (emphasis added).
38 Levinas, E., 1947: 85–6.
39 Ibid.: 117, emphasis added.
40 Derrida, J., 1997: 41.
41 Ibid.: 44–45.
42 Levinas cited on p. 44.
43 21 May 2008: 'We have in this country [Britain] at the moment a situation in which you can have two children, of exactly the same age and gestation, and one is in a cot with all the resources of medical science being poured into saving it and the other is quite deliberately being taken from the womb and destroyed'. British MPs vote to retain the 24-week limit for abortions. Marie Stopes International said it was "reassuring" that a majority of MPs were wise to what it called an emotive and misleading campaign to chip away at women's reproductive rights and had disregarded it in exercising their votes.
44 Dr Sarah Chan, Deputy Director, Institute for Science, Ethics and Innovation, Manchester University, speaking on *The Moral Maze* (BBC Radio 4, 9 October 2013) would allow infanticide under certain circumstances, as well as up to full-term abortions.
45 Paz, O., 1986.
46 *The New Scientist*, 23 February 2013.
47 Levinas, E., 1981: 127.
48 Ibid.: 127.
49 Baudrillard, J., 2001a: 52.
50 Baudrillard, J., 1999: 79.
51 We will return to this theme in the penultimate chapter.
52 Zupančič, A., 2000: 83.
53 Lacan, J., 1968.
54 Stavrakakis, Y., 2007: 4.
55 Robinson, A., 2005.
56 We will take up this revolutionary theme in Chapter 9.
57 Žižek, S., 2000: 160.
58 Capuder, A., 2004.
59 Žižek, S., 2004: 83.
60 Marchant, O. 2007, p110.
61 Lenin cited in Amis, M., 2002: 42.
62 Nafisi, A., 2003: 115.
63 Orwell, G., 1938: 207. Hitchens, C., 2002 refers to 'the deliberate subversion of the Spanish Republic by the agents of Stalin' (48). Andres Nin, the founder of the POUM,

was kidnapped, tortured and – refusing to crack – murdered. The Communist spokesman said he had fled to join the Nazis. Friends of Orwell, like George Kopp, whom Orwell tried in vain to get freed from jail, were tortured by confinement with rats, and other volunteers like Bob Smillie died of their treatment. Considering how the history of this period will be distorted, Orwell comments, 'The very concept of objective truth is fading out of the world' (cited on p. 50).

64 Žižek, S., 2002: 6.

6

THE POWER OF NEGATIVE THINKING

Analysis against therapy

There is a story about a husband who arrives home early from work to find his wife in bed with another man. Shocked by the situation he has come upon, he stumbles out a confused question as to *what on earth does she think she is doing*? She responds rapidly and indignantly by saying: never mind what *I'm* doing, why are you home so early; you're never home this early darling, why today? The wife's attempt to cover the truth could be seen as therapeutic and kind, insofar as she attempts to spare herself and her husband pain, whereas the analytic reading might demand the truth behind the covers of the bed. In the R. D. Laing version of this story the wife tells her husband emphatically that *there is no other man* – it is simply *his* delusion – the other man is not there; thus creating a psychotic confusion in the victim. A postmodern relativistic reading of the story would have the man with *his* perception and the woman with *her* denial as equally valid interpretations of the same contested and ultimately impossible reality. While a late Lacanian reading might insist on the woman's right to her own enjoyment. Anyway, the contemporary *therapeutic* advice for the husband would be for him to go and find his own therapist and work on his issues, particularly jealousy.

Everything is here for us. This gift has been given a quantum boost by the immediacy of the internet.

- *The sun rises and the sun sets and in between – everything is up for grabs.*
- *Run in New York. Fly in Paris. Surf in Rio. Pleasure hunt across the globe. The* New Magnum *Infinity for pleasure seekers.*

Michael Chorost[1] imagines a coming world of "telempathy," where there is no need to express your thoughts or feelings in words, where others experience your brain states *directly*, via nanowires, sending and receiving information effortlessly. No gap between stimulus and response; the gap, already identified as being what makes us human and not machinic. Ironically, Michael Chorost was born with severe hearing loss, partially restored with a cochlear implant in 2001. He later wrote about the experience stressing how the implant had made him *more* human.[2] The implant replaced the auditory sense and therefore restored a normal function. The essential gap remained between the sensory auditory cortex and higher cognitive functions.

With the abolition by techno-perfection of the NOT-ALL, the ontic swallows the ontological. Lacanians have held out for the gap, the *béance*, the lacuna, the ontological crack, the hole, the enigma and so on. Personally, I recall a precise moment in the mid 1980s, when an eminent Lacanian outlined this notion of the Real beyond being, and to me it was one of those moments of absolute illumination. For me this ontological crack was a space, above all, of forgiveness.

Now, everyone is upping their game. There is no excuse (i.e. no gap) these days for not being "worked-out" and living your dream. Love your life. We have now had at least one generation reared in this eutrophic firmament. A generation won over, via capitalistic logic, to addictive states.[3]

Positive thinking

In the West, we are constrained to be positive. This pervasive ideology underpins therapy culture. It first emerged with Calvinism. This branch of Christianity bears the name of the French reformer John Calvin from the sixteenth century, part of the Protestant reformed tradition. In this view human beings, in their "total depravity," are at the mercy of God and his divine intervention, which can change rebellion into obedience. To be saved, the person must believe the gospel and repent. Such faith compliance is a gift from God, and thus God completely and sovereignly achieves the salvation of sinners.

Most settlers in the American mid-Atlantic states and New England were Calvinists, including the English Puritans, the French Huguenots, the Dutch settlers of New Amsterdam (New York) and the Scottish-Irish Presbyterians of the Appalachian backcountry. Dutch Calvinist settlers were also the first successful European colonisers of South Africa, beginning in the seventeenth century, who became known as Boers or Afrikaners. However, it is to North America that we look for the origin of the Positive Thinking ideology. Its underlying purity belongs to its paranoid-schizoid structure. The tough-minded, punitive Protestant ideology enabled survival in the New World, but at a considerable cost in human suffering.

However, by the early nineteenth century things were changing radically. A post-Calvinist movement was emerging, the "New Thought movement," with such key influences as Emerson's transcendentalism, Swedenborgianism, popular science evolutionism, Hinduism and William James's *The Varieties of Religious Experience*. Phineas Pankhurst Quimby and Mary Baker Eddy, during the 1860s, were the originators of the Positive Thinking movement. It is Quimby, for instance, we have to thank for the belief that illness originates in the mind as a consequence of erroneous beliefs; a mind open to God's omnipotence could overcome *any* illness.

With this new development, God was no longer hostile, punitive and indifferent to human suffering. On the contrary, humanity, God, Mind or Spirit were all now part of the great universal harmony. Men and women could tap into the boundless and universal Spirit.

In the 1890s and early twentieth century, many New Thought books were published on all aspects of self-help, including how to be financially successful. A central tenet was the so-called "Law of Attraction:" the notion that thoughts seduce each other; good thoughts follow good thoughts and bad follow bad. 'You are what you think, not what you think you are'.[4] Thus, being follows thinking. The way is opened for self-empowerment or what James called "the Mind-Cure" movement. This has the added value of being utterly uncomplicated so that even the youngest children can follow the ideology. In biblical tones, William James declared, 'The blind have been made to see, the halt to walk. Life-long invalids have had their health restored'.[5] Popularised by Norman Vincent Peale,[6] Positive Thinking went viral. There were no limits to this movement.

Underlying this great ferment, the superego structure remained the same, only the *contents* changed. The Calvinist puritans became the New Thought puritans: the same punishing work ethic prevailed. The *same* agency was at work in punishing transgressions according to a strict moral code and its exact reversal in the strict new code of enjoyment and positivity without limit. The only difference being that the latter code seems more severe! Not just your soul is in peril, but your life, your thinking, your being.

Thus, Calvinist tropes remain in the New Thinking – pervasive judgementalism, discipline, the work imperative, work *on the self*, all dressed up in a positive light. Work done via therapy will produce the right kind of emotions, the right kind of thinking and speaking – tolerance and positivity. Negative emotions – anger, hate, rage, depression, will be left behind through hard therapeutic work. These emotions are not "wrong" but merely "inappropriate." Stay away from negative people and stay close to your angels. The formula was just four letters! CANI: Constant and Never-ending Improvement.[7]

Why not go the whole hog and bring together the mega-churches of Calvinism, Evangelical Protestantism, New Thinking and capitalism? Think positive and grow rich! Christian pastors and CEOs joined forces and exchanged positions to learn from each other. Businesses became cults; churches became businesses. CEOs were close to divinity. Any religious tradition can be purloined. Motivational speakers became gurus with shamanistic healing journeys to lead, vision quests to make. There were Native American healing circles for top managers, tribal story telling, even fire walking, bonding games and trust exercises, wilderness excursions and boot camps. Genuine mystics, it was argued, were more likely to be found in board rooms than churches. These mystics taught that 'reality is a product of human consciousness'.[8]

The relentlessly upbeat approach is for everyone, young and old. Everyone is caught within its positive sweep, as once again capitalism proves itself able comprehensively to neutralise/exploit the negative. Executives relax and meditate on the meaning of life while, in the background, a burgeoning army of invisible worker-ants, the new drudges, the "precariat" do the microtasks, boring service jobs outsourced to them at the lowest wages and with fewer and fewer rights, as each is required to be a *self*-entrepreneur and an indebted subject simultaneously. With a debt (for education, training, housing, health, etc.) that can never be paid back, they become the new "sinners" of the neo-liberal free-for-all increasingly in the *global* economy without a safety net. Now, increasingly, they are deemed the authors of their own sinning, with no chance of fight back. Indebtedness as risk is increasingly outsourced to them as workers. *They* take the hit if the business or the bank fails and the capital investment is immediately withdrawn and moved elsewhere.

The old will not die.[9] Even severe illness is an opportunity for positivity. Barbara Ehrenreich[10] experienced its impact when diagnosed with breast cancer; she was immediately introduced to the "pink ribbon culture" with a whole raft of pink themed breast cancer products, including four types of tiny bears, to inspire a positive and upbeat outlook. No self-pity was allowed, only "battling," "fighting," "bravely" and "fiercely," to come out on the other side of the treatments, as a "survivor." The self-improvement messages were clear: this was the hardest year, but it has made me stronger, happier, better, more sensitive, and so on. Cancer is initiatory; it is seen as a gift.[11] Academic, literary critic, queer theorist, Eve Sedgwick has written positively about baldness and mastectomy scars as these challenge positively negative heteronormative stereotypes.

Since the 1970s, it has been commonplace to link cancer to a weakened immune system caused by negative emotions. *You* are implicated in your cancer. Visualise your cancer cells being attacked by healthy cells. Although prolonged stress does damage the immune response, there is no evidence that the immune system can recognise cancer cells, only cells that are genetically *other*. 'The immune system does not appear to recognise cancers within an individual as foreign, because they are actually part of the self'.[12] Immuno-deficient animals are not more susceptible to cancers. Furthermore, it would make little sense to treat cancers with chemotherapy if the immune system played a key role in prevention. On the contrary, some activities of the immune system actually augment tumour growth by releasing growth factors. Ehrenreich concluded that breast cancer did not make her stronger, more feminine, spiritual, etc. What it did give her was an 'agonising encounter with an ideological force in American culture … one that encourages us to deny reality, submit cheerfully to misfortune, and blame only ourselves for our fate'.[13]

Awash with good emotion, feel-good chemicals and statements on social media linked to an endless spiritual high, people can still feel guilty. They stress how busy they are recycling and how they always buy "organic" and "hand-made," shop in "green" shops and buy "fair-trade" coffee. *Feeling good* is key and corporations stress their spiritual credentials. 'Every day, we go to work hoping to do two things: share great coffee with our friends and help make the world a little better. Our mission is to inspire and nurture the human spirit – one person, one cup, and one neighbourhood at a time' (Starbucks). 'We will work for positive social, ethical and environmental improvements in our supply chain' (Next). 'Looking for an ethical

Expresso or Cappucinio with a conscience? You'll find it in Marks & Spencer. It will be Rainforest Alliance certified'. Tesco is 'adhering to the Ethical Trading Initiative and making sustainable environmental impact a key business priority'. By paying for your plastic bags you are caring for the environment. By buying this food you are helping to save a child's life. Oxfam: 'Actually, we don't mail goats. But all of these gifts are real items that we use to fight poverty. When you purchase an unwrapped gift card, your tax-deductible donation will fund projects that your gift represents'.

Civilisation has become so thin it cannot bear any negative. To paraphrase Eliot, humankind cannot bear the Real:[14] we prefer the discourse of angels. Kundera saw angelic discourse as essentially a "shitless discourse," full of edifying kitsch. Kitsch characterises the postmodern. As Kundera explains, Kitsch in the original German 'is the absolute denial of shit, in both the literal and figurative senses of the word; kitsch excludes everything from its purview which is essentially unacceptable in human existence'.[15] The discourse of the postmodern is thus "unbearably light" and sassy. It should have nothing of the stain of shit about it. Unbearably positive and thus unbearably unreal, more recently kitsch has come to mean trashy, worthless, gaudy, imitative, derived and so forth, playing on bad taste ironically, like the bad art museum, or the "bad sex in fiction" award. The negative is overdetermined as bad, nasty or sad.

In the early 2000s, Irish growth rates were being massively fuelled by a building boom. Insisting on staying relentlessly positive and upbeat in July 2007, the Irish Taoiseach, Bertie Ahern, blamed those 'Sitting on the sidelines, cribbing and moaning … I don't know how people who engage in that don't commit suicide because frankly the only thing that motivates me is being able to actively change something'. Criticism was forbidden. The collective failure to heed negative thinking in this instance cost the Irish people €100 billion.[16]

In Peter Weir's *The Truman Show* (1998), Jim Carrey plays a small town clerk who initially is unaware that he has been living in a constructed reality television show since birth, broadcast to millions. Truman's hometown is a complete set built under a giant dome. The show's producer captures Truman's real emotions in certain contrived situations. Truman's family and friends are all played by actors under the producer's control. Despite such controls, Truman manages on occasion to behave independently. For instance, he falls in love with an extra on the set. In time, Truman notices certain aspects of his perfect world that seem out of place: a light bulb falls from the "sky;" his car radio picks up a conversation between the show's crew; the same people appear in the same places at certain times each day; Truman's "deceased" father reappears as a homeless man; a policeman seems to know his name. Truman starts seriously wondering about his life, eventually making a bid for freedom, trying to escape in a boat. His escape is blocked by various strategies, including a manufactured storm in which he nearly drowns. As he recovers, the boat reaches the edge of the dome, piercing the dome's painted sky. He discovers stairs, leading to a door marked "EXIT." The producer one last time speaks directly to Truman via a sound system, trying to persuade him to stay by arguing that there is no more truth in the real world than there is in his own, artificial world. However, unlike us, Truman has courage and steps through the door and into the real world.

Back in the 1970s, *The Stepford Wives* are turned into mindless, docile, fawning, submissive and impossibly beautiful wives. However, newly arrived Joanna Eberhart grows increasingly suspicious of their robotic type behaviour. Her friend Bobbie helps her investigate, but she too becomes docile and passive. Actually, the women are gynoids, manufactured in secret at the men's club in the town. At the end of the story, Joanna attempts to flee Stepford as well as warn her new friend Ruthanne, mother of the first black family to move into the town. But the men find Joanna and try to convince her that she's mistaken. They take her to her former best friend Bobbie's house, telling her that Bobbie will demonstrate her reality by cutting herself and bleeding. There is loud music playing to drown out the screams as we enter the house and see Bobby wielding a large knife. In the final scene, Joanna has become a Stepford wife gliding through the local supermarket, while Ruthanne is to become the conspiracy's next victim.

In 2003, philosopher Nick Bostrom put forward the idea that we are living in a Baudrillardian computer simulation run by our post-human descendants, so-called ancestor simulations. Such computing power will become possible at some point in the future. Furthermore, the simulators who control our universe may well be simulations themselves – a dream within a dream.[17] Popular notions such as *The Matrix* – a system that allows intelligent machines to harvest the humans' bioelectricity while keeping them plugged into a shared simulation of the world which they take for real – normalise the *psychotic* notion that there is no Real *out-there*, that what we naively take for Real is a fiction, a fantasy, someone else's dream that we are *powerless to control*, because in the post-human world there is no self to be in control. The growth of the internet and wild conspiracy theories lead to the spooky realms of "counter-knowledge,"[18] which is the softening up process of reality destabilisation's first stage.

Thus, liberal progressives, cultural theorists, geeks and postmodern subjects generally, successfully resist or foreclose the negative – any confrontation with the hard kernel of the real. Increasingly inhabiting a virtual-positive-dream-world of their own believing enables them to switch off the real of religious, scientific, artistic, political or philosophical truth, let alone personal truth – the truth of one's own history in psychoanalysis. Your real is your account of it. The rhizomal mat is centreless, fractal and amorphous. Reality destabilisation approaches psychosis. The self is an illusion, or maybe the last vestiges of the self involve regression to infantile omnipotence of great idealisation (positive thinking) alternating with great paranoid fears of extinction – *in the absence of the Real.*

Without the Real, religion, for instance, can become a positive mental health factor.[19] Only in a *post*-religious age could we think of "using," subordinating, and taming religion in this way to facilitate mental functioning. This rhizomic logic regards music as therapeutic, or laughter as therapeutic. Each distinct cultural form has to "lighten up" and justify itself with contemporary relevance, and not be afraid to mix it. The way you do this is to pretend there is no depth. The only test is: can I "relate" to it? Does it "speak to me"? Conflict is avoided.

Against this, older traditions lived inextricably with the gravity of being and the deep anguish of the void. Now, Jameson points out that anguish can be dispersed among language communities each speaking, 'a curious private language of its own, each profession developing its private code or dialect, and finally each individual coming to be a kind of linguistic island, separated from everyone else'.[20] With no overarching principle, no hierarchy, no privileged idea, nothing is more important than anything else. God is dead. *Nothing is total*, a BwO. Thus, the great irony of positive thinking is that *the reality of nothing now pervades everything*.

There are differing accounts of the death of Stalin's son, Yakov. Kundera again: Yakov was captured by the Germans and placed in a camp with a group of captured British officers. They shared a latrine, but Yakov habitually left a foul mess and denied that it was his. He adamantly refused to clean up his shit. Finally, humiliated by the camp commander, he ran at the electrified fence and killed himself. As Kundera suggests, maybe Yakov could no longer bear to see the poles of existence come so close that for him, 'there was no longer any difference between sublime and squalid, angel and fly, God and shit'.[21]

The modern Irish mystic, John Moriarty, aged 15, on being told the theory of evolution and thus discovering with horror the meaninglessness of life, ran away terrified across the bogs of his native Kerry.

Return to the Real

> *Then the Lord sent venomous snakes among them; they bit the people and many Israelites died. The people came to Moses and said, "We sinned when we spoke against the Lord and against you. Pray that the Lord will take the snakes away from us." So Moses prayed for the people. The Lord said to Moses, "Make a snake and put it up on a pole; anyone who is bitten can look at it and live." So Moses made a bronze snake and put it up on a pole. Then when anyone was bitten by a snake and looked at the bronze snake, they lived.*
>
> (*Numbers 21: 4–9*)

The true nihilists today are those very positive thinkers who deny the Void-Real, by turning being into an ever-expanding inflationary narcissistic froth of positivity.

As Heidegger claimed, Western metaphysics had fallen into nihilism, by default. 'Science wishes to know nothing of the nothing'.[22] Hence the aforementioned alienation of youth in the most technologically advanced countries. Even with its daunting capacity for mass destruction, materialist utilitarian concerns triumphed and the potential gap of wisdom was bought off through increasing wealth and prosperity. Meantime, people were encouraged to build little atomic bomb shelters at home and not go outside for a few days after a nuclear attack! What appalling estrangement must have been knocking at the margins of consciousness during the

1950s and 1960s; our science had brought us, Prometheus-like, to unlock the sacred energy at the heart of our sun!

> *Now I am Become Death, the Destroyer of Worlds.*[23]

As Heidegger notes, 'when science tries to express its proper essence it calls upon the nothing for help'.[24] Ironically, science underlines again and again the void that constitutes origin: the origin of the universe in the Big Bang 13.7 billion years ago; the step-change of the emergence of life from abiotic origins 2–3 million years ago; Rutherford's discovery in his famous gold foil experiment (1911) that the billiard ball atom is mostly empty space; Heisenberg's uncertainty principle; Freud's theory of infantile amnesia;[25] quantum theory and Feynman's intuition that any system has not one history but every possible history. Finally, the whole question of the void of human origins: the origins of the self, the origin of self-consciousness, the origin of language. Wherever we look, *each beginning is void*; we circulate around a void mystery.

Heidegger asks, what is the nothing? Alienated, we cling to being as totality, as a positivity, which he suggests bespeaks 'our profound boredom' that can irrupt into life itself, 'drifting here and there in the abysses of our existence like a muffled fog'.[26] But real attunement and testimony to non-being is revealed in the *mood of anxiety*, 'with the receding of beings as a whole'.[27] Speech falls silent, as the nothing reveals the strangeness of even the most familiar being(s). Such is the openness of beings to the void of non-being. 'Dasein means: being-[there] held out into nothing'.[28]

Heidegger envisages an *active* nothing, a "nihilating" that reveals the "openness" of beings as such. Thus all the antagonisms, conflicts and impossibilities, the rock-like kernel of the Real that psychoanalysis emphasises, forces man, as Heidegger says, to be 'a lieutenant of the nothing'.[29] Nothing is the ground of *Dasein*. So important is this analysis of the nothing, that Heidegger believes that it embraces the whole of metaphysics, namely, what is beyond or what transcends being itself. 'The question of the nothing puts us, the questioners [the analysts], in question. It is a metaphysical question'.[30] We hold ourselves out over nothing, into or over the "groundless ground." That is *Dasein*, which 'finds itself face-to-face with the nothing of the possible impossibility of its own existence'.[31] Not, face to face with *the other* in his accusatory proximity (Levinas), but nothing – no life contents, no past, no beauty, no kindness, but rather naked "facticity" and the immanence of death.

The nothing is key to the fundamental attunement of *Dasein*. An awakening, a shaking occurs. The existential theologian Paul Tillich called his well-known series of sermons *The Shaking of the Foundations.*[32] He cites Isaiah 24:18–20: *The foundations of the earth do shake/Earth breaks to pieces/Earth is split in pieces/Earth shakes to pieces .../Under the weight of its transgressions earth falls down/To rise no more.*

Heidegger wonders how it is that a momentous event of such gravity as WW1 can 'to all extents and purposes pass us by without leaving a trace?' His remedy: 'We must first call for someone capable of instilling terror into our Dasein'.[33] Heidegger sees the problem as the absence, 'the telling absence of any oppressiveness is what fundamentally oppresses us and leaves us most profoundly empty, i.e. *the fundamental emptiness that bores us*'.[34] The students sensed this alienated boredom of affluence and its emptiness. Once attuned to this phenonomen, opened by this boredom or anxiety, held out over the nothing, oppression can give way to a certain vision?

Heidegger thus accentuates indifference, emptiness, anxiety, and the void, to provoke a *negative* ontology of oppressive boredom and alienation, to attune *Dasein*, to open it – *be there*! He insists, 'Man must first resolutely open himself to this demand',[35] and continues, 'Freedom is only to be found where there is a burden to be shouldered'.[36] Heidegger exacerbates the "burden"– of boring empty modernity, by embracing the greater burden of utter precariousness and absurdity. For Heidegger, the essence of his new existential philosophical comprehension is that 'man, and man as a whole, is in the *grip of an attack* (*angriffe*) – driven out of everydayness and driven back into the ground of things ... [I]n philosophising the dasein man launches an attack on man'.[37] This attack on man is fundamentally to drive him out of his Oedipal home, out of his appalling complacency. He refers to Novalis who says that philosophy is mere homesickness. Burdened and terrorised, the fundamental antagonism is joined between the alienated, positive being and its negative void which must remain prised open and active as *the* creative site of *Dasein*.

Levinas stressed the ominous *presence of absence* in the "*there is*" (*il y a*) of existence and existing. Akin to the aforementioned boredom, the *there is* causes insomnia, not as a psychoneurotic condition, but as an apprehension of 'existing without existents', which returns at night as an involuntary wakefulness linked to Heidegger's concept of being "thrown" into existence (*Geworfenheit*).[38] Unable to master an originary dereliction, desertion or abandonment by the infinity of Being, the plenitude of the void, or, as Levinas puts it 'the irremissibility of pure existing', thus creates 'vigilance without possible recourse to sleep'.[39]

Paradoxically, this is being *without* nothingness, the murmuring of the Real of unabating flux. It is like the perpetual motion of the atmosphere, or the Brownian motion of molecules, the wakefulness of consciousness, or the sound of the sea in a shell. 'Nothing approaches, nothing comes, nothing threatens; this silence, this tranquillity, this void of sensations constitutes a mute, absolutely indeterminate menace'. Levinas describes arriving back in the city after an exhausting day, and 'beings strike us as though they no longer composed a world'. Things emerge in their pure [Real] materiality without their imaginary gloss, as a horror, like 'a corpse [which] already bears in itself its own phantom, it presages its return. This haunting spectre, the phantom, constitutes the very element of horror'. The haunting is the possibility of the return *within negation*, Banquo's ghost in Macbeth ... unreal mockery hence! Levinas asserts, 'We want to call attention to the existential density of the void itself, devoid of all being, empty even of void'.[40] Levinas calls it the negation of negation; as Blanchot has it, 'the return of being to the heart of every negative movement, the irreality of reality ...'.[41] Existing imposes itself when there is no longer any thing or any person! As Levinas says, 'Existing returns no matter with what negation one dismisses it'.[42] *It* is always lying in wait for us. *It* is being *without* nothingness, with no hole and no escape. Such totality deprives even suicide of its final mastery over being. With Camus, we should find the courage to confront the absurd full on without the rush to positivity and meaning.

The desert is growing. Not just culture, but the land itself is being degraded. Who, however, worries about the *human* climate and the growth of the inhuman? Where is the UN convention to combat *social* desertification and the culture of death?

The power of negative thinking, which initially showed such promise, has overrun the containing walls. John Gray calls our age the Eremozoic, the era of solitude.[43]

At this point we must make an all-important digression recalling that Heidegger's use of phrases such as, "instilling terror," "attack on man," "groundless ground," "nihilating," etc., in short his general *anti*-humanism (to subvert the totalising force of humanism), which cannot be separated from his support for the National Socialist Revolution. At the same time as teaching us 'a radically new way to think' (Steiner), the greatest paradox of all must be confronted: first, Heidegger's support for fascism, and, second, his failure to retract this monstrous political allegiance.

German philosopher, theologian, student of Heidegger, Karl Löwith[44] was an important witness in 1936 to Heidegger's allegiance to National Socialism. For Löwith, Heidegger's support for the "revolution of nihilism" can *only* be explained from his basic philosophical principle, namely, 'existence reduced to itself and resting on itself alone in face of nothingness'. Löwith stressed how Heidegger agreed with him, '*without reservation*', that, 'his partisanship for National Socialism lay in the *essence of his philosophy*', adding that 'his concept of "historicity" was the basis of his political "engagement"'. In a letter to Löwith (1920), Heidegger says, 'living in an actual revolutionary situation, I pursue what I feel to be "necessary," without caring to know whether it emerges from "culture" or whether my search will lead to ruin'. Like others before him, Heidegger noted that the bourgeois world had lost sight of the "ultimate instances" of human life. For Heidegger only death reveals our "facticity," our *Existenz*, stripped of all security. He deemed Europe an "exhausted pseudo-culture," impoverished and indigent, hemmed in by the double negative, between the death of God and the god still to come. Thus, his philosophy found "suitable terrain" in the inexorable Promethean will of the National (*Völkisch*) self-affirmation of the German *Dasein*, the "spiritual mission of the *Volk*," decreed by fate, both devastating and destructive. Revolution, awakening, disruption, duty, honour, exposure to danger; Löwith says that 'all these terms … are expressions of the bitter and hard resolve that affirms its [authentic] self in the face of nothingness, proud of its contempt of happiness, reason and compassion'.

For Löwith, Heidegger's huge influence during and since the war among French intellectuals in particular merits renewed attention. A towering figure, an inspired teacher, the greatest philosopher who in his life was also 'a secluded petty bourgeois', who could not bring himself to condemn German barbarity even after 1945. A symptom maybe of the lines of pure destruction, which must cause *real* barbarism – the collective acting out of *in*-humanism. The atrocities are symptomatic of the high-minded disdain for all things human, i.e. 'not caring to know … whether my search will lead to ruin'.

Steiner, like many academics, understates this calamity when he explains that 'Nazism comes upon Heidegger precisely at the moment in his thinking when the human person is being edged away from the centre of meaning and of being. The idiom of the purely ontological blends with that of the inhuman'. He says that while this posture in the early ''thirties is "tractable"', he continues, 'It is his complete silence after 1945 on Hitlerism and the holocaust *which is very nearly intolerable*'.[45]

Furthermore, Heidegger's *Black Notebooks* (*Schwarze Hefte*) containing his innermost philosophical thinking show the extent of his anti-Semitism. He accuses Jews of being "worldless," thus casting *Jews* out of *dasein*, i.e. eerily, out of actually "being-there" in the world. 'Jews', he writes, 'are "historyless" and merely "calculate with being"'. Thus, 'empty rationality and calculability gains a foothold in "spirit"'. Heidegger sees Jews as 'propagating the "machinational unessence" of beings, destroying the "wondrousness" of being'. For the phenomenologist, *any* objectification of human beings obscures the *being* of beings. In Heidegger's view, universalism meant "idealism" or the "philosophy of subject," all part of the "degeneracy of modernism." Heidegger strongly favoured *Lebensphilosophie* (philosophy of life) against the "empty" "religion of reason;" he favoured rootedness, belonging, and the primordial "forces of earth and blood," against neo-Kantianism, democracy, individualism, human rights and cosmopolitanism – all fabrication (*Machenschaft*) and deracination. Truly *authentic* life is bound up with the *Volk*. Thus the Jews are accused of "planetary criminality" [*planetarisches Verbrechertum*]'.[46] Heidegger asserts, 'The question of the role of world Jewry is not a racial question, but the metaphysical question about the kind of humanity that, without any restraints, can take over the uprooting of all beings from Being, as its world-historical "task"'.[47] *Jewish* "technological machinery" is the threat to civilisation and thus to the Jews themselves ultimately. According to an article in the Italian newspaper *Corriere della Sera*, Heidegger reverses truth by suggesting the death camps were part of *Jewish* "self-destruction."[48] Thus, 'the camps were only a logical outcome of this principle, the "supreme fulfillment of technology," [leading inexorably to] "corpse factories."' The real victims are the Germans. The Allies are guilty of 'repressing our will for the world'.[49] Indiscriminately, Heidegger accuses the "Western Revolutions" of ending up with the "despotism of No One."[50] For Heidegger, German defeat was not the end; the "peak of self-destruction" had not been reached. In terms of 'the history of being, the real immeasurable misdeed is the one committed against the German people, who were supposed to save the West'.[51]

Allowing for sensationalist and selective reporting, the above account suggests strongly a line of pure destruction justifying the camps *qua Jewish* self-destruction, the logical outcome of the *Jewish* invention of modernity, the worldless, annihilating machinations of technology leading to the end of Europe, which the German revolution with its spiritual mission of "struggle" and "annihilation" (*Kampf und Vernichtung*) decreed by fate would transform, had it not been stopped by those same (Jewish inspired) forces. Clearly across the Arab world the line of pure destruction in the name of Islamo-fascism continues towards Holocaust Two and the West in general.

The void-negative exists everywhere, extimately.[52] It constitutes the matrix out of which life emerges. Therein lies the nadir of the negative where "It" is likely to turn, scorpion-like, to sting its advocate. "It" is impersonal being. Heidegger says, 'it is It itself'; 'the advent of beings lies in the destiny of being'.[53] It – "Every [authentic] philosophy is in-human – a consuming fire."[54]

The consuming fire of *jouissance* reaches as far as the camps themselves – the twentieth century's passion for the Real. How could Heidegger seriously recant National Socialism without becoming inauthentic? Technological rationality, this way of "treating" people, leads *in extremis* to the camps (and doubtless further unknown horrors to come) on one line of pure destruction. And likewise, the radical Heideggerian critique of enlightenment rationality, Heidegger's anti-modernism becomes another line of pure destruction, coming from "below" and "within," this is the drive dimension, meeting the first one head-on, destroying the thin seam of civilisation for a generation. Evidently, Heidegger felt entirely justified in his anti-Semitic, anti-modernist rant wherever it was leading; it is no more than *the catastrophic revenge of being itself* for being forgotten, erased, and calculated in the modern scientific age. Heidegger is indifferent; he is *not* responsible for the outworking of being's revenge. SO BE IT!

No telling?

Notwithstanding the nihilating nihilism in the air we breathe, the *revolutionary* analyst presses on. She reports a patient's dream. In the dream the dreamer comes upon people who have died, but are somehow still alive enough to be able to speak and the dreamer asks them: 'What happens? Tell me how to live?' And the answer comes: 'We cannot tell you. Each one must go through this himself'. A suitably existential dream! No associations were reported for this dream; none were sought for. Maybe because the (non) answer given by the others in the dream was also the (non) answer unconsciously wished for by the patient *and* by the analyst: *Wanting* to be hung out over nothing with no answers?

We cannot tell you – although we, with our good life and our good education have *some* answers, we will not *help* you – no narrow footbridge. Each must go through this himself with only his insomnia, solitude and liberated orphan unconscious for "guidance." The dead and living refuse help. Surely, this is much more/much less than the *necessary* analytic space, the place-holding of the lieutenant of the nothing, a clearing in the forest,[55] a transitional space.[56] Is it not more of a desert space, a postmodern hyperspace, with no coordinates and zero gravity, pointless and uninviting? Each of us is "free" to re-invent values with all former values de-commissioned. Free! To be hung out over the void, abandoned to the meaningless roar of the "there is"?

Recall the parable of Kant's dove. It feels the resistance of the wind in its feathers and imagines it could fly much faster in a vacuum! Radical liberation has removed the Real – the resistance of the air – values, trainings, traditions, character, and so on – that alone enables flight and minimally supports being.

At the beginning of the modern period, Pascal *also* contemplated the immense nothing of the infinite and the immense nothing of the infinitesimal. But, he cautions us to consider what we are in comparison to the void: 'let him regard himself as lost, and from this little dungeon, in which he finds himself lodged, I mean the universe, let him learn to take the earth, its realms its cities, its houses and himself at their proper value'.[57] The key signifier here is "lost," which brings minimal order into the chaos of the infinite.

Against vanity, destruction (*jouissance*), and so on, of the *proper* value of the earth, its realms its cities, Pascal stresses, 'the finite is [already] annihilated in the presence of the infinite and becomes pure nothingness'.[58] Pascal engages in negative thinking. So it is with *our* minds before God's infinity as we can never *know* God rationally or cognitively.

While heading towards nothingness, *without* God, indifferent, hung out over the void, unaware of 'our little dungeon', until this word "lost" conveys its impact: for Pascal the wretchedness of man without the Other is the result of *making himself his own centre*. In his famous wager, Pascal invites the unbeliever to put aside his rational objections to Christianity and just *behave* as if he *was* a believer, to replace self-love by charity. 'They behaved just as if they did believe, taking holy water, having masses said, and so on'. Pascal is persuasive, telling the new "believers" that that they will gain faith, humility and do good works, while acknowledging that they will forego 'noxious pleasures, glory and good living'. The gains, he claims, will be great and the risk negligible. He summarises: 'Custom is our nature. Anyone who grows accustomed to faith believes it …'.[59]

"Each one, all alone," was the title of a Lacanian paper presented in Dublin recently.[60] It recalled yet again the anti-Oedipal moment. Now, each can claim his own mode of *jouissance* – gay, trans, autistic, etc. To each her own vice. Each is left to regulate his own *jouissance. Jouissance* exists independently of meaning. The symptom is a partner for the self. S1, the event of *jouissance*, infinitely repeated. The speaker makes reference to de Sade's *The 120 days of sodom*.

Pascal brings us back. He understood that Christ and the Apostles broke the cypher, 'broke the seal … rent the veil and revealed the spirit'. Pascal, in an almost conservative Freudian moment, concludes, 'They have taught us to this effect that man's enemies are his passions'.[61] For Pascal, no other religion has truly broken the cipher, to have known our greatness and smallness, our vanity and our wretchedness, sin abounding and grace even more so: 'Man is only a thinking reed, the weakest in nature, but he is a thinking reed. There is no need for the whole universe to take up arms to crush him: a vapour, a drop of water is enough to kill him'.[62]

We have been taught to celebrate only our narcissistic preoccupations, anti-Oedipally, with no thought for our 'smallness, vanity and wretchedness'. We have lost this negative thinking. Meanwhile the barbarians are not so much at the gates as inside the gates, and there are no longer any gates.

Analysing

Psychoanalysis, to be (in)credible must keep faith with the traumatic kernel of the Real – negative thinking. Insofar as therapy supports repression with its recovery programmes, our husband will try to focus on the fact that he did arrive home too early, or, even if he didn't, and whatever his wife was doing, *he* should work on his issues – to do with jealousy, dependency and so on. Mindfulness would help him relax.

The whole drama of psychoanalysis struggles *against* these false notions of recovery, growth and comfort which are legion, to find instead the "basic fault,"[63] where the story breaks, or the mask slips, the lip quivers and the cracks appear. The analyst struggles against all the various "fixes" that tempt the sufferer, from CBT programmes to drug therapies, all of which have their uses, but have to do with "doing" and "utility" rather than with "being" as such; to do with "moving on" rather than "being still," to do with continuous re-invention and re-branding, the "new me," and so on, rather than reflection. In this Heideggerian sense, therapies are indeed 'forgetful of Being', individual being and the larger Being.

Following the machinic anti-Oedipal logic, treatments for mental suffering resemble hit-and-run crashes, where drivers leave the scene of the accident never to return. 'My father was depressed; his brain was malfunctioning; he just needed a drug to fix it'. Return to the devastated surface. Is he okay now? Yes. Well fine! Within a very short time, the road is cleared, the traffic is flowing again. A few bits of glass remain.

How can an analyst ever be an authority again without the Oedipal compass that should orient everything analytic? Who is willing to believe that, for instance, a hyperactive child, let us take a hypothetical but not uncommon instance, is continually trying to evacuate from his mind/body, unbearable and unthinkable anxiety generated by his distressed mother, deserted by the boy's father, living in a part of town that is disadvantaged, now on her own and unable to cope herself? The child seeks a "container," his school, or the classroom to hold him together, but he continually destroys it as he repeats and "communicates" his psychotic distress about his (idealised and unreachable) mother who bore him and now cannot love him. *No*! He has a damaged brain, neuro-imaging shows it, and he must take his Ritalin.

Who is willing to investigate by listening to the narrative of the life of a middle aged woman who presents with, for her and her family, an unaccountable depression after her father died, which has continued too long. Medication is indicated. She believed that out of her four siblings she was secretly her father's favourite, enjoying really special times with him especially when her mother got sick. In adult life, she became his unofficial secretary and confidante and would even accompany him to functions as his career progressed. She got married, had children, but her imaginary father still held a special place in her heart. When he got sick and died suddenly just a few years back, she was distraught. But when his will was read, she was left with practically nothing. Who, without analytic insight and experience, can really appreciate the intense rage and hurt at the "betrayal" by her father and the self punishment and self-hate (depression) that ensue as she identifies with his rejection and abandonment, first by dying and second at the level of his final desire/will?

The analyst with an Oedipal compass understands the primitive oral omnipotence involved in anorexia, the master-slave fight to death with the re-discovered disappointing mother, over food – the ravaging greed coming from the id and the cannabalistic superego that that reduces her body to a skeleton that looks as if it might win the battle of will and counter-will in the war for total control and total perfection of the emaciated body. And the father was forced out to be a helpless bystander.

Everyone has a story to tell, but the analyst needs investigative powers, the skill and the desire to get beyond the story's manifest content – the very limited story – to the real scandals of Oedipal dynamics. Who understands and accepts as real, for instance, the intense emotions elaborated by Melanie Klein – matricidal, infanticidal, the insane mute limits of the human? And who in these non-judgemental days is prepared to find hidden sadism and masochism? Even analysts under supervision regularly miss human deviousness, complicity, deceit, double-dealing, and so on. They refuse *in toto* the real range of human dialectic, preferring instead the sentiments around a "damaged self," or now a "damaged brain," with minimal responsibility.

We believe what people say, but must also disbelieve, because revelation and resistance alternate. Resistance is always present. Only the gullible will just listen and believe, but this now passes for the highest therapeutic understanding and respect. To disbelieve is disrespectful and insulting unless you are a negative thinker.

Winnicott spoke of the true and false self. If we give it a Levinasian gloss, *conatus essendi* is the false self. The striving to maintain being, the false self *qua* caretaker self, or ego, begs the question of the status of the true self. Does it exist? Winnicott's answer is that it "exists" to a degree in secret,[64] until it finds a facilitating environment (in life, in analysis?) in which to express its emergent spontaneity, aliveness and real feeling, or in Lacanian terms, until it can speak. An analyst unaware of this distinction may allow years of analysis to continue unproductively – 'The patient's false self can collaborate indefinitely'.[65] The existential twist creates a necessary edge, not there with Winnicott. The delight with Winnicott was always his sense of ease and playfulness. However, analysis is bound to interrogate the false self, as it can become not so much a caretaker, but a minder, at worst a paranoid mind-body guard, protecting the subject from suffering, from the *other* within and without. With the loss of the "facilitating environment" over the half-century since this paper was written, the minder false self increasingly threatens to usurp the whole scene, *guaranteeing* security at the expense of life. Disturb this minder false self (via analysis) and he is likely to retaliate with terroristic threats against the subject and the analyst. What happens, observes Winnicott, is 'a need to collect impingements from external reality so that the living-time of the individual can be filled by reaction to these impingements'.[66] Thus, an analysis risks taking on the minders but with no certain outcome!

Rather than resolving the Oedipus complex, the anti-Oedipal "solution" is likely to end up becoming bogged down within it, or remaining pre-Oedipal. But who can detect this without the Oedipus compass? Like the young man with no history and no dreams, who lives from minute to minute, not thinking but reacting. His mother calls him many times a day as she worries about him. He lets her. She does his washing and sometimes she "feeds" him. He works a little but spends time helping out his sisters with their children. He says, 'they are always there for him'. There is never a mention of his father. Who without an Oedipal orientation can identify the "plague," the story spoken of around the forbidden/enjoyable/disappointing incestuous bonds?

A young woman was given medication to cope with the ongoing stress caused by her parent's acrimonious divorce 10 years previously. Her father left and re-married. She had no self-confidence in spite of significant success in her career. Her therapist gave her positive exercises to increase confidence but to no avail. Analysis revealed her secret Oedipal wish that her fighting parents would separate, countered by an equally strong reparative wish that they would stay together. When they really did divorce, her guilt was intense. *She* had caused it. She tried to excel at work to ward off her "badness." When her father re-married, his "betrayal" was complete, stirring up more jealous hatred and punitive self-condemnation. Only by proper analysis of Oedipal desire, confronting head-on the negative drives, is it possible to rebuild, repair, but not recover. The subject remains divided.

People used to fear their demons, derived from negative thinking and wishes associated with the Oedipus complex. Now, after anti-Oedipus there is shallowness. With positive thinking, not just some things are phoney, but *everything* may be phoney! *Semblants* everywhere forcing their dissembling reality on you like an insomniac roar to drown out the void. The closer the void, the louder the roar, which bespeaks the ultimate failure, the ultimate cynicism of positive thinking. The pendulum has swung so far in this direction that all moderation has been lost.

Heidegger reminds us that for the Greeks, truth is something *stolen* from concealment. For Heraclitus, the prevailing of things has in itself a striving to conceal. The risk of analysis is underlined by American satirist H. L. Mencken: 'for every nugget of truth, some wretch lies dead on the scrapheap'. The conceit of positive thinking is that it can definitely *improve* on the prevailing of things, whereas analysis, in creating a space for the saying of what is concealed, risks the radical contestation of "prevailing of things."

The criticism of modern "analysis" is that it does not contest. It listens well but does not analyse. Analysis *per se* belongs to a master discourse and must cease its search for truth. Listen but don't analyse; the end of analysis.

Freud's instruction to the analyst was 'to put aside all his feelings, even his human sympathy, and concentrate his mental forces on the single aim of performing the operation [analysis] as skilfully as possible'. Freud concludes his remarks by reference to the French surgeon, Ambroise Paré: 'I dressed his wounds, God cured him'.[67] At first reading, this is the best refutation of the comforting therapeutic you could imagine – *analysis not therapy*. This instruction should be read in conjunction with the aforementioned assertion by Freud that 'analysis is a cure through love' – clearing a space free of sympathy, pity, etc., yet dressing his wounds, and finally, the unknown – God's cure – through love. But who ever thinks of God?

Notes

1 Chorost, M., 2011.
2 Chorost, M., 2005.
3 Thompson, D., 2012. The author says that what worries him is the way addicted behaviour is 'spreading around society'. 'Impulsivity', he said, 'is becoming the default style of the cognitive elite'. Globally, he claims, 'there is an acceleration of addictiveness' (BBC Today programme). 'The amount of time we spend attached to our devices these days is not just an irritating twenty-first century habit, it is a sign that compulsive behaviours of all kinds are exploding in the modern world'. His thesis suggests that there is a cross-pollination between the social gaming companies of Silicon Valley and the gambling emporia of Las Vegas. Advances made in digital technology are hijacked by the gaming industry. 'With every passing day, technology finds new ways of distilling pleasure', producing sharper and smarter hits that create new cravings – for food, shopping, sex, gaming, pornography, phones, gadgets and so on. In particular, the goal is to create the "feel good" substances and actions that cause the brain to overproduce dopamine, the neurotransmitter associated with pleasure and desire. Digital technology has created an unprecedented demand for pornography. There is already plenty of evidence to suggest that men's growing fascination with rough porn is affecting their relationships. Food, drink, drugs and consumer appliances have all been very strategically modified to make them ever more engaging. As a result, we've got into the habit of liking things too much. As Baudrillard suggested we are creating a world that is dangerously seductive. Countries such as Brazil are moving from hunger to obesity in less than a generation. Also, places that previously never had much of a problem with alcoholism, such as northern China, are witnessing epic displays of drunkenness among young people. Increasingly, by being able to manipulate brain chemistry to produce intense bursts of short-term pleasure, cravings are sliding dangerously out of control. Thompson suggests that the primary purpose of government in the future will be the management and treatment of its citizens' addictions. Literally billions of people are beginning to have more fun and enjoyment than their minds and bodies can handle, thus developing life-sapping addictions. Nothing is new. In the mid-eighteenth century, parts of inner London suffered the world's first epidemic of alcoholism. The means to distil liquor from grain was developed in industrial quantities. The gin craze was eventually stamped out by legislation banning home distilling. Once cheap gin ceased to be available, addicted drinkers kicked the habit. A century later, in the late 1960s, new techniques for manufacturing heroin coincided with the arrival of troops in Vietnam. By 1970, 15 per cent of soldiers were addicted to heroin. President Nixon panicked at the thought of thousands of helpless junkies arriving back home after their tours of duty. However, as Thompson points out, the near impossibility of scoring high-grade heroin in Middle America meant that the vast majority of GI heroin users became almost instantly un-addicted. Therefore, Thompson suggests that addiction is not an illness, not an "irreversible" brain disease, but supply-driven behaviour. Kill the supply and the addiction stops. The fundamental shift demonstrated here is the progressive replacement of people by things, the inexorable drift towards narcissism and isolation. Not only do we obsess over the things we buy, but many of our "friendships" are mediated via systems bought with a debit card. And when we meet, it is in an environment so meticulously engineered and styled as to create an entirely artificial mood.

4 MacLelland, B., 1907.
5 James, W., 1902: 109.
6 Vincent Peale, N., 1952.
7 Tony Robbins. We only learn our limits by going beyond them. 'CANI! Is a principle designed to encourage you to make small incremental improvements daily ... and in doing so, you will be forced to find a way to go beyond your current set of self-imposed limitations'. See http://ezinearticles.com/?Tony-Robbins-CANI!-System-Explained&id=5380.
8 See, for instance, Malkowsky, E., 2007.
9 "Amortal" is the term coined by Catherine Mayer in a recent issue of *Time* (25 April 2011) when she visited Las Vegas where she discovered the "uniface" of those living agelessly and remorselessly positively, helped by the Cenegenics Medical Institute, allegedly 'the world's largest age-management practice'. The perma-tanned were remarkably devoid of the differential age markers that determine adolescence, young adulthood, middle age, retirement, golden years, and so on, even across the gender divide and income range. As Mayer observes, many of us now increasingly inhabit our own 'virtual Las Vegases', as we are now living 30 years longer than a century ago. It is no longer possible to answer when is the best age to have children (fertility treatments), to settle with a life partner, to retire, etc. Adults stay "young" with diet, exercise and cosmetic procedures, assuming all options are always open, attempting to live the same way and at the same intensity from youth right into old age! They get old without getting old, trusting that science will deliver them from the inevitable. Anti-aging supplements can exceed $1,000 a month including hormone replacement therapies, so that men in their seventies look young and virile again. And to prove that just thinking can make you younger, an isolated hotel in New England was retrofitted to the 1950s in every respect and the elderly guests were told to imagine that they had travelled back in time and live as though they were young again and within a week they had very significantly improved cognitive and motor skills, compared to the control group who were told that their stay was just an exercise in nostalgia.
10 Ehrenreich, B., 2009.
11 McNerney, A., 2004.
12 *Journal of Clinical Oncology* 2009, cited in Ehrenreich, B., 38.
13 Ibid.: 43–4.
14 From "Burnt Norton" (1935).
15 Kundera, M., 1984: 242.
16 See www.irishtimes.com/news/politics/oireachtas/patrick-honohan-cost-of-banking-crisis-more-than-100bn-1.2134967.
17 See www.youtube.com/watch?v=nnl6nY8YKHs.
18 Thompson, D., 2008. Previously unthinkable theories can make great headway, even entering the mainstream, because of the freedom and free market in ideas fostered by the internet. He cites the international publisher Penguin that has published a book, *Talisman*, by Graham Handcock and Robert Bouval, connecting 9/11 with ancient Egyptian religious cults. Or, to take some of his other examples, the US government was behind 9/11, a Chinese fleet reached America before Columbus and the structure of a cell is too complex to have evolved through natural selection. He cites Holocaust denial, the *Da Vinci Code*'s revision of ancient history, the *Book of Mormon*'s account of settling the New World, the belief in a link between the MMR vaccine and autism. He argues we're facing a pandemic of spurious claims and unproved theories, blurring the distinction between truth and fiction to dangerous effect. Each theory can have its own huge and loyal following without any checks and balances. Pseudoscience can be presented as real science. There is an "epistemological bubble" to suit every life-style. His plea is for sound *common* sense and science-based knowledge. He says we have well developed scientific techniques for testing truth claims. However, over recent years science itself has become discredited. For instance, where are the half million vCJD cases that were predicted? What about the millennium bug that was to bring nothing short of disaster and global recession? The *common sense* is just what has broken down in postmodernity. It

defines our era. Who could have imagined a few short years ago that creationism could have made headway against evolution, sponsored mainly, according to Thompson, by Islamic fundamentalism? Ninety-five per cent of Muslims do not believe in evolution. I wonder why we always blamed just the evangelical Christians from the US? Who would have ever believed that Holocaust denial would be gaining currency, and then, only opposed rigorously when propounded by white neo-Nazis, but not questioned when it is of Arab origin? The sign on the back of a car reads: *this car is protected by angels*. Maybe a joke, maybe ironic, maybe the driver believes it!

19 Casey, P., 2009.
20 Jameson, F., 1985: 114.
21 Kundera, M., op. cit.: 261.
22 Heidegger, M., 1929: 96.
23 Robert Oppenheimer, www.youtube.com/watch?v=26YLehuMydo.
24 Heidegger, M., 1929 op. cit.: 96.
25 Freud, S., 1905: 174–6.
26 Heidegger, M., 1929 op. cit.: 99.
27 Ibid.: 101.
28 Ibid.: 103.
29 Ibid.: 106. Lieutenant, means place holder (*lieu tenant*), a second-in-command. Therefore man holds a place for the Nothing. *The analyst holds a place for the nothing*. All the while, *being-there*.
30 Ibid.: 109.
31 Heidegger, M., 1927: Section 53.
32 Tillich, P., 1949.
33 Heidegger, M., 1929–1930: 172.
34 Ibid.: 164.
35 Ibid.: 165.
36 Ibid.: 182.
37 Ibid.: 21.
38 See Heidegger, M., 1927: 174, 223, 330–3.
39 Levinas, E., 1947: 44ff.
40 Taken from Hand, S., 1989: 30–5.
41 Blanchot cited in Hand, S., 1989: 36.
42 Levinas, E., 1947: 47.
43 Gray, J., 2002: 8.
44 Löwith, K., 1933.
45 Steiner, G., 1978: 118.
46 Wolin, R., 2014.
47 Polt, R., 2015.
48 Di Cesare, D., 2015.
49 Wolin, R., 2014.
50 Heidegger, quoted in Wolin, R., 2014.
51 Di Cesare, D., 2015.
52 Lacan's neologism (*extimité*) linking "inner" and "outer." See Lacan, J., 1959–1960: 139. Also Lacan, J., 1968–1969: 224. See also Miller, J.-A., 2008.
53 Heidegger, M., 1947: 234.
54 Heidegger, quoted in Wolin, R., 2014.
55 See Heidegger, M., 1959: 70 and 121.
56 See Winnicott, D., 1971a.
57 Pascal, B., 1670: fragment 199, p. 89.
58 Ibid.: fragment 418, p. 149
59 Ibid.: 150–2.
60 Alexandre Stevens' presentation for Irish Circle of the Lacanian Orientation – New Lacanian School's "The Names of the Real in the 21st Century" series, 10 November 2012.

61 Pascal, B., 1670: fragment 260, p. 108.
62 Ibid.: fragment 200, p. 95.
63 Balint, M., 1968.
64 Winnicott, D., 1960: 143.
65 Ibid.: 152.
66 Ibid.: 150.
67 Freud, S., 1912: 115.

7

TRANSLATION, INTERPRETATION AND RESPONSIBILITY

In interpretation, the metaphor of love is not far distant.

Translations is the title of a play by Brian Friel,[1] in which he explores the battle lines between the language of the coloniser and the colonised in the West of Ireland during the nineteenth century. Friel has said that *Translations* is a play about language. The action of the play takes place in 1833 at a hedge school in the townland of *Baile Beag* – an Irish-speaking community (or *Gaeltacht*) in Donegal. The "scholars" are a cross-section of the local community, from a semi-literate young farmer to an elderly polyglot autodidact reading and quoting Homer in the original. Nearby, in the fields around the town, is a detachment of British Royal Engineers, making the first ordnance survey of the area for the British military and government. The local place names have to be recorded, i.e. translated into a usable English form. Each of the Gaelic names – every hill, rock and little stream, each of which possess their own local names in Irish, have to be anglicised. For instance, *Cnoc Ban* is translated into Knockban or Fern Hill, *Bun na hAbhann* becomes Banowen, *Druim Dubh* becomes Black Ridge, *Baile Beag* becomes Ballybeg, *Lis na Muc*, the fort of the pigs, becomes Swinefort, *Tobair Vree* becomes Brian's Well because an old man called Brian with his face disfigured by a growth, used to bathe his face in the well, and one day he was found dead in the well.

One of the sappers, Yoland, who has fallen in love with Ireland – gone native – ponders: '*poteen – poteen – poteen*. Even if I did speak Irish, I'd always be an outsider here, wouldn't I? I may learn the password but the language of the tribe will always elude me, won't it? The private core will always be … hermetic, won't it'? He continues, 'I mean I feel so cut off from the people here. To meet people like yourself, who actually converse in Latin and Greek' (40).

'I like to think', comes the reply, 'we endure around truths immemorially posited … Indeed, [ours] is a rich language. A rich literature. You'll find sir that certain cultures expend on their vocabularies and syntax acquisitive energies and ostentations entirely lacking in their own material lives. A rich language, Lieutenant', continues the man, 'full of mythologies of fantasy and hope and self-deception – a syntax opulent with tomorrows' (42).

English, on the other hand, is the language of modernity; it standardises things, for exchange and commerce. The translations in *Baile Beag* are causing tensions to rise. Trouble is never far away. Fifty or more soldiers are spread out in a big line from Sean Neal's over to Lag and they're moving straight across the fields, prodding every inch of ground with their bayonets and scattering animals and hens in all directions, carelessly tumbling all before them – fences, ditches, hay-stacks, turf-stacks.

The hedge school will be replaced by a National School. 'And from the very first day you go, you'll not hear one word of Irish spoken' (22). Every subject will be taught through English. 'We should all be learning to speak English. That's what my mother says. That's what Daniel O'Connell says – the old language is a barrier to modern progress' (25).

The English captain voiced some surprise that the locals did not speak *his* language! He was told that, 'a few of us did, on occasion – outside the parish of course – and then usually for the purposes of commerce' (25). He was also told that English cannot really express Irish. But the place names will be changed, standardised into English? *The English that can't really express us.*[2]

Freud spoke of translation as the reverse of repression: repression was a failure of translation. The translation of the unconscious which Lacan said was structured like a language, fails in the case of repression. Opacity persists. Ireland is often referred to as Britain's Other, Britain's shadow, the idealised and dangerous "Emerald Isle." Ireland has always remained in some irrefutable sense, opaque to British consciousness.[3] In the psychoanalytic sense, translation, of the unconscious, is similarly a translation from an "archaic" language or "registration," to another – that of consciousness. More precisely, Freud speaks of 'successive epochs' each requiring transcription. 'At the boundary between two such epochs a *translation* of the psychic material must take place'.[4] Without translation, we a left with "*fueros*," which are "survivals" – ancient Spanish law still holding out in a particular city or province. The work of interpretation is precisely equivalent to translation – both work to make the (ancient) unconscious conscious – to make precisely what is opaque (therefore potentially dangerous, anarchic, foreign) transparent, relatively safe and modern, i.e. up-to-date. This was what the sappers in the West of Ireland were doing – colonising, modernising, up-dating, making transparent and relatively quiescent the opaque and dangerous.

Laplanche has made this equivalence between translation and interpretation much more explicit in terms of the child who tries to fathom or translate the fascinating enigma of the other's (sexual) desire (primal seduction). There is always an element of "failure" of this translating, leaving a remainder, an *á traduire* – which is the unconscious *qua* separate mental system, which must not be understood as a copy of past events in any simple archeological sense, but as an alien autonomous system, which intrudes itself into the otherwise smooth functioning of the ego.

Laplanche follows Freud in 1917, already referred to in the Preface above, putting the psychoanalytic revolution on the same footing as the Copernican one, striking at human narcissism. 'The ego is not master in its own house'. The signifiers "alien" or "foreign" (*fremd*) occur frequently. For example, 'these alien guests even seem to be more powerful than those which are at the ego's command'. Freud however retreated from his radical position in relation to the real *exteriority* of the other when he seemed to reassure us that we can 'explain these uncanny (*unheimlich*) disorders', and further, that 'nothing has entered into you from without; a part of the activity of your mind has been withdrawn from your knowledge'.[5] Laplanche, on the other hand, refers to a double de-centering whereby the alterity of the other-thing (*das Andere*), the unconscious, is inaugurated and guaranteed by the other person (*der Andere*) of the adult environment. True, this radical Other out there appears in the subjective moment as inevitably tied up with *my fantasy*, but what guarantees the alien-ness of the other is, in the full Lacanian sense, 'the priority of language'. Laplanche continues by pointing out that 'the adult transmits a message … he makes a sign from his own unconscious'.[6] These signs are the so-called "enigmatic signifiers," that came from the other,[7] which the child cannot decode. Signifiers that may become de-signified and lose their meaning but not the affective *force* of their operation in the Other. As Laplanche says, 'The language of the adult is enigmatic, not due to confusion or total strangeness, nor due to polysemy (for in the latter case all messages would be enigmatic), but through a one-sided *excess* that introduces a disequilibrium into the interior of the message'.[8] The distinction here is the famous one established by Ferenczi, between the traumatogenic intrusion of the "language of passion" into the innocent "language of tenderness" common to both adult and infant, namely, 'the precocious super-imposition of love, passionate and guilt-loaded on an immature guiltless child. The consequence must needs be that of confusion of tongues'.[9] Put simply, a child is disturbed by the sexual/aggressive overtones of her parents' fighting, talking, shouting, and so on. This disturbance will form the core of its unmediated unconscious which will insist on being acted out (from repression) rather than interpreted unless analysis intervenes to help with the translation.

Thus, translation from unconscious "language" to conscious language, from the old *fueros* to the contemporary, from Irish to English, all ineluctably involve a gap in understanding. There are *three* scenarios where misunderstanding is guaranteed: between the subject and his other *qua* unconscious; between one subject and another; between the subject speaking one language and the subject speaking another. Translating the Other involves some violation, some loss of its *Other*-ness *per se*. For instance, the modernisation of ancient place names – each one with its own story (like *Tobair Vree*, Brian's Well), means the story may be lost without trace. In an analogous way, the young child will grow up affected by the "language of passion" without knowing why.

To enter analysis is to violate one's deep opacity. Concealment is diminished and secrets revealed. Although, as Winnicott knew, the core of the self remains complicit with itself. The second violation will occur at the level of the analyst's specific training "language" – Freudian, Kleinian, Jungian, Lacanian, etc. These interpretations-cum-violations in turn are further reinforced by the analysts' supervisors who insist on ideological precision and exclusion. Every school has interpretative exclusion zones. Sometimes untrained subjects are shown to be better listeners than trained analysts with their hard-won theoretical filters!

Translation and interpretation define modernity. As Nietszche famously proclaimed there are *no* facts only interpretations.[10] Truth is on the move.[11] Thus, concerns about authenticity, originality and violation are nostalgic. The *á traduire* becomes a permanent feature of globalisation. The *fueros* have to go.

George Steiner, acknowledged by Brian Friel, could have been referring to the Ireland of *Translations* when he speaks of a 'civilisation … imprisoned in a linguistic contour which no longer matches … the changing landscape of fact'.[12] François Roustang theorises neurosis as "encystment."

It is tempting to view *The King's Speech* (David Seidler) in this way. Self-taught speech therapist Lionel Logue (Geoffrey Rush) helps King George VI (Colin Firth) overcome his speech impediment, a symptom with old imprisoning neurotic origins, arising from the excessive strictness of his father, George V (Michael Gambon) and the coldness of his mother, Queen Mary (Claire Bloom). In this fictional account, Logue acts like an analyst challenging the reluctant "patient" to assume his history by changing from the position of so-called master (Duke/King), regressing to a divided (stuttering) subject (Bertie) and *finding his own voice*, using a variety of techniques to overcome his massive resistance. Upon the 1939 declaration of war with Germany, the King is given a three-page speech to read over the radio. With only 40 minutes to rehearse, Logue takes the King through all of the freeing techniques he has learned over the previous months, which include swearing, body movements, humour and singing the words he has to say. As he reads the speech, to the whole country, it is clear that the King has found his voice with his stammer now sublated into significant pauses, silences, which, far from making him look vulnerable and weak, underscore the gravity and the momentous drama of the occasion! The symptom (stuttering) is "translated" into a sinthome[13] – The King has identified with his symptom in the most saintly way (*saint homme*).

For Steiner, there is a strain of femininity in the great interpreter, a submission, made active by the intensity of response, to the creative presence – 'Like the poet, the master executant or critic can say, *Je suis an autre*' (27). Rather than the reductionist tedium of classical psychoanalysis, interpretation that gives language *life* beyond the moment and place of immediate utterance or transcription is what attracts Steiner: '[w]ithout the unbroken animation of a chosen past, we become flat shadows' (31). The animation in the analytic process must come from the generous vitality of the analyst-interpreter if not from the analysand.

Steiner suggests that every individual has two sources of linguistic supply – what he calls the current vulgate plus his own private thesaurus – the latter being linked to his unconscious. Both together constitute a specific idiolect, towards which the analyst must 'turn his own unconscious like a receptive organ'.[14] Freud said as much in the dream book: 'we are thus obliged, in dealing with those elements of the dream content which must be recognised as symbolic, to adopt a combined technique, which on the one hand rests on the dreamer's associations and on the other hand fills the gaps from the interpreter's knowledge of [universal] symbols'.[15]

What fascinates Steiner is the prodigious supply of languages. Why not just one language or just half a dozen instead of four or five thousand, with many going into oblivion – each taking with it a 'storehouse of consciousness'? With the Irish language, for instance, it is reliably estimated that currently only about one in ten speak Gaelic fluently. Steiner reflects, 'What sense can be read into a situation in which villages a few miles apart use tongues incomprehensible to each other and morphologically unrelated'? (56). His central hypothesis is that 'the proliferation of mutually incomprehensible tongues stems from an absolutely fundamental impulse in language itself' (497), namely profligacy and excess, 'the almost bewildering built-in bias of the human spirit towards *freedom*' (497, emphasis added), from which we might surmise arises the potential exuberance of free association. The use of language merely to communicate empirical "facts" is clearly a secondary and minor part of human discourse, elevated to prime function only with instrumental reason and the enlightenment. To compare it with animal signalling systems is more reductive still. Steiner following Heidegger rejects 'the empirical inevitability of the world' (497).

Each language is an epiphany, ordering, shaping active cognizance of reality. Each language is an autonomous genius of 'infinite particularity' – a *Weltanschauung*, the only true *a priori* framework of cognition. Speech is poiesis, production and formation. Language is surplus.

According to Pavlov, such complexity must have involved a quantum step in evolution. More than 40 years ago, molecular biologist Jacques Monod speculated radically about the emergence of "a new realm" in the biosphere. His hypothesis was: 'language may have preceded the emergence of a central nervous system particular to man and contributed decisively to the selection of those variants most suited to utilize all its resources. In other words language may have created man, rather than man language'.[16] Unlike animal species, we are out of kilter within our world amidst linguistic superfluidity. Interpretation and translation, therefore, have in part a *conservative* function preventing linguistic excess from overwhelming meaning and dispersion.

Post-colonial guilt leads liberal propagandists to celebrate diversity and profusion. But a century before Lacan's 'The symbol as the murder of the thing',[17] Wilhelm von Humboldt, Prussian philosopher, diplomatic and linguist, sounded a note of warning that language's 'autonomous external identity and being does violence to man himself' (Humboldt cited on p. 86). Linguistic differences can breed hatred, 'zones of silence to other men and razor-edges of division' (58). In *Translations*, for example, the British sapper Yoland, who was most inclined toward Gaelic and Irishness, was murdered off stage by Republicans. Outside a particular language community, you will never be "one of ours," however earnestly you try to fit in. Erskine Childers senior, of British colonial stock, became radicalised, joining the old IRA. Before he was executed by the Free State army for gun running, he told his son Erskine to shake hands with his executioners. Young Erskine rose to become Irish President during the recent "Troubles." But both father and son, in spite of such exemplary loyalty and sacrifice, never lost the taint of being "British."

An Irish teacher working and living in Catalonia, who learnt Spanish *and* Catalan, found herself being spoken to in the hated colonial Spanish language in local Catalan shops – an insult to the "outsider" who has 'done everything correctly'. Liberals, multiculturalists, ex-pats, etc. make the covertly racist mistake of thinking that if they work very hard and vociferously at being "equal" they should be accepted!

Žižek points up the irony that language and speaking, presumed to promote peace and understanding between peoples, actually is a source of violence! *Fear thy (racist) neighbour as thyself.* For Žižek, language is the first and greatest divider. In the same street, we can live in different worlds. 'What this means is that verbal [racist] violence is not a secondary distortion, but the ultimate resort of every specifically human violence'.[18] We have papered over this division with our ideology of tolerance and "One World" mythologies. Worse still: *within* language communities, divisions occur between rich and poor, educated and uneducated, literate and illiterate, upper and lower classes, and so on, each of whom inhabits different more or less incommunicable worlds. Recall too, *there is no sexual rapport*: men and women speak "different languages," often explained as an evolutionary effect to do with our hunter-gatherer past, or a "wiring" problem, rather than properly a linguistic effect.

To explore the divisiveness of language, we must turn to the Babel myth, set out in Genesis, Chapter 11. A united humanity following the Great Flood, speaking a single language, migrating from the east, came to the land of Shinar, where they built a city (Babylon) with a huge tower up to heaven: *let us make a name for ourselves, lest we be scattered abroad upon the face of the whole earth* (Genesis 11:4). *God observed: here they are, one people with a single language … nothing they have a mind to do will be beyond their reach* (11:6). God said: *Come let us go down there and confuse their speech, so that they will not understand what they say to one another* (11:7). Thus, humanity was scattered. *The Lord made a babble of the language of all the world* (11:9).

Some primal error caused an explosion of linguistic chaos, like a Pandora's box event, or maybe language divisions were a punishment for the construction of a lunatic tower reaching up to the heavens to eavesdrop on the gods. Titans savaged one another and the splinters of their broken bones became the linguistic splinters of isolated diverse speech forms.

Babel was thus a *second* fall. In the first fall, mankind was exiled from paradise; in the second fall, mankind was exiled from any assurance of being able to grasp and communicate reality. For the Kabbalists, the pendulum might swing back again – there *was* the partial redemption at Pentecost with the gift of tongues – toward some messianic moment of restored unison. Maybe, mathematics, harmonics or the music of the spheres, or maybe, as Eckhart and Angelus Silesius assert, God has only ever uttered a single word, which all our babbling tongues shut out – the sound of Logos.

In the intervening time there is translation and interpretation, marking our radical exile, our non-rapport, seeing through a glass darkly (*For now we see through a glass, darkly; but then face to face: now I know in part; but then shall I know even as also I am known.* 1 Corinthians 12:13). As Steiner says, 'translators are men groping towards each other in a common mist' (80).

Benjamin believed that *die reine Sprache*, the pure language, was trying to make its way back through our differing tongues. This gives to translation and interpretation a radical philosophical and ethical import. Not only are we trying to enable the unconscious to speak, but also the speaking subject is linked however faintly to a wider *telos*, which cannot be possessed in any way.[19]

For Steiner, both Luther and Hölderlin move the German language back closer to its universal origin. The tower is an assault on Heaven, but also a vast Jacob's ladder of stone on which man would ascend towards his creator: thus rebellion *and* worship – the move towards and away from God. Borges advanced the occult belief of alternative cosmologies, "counter-worlds," today's multiple universes, interpenetrating our own free energies of thought. Likewise, "free association" as the guiding principle in psychoanalysis to circumambulate the truth of the unconscious that Lacan believed contained its own revelation.

Rather than bemoaning the loss of the *Ur*-language with its splintering, this apparent failure/punishment should be seen as a blessing. Ontological incompleteness,[20] "failure" of translation is also a forgiving space, a liveable space where we can think and be complicit with ourselves. God smashed the tower out of love, just as he withdrew from his creation out of love, fostering atheism.

For Bion, Babel represents God or fate punishing mankind for reaching out for total knowledge. This fateful blocking acts as the envious superego of the psychotic, understood in Bion's terms as having the capacity to destroy thinking, judgement, reality, all functions of the mature ego. Thus, the psychotic aspiration to *total* knowledge, *too much* meaning – the psychotic sees meaning in everything – is matched by the talion of the equally envious superego. The pursuit of absolute knowledge comes with devastating consequences. Thus the psychotic is persecuted by meanings and meaninglessness. Bion understands a number of myths – Oedipus, Eden and Babel – as "pre-conceptions." Preconceptions are unconscious intuitive, "unsaturated" elements, "thought-without-a-thinker," awaiting realisation by mating with conceptions, level D in his famous grid.[21]

Recall *The Nine Billion Lives of God*, the prescient science fiction short story by Arthur C. Clarke. It is a parable of extermination. Tibetan monks have been laboriously deciphering the names of God for centuries. They work out that there must be nine billion names when all combinations are taken into account. Writing the names out by hand, eliminating nonsense combinations, will take many thousands of years. They then turn to modern technology to finish the task more quickly. They hire Westerners with computers powerful enough to do the job in just three months. Now the monks' prophecy is that once the listing of the names of God is complete, the universe will come to an end. The computer analysts are sceptical. Nevertheless, the experts prefer to delay the completion of the process until after their departure. They leave on ponies. They pause briefly on the mountain path leading to the airfield, where a plane is due to take them back to civilisation.

Under the clear night sky, at about the time when the monks will be getting the final listings, they look up to wonder at the heavens above them. Overhead, the stars, one by one, were going out.[22]

Four stages

Each language is *a* world. Irish, for instance, is a language of myths and of fantasies, hope and self-deception, humour and cursing, as against English which is empirical, practical, colonial, yet travels well. Greek syntax helps explain the divisiveness of Greek politics – excessive trust in rhetoric, the falsehoods that corrode the affairs of the *polis*, while Latin offers a grave contrast – stern, masculine, sober, correlating so well with the weight and tenor of Roman culture.

Žižek went as far as differentiating language worlds at the level of their sewage disposal systems. In the German toilet, for instance, the shit lies on the pan (for inspection?) before being flushed away. The Germans are reflective, contemplative, philosophers and poets. In the old French toilets, the shit immediately disappears down the hole, symbolising the revolutionary spirit of the French. The obsessive British allow the shit to float for inspection and the suppression of odour.

Steiner holds to the notion that 'languages are different [other], inherently creative counter-proposals to the constraints, to the limiting universals of biological conditions …' (300). Languages are profusely expressive, yet complicit within themselves. Languages communicate inwardly to the native speaker with a density of shared unspoken knowing impossible for the outsider. When Lacan said that the unconscious is structured like a language, it is true to say that language is also structured *with* an unconscious.

For Steiner, there are four movements to the process of interpretation and translation of interest to psychoanalysts and hermeneutics. First, *trust* or belief in the text – it is saying something and thus stimulates the desire of the interpreter/translator.

Second, *aggression*. The translator appropriates, seizes hold of the material – all cognition is an inroad, a tactical intrusion into opacity, a betrayal of the secret. For the analyst, deconstruction, punctuation, scansion, even the *interrogation* of the unconscious are intrusive. Lacanian analysts employ variable length sessions, ending the session at a key moment that raises a question for the analysand; this implies aggression. This is the "Zeigarnik effect."[23]

Third, *incorporation*. Incorporation changes the recipient, insofar as the recipient analyst remains open. This transference to the analyst thus begets a countertransference at the level of the body as well at the level of speech. Bion elaborated a spectrum of effects to do with the analyst's necessary incorporation of the analysand's discourse. The analyst becomes the "container" of words and feelings – the "contained." Bion suggests three types of container/contained relationship: commensal, symbiotic and parasitic. As Bion says, 'In the commensal relation there is coexistence on each side of the relation in such a way that each is inoffensive to the other'. Here the container's translation of the contained is quite ineffective. In the symbiotic relation, 'there is a confrontation [incorporation] and the result is growth-producing'. However, 'In the parasitic relation the product of the association is something that destroys both parties'.[24] Bion points to envy, the death drive *per se*, already destroying the parasitised-analysand, extends to the host-analyst-translator and her translation. In other words, whatever the analysand produces by way of speech and feeling becomes more or less untranslatable. Bion has in mind here the risk involved in "translating" the language of psychosis. The container is damaged and the contained leaks out into the void. Something other than translation is required, which we might come to.

The fourth movement is *restoration*. In the first three movements the translator leans towards, confronts and incarnates the other, experiencing maybe rapture even mania, or on occasion, indifference, catastrophe or failure. Finally, there is a need for a re-balancing, or restitution as recompense for the original appropriation. As Steiner says, 'the arrows of meaning … move both ways' (318). This fourth stage involves reciprocal enhancement, in which the translator gives back, even in an enhanced form, what he has (aggressively) appropriated and incorporated.

Steiner believes that the foundational Greek and Latin classic texts have been given a reprieve from silence through translation. Without translation they might have been ignored. Likewise, in modern times, Kierkegaard, Ibsen and Strindberg have had their considerable impact *in English*. Faulkner was returned to American awareness after critical appreciation in France. As for the analytic process, this fourth restorative stage may come late in an analysis: the analysand may feel that she has been both listened to and heard, been enabled to speak, while the analyst welcomes the opportunity to analyse.

To summarise, the analyst *trusts* that the analysand has something to say. In order to get beyond the resistance which is always present, some *aggressive* appropriation will be required by the analyst and some reciprocal submission by the analysand, a divided subject. The analyst is transferentially affected by *incorporation* of the other's discourse being led astray by the personal ideology, ideolect of the analysand. At stage four (*restorative*), something of value is given/revealed by way of interpretation/translation. And the reverse is undoubtedly true: failed translations that do not keep faith with or trust in the text are less than, diminish or subtract from the original.

The Heideggerian concept of *Ereignis* (appropriating event) points to two important considerations here. First, the fundamental historicity of being: each subject is formed (interpreted/translated) in a unique and entirely contingent cultural context. Second, *Dasein*, being-there, is the miraculous event arrival of being itself. Being makes its fleeting appearance precisely through this being *there*. The significance of the event-arrival of being should recall Bellow's notion that being makes its temporal appearance by the *vividness* with which the physical world appears to us. As Adam Kirsh suggests in his review of Bellow's letters, 'the wager of Bellow's fiction is that this very energy can be harnessed to affirmation. "The Universe itself being put into us, it calls out for scope. The eternal is bonded onto us. It calls out for its share"'. Against the naysayers who complain about the broken world, or the Wasteland outlook, as Herzog calls it, Bellow says that he cannot accept such "dreariness," such "cowardice." 'What were we here for, of all strange beings and creatures the strangest? Clear colloid eyes to see with, for a while, and so finely, and a palpitating universe to see, and so many human messages to give and receive ...'.[25]

Steiner's excitement about translation and interpretation, the palpitating universe, implies also that translation *has a direction*. What waits in the appearance of being, *behind* the lines of the text, the scattered tongues of the Babel disaster and ruin, so to speak, Benjamin detects the more "final realm" of language. Ultimately, according to Jewish philosopher Franz Rosenzweig, the translation into German of the Old Testament 'is a messianic act, which brings redemption nearer' (Rosenzweig quoted on p. 257). Likewise, the Tyndale translation of the Bible, 'the keystone in the bridge to democracy', stemmed from the need to disseminate the Gospels to the common folk.[26] Only translation would ensure that modern man would not be deprived of the wisdom of the past. Pushkin defined the translator as the 'courier of the human spirit', having respect for the mystery, for the "final realm" forever veiled yet waiting.

The fourfold hermeneutics replaces the older triadic model of translation: literalism, paraphrase and free imitation. We will limit the discussion to literalism, which carries the translation process to an extreme of technical violence, so much so that Benjamin warned against distortion, language 'wrenched from its hinges'. For Steiner, Hölderlin, for instance, sought to break open modern terms to elicit their root significance. He believed that the name if closely pressed would reveal its secretive presence, the "pre-logic" or universality of inspiration, 'a bodying forth of implicit meanings' (345) in a search for the numinous, the sacred. Steiner observed that for Hölderlin translation was a dialectical *crashing* to break open the core of an alien meaning, going as far as annihilating his own ego in the process to fuse with the Other. Steiner adds the antithesis: 'The frontiers between languages are "alive"'. To feel difference, 'is to *re-experience identity*' (381, emphasis added). Otherness can overwhelm, and/or Otherness compels presence, a "close distance," energised by differentiation. The way, for instance, ex-pats can become intense loyalists for the old country. In the quantum realm, high-energy attraction and repulsion are most intense *at proximity*. Consider the proton and the electron, the strong electromagnetic force of opposites, consider the gravitational force between Io and Jupiter. Io is the most volcanically active body in the solar system. The energy for all this activity derives from the proximity between Jupiter and its moons.

Against postmodern inclusiveness, conflict, difference, otherness *energises*. Good translation, according to Steiner involves a real 'dialectic of impenetrability' (413). Against tepid integrationism, attempts to break into the Other will be met with the greatest resistance – slamming shut. Nothing less than a tactical duel, a subtle fight, must be joined, at close quarters. Difference resists the Same. Difference, as we have seen, can strategically dissolve itself in a masquerade of the Same. Yoland, who thought he loved rural Irish life, thinking the natives would love him in return, was the one murdered in secret by the Donnelly twins. The Other holds to itself with a secret *nuclear* energy. This is the essence of racism.

Nevertheless, 'because the translator's vision of the original [Other language] is diachronic … the correction made by the translator is latent in the original' (345), maybe bringing it to life out of its sclerotic seclusion. The Other can be "improved" in its otherness! An ethnic cuisine, for instance, might become *more* itself by being "translated" into the modern context? John Coltrane's 1961 "translation" of the trivial "My Favourite Things" from *The Sound of Music* became a modern jazz masterpiece? Likewise, Miles Davis and Gil Evans with "Summertime" on the *Porgy and Bess* album in 1958? In April 1994, the seven-minute performance of *Riverdance*, combining the music of Bill Whelan with a reinterpretation of traditional Irish dance, had a worldwide impact. *Contra* Baudrillard, is not the hyper-real an improvement upon the real? In the same vein, is not the anti-Oedipal impulse correct in its revolutionary 'wrenching from its hinges' transformation-translation of the original sclerotic Oedipus?

Controversially, the analyst, because of his training, reading, experience, etc., may have a similarly liberating vision of the patient way in excess of the latter's repetitive self-positing. Far from fearing the analyst as grandiose or becoming a subject-supposed-to-know, might not such a vision, properly understood, *but not claimed, forced or possessed in any way*, energise the psychoanalytic process?

Steiner stresses that translation is no more than the heightened form of communication and reception in any given speech act. The same possible "heightening" is facilitated by the rituals pertaining in the analytic situation. The challenges implicit in any *inter*-lingual translation are there too in the analytic situation – discovering through free association, the shift from mute feeling to speech, from the Real to the Symbolic.

Optimally, what transpires will be revelatory to some degree, 'an understanding of understanding' (436). The obverse is also possible: failure and violation. Recall the Irish complaint about the anglicisation of ancient place names – an undoubted case of translation as *subtraction*. Likewise, the use of the old clichés of classical psychoanalysis risk the same kind of subtractive translation, where the analyst-master interpreted the analysand-slaves's words in the reductive jargon of infantile sexual strivings.

So what has been our aim here? First, to situate the practice of analysis into the larger translative-interpretative frame that Steiner so comprehensively provides in *After Babel*. Second, to consider how day-to-day "translations" of the analysis might be helped, expanded and deepened by consideration of inter-lingual translation. While Steiner generates excitement about the enterprise of translation and interpretation, another darker theme is always present, "splintering" being fertile ground for inter-ethnic conflict. The universalising tendency of modernity, represented by the British engineers, with which we started, effectively covers over with an iron fist the lethal potential for internecine rivalry.

Recall the eruption in 1992 in the former Yugoslavia, where Serbs (Orthodox Christians), Croats (Catholics) and ethnic Albanians (Muslims) were living together in close proximity. After WW2, Tito reunified Yugoslavia under the modernist-Communist slogan "Brotherhood and Unity," merging together Slovenia, Croatia,

Bosnia, Serbia, Montenegro, Macedonia, along with two self-governing provinces, Kosovo and Vojvodina. With the apparent end of Communism, the old (unconscious) pre-modern ethnic tensions resurfaced. In the subsequent conflict, 200,000 people were killed *in modern Europe*. How much greater the potential for violence in say modern China, where the 55 *recognised* minority groups total about only eight per cent of the nation's population, all "held down" by an aggressive monopolistic state bureaucratic capitalism. Everywhere, the ever-present danger of violent ethnic re-tribalisations in the twenty-first century will require unimaginable hypermodern violent surveillance-repression systems.

Likewise, the atomised discontents of civilisation come to analysis in the hope that instead of aggressively acting-out their distress in "the community" they will translate their archaic feelings into civilising speech. Thus, culture is protected by the priests and priestesses of modernity, as the schizoanalysts jibe. Translate your distress and rejoin the mainstream; there is no alternative! The analyst oils the megamachine of universalising modernity.

Responsibility

But a subject is more than just his text. The translation-interpretation analogy works only up to the point of responsibility. Responsibility is central to psychoanalysis. One answers for oneself before the law. *We* are (held) responsible for our lapses, slips, dreams, jokes, fantasies, for our unconscious and so on. Although the originary "choice" was so-called *forced* choice, nevertheless we are responsible. Castration or *jouissance*? You must choose castration and enter the Symbolic, or you lose both.[27] Your money or your life? Hand over your money or you lose your money *and* your life![28] This implies a strong social contract – you *must* choose to join civilisation, and you alone are responsible for this joining, or else. There is no alternative. In recent times, as we have been emphasising, there has been equivocation about the need for castration coincident with the weakening of Oedipus and the Symbolic register.

In *The Mission* (1986), mercenary and slaver Rodrigo Mendoza (Robert De Niro) makes his living kidnapping natives and selling them to nearby plantations, including the plantation of the Spanish Governor Cabeza. Mendoza finds his fiancée and his younger brother Felipe in bed together. He kills Felipe in a duel. Acquitted of the killing by Cabeza, Mendoza becomes severely depressed and guilty about his crimes and retreats from the world. Father Gabriel (Jeremy Irons) visits Mendoza and challenges him to take responsibility for his violence and thus to undertake a suitable penance and to avow non-violence. Later, we see Mendoza, now converted, accompanying Father Gabriel and the Jesuits on their return journey, pulling a heavy bundle up the steep mountainside; their mission being to convert the Guaraní community above the perilous Iguazu Falls. They die defending the natives against the overwhelming might of the Portuguese and Spanish colonists. Father Gabriel carrying the cross is gunned down, while Mendoza, in another act of responsibility, returns to violence after all, to defend the defenceless.

Sebastian Faulks' fictional Mike Engleby[29] is a bright working-class boy from a small red-bricked terrace house who wins a place at an esteemed English University to study English in the 1970s. In his second year, he becomes besotted with Jennifer Arkland, from a wealthy family, in her second year studying history, but he cannot talk to her. Engleby has a drug and alcohol problem. He is a loner. Jennifer is upper class and out of reach. *He seeks to get inside her being.* He steals her diary and learns it verbatim. There is a letter to her father where we glimpse their wonderful unreachable world of love and goodness.

Experts classify Engleby as borderline, schizoid, etc. Inspector Cannon discovers the blood-stained tee-shirt. The criminal is unmasked and Engleby wants to take responsibility for his criminal act. Instead he gets the Imaginary-diagnosis-treatment-care option: 'I was no longer a prisoner or a criminal; they'd taken off my handcuffs; I was a patient now. My identity was changed, from an object of vilest hatred to something broken that must be cured'. Engleby becomes part of the *no* fault, *no* judgement, *no* stigma unreal therapeutic world. No shame is attached to him. He knows he should be shamed: 'Take shame from me and you are calling me pre-human'.[30]

Instead of holding him responsible for his crime, the therapist told Engleby to work on his sexism and racism. Apparently, trawling through his diary, she found his theft of women's bikes, attitudes to the women students generally, criticism of the therapist in the transference, all pointing to his misogyny! Similarly, covert racism was detected in his jokey sympathy for West Indians 'trying to have a street culture in the pouring rain' Engleby's "disfunctionality" makes of him a machine without responsibility.

Lacan in 1950 is clear about responsibility and punishment. However, 'A civilisation whose ideals are ever more utilitarian … can no longer understand anything about the expiatory signification of punishment'.[31] Rodrigo Mendoza understood expiation. Engleby acted in a trance and only *afterwards* realised what he had done. Only then is the act "subjectivised," i.e. translated into terms of experience, thinking and responsibility leading to punishment and possible atonement. His was a violent *passage á l'acte*. The *passage* in question here is the passage from an idea to an act directly, *without* the conscious intervention of the subject.[32]

Engleby discovers the truth. Lacan says, 'Through the analysis the subject discovers his truth, that is to say the signification taken on in his particular *destiny* by those givens which are peculiar to him and which one can call *his lot* …'.[33] Engleby's destiny was to be a dog. He said of his father, 'I don't think dad ever reached a level much above a dog's. He'd been beaten and he beat. He was beaten by his life as a slum child, as a young man in the navy, then as a worker in a factory …'.[34]

In his Rome Discourse, Lacan makes clear, 'Analysis can have as its goal only the advent of true speech and the subject's realisation of his history in its relation to a future'.[35] This involves the subject taking responsibility for, making judgement about his own history. The subject's "lot" or let us say, misfortune bound up with hubris, folly or arrogance, goes by the Greek word – *Atë*. Lacan outlines the tragic dimension that grounds psychoanalysis uniquely among the psychological disciplines. The subject is obliged to accept 'something that began to be articulated before him in previous generations, and which is strictly speaking *Atë*. Although this *Atë* does not always reach the tragic level of Antigone's *Atë*, it is nevertheless closely related to misfortune'.[36]

The reference to previous generations recalls Laplanche's notion of the "psychotic enclave," transmitted down the generations, *without interpretation*. 'I think that in some way the [introjected adult] messages that become super-ego messages are messages that *are not being translated* .... I would speak of the super-ego as some kind of psychotic enclave in everyone, something that consists in part of messages that cannot be translated'.[37] No one has taken responsibility for "it." We must take responsibility for the other's responsibility – the sins of the fathers.

Of Gods and Men (*Des Hommes et des Dieux*) (2010), directed by Xavier Beauvois, is a film about seven French Cistercian monks who were kidnapped and then killed at Tibhirine in impoverished Algeria in 1996. Their murderers were never found. The monks lived a simple life dispensing medicine and comfort to their poor Muslim neighbours. As the countryside is terrorised by Islamist mujahideen, an order comes for all foreigners to leave. Do the monks leave, or do they stay to protect their flock, knowing that they are a target? Producer Etienne Comar comments, 'Every one of these monks made a personal decision to stay, and it was very courageous. I don't know if I could have done the same. Yet they say, "there is no better proof of love than to die for people"'. They assume responsibility for themselves and for the other's crime á la Levinas *beyond* Lacan. The community sing to drown out the roar of a military helicopter overhead. The men share a supper with red wine as Tchaikovsky's *Swan Lake* plays in the background on an old tape deck. They are then force marched through the snow supporting each other until the end.

Breathing (*Atmen*) is a 2011 Austrian art house film directed and written by Karl Markovics. Kogler (Thomas Schubert) prepares for release from juvenile detention. He is applying for a job in a mortuary while waiting for his parole hearing. His parole applications depend very much on his being able to hold down a job. After freaking-out on a previous welding job, he *must* now succeed. He is signed out each day to take the train to his work before dawn and returns in the evening having to undergo a humiliating full body inspection each time. In the mortuary, he has to handle corpses, rolling them into and off gurneys, with his workmates. In contrast to the unremitting greyness of the movie, we are shown the tender ministrations by the mortuary team who have to dress the body of a naked woman in her bedroom, while her distressed daughter-in-law waits outside. Kogler grew up in an orphanage. A chance discovery leads to the identity of Kogler's mother, which results in a meeting in which she tells him that giving him up was the best decision of her life. Against misfortune, *Atë*, his fate, the little that was handed down, we feel that Kogler is holding on.

As Cormac McCarthy says in his apocalyptic *The Road*, 'There is no god and we are his prophets'.[38] The Lacanian imperative to take responsibility before the

Law, including the unconscious (law) and *jouissance* – our radical eccentricity with respect to ourselves, greatly extends the notion of responsibility. Even, or especially in the *absence* of God – 'Darkness implacable … The crushing black vacuum of the universe. And somewhere two hunted animals trembling like two ground foxes in their cover'.[39]

Lacan, clearly one of the no god prophets, invented the register of the Real. '*Wo Es war, soll Ich werden.* Where It was, I must come into being'.[40] Lacan reverses Freud's explanation, at the end of Lecture 31, where Freud talks about 'the strengthening the ego … so that it can appropriate [translate/interpret/take responsibility for] fresh portions of the id. Where id was, there shall ego be'. He explains, 'It is *a work of culture* – not unlike the draining of the Zuider Zee'.[41] Here, Lacan implied that Freud was 'reneging' or 'being fundamentally dishonest' about the 'radical heteronomy' of his discovery. For Lacan, it should be the strengthening of the Id's authenticity over the Ego, in the grey-black landscape. In *Seminar 6*, Lacan explains, '*it* must be, this *I* must become'. I, the subject, becoming It, the unconscious – It is a "duty."[42] Thus, the subject must assume responsibility for her own desire even to the point of being subsumed in destruction and the anti-human, entirely alone in the universe.

Close by is the subject's *destitution*. *Frost/Nixon*, directed by Ron Howard, dramatises David Frost's (Michael Sheen) legendary TV interviews in 1977 with disgraced ex-president Richard Nixon (Frank Langella). The encounter turns into a duel, with Frost risking his own money as backers fall away, and Nixon trying one last time to rehabilitate his good name after the Watergate fall from grace, three years before. The erotic bond between the two men becomes apparent, especially late one Friday night when Nixon unexpectedly calls Frost by telephone. Nixon has been drinking and he asks Frost, who like Nixon also came from humble origins, if he ever felt looked down upon by the liberal elites. Frost says he has never felt snubbed in this way. Disbelieving, Nixon continue more and more bitterly, saying how he can never win, never be accepted by them, however hard he tries.

During the taping sessions themselves, Nixon successfully combats Frost's line of questioning on the carpet bombing and the mass killings of civilians in south-east Asia. Until, that is, he is caught by the sudden emergence of the traumatic real. Frost confronts Nixon with his (disavowed) knowledge of the authorisation of the Watergate break-ins. Here, Nixon, hesitates, then assumes his guilt *for the first time*. He leaves the interview a broken man. Nixon knows he will have to bear his loss full on, i.e. take responsibility for his crime. He has reached the point of "symbolic destitution." His world has collapsed.

At their last meeting at Nixon's home in California, Nixon asks Frost what they had talked about that Friday night on the phone. 'Oh, burgers', says Frost, the moment for the more humiliating Real having passed. Frost leaves Nixon with a present of men's slip-on Italian shoes. Nixon has earlier referred to these as 'kind of effeminate'. The rather trivial hint is clear: these shoes are the ones worn by the winners, by the liberal elites.

Notes

1 Friel, B., 1980. Page numbers in parentheses refer to this volume.
2 The writer Hugo Hamilton, whose father was Irish, insisted on Irish being spoken in the house at all times. No English music was allowed, but his German mother always wanted to learn English simply because English was the cool thing to learn and to speak. Hugo was caught between the two "worlds," with his father violently defending the tradition of the Irish language against the inevitability of modernisation. See Hamilton, H., 2004.
3 See, for instance, the first chapter, "Ireland – England's Unconscious," in Kiberd, D., 1995: 29–66.
4 Freud, S., 1950 [1892–1899]: 235.
5 Freud, S., 1917: 141–2.
6 See, for instance, Laplanche, J., 1997: 660.
7 Laplanche, J., 1989: 45.
8 Laplanche, J., cited and translated by Fletcher, J., 2007: 1253, emphasis added.
9 Ferenczi, S., 1933.
10 Nietzsche, F., 1888: 458.
11 Caputo, J., 2015.
12 Steiner, G., 1975: 22. Page numbers in parentheses refer to this text.
13 *Sinthome* is another Lacanian neologism (saintly man, *saint homme*). It is a concept introduced by Lacan, J., 1975–1976. The sinthome is a signifying formulation beyond analysis as such. It enables one to live by providing an essential organisation of *jouissance*. The Lacanian aim of the cure is to identify with the sinthome that knots the three Lacanian registers together.
14 Freud, S., 1912: 115.
15 Freud, S., 1900: 353.
16 Monod, J., 1969: 15–16.
17 Lacan, J., 1970: 262/319.
18 Žižek, S., 2009: 56–7.
19 See, for instance, Weatherill, R., 2011: 113ff, and in the last chapter we will return to teleology.
20 See discussion of parallax in Chapter 5.
21 Bion, W., 1963.
22 Clark, A. C., 1992: 17–23.
23 Lacan, J. 1954–1955: 86.
24 Bion, W. 1970: 78.
25 Adam Kirsh reviewing Saul Bellow in TLS, No. 5621/2, p. 5.
26 See Bragg, M., 2011: 355.
27 'Castration means that *jouissance* must be refused, so that it can be reached on the inverted ladder (*l'échelle renversés*) of the Law of desire' (Lacan, J., 1960: 700/827).
28 Lacan, J., 1964: 212.
29 Faulks, S., 2007.
30 Ibid.: 318.
31 Lacan, J., 1950: 112.
32 The best known example of the *passage á l'acte* was the case of a writer who consulted Ernst Kris. The writer complains that whenever he writes he is plagiarising someone. Kris examines his patient's work and tells him that he is not a plagiarist, but is using the notion of plagiarism as a defence against having ideas of his own. The man leaves the analyst's office and goes to a restaurant and orders fresh brains! Other examples come to mind. A woman, told by her lover that he loves best of all the way she *looks* at him, sends him one of her eyes beautifully wrapped. A man who feels he is no more than human waste throws himself into a skip. He is pulled out and he jumps in again. A man injured his leg badly in a motorcycle accident. The doctors thought of amputating it, but decided in the end that they could save it. They did so, but the leg was deformed. In order to bring about a real amputation, this man laid his leg across a railway line in

a very careful manner so that a train sliced it off cleanly. In another case report, a man wanted to disable himself. He had the overwhelming desire to cause one of his legs to be amputated. No doctor obliged him with an operation. In desperation, and with elaborate precautions, he fired a gun shot at a precise distance from his leg. He then tied the tourniquet. Covered in blood, he phoned for an ambulance. Relief, the amputation was necessary.

33 Lacan, J., 1954–1955: 325–6.
34 Faulks, S., 2007 op. cit.: 162.
35 Lacan, J., 1953: 302/249.
36 Lacan, J., 1959–1960: 299–300.
37 Caruth, C., 2001. An Interview with Jean Laplanche http://pmc.iath.virginia.edu/text-only/issue.101/11.2caruth.txt.
38 McCarthy, J., 2006: 181.
39 Ibid.: 138.
40 Lacan, J., 1957: 524/435.
41 Freud, S., 1933 [1932]: 80, italics added.
42 Lacan, J., 1958–1959: Lesson 21, 20 May 1959: 4.

8

NEW SUBJECTIVITIES IN THE VIRTUAL WORLD

Implications for practice

Active nihilism

Marxist philosopher Fredric Jameson observed, 'We went out one morning and the thermometer was gone'. In some countries to know the thermometer reading before you leave the house in the morning can be a matter of life and death. How do we take the temperature of the times 'without instruments and in a situation in which we are not even sure there is so coherent a thing as an "age" or "zeitgeist" or "system" or "current situation" any longer'.[1] We have no way of figuring things.

Alain Badiou has defined the contemporary, again following Marx, as "atonal" (*monde atone*) which means unaccented, without tone, debilitated, or pointless.[2] There are ever fewer quilting points or buttoning points that will hold the social fabric in place. Many of us already, post Deleuze and Guattari, find ourselves "deterritorialised," under the frenetic conditions of late capitalism.

Baudrillard speaks of an 'act of prestidigitation'; the tablecloth is pulled off leaving the objects in place, 'a material presence of objects, from which, however, *the meaning has been removed*'.[3] Modernism clears the pitch, next everything has to be reinvented artificially, with some reality (special effects) added. For example, electric cars are so silent that people don't hear them coming. Engine noise has to be added to the level of 40 dbs to make them sound real.

All paths lead to what Nietzsche terms "*active* nihilism." Everything is available so youth, which presents an impossible burden of "choice" and "consumption" – signifiers of late capitalism – requiring hyper-adaptability. Everything is knowable – the democracy of knowledge. All truths are out there – the democracy of truth telling. Everything is do-able – the democracy of effort. For Nietzsche, this active ingredient of nihilism, the 'will to truth' is inherent in Christianity itself no less, which thus wills its own destruction. '[I]t is an awe-inspiring catastrophe', declares Nietzsche, 'the outcome of a two-thousand year training in truthfulness, which finally forbids itself the *lie of belief in God*'. And, 'it is this rigour … that makes us good Europeans and heirs to Europe's longest and boldest process of self-overcoming (Selbstüberwindung)'. '*Patere legem, quam ipse tulisti* – submit to the law that you yourself have decreed'. He forecasts quite correctly that morality will perish over the next two centuries – 'perhaps the most hopeful of all spectacles'.[4]

This echoes the Lacanian–Kantian imperative to submit to desire: morality is destroyed by truth; meaning is destroyed by truth. Nietzsche's exhilarating claim is that, 'Behind every great human destiny there sounded a yet greater "In vain"!' Nietzsche is ecstatic. Everything is vanity. Everything is pointless, empty (*vānus*)! Man is 'surrounded by a fearful void'.[5]

Nietzsche celebrates the courageous spirit and its will to truth – 'unconditional honest atheism (and it is the only air we breathe, we more spiritual men of this age!)'.[6] Nietzsche was excited about the "beautiful ruins" of Europe, long before Germany actually reduced Europe to ruins in two world wars.

Nietzsche traced this specifically *German* philosophical path to destruction. First, Leibniz's insight that 'consciousness is merely an *accidens* of experience', i.e. only one of many possible states of our psychical life, paving the way for Freud. Second, Kant's questioning of the *a priori* status of "causality;" events are not simply given, but rather constituted by the mind by the principle of causality. For Kant, we only see appearances. Third, there is Hegel's notion that 'species concepts (*die Artbegriffe*) develop *out of* each other',[7] leading the way for evolution and Darwin. Hegel, however, delayed somewhat the triumph of atheism with his 'grandiose attempt to persuade us of the divinity of existence'. But Schopenhauer, the "inexorable atheist," asks whether existence has any meaning at all, as he stares out 'into a de-deified world that has become stupid, blind, mad and questionable; his honest horror was not merely an exceptional case among Germans but a *German* event'.[8]

For Nietzsche, the sign of a strong intellect is one that is not afraid to doubt everything absolutely. The default nihilist of today hardly exemplifies this great Nietzschian rigour which demands that 'Every achievement, every step forward in knowledge, comes from courage, from harshness towards yourself, from cleanliness with respect to yourself'.[9] On the contrary, we appear to need every kind of psychological crutch and therapy *against* Nietzsche's active nihilistic notion of *becoming*, without fabrication, without belief in any true world, without any metaphysics.

Nietzsche's "becoming" is the unbearable schizo real – *without* ego, without *papamummy*, without moorings, each alone with his machinic *jouissance* and orphan unconscious. Writing with his blood, Nietzsche could not be further from the cool dudes of today with their ironic indifference. It was Nietzsche's acute sensitivity to the pain of the world that led to his final breakdown.

Recall *I'm All Right Jack, a* 1959 British satire, based on British industrial life in the 1950s, showing the corrupt and cynical nature of industrial management and trades unionism after the war. The title was derived from the original "Fuck you, Jack, I'm all right" coined by sailors (jacks) returning home after war, not heroes or victors, but ignored, disdained by the newly emergent, complacent, competitive "get-ahead society." The new twenty-first century "I'm all rights" are the burgeoning private and professional high-earning elites and the new "jacks" are in the front-line services – teachers, nurses, police, psychiatrists, social workers, GPs, as well as migrants, refugees, asylum seekers and so on, exposed as they are to the Real and growing antagonisms of globalisation.

Simon Stephens' play *Punk Rock*, set in the sixth form of a private school in Stockport, is edgy commentary upon the rage, dislocation and sexual despair across the class structure in Britain today – just as real in the middle classes as on sink estates. Stephens wants to capture the violence in kids as young as ten, and not just black and Asian kids. What first drove him was the massacre at Columbine, an event that left its scar over the beginning of the new century. In his school there are *no* adult figures, *no* teachers, *no* police, *and no* parents. Stephens refers to Dennis Kelly's *Orphans*, in which Kelly explored precisely this anti-Oedipal "psychological orphaning." According to literary critic Kate Kelloway, Stephens describes his schoolboy assassin as 'romantic, violent, funny, charming and ironic – suffering from an increasing dislocation from himself'.[10]

Verleugnung

The schizos' revolutionary dream of orphanising, dislocating, de-familiarising and so on, coincides with the border*less* condition of the "borderline" personality – without history, without response-ability, on edge, on the verge, in transit, refugee without shelter or asylum, migratory, temporary and marginal. Incontinent feelings drain away. Mania alternates with depression. When André Green's long-term patient says to him, *ça ne chante pas* – it doesn't sing any more – Green says, 'this is one of the most mysterious things: why [with some patients] the playing stops, or the song stops, or the vitality disappears'.[11] Life goes out of things; the urge to live dissipates.

The collective anti-Oedipal thrust has become the norm. The proximity of psychosis and perversion had led to the key defence of our time, disavowal (*Verleugnung*), linked for Freud to the warding off or denial of (traumatic) external reality. *We know but we do not want to know.* Things we know but refuse to think about. How often did we hear in the early years of this century, 'there is no economic crisis in Europe?' Until it happened.

While Nietzsche anticipated Europe's nihilism, Bruchner confirms that Europeans no longer know who they are, 'Timorous and all devouring, the Old World is in danger of dying, like Rome, of obesity, and ectoplasm that grows larger as it loses its substance'.[12] In European cities, the "call to enjoyment" parallels the "call to prayer." The former is postmodern and the latter is premodern. Behind the latter, the "call to jihad" – the violent counter-reaction to anti-Oedipus, the blind injunction to *destroy* enjoyment. The four-century domination by European ideals is waning,[13] just as Nietzsche predicted.

Verleugnung causes the segmental loss of reality – great chunks of the real go unnoticed. Baudrillard goes further: 'Reality asks for nothing other than to submit itself to hypotheses. *And it confirms them all*'.[14] Such passivity he suggests is like an 'irreversible coma [where] everything continues to function all the same, and eventually can even seem to amount to history'.[15]

The severing of binding social bonds leads to the absence of the normative regulation of societal relationships. More than a century ago, Durkheim believed this *collective* loss was the key to male suicides.[16] In Ireland in the twenty-first century, suicides among men are running at five times the rate in women, as men are de-meaned by an endlessly justified anti-Oedipal rage. A poster in a local pharmacy reads: "Grow your own dope; plant a man." Such casual sexism displayed in public places passes without comment.

Virilio considers the internet to be a key component of the 'third age of military weaponry' or what he calls the *The Information Bomb*.[17] What he terms "information monotheism" has come into being all at once leading to 'the loss of social bonds linked to the *demise of the proximate human being*'.[18] No longer the monotheism of the Word – the Bible, the Koran, the New Testament – but an inhuman digital monotheism. This may prove to be the biggest *unknown known.*

We perceive the traumatic reality, as Freud says, 'we see that the perception [prototypically the woman's lack of a penis] has persisted, and that a very energetic action has been undertaken to maintain the disavowal'. More precisely, 'In the conflict between the weight of the unwelcome perception and the force of his counter-wish, a compromise has been reached, as is only possible under the dominance of the unconscious laws of thought',[19] that is, the law that permits opposites to coexist in the unconscious.

Thus, we can welcome the information bomb on condition that the loss it represents is for the very best in the long run. We can wring our hands about male suicides, while at the same time hollowing out masculinity. We can disavow the social crisis if we can hunker down and protect *our* homes. We can lose the whole substance of reality providing we have the virtual.

Dissident feminist Camille Paglia envisages the traumatic real of "Generation Gaga," 'marooned in a global technocracy of fancy gadgets but emotional poverty ... raised in a relativistic cultural vacuum where chronology and sequence as well as distinctions of value have been lost or jettisoned by politically correct educators'.[20] She depicts the ideal anti-Oedipal world of de-differentiation, where you can self-identify as gender *x* without biological referents.

Author Nicholas Carr argues that as we skim, extract, hyperlink, we are losing *deep* thought: 'The strip mining of relevant content replaces the slow excavation of meaning'.[21] In a Freudian vein, he suggests that the story of human civilisation has been to master and move beyond primitive instincts to train the mind for focused argument and deep contemplation and reflection. By contrast, the web is returning us to "the shallows" and the loss of centuries-long meta-thinking can only be tolerated if we can energetically counter-believe along with, for instance, innovation expert Vijay Govindarajan,[22] that internet multitasking enables ultra-rapid innovation as per the Silicon Valley slogan: 'Fail early, fail fast and fail cheap'. Thus we can bear loss if we can disperse it with manic experimentation.

The borderline is shallow – all edgy chaos with no depth. All affirmation and no negation. Childish, regressed, fragile, futile, *Verleugnung* is the psychotic's first step, involving a splitting of the ego. If anti-Oedipally repression is no longer tolerated, disavowal is the only option; shallowing, scotomising – seeing and not seeing. Even Lacan's foreclosure (*forclusion*) seems attractive. Here important signifiers are abolished in a double movement along the familiar lines of first known, then unknown. More precisely,

> The first of these operations is what Lacan also calls "symbolisation" or "primary" *Bejahung* (postulation, affirmation); the second "constitutes the Real inasmuch as this domain subsists outside symbolisation." So foreclosure is not symbolising what ought to be symbolised (castration, [loss]): it is "symbolic abolition."[23]

From the beginning, splitting (*Spaltung*) was part of Freud's psychoanalytic thinking coming from Breuler, Breuer and Janet. He referred to 'a splitting of consciousness, accompanied by the formation of separate psychical groups'.[24] Doubling, dissociation, double conscience, dual personality, doppelgangers and so on, has a long history in psychiatry. Freud observes, however, that even in the worse cases the ego's detachment or dissociation from reality is *not* complete: there is 'the normal one [split], which takes account of reality, and another which under the influence of the instincts detaches the ego from reality'.[25] Decommission "reality" via cultural relativism and confusion abounds as opposing "separate psychical groups" approach equivalence.

However, the key *triplet* of psychotic defence mechanisms – disavowal, splitting *and projection* – underpins and "stabilises" the sleep-inducing confusion of "realities." At the behest of the death drive, the "bad-object" that will be split-off, disavowed and projected, while the "good object" will be avowed and idealised.[26] The result, as Segal tells us: '"perfect babies," never protesting and never crying, as though all experiences were experienced by them as good ones. In adult life these mechanisms lead to lack of discrimination between good and bad and to fixations upon bad objects that have to be idealised'.[27] Bion imagines a weak ego whose contact with the real world is dominated by 'an omnipotent phantasy that is intended to destroy either reality or awareness of it, and thus to achieve a state that is neither life nor death'.[28] The omnipotent fantasy becomes normalised. Bion even speaks of the evacuative process: 'The unburdening of the psyche by hallucination, that is, by the use of the sensory apparatus in reverse … reinforced by muscular action'.[29] The splitting, fragmentation, the shattering, unlinking and evacuating brought about in the paranoid-schizoid mode of functioning enable hallucinating *without feeling or thinking*. The result is the paradox of the un-known, un-thought, un-felt, knowns; things that we know but disavow, that Bion conveniently symbolised as "minus-K."

Our courage has largely vanished; along with strength, nobility, character, etc., thrown out ecstatically along with patriarchy. With the onset of reality fatigue we welcome instead minus-K: hallucinosis, regression, relativism, being mindful of nothing. Graffiti artists everywhere agree by masking signs and uselessly spray painting the rich old fabric of cities.

Ressentiment

The Nietzschean exposure of European nihilism is accompanied by the imperative to overcome nihilism, to not get stuck at the nihilistic/disavowal stage by either 1) passive nihilism (e.g. European Buddhism, Spirituality), or 2) terroristic nihilism (Russian anarchists, Situationists, Fascists), or 3) the nihilism of mental apathy, exhaustion, depression disavowal. Nietszche's *active* nihilism and the '*reality of becoming*' rest on his notion of "eternal return," a neo-Kantian sublime duty, not based on any self-serving interest, or ultimate hope for happiness, any prior identity or simple repetition, but the courage continuously to think and rethink the world in terms of becoming, beyond Kant, without God, without theological meaning, without the immortality of the soul. Unlike *Verleugnung* which denies the negative, 'becoming' takes nihilism to the full in order to overcome in full, beyond good and evil. This is the *true* anti-Oedipal spirit, whereas the Oedipal spirit is *dis*pirited and mired in the reactive stage described by Nietzsche as *ressentiment*, closely allied to the English, resentment – an unforgiving feeling of bitterness, a fixation on the bad object, preventing the boundless possibilities of becoming.

As Deleuze has it, 'The man of *ressentiment* is characterised by the invasion of consciousness by mnemonic traces'.[30] His problem is not so much what he knows but what *he cannot forget*. Nietzsche distinguishes two systems within the reactive apparatus, conscious and unconscious. The reactive unconscious is characterised by imprints of mnemonic traces which are ruminative, undigested and indelible, while the conscious reactive forces aspire to freshness and fluidity. They require the specific *active* force of forgetfulness! Forgetting is 'an active and in the strict sense positive faculty of repression'.[31] Forgetting is an active curative force without which 'there could be no happiness, no serenity, no hope, no pride, no present'.[32] The man of *ressentiment* is like a dog that can *only* react to traces, because everything offends. He takes on a slave mentality that requires the other to be evil. As for 'The memory of traces [it] … embodies the spirit of revenge and engages in the enterprise of perpetual accusation'.[33]

Although we can envisage *becoming* in the strong Nietzschean sense, we frequently fall short at the nihilistic becoming-*reactive* stage, where *ressentiment* and bad conscience accompany nihilism. The active becoming turns against itself, turning inwards and becoming reactive: pushed back, repressed, incarcerated within, venting itself on itself, full of pain and bitterness, unable to forget, unable to love. This is not a matter of psychology but *foundational* for man. For this reason, Zarathustra refers to man as 'one of the skin diseases of the earth'.[34]

Ressentiment is never about justice. 'To sanctify revenge under the name of justice … to rehabilitate not only revenge but all reactive affects',[35] is how 'this plant blooms', says Nietzsche, although it 'does not smell of violets' – maybe instead a whiff of anal sadism. Can reactive feelings such as hatred, envy, jealousy, mistrust, rancour, revenge (Nietzsche lists them), become justified? Absolutely not! According to Nietzsche, 'the *last* sphere to be conquered by the spirit of justice is the sphere of reactive feelings'.[36] Nietzsche anticipates MacIntyre's critique of our descent into emotivism. If you *feel outrage* it must be justified. As MacIntyre says, 'Emotivism entails the obliteration of any genuine distinction between manipulative and non-manipulative social relations'.[37]

For the reactive type, 'One cannot get rid of anything, one cannot get over anything, one cannot repel anything – everything hurts. Men and things obtrude too closely … memory becomes a festering wound. Sickness itself is a kind of *ressentiment*'.[38] One is burnt up, used up by *ressentiment.*

Irish analyst Hanaghan spoke similarly of such spiritual sickness and unresolved Oedipal hatreds and resentments. The injunction to forget was aided by what Hanaghan termed "forth-giveness," going forth to the other in fellowship. In this he believed we are guided by the "visionary" nature of the ego ideal. Neurotic *ressentiment* is the massive defence that prevents this happening. Paradoxically, forth-giveness can only occur actively on the basis of a full acknowledgement of/memory of/working through of the thorough-going hatred that can then be "forgotten."

For Nietzsche, the paradoxical remedy for *ressentiment* was Russian fatalism, exemplified by the Russian soldier who exhausted by war lies down in the snow, ceasing to react altogether. This is not the courage to die, but a kind of hibernation, maybe a holding oneself in reserve, biding one's time, accepting the given. As Nietzsche says, calling on a Stoic tradition of love for an all-pervading necessity that governs the universe,

> My formula for greatness in a human being is *amor fati*: that one wants nothing to be different, not forward, not backward, not in all eternity. Not merely bear what is necessary, still less conceal it – all idealism is mendacity in the face of what is necessary – but *love* it.[39]

However, read *amor fati* in its Nietzschean context, lest it slip into mendacity and become an easy slogan for postmodern healers. Kaufmann signals the paradox: 'Without ascetic ideals, without self-control and cruel self-discipline, we cannot attain to [*active*] self-mastery which Nietzsche ever praises and admires'.[40] *Ecce Homo* as a whole exemplifies this *amor fati.* Throughout the previous decade Nietzsche had been troubled by ill health and excruciating physical pain and up to this point all his books had been totally unsuccessful.

The discourse of *ressentiment* leads us to the contemporary discourse of the victim: *the other will hurt you.* There are *real* victims of misfortune or evil, but the ideological recalibration of the senseless real into *virtual recrimination* creates a burgeoning slave culture with an expectation of abuse, harassment, victimisation and exploitation leading quite "rationally" to pay-offs and compensation and worse – to violence and terrorism. There is *someone* to blame. Hate the other as yourself – the narcissistic infantile imperative, paranoid, reactive and intolerant, creating "survivors" and "survivors' networks," self-help and the demand for redress. Another triad: hate, self-hate and self-pity. To question the "victim" risks immediate claim of *re*-traumatisation. Everything hurts.

One can be a victim of *anything* – the environment, smoking, drugs, toxins, stress, corporations, AIDS, aliens, even genetics. *Real* encounters with others (erotic or otherwise) are therefore best avoided. Instead, the reactive readiness to be a victim gives endlessly, for a number of reasons: 1) New causes of abuse/harassment/hate crimes are always being discovered or created. 2) The past can be reinterpreted through the new vision of these crimes. 3) It is based on an impossible childish idealism that nothing bad must happen: no one should be bullied; no animal can be hurt. *The other will hurt you.*

While there is undoubtedly widespread compassion fatigue as well as reality fatigue, we nevertheless feel drawn towards victims lest we, in our good fortune, join their ranks or indeed unconsciously become their humiliators and tormentors, accused on the spot of being an insensitive "phobic," shunned as a non-person. With a bad conscience and the sickness that is contagious, we feel duty bound falsely to promote the ideology of suffering and swell its coffers. We cede ground to the moral superiority of the victim. We not only treat the victim with compassion, but increasingly with reverence, with deference owed to the new authority. We secretly admire their negative power and with our chains, piercings and scarifications, long to join them. Look at the attention they get! Maybe I can join an oppressed group, maybe I can be a victim. Blacking-up. Books and buildings get burned; victimhood has become weaponised. To share in some of this "authenticity," people dumb down their accents; parade their humble origins, their stigmata, and show solidarity with the poor for fear of being "outed" as privileged or elitist. Walk on egg shells around victims lest you cause offence. The politics involved here is based on identity and emotion rather than reason.

No allowance can now be made for what Baudrillard simply calls, 'the intelligence of evil',[41] the way in which the slave is complicit and connives in his own slavery, the way the patient gains from his illness, the way the addict can be proud of his addiction, the way David welcomes Goliath. Such is the hidden libidinisation of pain and suffering that Freud discovered, the mere mention of which would be the most outrageous slur on the victim! For instance, one no longer *commits* suicide; the discourse of the victim states that one dies *by* suicide, thus the suicidal subject is even deprived of his final and fateful act.

What should the analyst do?

With increasing numbers of people living without "a world" to inhabit, *ressentiment* abounds. *Ressentiment* and *jouissance* are tied, knotted together as a negative sinthome, a failure of "becoming," and a failure of the real schizo project of radical transformation. Bleak: no world; no change; no real.

For modern psychoanalysis, man is symptomatic! In other words, where there is a subject there is a symptom, i.e. disease, a fallen being (*syn*, with; root of *piptein*, to fall). Fixations for Freud were the *primal* symptoms, and for the Lacanians, Verhaeghe and Declercq explain: 'The symptom is what defines mankind, and as such it cannot be rectified or cured. That is Lacan's final conclusion: *there is no subject without a symptom*'.[42] Thus, psychoanalysis with its dismal priestly vocation is confirmed. The bar is set low. Expect nothing. No vitality, not nobility. No affirmation of life itself.

Lacan uses the image of the jar or pot, whose material shape encloses an empty space (the Real), while the jar itself acts as a container or creator of this real with its signifiers. Analysis is a "sounding" of the jar. By no longer believing in resolving the symptom in analysis, the question arises what to do with the symptom? You can either "believe" in it, believe that you can indeed resolve it with a "final" signifier, a final answer *out there*. Or, you can "identify" creatively with your symptom, now called by Lacan a sinthome – *some way of living your own unique enjoyment that is not "alienated" in the Other.*

Verhaeghe speaks of contemporary mental disorders, so different from Freud's descriptions of the psychoneuroses. Panic attacks, stress disorders, addictions, cutting phenomena, suicide, promiscuity, somatisations, all have much in common with Freud's descriptions of the "actual neuroses." They are *action* oriented, with the focus on the Real of the body and of the drive, the here and now with no meaning or historicisation. The transference is likely to be not just a negative transference *per se*, but sometimes an immediate challenging of our position as analysts. These patients do not have a "jar," they do not even believe in a "jar maker." These subjects have not constructed symptoms that *repress* the drive, they haven't the luxury of a sinthome. Rather, they are over-exposed to the drive and under-exposed to the Other. Thus the analyst must create a therapeutic alliance by attempting in various ways to 'create a jar', to provide 'a coating for the drive'.[43]

Commenting on the changing nature of the Lacanian theorisation of the subject Verhaeghe and Declercq point out that 'the essence of the Lacanian subject comes down to its lacking any kind of essence whatever, and that the whole accent has to be put on its divided character'. However, in later Lacan comes a surprise reversal: the notion of 'another subject, one that has, after all, a *kind of substantiality*. It is tempting to consider this, in the light of what we inherit from the "sixties, as a Lacanian version of the existential "authentic self"'. Authentic to the extent that, 'this neo-subject tries to come and go with the Real of the *jouissance* dictated by its own drive',[44] without recourse to the signifiers of the Other.

From the opposite orientation, Otto Kernberg, speaking in Dublin in August 2010 about the borderline patient, stated that the analyst's position should be one of "concerned objectivity." His is a master discourse. He assumes patients want to get well and makes them sign a contract initially to that effect. Any destructiveness, self-harming and so on will not be tolerated. He is clear about ending the sessions or ending the treatment if destructiveness is acted out instead of being thought out or "mentalised." And where violence is concerned, he is clear that the safety of the analyst or the analyst's family *comes first*. His aim is to interpret the "here and now" transference and counter-transference manifestations, in terms of the "there and then," with the analyst exploring who he represents at any given time in the patient's past (the parent imago or indeed the child in the presence of parent, or both).

The more disturbed the patient, the more the analyst's counter-transference will be felt and must be analysed rather than acted out. The aim is to achieve more flexibility, adaptation and to resolve the "identity diffusion" that lies at the heart of the borderline patient's problems, by bringing the good idealised and bad threatening objects to light in the transference and integrating them.

The two radically incompatible psychoanalytic currents have an ocean of clear water between them.[45] The gulf, created by Lacan, was an attempt to divide and conquer the psychoanalytic movement. Editing *The Later Lacan,* Voruz and Wolf make clear, 'Subjects are *not* to be cured; they are neither deficient nor helpless victims of their family circumstances'.[46] Further on, 'Psychoanalysis refutes the universalisation of the discourse of science exactly because the latter forecloses singularity … It stands against the dehumanisation proposed by CBT whose pernicious appeal lies in that it feeds fantasies of normalisation'.[47] Ultimately, analysis can bring about change and a new dignity for the subject once a proper separation is achieved from one's own investment in the fantasy of what one is or might be, or still hopes to be, for the Other (What do you want from me? What do you expect from me?). Separation, in the full sense that Lacan gave it, is *se parer*, to dress oneself, or defend oneself, to give birth to oneself.[48] The point being to separate oneself from all the former detritus of one's life and expectations from others.

Even psychotics can expect something from a Lacanian analysis, insofar as the psychotic subject is helped to 'find ways to treat his *jouissance* with the signifier', enabling over time a stabilising shift, as it were, from the Real to the Symbolic.

For J.-A. Miller, we inhabit a post-interpretive world, because the signifier itself has a way of interpreting; all that is required of the analyst is to hear it and maybe repeat it, putting it in quotation marks, decontextualising it – to allow new senses, new directions to emerge. As in the Ratman case,[49] the mobility of the signifier "rat." Or the case of the patient who dreamt of giving her analyst six roses. Hear this "six roses" slightly obliquely realising that the patient's father had died of *cirrhosis* of the liver and a new sense flashes before us. Or the man who dreamt of raking the autumn leaves. Once it was recalled that his absent father was known as "the rake," the analysis took a new direction.

"Insights," self-understanding, any appeal to "normal" or "healthy" and so on amounts to "dehumanisation." Lacanians prefer perplexity – *not* explanation but evocation and provocation: "punctuating" the bla-bla-bla, underlining certain words, placing words in quotes, italicising, bolding, bracketing, full stops, and so on. All this has to be done with tact or *tactically* to create an effect of interruption and deconstruction, with no time for the ego to intervene defensively.

In the twenty-first century, the conflict of psychoanalytic orientation seems long over, although apparently J.-A. Miller still refers to "the war." Ultimately, it is more than ever a war against the hegemony of "health science" and behind that neuroscience – the long history of body-brain as machine to be "treated" as such. Consider EST – "empirically supported treatment." This is treatment via the manual. Here best practice dictates a particular sequence of predictable interventions that the therapist, any briefly trained practitioner, or soon a robot, can make.[50] It is this dehumanisation by science that the Paris students were against – structuralism, dominating French thought in the 1960s, as well as hard science.

However, bearing in mind the "slavery of *ressentiment*" and the contemporary failure of courage, the lack of "thymos" (Sloterdijk), the "singularity" of the individual, is unique indeed, but often not dignified still less noble. The Kleinian *naming* of "destructiveness," or Rosenfeld's "negative narcissistic omnipotent organisation,"[51] where a (silent) rage/contempt holds the subject and others in fear and terror, does not automatically imply any loss of dignity, or demeaning of the subject. To be disturbed, to be resistant, confrontational even, might but does not always patronise or stigmatise the other. However, Rosenfeld himself warned that patients traumatised in their childhood could be re-traumatised in their analyses if the analyst put too much emphasis on innate destructiveness.

To challenge, to question, to interrogate must be part of an analytic approach, not from the position of master, adaptation, normalcy, or conventional "right" or "wrong," but in the name of something other, something real, something different. We should shake off any politically correct silent complicity with the other (Lacanian, Kleinian, etc.), while realising that sometimes it is the only option for a time. Likewise, 'the path of perplexity' can lead to just that, more perplexity, confusion without end.

Case material

An example will illustrate the schismatic Lacan/Klein complexity.[52] Joanna Swift talks about a young patient of hers, with whom she has a rather intense relationship, who tells of wanting to take grapes from the front of her analyst's house. The patient reported stealing a bunch and putting one in her mouth, saying, 'it was a sacrament'. Swift replies, 'My body, my blood', playing on the language of the communion service. However, Swift was in supervision with a Kleinian analyst, who asserted that the grapes were the nipple, etc., explaining the girl's utterance in terms of primal fantasy. But Swift already had a chain of associations connecting the grapes with the girl's father's alcoholism and the past, now closed off by the *sole* emphasis on the breast and oral fantasy. Surely, the narrative connected to the grapes, living with an alcoholic father, AND the "intense-relationship" of transference and counter-transference, how this child *affected* her analyst during their sessions week after week; *both* are important.

In her paper on transference, Betty Joseph explicitly eschews consideration of specific associations in favour of attempts at understanding the patient's current internal state in terms of the total interpersonal situation the patient creates in the transference with the analyst.

> If we work only with the part that is verbalised, we do not really take into account the object relationships being acted-out in the transference … for example, the relationship between the uncomprehending mother and the infant who feels unable to be understood, and it is this that forms the bedrock of her personality.[53]

It gets more complex still, according to Fonagy.[54] As psychoanalysts, we know that patients cannot possibly remember why they behave as they do. Nor will they necessarily learn about the events or experiences that have caused them to be this way. Primordial, pre-biographic "experiences" that may lead to what he calls, 'deeply pathological ways of experiencing the other' often antedate the development of the memory system, which is capable of encoding and retaining the experience in a way that can be ever represented, consciously or unconsciously, as a story with its key signifiers. This is the problem with a *sole* reliance on Lacan.

According to the standard Kleinian-object relational view, the only way we can know what goes on in our patient's mind, what might have happened to them, is to sense how they are with the analyst in the transference. They come to us with a model – a network of unconscious expectations or mental models of self–other relationships. What complicates things further is that the affective fragments are not *replicas* of actual experiences but are undoubtedly defensively distorted by wishes and fantasies current at the time of the experience. Thus, in no sense can they be thought of as bearing testament to actual historical truth.

For Fonagy, the therapeutic work needs to focus on helping the individual identify regular patterns of behaviour and fantasy based on childhood fantasy and experience, for which autobiographical memory is marginal at best. He is suggesting that psychoanalysis is more than the creation of a narrative; it is the *active* construction of a new way of experiencing self with other, against the danger of mere repetition in the transference of the original failed relation with the Other.

Self-harming is an all too familiar repetition of the failure of early object relations. According to a recent article researched by Roisin Ingle (*Irish Times*), rates of self-harming increased by a third in 2010. A case is given of a 20-year-old woman who began cutting herself aged 11, using the blade from a pencil sharpener. Her home life had always been very difficult, shunted between feuding separated parents; she found the family situation painful but couldn't discuss her problems for fear of worsening the disaster. 'Cutting myself was something I did nearly every time I got upset. Over the years it got worse, I started getting what I now know were panic attacks and the cutting became more regular. By the time I was 15 or 16, I was doing it every other day'. While there are currently in Ireland about 12,000 hospital admissions a year for self-harm, it is estimated that there are as many as 60,000 cases of self-harm going unreported each year.[55] She has a particularly unsightly scar, one of the most recent, the result of a night out when she had a row with her boyfriend, the father of her now 1-year-old son. 'I smashed a glass and used it on my arm', she said. 'There was blood everywhere. I had to go to hospital'.[55a]

The standard explanation for the "illness" is that it represents a form of *bodily* "communication" for people who haven't learnt to express fear, pain or distress in any other way, i.e. through speaking, representation, etc. Self-harm represents a breakdown in the primordial symbolisation process, normally brought about by proper attachment to the first Other (Mother). Without this graduated, mediated passage from the Real to the Symbolic, strong feelings and emotions, especially levels of rage are expressed violently, intensely and impulsively, in the Real, here and now, where the self-injury serves to "say" to the present other (harking back to the failure of the first Other): *look how much you have hurt me, look how much you are killing me*. Or *I hurt myself for not being able to cut-loose from you. I hurt myself to hurt you.*

In such a false/virtual/no world, increasing numbers of people require violent acts to feel Real, the so-called "passion for the Real." The warm flow of blood is real, as are all other extremes of addiction, sex, etc., providing violent self "initiations" in the profane world – means of bypassing the process of symbolising, just as the social question of the father, the family, Oedipus are bypassed by all the *bien pensants* post '68.

In one scene from ITV's 2010 remake of *A Bouquet of Barbed Wire* (based on a 1969 novel by Andrea Newman), set in a farmhouse holiday home in Yorkshire, Gavin (Tom Riley) the disturbed young English teacher boyfriend of sixth-former Prue (Imogen Poots) holds his arm over a candle flame with rising tension and pain. Eventually he explodes in rage leading to a violent assault on Prue, who is pregnant and about to be married to provoke her father's ongoing love for her.

The causative factor in what Freud called "actual pathology" lies simply in the fact that the drive excitation has not been adequately encountered and answered by the big Other. The transition from "a," the object of the drive, to A (*Autre*) through which the Other supplies an answer and sets the secondary process into action does not properly occur and therefore the initial arousal remains unprocessed leading to anxiety, panic, rage and various forms of acting-out.

The Kohut formulation is also helpful. He burrowed his atomic analogy of the self from Dr Douglas Levin – particularly relevant now in an *atomised* culture. Just as splitting the atom releases an enormous quantity of energy, so does the break-up of the "nuclear" self, leading 'to the appearance of an isolated "drive," e.g. the eruption of narcissistic rage',[56] the most violent of which occurs after an injury to a fragmenting or almost destroyed self.

Here, the shift is from A to "a," from the coherent other to the drive explosion. For Kohut, what he terms 'the life-sustaining matrix' is key. Without it, "a" manifests in 'oral, anal, and phallic sensations … of great intensity'.[57] Appearing to reverse Freud and Klein, Kohut suggests that drive manifestation, chronic narcissistic rage, is disintegration, fission product of the self and by extension, the social bond.

Freud's and early Lacan's preoccupation with the father, Winnicott's descriptions of the ordinarily devoted mother, Bowlby's attachment theory and Bion's "reverie," to name a few of the key figures which reoriented psychoanalysis in its heyday in the mid-twentieth century, have been overtaken by the libidinal politics – feminism and gay activism, on the Left and capitalist commercial neo-conservatism on the

Right that demanded women in the workplace, new types of families and everyone as consumers. Thus the one-time devotional givens of "mother" and "father" are replaced by significant carers, universal child-care – a whole generation reared in this glacial climate, at the behest of a global system. We get the mental health we deserve.

The "devotional desert" has created excessive demands that the contemporary psychoanalytic clinic seems quite unprepared for. Instead of *de*construction, what is required is *reconstruction* – the recovery of or even the installation of the primary relationship between the subject and the Other, helping, enabling the secondary elaboration that failed so badly in the first instance, thus helping to embed the original and still excessive bodily arousal – rage and anxiety – into signifiers and signifying chains. There are *two* parallel tasks here: the elaboration of narratives of the original relation between the subject and his others with particular emphasis on separation anxiety, the minimal initial inscriptions of the drives into the symbolic-imaginary universe; and, at the same time, the present day, here and now transferential repetitions that represent a chance to re-live the initial separations but this time with insight and better comprehension. Again we must follow the parallax between the Lacanian emphasis on language and the affective dimension-repetition so familiar to Kleinians and others.

Special mention should be made of the archaic superego.[58] If the superego is the heir to the Oedipus complex, the archaic superego becomes heir to the anti-Oedipus complex, i.e. the absence of the Other. The absent Other absents the self, nullifies the self, after torturing it with its worthlessness. The subject thus identifies with a nothing, an absence. Again, the paradox of modernity, the "freer" the external world, the more abject and servile the internal horizon. This is the *a*-logic of extremism, radicalisation and suicide, the archaic superego wipes out the subject by assuming *total* control.

Christopher Boone has a favourite dream.[59] 'Nearly everyone on the earth is dead, because they have caught a virus. It's like a computer virus … and I can go anywhere in the world and I know that no one is going to talk to me or touch me or ask me a question'. Christopher is apt to lie down and scream, or groan when confronted by the outside world, because his computer brain is easily overwhelmed. He prefers "white noise" to listening to his parents arguing, mainly about the difficulties posed by him and his rigidities. He has the safety of his Swiss army knife in his pocket with its saw blade ready when people come too close and his only "friend" is Toby, his pet rat. Although both his parents try to help him, Siobhan, his special needs assistant at school, is the most consistent. Christopher is unable to deal with emotions. He is told of his mother's death and he records his Scrabble score and writes what he has had for dinner. Yet, he hugs the dog that was killed, and is nearly killed himself while rescuing Toby who has run onto the track in front of a train. Humanity and empathy, as it were, hover in the margins of the story – always a link, a contact, a bond just missed.

Christopher is the child of the present future locked in with his prime numbers, his noughts and ones, a digital child, without the Other, without hope of the Other.

The reader is positioned counter-transferentally, moved to bring life to the lifeless, but believing all along that this is an impossibility.

Milan Kundera created a girl without a name, who nobody knows, who went out on a highway at night and sat down with her back to the oncoming cars. Several cars swerved and crashed. She got up, walked away and nobody ever found out who she was. Her longing for suicide 'was planted in the very soil of her being, and it grew slowly and unfolded like a black flower'. The longing for self-destruction slowly grew until one day she was no longer capable of resisting it. 'She longed to die like a beetle, crushed by a sudden fist'.[60] Kundera's subject has *no* name, *no* voice, *no* body and *no* image. She is not part of any circuit of human exchange or community. She is pure desertion. Her suicidal impulse, therefore, cannot be a "cry for help," for instance, because this implies a place, however tentative, within the symbolic. Her position is one of maximal distance. She is a negative object, a piece of anti-matter in a universe where everything is reversed. Black flowers unfold and death grows.

These two examples dramatically illustrate the absence of the Other. And in the absence of the Other, there is nothing – but *jouissance*. Lacan's *Seminar 20* is said to be 'host to an uncompromising staging of *jouissance* as the key concept of psychoanalysis, and it is in this sense that the phase described here as the "later Lacan" is inaugurated'. And however we describe the new subjectivity – post-human subjectivity – it involves an 'uncompromising staging of *jouissance*'.[61] The Kleinians would call this the death drive and Bion in particular would call it an anti-thinking, anti-linking process – thoughts without a thinker, thoughts without a subject. Whatever we call it, it is a quasi-totalising phenomenon; it is saturated, complete and closed off to the other; we have no point of entry, we are presented with a *fait accompli*. *Jouissance* is the answer, to the question posed by *Dasein*, by existence. Clinical work with "extreme" cases of, for instance, drug addiction and anorexia confirm our analytic pessimism.

Nevertheless, the Lacanian "answer" is similar to the Kleinian one in outline at least, forever hopeful and naively optimistic: language is a means of treating *jouissance*. The symptom will be 'drained of its *jouissance*' and this is procured through its articulation with the fantasy so that eventually the subject can make use of his sinthome to love, work, and desire. The neologism "sinthome" connotes saintly forbearance, finding a way of turning one's symptoms, through a long period of analysis (but not always) to one's own advantage, not unlike sublimation. The sinthome is a way, a unique way of holding all the registers of being together, not unlike the "container-contained" of Bion.

In this respect, consider Philippe Lacadée's case of a young woman, Virginie, in analysis with him for 8 years. She suffers from "ordinary psychosis," an un-triggered psychosis.[62] She is not deluded and can hold together her psychical reality, which she achieves by the ingenious and inventive use of a hairdryer in the first instance at least, which has a sinthomal effect.

On entering analysis she spoke of serious relational and social difficulties. Things were going badly with her partner and she was unable to complete her studies.

However, in the intervening years, she became a teacher of French literature and language, married, had a young son and is expecting another child, whose birth she fears will trigger more severe anxiety. Her excessive vulnerability was caused by her father's paranoid control of the family and his denial of external influences even to the extent of not turning on the gas central heating for fear that it will admit germs from the outside. In Lacanian terms, there has been no proper installation of the paternal signifier.

There were two key triggering events in puberty. First, the arrival of her period for which she was quite unprepared, thus plunged into the Real of her body and its products. Second, she arrived down early one morning to discover her little brother of seven months dead in his basket next to the wooden stove – his inanimate body was staring up at her. She describes this dead gaze as like an electric shock.

In the unmediated experience of her body with its issuing forth, Virginie heard a disembodied scream and her heart pounding like a piercing mechanical sound – my body is a machine – and a voice that was a clamour that seemed to be incessantly addressing her. These phenomena are *outside* of discourse, part of the Real. The hairdryer comes in, maybe three times a day, to calm her, pacifying extreme anxiety. The noise of its motor covered the noise of her "mechanically unregulated body," heating up her body, described by her as *frigorée* – a dead, cold thing – outside meaning. The signifier *frigorée* creates a symbolising entry point, a condensation back into meaning, back towards human discourse. She refers to herself as 'a cold, lonesome, glacial woman'. The use of her hairdryer on her abdomen has a subjectivising effect, heating her up, giving her the feeling of being a young woman. In other words, with this trick of the hairdryer, Lacadée suggests, she can now tolerate the Other, i.e. come and speak in the analysis, thus elaborating and stabilising her world. The hairdryer reminded her, aged four or five, of her mother when its hum calmed her. Its warmth reminded her of the hot water bottle her mother used to put on her abdomen when she had period pains.

She discovered the world of books which greatly angered her father, who, grabbing the books and throwing them on the refrigerator (*frigidaire*) shouted, 'I am life; I know what you need'. He was paranoid; his words carried only *his* meaning. As a child, she answered only to *his* meaning. She knew that she had to separate from his *mad* language, so she became a *teacher* of language and literature. There was a key moment in third grade when the teacher read the following poem entitled: *l'enfant qui battait la campagne*, by Claude Roy. (*Battre la campagne* means to search without knowing what one is looking for.) She said that she *knew* in that instant of the poem that she would be a teacher. She would have to face up to the problem of this word *battre* (to beat) – what her father did to her – and *battre la campagne* – go on her own search. At that point, she realised her alienation in her father's world and her need to separate from him.

An object-relations view would have emphasised the dominance of the maternal grandmother in the household, 'annihilating my mother', noting that the perverse couple was the strong grandmother and the weak father who became authoritarian and paranoid as a consequence. The grandmother said to Virginie that 'one has a bad start in life if one is a girl'. But this grandmother had lost a child, a four-year-old boy called Claude, just before the birth of Virginie's mother, whom she called Marie-Claude in his memory. Her mother was named after a dead child. Virginie's mother, who also has a child that died, might have resembled Andre Green's "dead mother."[63] Indeed, Virginie saw her mother as 'wasting away before my eyes so I decided to eat more and gain weight'. Thus, Virginie was faced with a paranoid father and a depressed mother. The resulting frigid and persecutory void could be filled with food and soothed and warmed by the hairdryer, the good object that warmed-up her dead mother and later warmed her, the frozen *girl* with a doubly 'bad start in life'. She surely had to beat (*battre*) her way out of that claustrophobic family by identifying with the *sanity* of her teacher and later with the *sanity* of her analyst.

Against the pathos of mental illness, Nietzsche longed for a new heroic age of cheerfulness (*Heiterkeit*), patience, unpretentiousness and contempt for the great vanities, *without God*. Sounding quasi-religious, he celebrates the free spirits, the new dawn – 'our heart overflows with gratitude, amazement, premonitions, expectation … our ships may venture out again … the sea, *our* sea lies open again … there has never yet been such an "open sea"'.[64] He is celebrating the "Good News," but *without God*! Nietzsche longed for the nobility of the aristocratic Greek heroes. We are closer to the "last man," the subject divided, flawed, neurotic, full of *ressentiment*, passively nihilistic, devitalised, a slave morality. 'Is there another becoming?' asks Deleuze on behalf of Nietzsche. 'Everything tempts us to think that perhaps there is. But, as Nietzsche often says, we would need another sensibility, another way of feeling'.[65]

Notes

1 Jameson, F., 1991: xi.
2 Badiou, A., 2006a: 442–5.
3 From a discussion between Baudrillard, J., and Noailles, E. 2005: 7, emphasis added.
4 Nietzsche, F., 1967: 161.
5 Ibid.: 162.
6 Ibid.: 160.
7 Nietzsche, F., 1982: 305.
8 Ibid.: 309.
9 Nietzsche, F., 1967: 218.
10 See www.theguardian.com/stage/2009/aug/30/simon-stephens-theatre-punk-rock.
11 See Kohon, G., 1999: 57.
12 Bruchner, P., 2006: 190.
13 Ian Traynor, in *The Guardian* (17 September 2012), suggests the West's efforts to use the United Nations to promote its values are failing, according to a detailed study. There has been a shift in the balance of power to favour China, India, Russia and other emerging states, hindering efforts by Europe and the US to entrench human rights. Western policies are in crisis and suffering serial defeats in what the study identifies as a protracted trend. The haemorrhaging of Western power, as reflected in longer-term voting patterns in key UN bodies, is mirrored by the increasing clout of China, Russia and the Islamic world, according to an audit of European influence at the UN by the European Council on Foreign Relations. 'The EU is suffering a slow-motion crisis at the UN', says the

report, noting that the West is now being regularly outwitted. The West is in disarray. The EU's rifts with the US on many human rights issues at the UN in the Bush era have weakened both. This is part of a broader decline over the past decade. China and Russia defend national sovereignty and non-intervention in sovereign countries *no matter how grievous the atrocities and human rights violations* blamed on national governments.
14 Baudrillard, J., 1995: 99, emphasis added.
15 Baudrillard, J., 1977: 72.
16 Durkheim, E., 1897.
17 Virilio, P., 2000b.
18 Virilio, P., 2001: 103, emphasis added.
19 Freud, S. 1927b: 154.
20 Paglia, C., *The Sunday Times Magazine*, 12 September 2010, p. 21.
21 Carr, N., 2010.
22 In discussion with Nicolas Carr on BBC Radio 4, *Today*, 2 September 2010.
23 Laplanche, J., and Pontalis, B., 1974: 168.
24 Freud, S., 1894: 46.
25 Freud, S., 1940 (1938): 202.
26 See Klein, M., 1946: 1–24; also Segal, H., 1986: 24–38.
27 Segal, H., 1986: 27.
28 Bion, W., 1957: 46.
29 Bion, W., 1958: 83.
30 Deleuze, G., 1962: 107.
31 Nietzsche, F., 1967: 57.
32 Ibid.: 58.
33 Deleuze, G., 1962: 116.
34 Nietzsche, F., 1883–1891: 153.
35 Nietzsche, F., 1967: 73–4.
36 Ibid.: 74.
37 MacIntyre, A., 1982: 25.
38 Nietzsche, F., 1967: 230.
39 Ibid.: 291.
40 Ibid.: 12.
41 See Baudrillard, J., 2004.
42 Verhaeghe, P., and Declercq, F., 2002: 59–83. See also www.psychoanalysis.ugent.be/pages/nl/artikels/artikels%20Paul%20Verhaeghe/English%20symptom.pdf p8.
43 This formed part of a presentation by Verhaeghe at the annual conference of the Association of Psychoanalysis and Psychotherapy in Ireland, November 2007.
44 Verhaeghe, P., and Declercq, F., 2002. See also www.psychoanalysis.ugent.be/pages/nl/artikels/artikels%20Paul%20Verhaeghe/English%20symptom.pdf p11.
45 This difference amounts to a parallax situation, outlined in Chapter 5.
46 Voruz, V., and Wolf, B., 2007: xiv, emphasis added.
47 Ibid.: xvii.
48 Lacan, J., 1964: 214.
49 Freud, S., 1909: 151–318.
50 Fonagy, P., 2001.
51 Rosenfeld, H., 1987.
52 Burgoyne, B., and Sullivan, M., 1997: 170–1.
53 Joseph, B., 1985: 448.
54 Fonagy, P., 1999: 217.
55 Self-harming does not just include drug overdoses or cutting, the most widely used methods, but can range from chronic nail picking and biting to scalding or swallowing dangerous objects.
56 Kohut, H., 1977: 122.
57 Ibid.: 123.
58 Weatherill, R., 1994: 140–51.

59 Haddon, M., 2004.
60 See Kundera, M., 1991: 280–300.
61 Voruz, V., and Wolf, B., 2007: x.
62 Brousse, M.-H., 2009.
63 Kohon, G., 1999.
64 Nietzsche, F., 1882: 279–80.
65 Deleuze, G., 1962: 60.

9

FROM THE GREATEST GOOD TO THE DUNCE'S CAP AND REVOLUTIONARY SUBJECTIVITY

A young French black woman speaking to camera looks forward to discovering sexual pleasure after female sexual mutilation (FSM) reconstruction surgery offered her by the French health service.[1] The French government has banned FSM, overriding ethnic sensibilities.

As Baudrillard says, 'something [sacred] has been given to women that must be exorcised by a deliberate campaign to dispossess her of her powers'. This dispossession involves 'the innumerable rites for the exorcism of female powers ... to cast out women's power of fertility, to encircle and circumscribe that power, and eventually simulate and appropriate it, is the purpose of the couvades, the artificial invaginations, excoriations and scarrings ...'.[2] Most FSMs are carried out by women – mothers or grandmothers – i.e. done by those who "know" the Other *jouissance* and its secret power over the Symbolic universe.

Men (and women) dream of *complete jouissance* beyond the interrupted and incomplete *phallic jouissance*, a pleasure which never comes up to expectations. But is this Other *jouissance*, as the cliché goes, just male fantasy? Does such a beyond exist? The answer is both: it *is* a male fantasy, but it is also real![3] It is the *jouissance* of the erotic, a *jouissance* also of hatred and violence as we have amply demonstrated, ultimately the operations of the death drive – a sacred unfathomable power.

With this "beyond" in mind opened up by psychoanalysis, what now can be made of the universal commandment to love thy neighbour? Lacan underlines this problematic specifically delineated by psychoanalysis. First, he acknowledges that Freud makes quite moving comments on what is truly worth loving. Lacan affirms that 'the Aristotelian conception of the good is alive in this man who is a true man; he [Freud] tells us the most sensitive and reasonable things about what are worth sharing the good that is our love with. But what escapes him', emphasises Lacan, 'is perhaps the fact precisely because we take *that* path we miss the opening on to *jouissance*'.[4]

For Lacan, there is no "objective good." Such a notion is for Lacan a betrayal of desire. 'What I call "giving ground relative to one's desire" is always accompanied in the destiny of the subject by some betrayal'. And, without this sense, Lacan imagines such a subject saying to himself, 'well if that's how things are, we should abandon our position; neither of us is worth that much, and especially me, so we should just return to the common path'.[5]

Freud himself also has some fun with the commandment to "love thy neighbour:" how can I spread such love around even to people that I do not know, and, especially as my neighbour *is my enemy*. He cites Plautus: *Homo homini lupus*. Therefore, Freud concludes, 'Civilisation has to use its utmost efforts in order to set limits to man's aggressive instincts'. As for the commandment to love one's neighbour, 'nothing else runs so strongly counter to the original nature of man',[6] that means, *nothing runs so counter to his jouissance*.

Freud underlines our dilemma: 'A good part of the struggles of mankind centre around the single task of finding an expedient accommodation – one that will bring happiness – between this claim of the individual and the cultural claims of the group'. Our fate depends upon 'whether such an accommodation can be reached by means of some particular form of civilisation or whether this conflict is irreconcilable'.[7] Freud refers to "accommodation" whereas Lacan speaks of "betrayal."

Ultimately, *jouissance* trumps everything. And Freud is *not* denying *jouissance*, quite the contrary; his sole preoccupation is whether or not civilisation can cope with it. He sees the greatest danger and problematic here. And finally, at the end of his civilisation book, he makes his difficult position clear. On the one hand, he says we understand the 'obligatory nature' of civilisation's repression of sexuality, etc. On the other, he follows the libertarian position, 'where [repressive] trends … which were considered insurmountable, have often been thrown aside and replaced by other [libertarian] trends'. But he honestly concludes, 'I have not the courage to rise up before my fellow-men as a prophet, and I bow to their reproach that I can offer them *no consolation*: for at bottom that is what they are all demanding – the wildest revolutionaries no less passionately than the most virtuous believers'.[8]

While Freud and Lacan have taught us to stare into the abyss, Lacan has a good laugh about St Martin sharing his cloak with a beggar who is naked, wondering what the beggar is *really* begging for – to be fucked or be killed?[9] Lacan's smirking is already beyond civilisation. Fuck or be fucked; this is the bottom line, the law of *jouissance* beyond the law. What chance has the common good? What chance has anyone? Once you have stripped away the civilising reserves of courtesy and modesty? Beyond betrayal, beyond accommodation, the abyss beckons. The cul-de-sac of *jouissance*, of Ballard's twitching frog's leg.

Historically, it has always been a question of accommodating excess pleasure – *jouissance* – to the final Good. There is no doubt; Freudo-Lacanianism confronts the moralists! Lacan declares: 'There is no Sovereign Good – the Sovereign Good, which is *das Ding*, which is the mother, is also the object of incest, and is a forbidden good. Such is the foundation of the moral law as turned on its head by Freud'.[10] To link *das Ding* with the Sovereign Good plays deliberately on "Good." The only "good" for Lacan, the anti-humanist, is the forbidden exciting extreme one. The "link" between pure desire and the Law is thus complete. *Pure* desire is desire uncontaminated by human concerns. Lacan is following the Copernican revolution into ethics and desire, bringing the emptiness, objectivity and the bleakness of the universe to bear on *acephalic* desire – desire for itself alone is ironically pure and even ethical!

Several centuries after Copernicus, we know that at the heart of our galaxy, the affectionately termed Milky Way, is a black hole.[11] We need an ethics that is commensurate; that has nothing whatsoever to do with human affection. This is 'the insane corner we have been backed into', as Lacan himself admits, by science. Beyond the good, detached from it, remote, universalising, operationalising, Kantian, Deleuzian: 'Never act in such a way that your action may not be programmed'.[12]

Das Ding is key, everything else is mirage. Explaining sublimation, Lacan refers to imaginary and cultural elaborations, 'useful objects', he calls them, where the 'collectivity … finds rather a space of relaxation where it may in a way delude itself on the subject of das Ding, colonise the field of das Ding with imaginary schemes'.[13] How we might take comfort from these "mirages." The tone is condescending, *we* know the truth! Deluding ourselves with cultural artefacts – mirages and relaxation! All rather pointless and tame when compared to *das Ding*. Lacan makes much of the potential for difference and variability of the object of the drive in sublimation and perversion; the drive is not an instinct with a "natural" more or less fixed object, as Freud indicated, 'the pulsating sexual excitements are extraordinarily plastic. They may appear in each other's places. One of them may accumulate the intensity of the others … like communicating channels that are filled with water'.[14] Thus the drives cannot be satisfied in moderation, Lacan wants to stress, no use for the "taming" word that Freud's translators use in relation to the drives.[15]

Das Ding never appears as such, but is always veiled in an object, like the lady in courtly love, or Lacan's friend's long string of match boxes raised to the level of an art form. Thus *all* objects are no more than the *re*-found object, *das Ding* that is always nearly found again, from which we must always keep our distance. Thus, for Lacan, *das Ding* will always be represented by emptiness, by the vase, by the vaulted cathedral or temple, which outlines the emptiness to be filled, or the cave paintings at Altamira, which begin the human mastery of emptiness. Or emptiness represented by the vacuole of the cell, or the the heart's ventricles. Or the emptiness of the most refined sublimation, masking maybe what hides in the core of the most refined signifiers of courtly love.

Lacan refers to what he has to acknowledge is a therapeutic form of ethics – 'a form of analysis that boasts of its highly scientific distinctiveness gives rise to normative notions that I characterise by evoking the curse Saint Matthew utters on those who make the bundles heavier when they are to be carried by others'.[16] Matthew was referring to the scribes and Pharisees (The Ego Psychologists?) who say much yet do nothing; they do everything for appearances, for the imaginary, and they like the uppermost rooms at feasts and the best seats in the synagogues, and they just want to be called Rabbi, Rabbi! That is, unlike the Lacanians, they are just normatively bourgeois.

Staying with Freud and Lacan, and abandoning any hope of an ethical notion of the Good that would take us away from the hell of ourselves, we must agree with Lacan when he says that 'the first thing that poor, defenceless man can do when he is tortured by need is to begin to hallucinate his satisfaction, and after that he can only monitor the situation'.[17] After the Lacanian revolution, man is reduced more or less to the status of a starving camp inmate hallucinating food in the desolate snow of the European winter. The worst winters may be coming. Lacan is inclined to sneer at the "defenceless man."

Does the circuit of exchange inevitably get tighter, smaller and smaller, closer and closer to *das Ding*? What will prevent this happening, save some centri*fugal* force, an ethical force no less? What should be made of the Lacanian utterance which on the one hand protects *jouissance* and on the other agrees with Freud that *jouissance* is malignant[18] yet kicks away all the supports that might contain it, limit it and protect us from what we might ultimately slavishly "want"?

The stranger is unworthy of my love not least because he has his own violent *jouissance*; he more often than not means me harm – 'he thinks nothing of jeering at me, insulting me, slandering me …'.[19] And when it comes to the scandalous *loving my enemies*, Freud cites Heine's joke about being of a peaceable disposition, when all Heine wants is a humble cottage surrounded by trees, good bed, good food, etc., and the joys of seeing his enemies hanging from the trees, after which point he will indeed forgive his enemies!

The best we can do in respect of love is loving someone in our own image, someone who is like us. Freud (and Lacan) invoke the Hobbesian and Darwinian universe plus *jouissance* – not only does the other potentially hate us and want to destroy us, but will also get his highest enjoyment from doing so, reaching its apogee with de Sade's absolute badness – *mauvaisité*.

'Lend me the part of your body that will give me a moment of satisfaction and, if you care to, use for your own pleasure that part of my body which appeals to you'.[20] No longer a whole person, but the break into "partial objects," recalling today's recreational sex, playfully negating the whole person – *go do it*. Beyond Freud, Lacan explores the abyss to the *n*th degree, in the name of his anti-ethical ethics – *should you care to use for your own pleasure*. The contemporary signifiers are there – "caring," "using" and "pleasuring."

Wanting the Good is for Lacan a 'benevolent fraud of wanting-to-do-the-best-for-the-subject'.[21] Lacan explains for the umpteenth time that the subject is *nothing* beyond the signifying chain, beyond this fault-line – the abyss, the void of structuralism. And he celebrates de Sade's evocation of anarchy, war, discord and magnitude in crimes – 'nature wants annihilation; it is beyond our capacity to achieve the scale of destruction it desires'.[22] But as man clings defensively to the signifier, Lacan asks: 'What relation can there be between man and the return of the sunrise, if it is not the case that as a speaking man he is sustained in a direct relation to the signifier?'[23] Lacan wills the subject's full exposure to the zero; the sunrise is a token!

Lacan deliberately confuses the Good with goods, as in consumer goods.[24] *Who's* good? *Whose* goods? When the good is invoked, who secretly pulls the strings? A Master of some sort. Lacan is almost Catharist in his suspicion of the world and its alleged corrupting effects, which are everywhere. Anyone who wants the good is suspicious, attempting to take away from and constrain the unique desire-good for the individual subject. Lacan's suspicion is total. For Lacanians there is no distinction between a manipulative "good" and the genuine wanting-to-do-the-best-for-the-subject. "Genuine"! what's that? More fraud? There is no such integral "genuine." What is the do-gooder's (normative) motive? Whom does he want to impress, dominate or control? Tear all this down. Purification by elimination and divestiture; no doubt the bundles are lighter.

Recall the group of Californian Catholic nuns in the 1970s who forsook their vows *en masse* after a workshop given by a radical sex therapist from Esalen. Let us say, it took years to bring them through their novitiate and formation and only a few days to destroy it all – through "liberation." Not unlike young Muslims in alien European cultures who have achieved well in school, then higher education, degrees and so on, yet, with just weeks of indoctrination can turn to violent jihadism. The collapse into *jouissance*. The simple point being an essentially asymmetrical one: it takes so long to build something and zero time to destroy it. And Lacanians, again and again, cannot resist celebrating the *jouissance* of destruction.

Lacan is on Antigone's side against Creon, on the side of "criminal desire" against the burdened ruler, and against her sister Ismene, who wants the general good to prevail. Be on the side of the radical sex therapist; on the side of the jihadist; on the side of the *jouisseur*; on the extreme side. This zero brings absolute clarity and purity. The purity of widespread destruction and the hope of creation *ex nihilo*. Antigone is a martyr: 'Only the martyrs know *neither pity nor fear*. Believe me', says Lacan, 'the day when the martyrs are victorious will be the day of universal conflagration'.[25] Lacan asserts conflagration as desire, versus conformity. Don't give ground. Don't give ground!

> My brother is my brother
> I will speak for me
> That's how it is because that's how it is.

The "it" (*ça*) here clearly refers to the inhuman or extra-human, the *un*-divided dimension. That's how *it* is: totality, finality. Lacan refers to the *absolute* individual as being in the domain of the sacred, where *the race is run*; it is over and done with. Death has already occurred before corporeal death. All is savagery, pitilessness, harshness. He refers to the "inanimate" condition as Antigone identifies herself with Niobe becoming petrified – a good example of Freud's description of the death drive as a return to the inorganic. Recall, Niobe's entire family were killed in revenge for an arrogant comment she made at a ceremony in honour of Leto, the daughter of the Titans, Coeus and Phoebe. In shock, she cradled the youngest daughter in her arms, and then fled to Mt Siplyon in Asia Minor. There she turned to stone.

Antigone allegedly becomes beautiful as she becomes more thin and emaciated, once she enters the zone 'between two deaths' – her symbolic "death" for the community, 'walled up alive', and her early biological death. Then, there was her realisation, her lament about never knowing the conjugal bed, never having children. Antigone's beauty is an enigma in itself to do with the "purity" of and the uncompromising nature of her desire, her 'ethics of the Real', which as Zupančič says, has nothing whatsoever to do with the Law or the transgression of the Law. For instance, 'Antigone is not an activist, fighting for "human rights" that are being trampled down by a tyrannical state'.[26] Antigone refused to '"live in peace," sheltered from *jouissance*, sheltered from the drive that makes us do things which go against our well-being'.[27]

Sophocles's Chorus of Theban elders say: 'Do you not leave for the enclave of the dead with glory and praise, neither withered with illness nor cut down by the sword? Alone of mortals you go down to Hades a law to yourself and alive'. In Seamus Heaney's translation this becomes: 'Steadfast Antigone./Never before did Death/Open his stone door/To one so radiant./You would not live a lie./ Vindicated, lauded,/Age and disease outwitted,/You go with head held high'. The original rhetorical question becomes a trumpet blast. 'A law to yourself', becomes, 'you would not live a lie'.[28] Heaney is with Lacan here.

Contrast this with Pol Guillard's assertion that Antigone's gesture is entirely devoid of human value: 'Antigone thus dies for nothing, and the whole play expresses the failure of human effort in general'.[29]

Even the name, Antigone, Graves suggests, means 'opposed to motherhood', or 'in place of a mother'.[30] Or, as Judith Butler suggests, it may also mean '*against men*' since men were dominant in the ancient Greek family structure, and Antigone clearly defied masculine authority, or was 'anti-generative', from the root *gonē*, 'that which generates', related to *gonos*, seed or semen.[31] Antigone is not a radical, but more of an aristocrat fighting the new order. Her sacred duty is to be true to "one's own" *philoi*, not fellow citizens but family and allies. Yet she turns against her family, her sister, Ismene. She is loyal only to *one* member, Polyneices, with a fixation that is incestuous.

Antigone is not political, not an activist or a dissident. She is not acting in any way for the human Good. Recall Thomas More, recall the dissidents of more recent times, Sakharov, Solzhenitsyn, Mendela, the Tiananmen Square dissidents, fighters for freedom in the Middle East and Iran. Antigone is not here. The test for our discussion here is whether or not the unique dissident stand, the heroic singular desire will ultimately, maybe indirectly, contribute to the *sovereign good*! Not so with Antigone. However, in each case dissidence (*dissidēre*, to sit apart) can be read initially as an "evil" disruptive and self-destructive act of defiance *against* the community of which he/she is a part, in the name of a greater good. In Roosevelt's words, they may start out as sons of bitches but ultimately they are *our* sons of bitches.

Lacan is contradictory. On the one hand he says the sovereign good is a 'question that is closed' for the analysis, and then in the next paragraph, he suggests that in the process of an analysis, the subject will encounter 'much that is good for him … if at every moment he eliminates from his wishes the false goods, if he exhausts not only the vanity of his demands, given that they are all no more than regressive demands, but also the vanity of his gifts'.[32] Clearly, Lacan is hinting here at some discriminatory notion of the Good.

The question of the sovereign good cannot be avoided. However, as regards psychoanalytic practice as an *individualist* preoccupation, it is left to one side. No one can tell the other what to do. The analyst must not propose themselves as some imaginary good person. This remains barred. Nevertheless, with the Good in the background, everything changes; a tension is introduced. Without this tension caused by the Good, *my* desiring for the sake of desiring – wherever it might lead, whoever might be hurt, whomsoever's life might be damaged by the ethical purity and non-compromise of my desire, matters little. *My* desire alone trumps everything; do not give ground (*ne pas céder*).[33] Anything less is a betrayal of unknown desire, a self-betrayal, or a giving in to the other, or to some supposed "good," less than your categorical duty, no matter how boring, how corrosive, how pathetic, your desire may turn out to be! Or like Antigone, you may feel a subversive, anarchic duty to go to the end without compromise, be it diabolical evil or the highest good. It may be the latter – the highest good – but there is no gainsaying that.

This Kantian shaking off the human with all of its compromises to prevent a greater evil is reflected in the chorus at the beginning of Anouilh's *Antigone*.

> The machine is in perfect order; it has been oiled ever since time began, and it runs without friction. Death, treason and sorrow are on the march …[34]

It is the machinic that attracts Lacan to Kant and Sade, whereby we pass through the Symbolic to the Real, from morality to ethics, from desire to the drive – the *death* drive. So instead of colonising the Real with the Symbolic (an allegedly cowardly strategy into which we are all forced during Oedipus), why not anti-Oedipally plunge straight into the Real of creativity and destruction *ex nihilo*. A clean break with the Symbolic!

Once again, the break with the Symbolic is now mandatory. Consider, for example, the "criminal duties" of Martin Amis's psychopathic anti-hero in his disappointing novel *Lionel Asbo*.[35] Lionel, who changed his name to identify himself with England's notorious Anti-Social Behaviour Order – *wants* to be anti-social – law, criminality and prison make up his "vocational trinity." Lionel with Joe and Jeff his vicious pit bulls, has made stupidity into an art form, proud to be an anti-father, a man with a genius for "disseminating tension." He also does not give ground! 'Each thing is hostile/To every other thing: at every point/Hot fought cold, moist dry, soft hard, and the weightless resisted weight'. In the background, nephew Desmond Pepperdine, a mixed-race 15-year-old, writes to an agony aunt about his incestuous relationship with his Nan, Grace. Pervert and psychopath: *The State of England* – the subtitle of the book.

Include too, Anders Behring Breivik as "not giving ground," when he perpetrated the 2011 Norway attacks with a sequential bombing and mass shooting on 22 July 2011. First, he bombed government buildings in Oslo, killing eight, then went on to carry out a mass shooting at a summer camp of young Labour supporters on the island of Utøya, killing 69 people, mostly teenagers. He was quite logically, pitilessly, coldly following his militant ideology contained in a collection of texts entitled *2083: A European Declaration of Independence*.

We must stop there because so-called ethical act(s) in the line of pure desire can only come from the Left, *not* from the Right. So Breivik, Asbo, and so on are ruled out, as they come from the neo-Fascist Right. Only Leftist ethical acts (in spite of their often fascistic colouring and antecedents) are counted in, prototypically the French Revolution and the Bolshevik Revolution. According to Žižek, the World Trade Center (WTC) atrocity, for intance, is ruled out as an ethical act as it has not changed the politico-historical coordinates. It is too early to tell. It is entirely possible that the WTC attacks stand for a reversal, the beginning of the end of human rights as we know them in the West. Time will tell.

Mao

Pure desire always turns around the old call like, *épater le bourgeois*.[36] Hit the middle classes for their provincialism, their small "c" conservatism, their family values, their attachment to place, nationality, identity, their social bond, their humanism or their Christianity, their alleged hold on political power, their money, their inauthenticity, and so on. Stun the silent majority into utter silence. This is the heartless heart of the anti-Oedipal ethical call. The family with its ties to the rural, custom, tradition and so on, is regarded as ignorant and backward, trapping women and children in slavish silence. The family is where the pathology lies. It needs to be broken open with its content scattered. Worldwide the family has been regarded as the nucleus of life and community, but where there is *no* community and *no* life, the family is deemed *the* source of disease. From domestic violence to child sexual abuse, the family is where it happens. As the door (to the family home) slams shut, it is alleged that the screaming within begins.

This is in effect an elitist call, whereby a tiny group of highly committed influential radicals – urbane, cosmopolitan, metrosexual, transnational – have taken it upon themselves, i.e. undemocratically, to deconstruct all constructs from inside government, top-down. For the Left this is an ethical call. But the neo-conservative Right with its global economics shares in the hollowing-out of the old institutions with the shake out of middle management and public service jobs, formerly safe jobs become unsafe and disappear, as nations become internationalised, work areas are automated, and so on. No guarantee of an identity, a relationship, a family, a job. All liberation calls for celebration.

As exemplary emancipatory violence goes, we turn to the Chinese Cultural Revolution, contemporaneous with *Anti-Oedipus*, for which the historic details of the suffering inflicted are available. Later we will turn to Alain Badiou for his analysis of these events. For more than four decades, Badiou has remained an avowed Maoist.

In their book on the Chinese Cultural Revolution,[37] the sinologists Roderick MacFarquhar and Michael Schoenhals assert that in rural China alone some 36 million people were persecuted, of whom between 750,000 and 1.5 million were killed, with roughly the same number permanently injured. This orchestrated social upheaval lasted from 1966 to 1976 and left deep scars upon Chinese society, following on from the catastrophic Great Leap Forward, in which more than 20 million people died, twice as many as in WW1.

In the early 1960s, Mao's influence was declining; the old revolutionary spirit was waning. Lin Biao, the head of the People's Liberation Army (PLA), was perhaps Mao's strongest ally. Lin organised hundreds of Mao's quotes into the *Little Red Book*, required reading for every Chinese soldier. Mao became a prophetic figure for many Chinese, because by 1965, people were openly criticising the increasingly bureaucratic Communist leadership. By May 1966, radicals in the leadership, such as Jiang Qing, distributed armbands to squads of students and declared them to be Red Guards – the front line of the new revolutionary upheaval and radicalisation. The descent into chaos followed. Anyone could become a target of abuse and be denounced as a reactionary. In the greatest anti-Oedipal gift to the youth of the day, the Cultural Revolution provided a massive release from all repressions, frustrations and feelings of powerlessness. The Red Guards could act out revenge on those deemed "class enemies," settling old scores. They not only inflicted violence upon their own communities but also each other.

In the summer of 1966, 34,000 homes were raided, 1,700 people in Beijing alone were beaten to death, some by having boiling water poured over them, and some were forced to swallow nails. Eighty-five thousand were exiled to the countryside, where they were forced to work a programme called "reform through labour camps." Teachers were forced to confess publicly their "problems." Twenty-three faculty members at Beijing University were persecuted to death.[38]

The Red Guards were used by Mao as proxy bandits, stealing gold, silver, jewellery, hard currency, antiques and paintings – for the state coffers. They also burnt books, broke up phonograph records, musical instruments, and "confiscated" valuables, and wrecked anything "cultural." Some of the few top leaders were to have the pick of the confiscated booty. Apparently, Mme Mao selected an 18-carat gold French pendant watch, studded with pearls and diamonds. In that summer, Red Guards ravaged every city and town. Some people pre-empted the raiders, burning their own books and destroying their own art objects before any raid could happen.

The chaos and violence increased in the autumn and winter of 1966, as schools and universities closed so that students could dedicate themselves to "revolutionary struggle." Many of China's temples, valuable works of art, and buildings were raided.

They also attacked authority figures in society, their teachers, school administrators, Communist Party members, neighbours, and even their friends, relatives and parents.

The desecration of the home of Confucius in Shandong, a rich museum of donated art objects, where emperors and artists had come to pay homage, was ordered from Mao's office. According to Chang and Halliday, Mao hated Confucius, because Confucianism enjoined the ruler to care for his subjects. But true to the anti-humanist moment, Mao apparently declared, 'Confucius is humanism … that is to say, People-centred-ism'.[39]

By September, with the whole country terrorised, Mao thought it safe to go against his party officials. Lin Biao instructed the Red Guards to go in search of "capitalist-roaders" without mercy. New groups of Red Guards were formed to move against Mao's enemies indiscriminately, Party officials, even the most loyal. On 1 January 1967, newspapers urged the overthrow of the entire class of decision makers. The Red Guards were told to treat the Cultural Revolution as a class struggle, in which 'everything which does not fit the socialist system and proletarian dictatorship should be attacked'.[40] In that month, Mao called on the Rebels to "seize power" from their Party bosses. Stalin preferred hustling his victims quickly out of sight, taken off by the KGB to prison, gulag or death; Mao preferred to carry out violence or humiliation *in public*. Filming torture became popular during the Cultural Revolution, especially for Mao's personal enemies, not for proof or record-keeping, but more for his own satisfaction. Many officials were exiled to "May 7 Cadre Schools" where they also joined artists, writers, scholars, actors and journalists. According to Sing-Nan Fen, the hope was that through such "training," civil servants would become one with the masses. Emphasis on the "mass line" has been abandoned since Mao's death, but as Sing-Nan Fen observes, 'Insofar as it represents the purists' view of communism, it is worthy of our attention, *for the purists are surely waiting in the wings for their moment to return in history*'.[41]

Overall, the Red Guards and other groups of workers and peasants terrorised millions of Chinese during the 1966–8 period. Intellectuals were beaten, committed suicide, or died of their injuries or privation. Thousands were imprisoned, and millions sent to work in the countryside for "re-education" labouring among the peasants. The breakdown of order reached its peak in the summer of 1967. Intense violence in Beijing and Guangzhou, fighting between local militant groups and the PLA in Wuhan, led to the deaths of more than a thousand protestors. Radicals even took control of the Foreign Affairs Ministry in August 1967 and began to appoint their own radical diplomats to Chinese embassies around the world.

In fear of real anarchy across the country, troops were brought in to restore order that summer. The Cultural Revolution continued with the "Campaign to Purify Class Ranks," which lasted from late 1967 until 1969, attempting to rid the Party of those with "bad" class backgrounds, which included those radicals who had tried to disguise their bourgeois pasts by appearing militantly Red. In 1969, Lin Biao was named Mao's successor at the National Party Congress. However, in 1970 Mao blocked Lin Biao's accession to the post, in spite of his gain in popularity leading the PLA to victory during a Russian incursion in the North. Then, in late 1971, the CCP announced that Lin had attempted to assassinate Mao. In September, a plane carrying Lin and his family mysteriously crashed killing all on board. After being a hero for almost a decade, the Party now cast Lin Biao as a "renegade and traitor," an enemy of the people.

With the education system broken by the violence, it was not until 1973 that examinations for entrance into universities were reinstated. In effect, 16 million urban Chinese youth had been sent to work in the countryside during the Cultural Revolution, ostensibly to develop solidarity with the peasants, but also to ease the overcrowding of Chinese cities. A generation had forgone their education. President Richard Nixon's 1972 visit to China enabled the signing of trade deals with Western nations. Lest he be seen as pro-Western, Mao simultaneously launched the "Anti-Lin Biao Anti-Confucius" campaign, urging Chinese to stay true to Marxist values. However the Cultural Revolution was at an end by 1974; China's two most powerful leaders, Zhou Enlai and Mao, were seriously ill and both were to die within two years. Hua Guofeng, the CCP's second-in-command, seized power and arrested the so-called "Gang of Four" leaders of the Revolution, scapegoating them by accusing them of various crimes and causing all the problems of the Revolution. Their arrest on 6 October 1976 is generally considered to mark the end of this active revolutionary phase.

This Revolution in particular forms the backdrop to our own Western cultural revolution of the 1960s and 1970s, which in turn informs the arguments being developed, discussed and debated in this book. It is a case illustration of an influential revolution broadly in our time, in living memory. What happened can be examined in detail. Radical analysts, social activists, militants and so on, were and continue to be inspired by Maoism, most notably in France.[42] How much are "cultural Marxists," as conservative commentators dub them, still in thrall to Maoist thinking and praxis? With the rising influence of its structural antithesis, a ruthless State capitalist China around the world, the so-called "cult of Mao,"[43] may be no more than kitsch nostalgia for the benevolent and all-powerful leader. However, unlike Hitler, Mao has never been held to account for the 70 million dead. There has been no redemption.

Badiou

Badiou remains inspired by Maoism four decades on. 'The Maoist current', he argues, is 'the only true political creation of the sixties and seventies'. He refers to the Chinese revolutionaries' untiring inventiveness 'to change subjectivity, to live otherwise, to think otherwise ... to change the human being in what is most profound ... we must be both the arrow and the bull's eye, because the old world view is still present within us'.[44] Badiou points out that the term "cultural" is strongly ideological, aiming 'to touch people in their very souls'.[45] People must 'put daring above everything else', cast off 'mental burdens', create mass democracy against party authority. Badiou observes that within the Maoist movement there was a huge popular ferment – mass political mobilisation and turmoil, confrontation, discussion, journals, tracts, banners, murals, political declarations and so on.

Rather late in the day, maybe realising the true extent of the excesses of the Red Guards, Badiou concludes that political organisation must be "transgenerational," it is a bad idea to organise the political separation of youth. However, *every* revolution plays anti-Oedipal youth against age to good violent effect. He adds there never has been 'a global political space' for this kind of youthful political revolution. Badiou refers to "well-known revolutionary practices," "exorcisms," where the hated bureaucrat 'wears a dunce's cap and a sign describing his crimes; he must lower his head, and receive some kicks, or worse'.[46] He notes that the peasants who for so long counted for nothing at last get to do the humiliating.

Likewise, every Revolution has its anti-intellectualism. Badiou recalls Lavoisier's execution during the French Revolution, with his public accuser declaring, 'The Republic has no need for scientists'.[47] Indeed, a quip circulated after Mao's death that the Cultural Revolution's goal was to do away with culture *per se*! Badiou wants us to respect this "creative absolutism" – it was better to be "Red" than be an "expert."

The rebellion and anarchic factionalism was only seriously challenged when, early in 1968, thousands of unarmed workers were called upon to occupy the University of Beijing and confront the students head on. Some workers were killed, but Mao stood with the best known Red Guards, expressing disappointment only with their factionalism. The "Leftists" were thus subdued, without recourse to a military crackdown.

Badiou praises Mao's development of mass political mobilisation as a model of 'communist political subjectivity' which came *between* the Party's rule congealing into bureaucratic formalism on the one hand, versus terroristic purging on the other. In other words, the "class struggle" continues even *within* the proletarian state, where, 'under socialism, the bourgeoisie reconstitutes itself and organises itself *within the Communist Party itself*'.[48] However, what impressed militant minds across the world, for a time at least, was nothing short of the end of the party-state itself. However, Badiou concedes this could not be allowed as there would have to be a call to order at some point involving 'extraordinary brutality'.

Quite clearly, the so-called ethical Real of such continuous revolutionary *action* cannot be subsumed under the 'strict logic of class representation' (Symbolic). It is and always remains a real revolutionary potential. The continuous revolutionary "counter-model" against the party-state has no possibility of development beyond a certain point and even Mao conceded that Zhou Enlai as the head of state would remain to guarantee the minimal functionality of the State apparatus.

Mao liberated simultaneously the Chinese peasant from the brutal Japanese invasion, from colonialism of Western powers and pre-capitalist feudalism in the countryside. Declaring that politics must be 'a procedure of truth', Mao for Badiou becomes a 'representation of representation', a guarantee, a genius; Mao is 'a revenge of singularity upon representation'.[49] Mao simultaneously identifies the bourgeois tendency *within* the Communist Party and also declares *it is right to revolt.* He is the rebel in power; he is the party-state and its overcoming.

French Maoism lasted in effect for only six years (1968–74). Revelations about the violent excesses of the Cultural Revolution, the mysterious plane crash involving the popular Lin Biao, the unlikelihood of the staunchly pro-Soviet French Communist Party ever transferring its allegiance to Mao, the gulag exposé, otherwise known as the "Solzhenitsyn effect," spurred most former adherents to become *ex*-Maoists, turning towards human rights advocacy instead. Not so Badiou, who, early on, broke with the Maoist *Gauche prolétarienne*, when, as he saw it, they turned towards "libidinal politics," away from serious revolutionary aspirations.

Influenced by Sartre's phenomenological subjectivity against the objectivist dogmatism of Stalinism, Badiou was also a *normalien* (a graduate of the elite ENS – *École normale supérieur*), where he came under the influence of Althusser, who taught that Marxism embodied an unassailable theoretical rigour and doctrinal purity, proof against any "deviationism." However, the Althusserian Marxist-structuralist notion of "history-without-a-subject" was a theory of anti-humanism and anti-subjectivity, at odds with Sartrean committed political subjectivity on the one hand and Maoism's energetic renewal of revolutionary political subjectivity on the other.

However, a generally sympathic commentator such as Wolin calls attention to what Badiou himself refers to "terroristic nihilism" driven on by the sheer destructive force of "subjectivisation." As Nietzsche 'philosophized with a *hammer*', so Badiou believed that even if something was not dilapidated and falling, one should give it more than a push until it collapsed in rubble.

As if to answer Lacan's question, *is there a discourse that is not a semblance?*[50] Badiou asserts 'the passion for the Real', real identity, unmasking copies, semblances, fakes, and so on, in short, 'a passion for the authentic … that belongs to Heidegger as well as Sartre. *This passion can only be fulfilled as destruction*'.[51] Thus the *latent* content of the revolutionary dream is laid bare.[52]

From Mao to Pol Pot and the Khmer Rouge, Badiou's support is denounced variously as "bone-chilling," "atrocious," and so on. Here, Badiou's final push, his unique passion for destruction has reached year zero. Almost contemporaneous with Mao, from 1975 to 1979, the Khmer Rouge waged a campaign of genocide on Cambodia's population.[53] The Khmer Rouge believed that cities were a capitalist tool, and could not be a part of a true Communist regime. The capital, Phnom Penh, was emptied of its 2.5 million inhabitants, schools and factories were closed, intellectuals were singled out and killed, thousands of teachers were executed. Even Phnom Penh's hospitals were emptied of their patients.

Commenting upon the mass immiseration of these revolutionary "events" to which we should be bound by "fidelity," Badiou seems resigned and indifferent: 'What about the violence, often so extreme? The hundreds of thousands [millions] of dead?' He claims *á la* Nietzsche that violence always has 'marked the History of every somewhat expansive attempt to practice a free politics'. He continues, 'The theme of total emancipation, practised in the present, in the enthusiasm of the absolute present, is always situated beyond good and evil'. His conclusion: 'Extreme violence is therefore the correlate of extreme enthusiasm, because it is in effect a question of the transvaluation of all values .... *Morality is a residue of the old world.*[54]

Saint Paul

Morality belongs to the Symbolic and the sovereign good; the 'beyond good and evil' belongs to the so-called 'ethics of the Real', another register, a pitiless revolutionary register of mass disorder and sacred violence. Badiou invokes St Paul.[55] For the radical Left over the past two decades, Pauline Christianity has torn through Roman and Jewish law to proclaim a universal gospel of justice and redemption based on interior faith. Paul has been co-opted for the militant wing of Christianity (Paul is placed above Christ), to blast a way through the ontological wall of Being and representation, to smash totalities. *We wrestle not against flesh and blood, but against principalities and powers, against the rulers of darkness of this world in high places. Wherefore take unto you the whole armour of God ...* (Ephesians 6:12, 13).[56]

There is more to Paul than the well known dialectic Law/Sin; Sin/transgression, and so on.

> *But except by the law I should never have become acquainted with sin. For example, I should never have known what it was to covet, if the law had not said 'Thou shalt not covet'. Through that commandment sin found its opportunity, and produced in me all kinds of wrong desires.*[57]

Paul is not blaming the law as such (as Badiou *et al.* appear to do) but praising the law: *the law is in itself holy, and the commandment is holy and just and good ... We know that the law is spiritual; but I am not: I am unspiritual, the purchased slave of sin.* (Romans 7:12–14).

Translated into Lacanian terms, the law invokes or provokes *das Ding*, or the death drive, leading to the 'night of the world' and total collapse of the Symbolic: 'the commandment that was supposed to lead to life turned out to lead to death, for the Thing found a way and thanks to the commandment seduced me; through it I came to desire death'.[58] For Lacan, the death *drive* will bring us beyond this morbid repetitive cycle Law–Sin. Total symbolic collapse will purge, will clear a space or wipe the slate for creation *ex nihilo*. *Moreover the law entered, that the offence might abound. But where sin abounded, grace did much more abound* (Romans 5:20).

The image is of tanks crushing whole villages, creating a smooth unstriated space for the new beginning. 'Love without cruelty is powerless', says Žižek paraphrasing Kant and Robespierre.[59] 'Divine violence (Benjamin) is the subject's work of love'.[60] The distinction is made between mythic violence, i.e. the violence of the State imposing the rule of law – "bad" violence – on the one hand, and divine violence on the other, which is purely expiatory "good" violence – putting right a wrong, from mob lynchings to revolutionary terror. It appears from nowhere, beyond the Law, and has no immediate justification. There is only the Event and those who are and remain faithful to it. A new "political theology," orthodox Marxism recharged with the biblical language of redemption, emerges, inspired allegedly by Paul's declaration that *sin shall not have dominion over you: for ye are not under the law, but under grace* (Romans 6:14), heralding a continuous new world ordering. The greatest paradox: grace (kindness, pardon, mercy) becomes synonymous with the total creative destruction of the death drive. Agape becomes: *Love is a war machine*.[61] Saint Paul appears here to underwrite cycles of purifying revolutionary barbarism. Words like "grace" and "love" become monstrous words of liberation transcending any mediocre congealing 'residue of the old world' – Law, State, Party – blasting a way through for grace and love.

Twentieth century French philosophy's radical wing crashes into the New Testament. Just as twentieth century philosophy crashed into the Chinese peasantry with untold and untellable consequences for the masses of ordinary people – left imperialism's tiny elites claiming "love" for their new colonial peoples bringing on, exacerbating their collective immiseration. After all, did the peasants demand it – their "liberation," their "re-education"? Did they demand wholesale destruction of the old, of tradition? Did they say, oh yes! This is "creation *ex nihilo*"? Now, thank God, we will be beyond good and evil! Did we ask for such violent unmasking and real-making? When did we make this request? Did we ask for this "hammering" and this violent subjectivisation? This night of the world? Did we ask for these (mostly young) men/thugs to destroy our communities – kill, rape and humiliate the old and kill each other? Did we want this purification, this cleansing?

On 19 March 1988, corporals David Robert Howes and Derek Tony Wood, two British Army soldiers, were shot by the Provisional Irish Republican Army, after they drove into the funeral crowd of an IRA volunteer. Three days earlier, former loyalist gunman Michael Stone had attacked an IRA funeral, killing three people. Believing it to be another loyalist attack, dozens of mourners attacked the soldiers' car. During this, Corporal Wood drew his service pistol and fired a shot in the air. The soldiers were then dragged from their vehicle, beaten, driven to nearby waste ground, stripped and shot dead, in full glare of the TV cameras. Amnesty International accused the IRA of a 'gross breach of minimum humanitarian standards'.[62]

Recall the violent scene in *Germinal* when the starving crowd pursue the shopkeeper, Maigrat, who had charged them and their daughters in "sexual favours" when their money had run out. He falls from the roof onto which he has retreated in terror of the mob, and his head is smashed as he hits a stone post on the road in his fall, with his wife looking down from the window. For a moment they were horror struck, then yelling began, and it was the women, screaming into his face, stuffing earth into his mouth, then came the shout – doctor him like a tomcat! They pull off his trousers, part his legs and with great difficulty 'pull away the lump of hairy bleeding flesh'. They bared their teeth, and spat on it. 'Never again shall we have to go through that, offering our backsides for a loaf of bread'. They put his severed genitals on a stick and raised it high as they walked down the street – 'the evil beast crushed at last and stuck on a pole'.[63]

In late March 2004, four civilian contractors working for Blackwater Security Consulting, based in Moyock, North Carolina, hired by the Pentagon to provide security for convoys that delivered food in the Falluja area of Iraq, were brutally killed. Masked men attacked the two cars in which the four were travelling with grenades and heavy gunfire as the vehicles entered the city from a nearby US army base. A mob then descended on the wreckage. One of the bodies was tied to a car with cord and dragged through the streets. Other bodies were hacked with poles and farm tools. At least two were hanged from a bridge. Television film of the attack showed a large crowd stoning the burnt-out cars and celebrating the killings. Footage showed an American passport and a US Department of Defense identification card lying beside the remains.

Žižek makes his own contribution. After reading reports about torture in Latin American authoritarian regimes he wonders what he might do with the doctors who aid the torturers by monitoring precisely how much their victims could endure to the maximum of unbearable pain. '[I]f I were to encounter such a person', he concludes (many of us would), 'knowing that there is little chance of bringing him to legal justice, and being given the opportunity to murder him discreetly, I would simply do it, with a minimum of remorse about taking justice in my own hands'.[64]

Divine violence belongs to the order of a Badiouian Event, a happening that may or may not retrospectively garner significance politically. According to Badiou's ontological theory, Being as such is purely mathematical. Being is multiple, but not yet a multiple of ones, as "ones" belong to counting and the structured Symbolic register. The multiple can only be unrecognised – the formless chaos of the Real, i.e. *nothing*. Then, in wholly unpredictable and contingent ways, an Event can emerge *ex nihilo*, that is revelatory. It is an epiphany which reveals the hidden truth of the so-called "official" state of things. Classically, the French Revolution was the Event that revealed the "lie" of the *ancien régime*, linked across time through later revolutionary events as far as May 1968. The Event is not an objective fact, but a *subjective* phenomenon, named by the instigators and followers themselves, *après coup*. The subject is defined/created by his or her fidelity to the Event and its traces in their subsequent lives. If I fall in love, the link to my beloved will be an Event, named as such by us alone, emerging from the vast multiple of possibilities of love, to which we might remain faithful for the rest of our lives. In this sense miracles do happen. Unlike Lacan, where the subject is divided, typically an hysteric, for Badiou the subject is a master who names and remains faithful to the event.

Christian *agape* is the event linked to a militant (and universalised) mode of affirmation of the outcast, *qua* excluded other. Clearly, not the charitable disposition of bourgeois or Christian philanthropy, but quite the opposite, a shocking exposure through love revealing the ills we allegedly suffer by being inserted into the prevailing socio-economic order, with its violently disavowed underbelly. Subjective conversion is always possible, via Christianity. Saint Paul is exemplary, as long as we understand his conversion (subjectivisation) via Badiou as something of a once off 'thunderbolt, a caesura, and not a dialectical reversal'.[65] And for those who might follow him, Badiou claims that, 'Through their commensurability with a truth, anonymous individuals are always transformed into vectors of humanity as a whole'.[66]

However, *agape* remains Franciscan, extreme, austere, eposodic, with no allowance made for the ordinary Christian masses, whose rights will be trampled, and worse, whose lives will be lost. They are the millions of ordinarily devoted people who lead unselfish lives, caring for their families, for their children, for their communities. They are the unseen cement of civil society, whose work and dedication enables everything to continue to function normally and reliably. The shops get produce, the trains and buses run on time, the streets get cleaned, the hospitals care for the sick, buildings get built, roads are repaired, and so on. Without this centre of gravity, civil society would cease to exist. Millions of small silent unknown creative acts maintain life, living and well-being. Without this love civilisation would be over in an instant.

Badiou and Žižek assert the radicality and superiority of the Event of Pauline Christianity-cum-Communism, over other religions and none, including ordinary Christianity. This superiority is not elitism, quite the reverse – it asserts the truth about the illusory nature of the contemporary normalcy, on the one hand, and the truth about elitism of *any* group, on the other. Therein lies its universality, its intense/impossible ethical reach and its *post*-modernity. Normalcy is specific; the Law is specific to a particular culture and time; elitism is specific to a particular privileged group or culture. Love, *agape*, is universal, transcending, undercutting, erupting within all boundaries and classes. However, the "Event" is named by a master! The radicals by choosing to act, when they do, posit *themselves* as a new elite, masters of a new revolutionary order – the Party – or maybe becoming in Badiou's terms "Event reactionaries;" or worse, becoming old Masters (like Creon or Stalin!) knowing that they are castrated but prevailing (violently) all the same, unwilling to give up power.

After the catastrophic failures of Stalinism, Maoism, the Khmer Rouge, what is Left?[67] Are not the countless examples of divine violence, expiatory justice and the like, just another return to escalating sacred violence, "love" plus mimetic cruelty now potentially on a planetary scale *á la* Girard? Girard warned, 'the West is going to exhaust itself in its fight against Islamic terrorism … Violence can no longer be checked. From this point of view we can say the apocalypse has already begun'.[68] Our weakened Europe, he suggests, is 'like a medieval village facing the vikings'.[69]

Houellebecq describes himself as *depressionist* because he believes 'our societies have come to a terminal stage where *they refuse to recognise their malaise*'?[70] The silent Christian masses watch the news; live their lives keeping their heads down, not wanting to know but secretly fearing the worst which is quite beyond their control. But the "triumph" of libidinal anti-Oedipal politics is key to this failed recognition. The sixty-eighters are dying off, leaving their children and grandchildren who have known little other than the libidinisation of life, the call to enjoyment, born of the calamitous retreat from the Other. They have been told they are free to enjoy the extremes of techno-capitalism, which in the view of Deleuzian philosopher Brian Massumi has overcome the former enlightenment logic of totalising normality and adopted the postmodern illogic of erratic excess, the more varied and erratic, the better. 'Normalcy starts to lose its hold. The regularities start to loosen … the oddest of affective tendencies are okay – as long as they pay'.[71]

Between the impossible extremes of capitalism and anti-capitalism, the former pressing onwards with unlimited post-human technologies, the latter imbued with the righteous high-minded romance of violence, a return to the sacred, with support for the exception, for jihad – anti-American, anti-capitalist, anti-Semitic – we inhabit the brief and ever-shrinking "postmodern indifference zone" of the libidinised masses, recalling the lab mice of long ago who gave up living when they were offered a "pleasure button" to press.[72] Without the Oedipus complex as a structural limit, the way is wide open for incest and murder. Without Oedipus, there is only schizophrenia. Without reason, one will be quite unable to fathom and uncaring about the difference between good and evil.[73] The stakes are high. We can only have the pretense of a peaceful, harmonious and multicultural society if we continue to refuse to live up to our best values (which we no longer really believe in), because those values allegedly threaten those who hate our values.

Generations to come will have to negotiate their survival mentally and psychically through a bewildering array of lethal substances and, as mere nodal points in an infinite network, avoiding violence by skulking in safe areas in cities, staying "below the radar," grabbing a few intense but brief "highs" followed by the darkest nights imaginable. We should note that the latest findings in astrophysics suggest that 96 per cent of the universe is composed of dark matter and/or dark energy.[74] And the best that the radically helpless, unjudgemental and indifferent liberals, democrats and educationalists, all decent souls, will ever manage or muster is "damage limitation:" *warn them of all the dangers and let them decide.*

> The secret of the radical thing is that it is about nothing!
> Nothing *per se.*
> Clearing the space – *for nothing.*
> Nothing is the greatest power.
> Millions of dead for nothing.
> The death drive for nothing.
> To destroy the other (peasant, worker, woman, child, bourgeois, Christian) for nothing.
> To desecrate for nothing.
> To push over or pull down for nothing.
> Unmasking for nothing.
> Destroy consumption for nothing.
> Destroy education for nothing.
> The long march through the institutions for nothing.
> Destroy orthodoxy for nothing.
> But clear a space.

Notes

1 According to the WHO, FSM is practised in 28 countries in western, eastern, and north-eastern Africa, in parts of the Middle East, and within some immigrant communities in Europe, North America, and Australasia. The WHO estimates that 100–140 million women and girls around the world have experienced the procedure, including 92 million in Africa.
2 Baudrillard, J., 1979: 101.
3 Hélène Cixous; she uses the term *jouissance* to describe a real form of women's pleasure, or sexual rapture that combines mental, physical and spiritual aspects of female experience, bordering on mystical communion. Cixous maintains that *jouissance* is the source of a woman's creative power, and the suppression of *jouissance* prevents women from finding their own fully empowered voice. Thus, *Écriture feminine* was born. See Cixous, H., 1981: 253.
4 Lacan, J., 1959–1960: 186, italics added.
5 Ibid.: 321.
6 Freud, S., 1930 (1929): 112.
7 Ibid.: 96.
8 Ibid.: 145.
9 Lacan, J., 1959–1960: 186.
10 Lacan, J., 1959–1960: 186.
11 Matson, J., 2012. 'At the centre of our galaxy is a sleeping giant, a black hole more than four million times as massive as the sun'.
12 Lacan, J., 1959–1960: 77.
13 Ibid.: 99.
14 Freud, S., 1916–1917: 345.
15 See, for instance, Freud, S., 1937a. "Analysis terminable and interminable;" 224ff.
16 Lacan, J., 1959–1960: 133. The biblical reference is Matthew 23: 4.
17 Ibid.: 138.
18 'If we continue to follow Freud in a text such as *Civilisation and its Discontents*, we cannot avoid the formula that *jouissance* is evil'. Lacan, J., 1959–1960: 184; also 194.
19 Freud, S., 1930 (1929) op. cit.: 110.
20 De Sade quoted in Lacan, J., 1959–1960: 202.
21 Ibid.: 219.
22 Sade cited on p. 211.
23 Ibid.: 224.
24 See p. 216, n2.
25 Ibid.: 267, italics added.
26 Zupančič, A., 2000: 58.
27 Ibid.: 254.
28 *Burial at Thebes*, a translation by Seamus Heaney, was specially commissioned to mark the centenary of the Abbey Theatre in Dublin in 2004 (31 March to 1 May). Subsequently published by Faber on 4 March 2004.
29 Cited already in Weatherill, R., 1998: 96.
30 Graves, R., 1960 [1955]: 380.
31 Butler, J., 2000: 88.
32 Lacan, J., 1959–1960: 300.
33 The true quotation is a paradox as Lacan acknowledges: ' …from an analytical point of view, the only thing of which one can be guilty is of having given ground relative to one's desire' (Lacan 1959–1960: 319). This, of course, can mean feeling guilt for having not *fully* desired according to one's own unknown being, or, feeling guilt for having given in to or yielded to one's forbidden desires
34 Quoted in Cudden, J., 1977: 985.
35 Amis, M., 2012.
36 See, for example, Sartre here https://www.youtube.com/watch?v=USsUQUTpYyA&feature=youtu.be.

37 MacFarquhar, R., and Schoenhals, M., 2006.
38 See Ferguson, N., 2006: 620.
39 Chang, J., and Halliday, J., 2005: 542.
40 Spence, J., 2001.
41 Fen, S.-N., 1986. The so-called "mass line" is the communist equivalent of the formula, 'Of the people, by the people, and for the people'.
42 Wolin, R., 2012.
43 See, for instance, Ian Buruma, "Cult of the Chairman," *The Guardian*, 7 March 2001.
44 Badiou, A., 2006b: 291.
45 Ibid.: 291.
46 Ibid.: 310.
47 Ibid.: 307.
48 Ibid.: 298.
49 Ibid.: 320.
50 Lacan, J., 1970–1971.
51 Badiou, quoted in Wolin, R., 2012: 162. Emphasis added by Wolin. See also the discussion on Heidegger in Chapter 3 and later in Chapter 6.
52 See discussion of the Easter Rising in Weatherill, R., 2016.
53 *S-21: The Khmer Rouge Killing Machine* (2003), a documentary by Rithy Panh, recalls our earlier discussion on the machinic. See also Weatherill, R., 2011. Chapter 7: pp. 131–56 and 209.
54 Badiou, A., 2007: 62–3, emphasis added.
55 See, for instance, Badiou, A., 1997. For an interesting overview of Pauline radicalism, see "A new political Saint Paul?" The Jarvous Arcades Project, http://javous308.blogspot.ie/2011/05/new-political-saint-paul.html.
56 There is doubt about Paul's authorship of Ephesians.
57 Romans 7:7, 8.
58 Lacan, J., 1959–1960: 83.
59 Žižek, S., 2008: 173.
60 Ibid.: 172.
61 Deleuze, G., and Guattari, F., 1980: 307.
62 However, they also report that the subsequent prosecutions and ensuing trials have failed to satisfy 'international fair trial standards'. See www.amnesty.org/fr/library/asset/EUR45/007/1993/fr/c34d72cc-f8fd-11dd-92e7-c59f81373cf2/eur450071993en.pdf.
63 Zola, E., 1885: 350ff.
64 www.theguardian.com/commentisfree/2013/aug/12/agota-kristof-the-notebook-slavoj-zizek.
65 Badiou, A., 2003: 17.
66 Ibid.: 20.
67 Nick Cohen has detailed the failure of the Left, since the 1980s, in Cohen, N., 2007.
68 Girard, R., 2010: 209–210.
69 Ibid.: 214.
70 See Houellebecq, M., in Henri-Levi, B., and Houellebecq, M., 2008: 63, italics added.
71 Massumi, B., 2002: 224.
72 Olds, J., 1956.
73 See the extended discussion in Chapter 3.
74 Panek, R., 2011.

10

MATERIALISM OR MAGISTERIUM

"Events" as miracles are clearly not objective as such, but only appear to believers – those who have ears to hear, eyes to see.[1] Christianity, more specifically the incarnation, word-made-flesh, "in" Christ, is *the* event for Christians. For non-believers the Christian event is nothing. But the theological legacy persists even in emancipatory circles, from animal magnetism or mesmerism to para-psychology, the occult, homeopathy and hypnosis, right down to psychoanalysis. All have the whiff of the miraculous about them. Žižek quotes from Lacan's *Seminar 18*, on the *truth* of psychoanalytic interpretation: 'Interpretation is not tested by a truth that would [be] decide[d] by yes or no, [instead] it *unleashes truth* as such. It is only true in as much as it is *truly followed*'. Žižek adds, 'the "test" of the analyst's interpretation is in the truth effect it *unleashes* in the patient'.[2] "Unleashing" and "truly followed:" you get caught up in the revolutionary fervour. First, truth is unleashed and then you follow it passionately – *your* desire, *your* belief. This is miraculous–ideological–fanatical.

Maybe Lacan was referring to Freud's late paper on constructions in analysis, where indeed Freud says that the patient's "yes" or "no" is *not* the key to a truthful construction/interpretation. Affirmation or negation of the analyst's remarks are ambiguous and may be an effect of the resistance. However, a "yes," or even a "no" that nevertheless 'produces new memories which complete and extend the construction' indicate that the analyst is on the right track. Freud also points to indirect forms of confirmation, such as 'I didn't ever think', or 'I shouldn't ever have thought',[3] this or that about my unconscious, is indeed the truth about what I think. Freud is balanced and nuanced. If the analyst is near the mark, new material will follow to confirm the hypothetical construction. This can even apply to dreams, so-called 'corroborative dreams', that 'tag along behind' the analysis obligingly amplifying what the analyst has interpreted.[4] Freud is moderate, *not* ecstatic and revelatory.

We must clarify the sort of psychoanalysis we want, even though it is probably too late. First, we reject the revolutionary unleashing trends of Freudo-Lacanian psychoanalysis.[5] Second, like Lacan we reject the presumptive humanistic version of ego psychoanalysis that seeks without question merely to correct maladaptive behaviour. Third, we reject the reductive utilitarian universe that both these approaches espouse. Fourth, we deplore the unctuous tendency in therapeutic circles, who already know how "fragile" you are, how much "pain" lies hidden and how much "caring" you need. Instead, like the late Christopher Hitchens, we are against totalitarianisms of Left and Right; of the former, he paraphrased Wilde who declared 'on an occasion of this kind it becomes more than a moral duty to betray the Left. It becomes a pleasure'.[6]

We have a similar urge to clear a *free* space. Then maybe the ethical, some notion of the common participatory good, of universal justice to break the lack-lustre non-commitment and disengagement generated by postmodern cynical materialism. Derrida refers to 'a donating affirmation', more ancient than the origin, 'that remains the ultimate unknown for the analysis that it nevertheless puts in motion'.[7]

Subtraction

With the ethical in mind, by way of clearing the space, creating/maintaining the gap for speaking, we will explore a Catholic sensibility to ground, frame and disturb the meandering road that psychoanalysis takes. In fact, properly understood, the theological provides *the* ground and guards it against the violent unleashing forces we have been considering throughout.

First, the big question: how did we lose the great and medieval Catholic vision over the last half millennium? Charles Taylor argues against the standard notion that secularism arose merely by the "subtraction" of religious elements from medieval society to reveal a "secularity" that lay buried all along. Taylor asks, 'Why was it virtually impossible not to believe in God in, say, 1500 in our Western society, while in 2000 many of us find this not only easy, but even inescapable?'[8] In the most radical version of the subtraction theory, 'ordinary desire undergoes a reversal in value. Formerly it was comprehensively condemned in the name of other-worldly salvation. Now it is affirmed. Sexual fulfilment, instead of being condemned as the path to perdition, is now seen as one of our greatest joys'.[9] Get rid of the false mythologies is the subtraction story, in which Freud plays an important but complex part.

Against this oversimplification, Taylor argues that the movement of reform emerges from *within* the Christian matrix itself that aimed to raise all people to the higher levels of *religious* devotion and practice, which in turn paved the way towards secularisation. Taylor explains that the Catholic Church has always been at the *centre* of reform. 'Probably no other branch of Christendom went through such repeated, far-reaching and global attempts of reform as Latin Christendom has done in this second millennium of our era'.[10] In medieval times, there was Augustine's "City of God" on the one hand, and the earthly city, the *saeculum* (*saeculum* = aeon, earthly time) on the other, each with its own domain. The ascendancy of the secular at the expense of religion started as early as the eleventh century quite paradoxically when the laity, living in the *saeculum*, were being urged to become *more* devotional and ascetic, in short, more Christian. Reformist tendencies got a major boost with the Reformation, when Protestants rejected what they believed was the "spiritual pride" of practices of ascetic withdrawal. They believed you should be a proper Christian *within* the *saeculum*, not in a special sphere outside.

All reformist approaches *within* Christianity tend to bring gradual disenchantment which progressively collapses the sacred/profane divide. The great achievement of modernity and civilisation over the past half millennium has been the slow discovery of disengaged human agency; the "immanentisation" of moral sources, without the transcendental help of God. Purely humanly grounded motivations and flourishing became possible with the creation of self-given laws. With the increase in cognitive abilities via demystification through the new sciences, the old demons of the former "porous self," vulnerable to outside malevolent powers, could be faced down with renewed confidence. Descartes' *cogito*, abstracted from its surroundings, isolated and controlling, was a key development.

In religious life also, there developed a process of interiorisation, a move away from "external" ritual observances, fasting, prayers, Masses, etc., towards *in*-tentionality, piety and faith, particularly during the Reformation. Eventually, the secular so-called "buffered self" developed the new myth of confident *exclusive* humanism, escaping parochialism through the universalism of enlightenment, discipline and rational self-control *á la* Locke, Helvétius and Kant. The new identity, grounded firmly in rational autonomy, was buffered against demons, tyrants and magic forces including the aura of desire itself. Alone in a vast universe, blind and indifferent to our fate, with no personal God or self-evident purpose, we were obliged to adopt an austere Universalist, autonomous, impersonal standpoint within. Taylor notes, 'Not only is there a firm inner/outer boundary in a world that has been disenchanted, but further barriers are raised against strong physical desires and the fascination with the body'. As if anticipating the arguments here, he warns that a disengaged buffered self believing itself invulnerable 'falls easily prey to ideologies of atomism, in which men might well have "grown like mushrooms out of the earth"'.[11] The "condescension," the "unflappable tone," the belief in being "civilised," were all part of the sure-footed eighteenth century enlightenment historical sense.

However, over-confidence brings its own reaction. Against the perceived flatness and levelling of materialist atheism – the "nova effect" – an explosion of spiritualism exemplified the return of quasi-religion within the multitude of spiritual forms that grew up *between* orthodoxy and atheism, as the buffered self remained vulnerable, lacking real gravity and substance without transcendence. Taylor summarises what he calls the "malaise of immanence" under three headings: 1) The loss of over-arching meaning; 2) the lack of solemnity at crucial moments of significant life events; and 3) the threat posed by the emptiness of the ordinary.[12] Mention has already been made of the loss of the Real and the loss of Otherness. Subtraction becomes more than disenchantment by taking away the transcendent; subtraction risks nihilation, the loss of the capacity to register loss itself. Subtraction can be total.

The direction of humanity's so-called progression becomes clear. Beginning with the axial period, when the spiritual foundations of humanity were laid simultaneously and independently in China (Taoism, Confucianism), India (Hinduism, Buddhism), Persia (Zoroastrianism), Judea (monotheism), and Greece (sophism, Plato, etc). With the eclipse of paganism and polytheism, orthodox monotheism was clearly a step forwards, but believers were still in thrall to a capricious God. Post-axial equilibrium allowed for private religious devotion on the one hand, and the older collective cosmic rituals and carnivals on the other, until the increasingly serious imposition of rational order led to the Reformation, disenchantment and the end of any sense of cosmic "embeddedness." The evolution of the impersonal order inspired by the infinite universe without, and the universalist moral code within, led to a disengaged subjectivity, and finally, with *Anti-Oedipus,* to the end of subjectivity and the personal itself.

Eventually, as Taylor says, 'There is just this one relentless order of right thought and action, which must occupy all social and personal space'.[13] Thence, it is only a short step to exclusive secularism – to decide that the 'relentless order of right thought' be a neutralised code to encompass the goods of life *without God.* Humanism becomes the alternative faith of humanity.

Anger at the Church was always a key factor. Catholicism was perceived as obscurantist and irrational, associated with oppression, suffering and the denial of happiness. The Church offended against reason and freedom. The doctrine of original sin, the doctrine of predestination, the juridical-penal model, caused revulsion and rejection, fuelling the anthropocentric turn. Such religious practices as celibacy, fasting, penance, mortification, self-denial, humility, silence, solitude were dismissed as "monkish virtues" by Hume, and were said to contribute nothing to *human* welfare. The rise of city-states and national monarchies, the break up of the old feudal structures, contributed to the increasing failure of the Roman Catholic Church to maintain a stable and unifying framework for the organisation of spiritual and material life.

However, the rise of *exclusive* humanism plus its liberal democratic counterpart consolidated at the end of the last century after the dramatic fall off in "faith" in Communism, was thought to be the Hegelian "the end of history."[14] However, the new threat from Islamo-fascism aligned with the revolutionary Left may send history into reverse gear. The point may have been reached where the confident emancipatory philosophies developed in Europe over the last half millennium, like the vast universe they celebrate, may have ceased to expand and may be already in retreat.[15] Was not postmodernism already a retraction and equivocation, the recycling of tradition?

The secular was really unthinkable from scratch. It rides on the back of this enormous history of religious reformation with its battery of the most powerful ethical ideas and only at the last minute drops the religious reference in order to espouse values in purely human immanentist terms. A-theism does not stand alone; it is essentially a denial of theism. Hence there is a Jewish atheism, Marx and Freud being the most obvious examples. There is a Protestant atheism of rational disciplined responsibility without God. And Lacan, the Catholic atheist who jokes *God is not dead, but merely unconscious.*[16] However, even the most radical atheistic materialist buffers herself with *belief*, that instrumental reason and liberal democratic freedoms (against the void) will continue to triumph. The idea that the *self*-authorising of reason alone has a strong hold and there is no going back may be just one more illusion.

Radical orthodoxy

Was the momentous, the courageous shift to exclusive humanism inevitable? John Milbank thinks not. He argues that secularism had to be positively imagined and constructed. Milbank famously said, 'Once, there was no secular'.[17] Instead there was a single participatory and interconnected community of Christendom, living in the space between the fall and the *eschaton*. The secular is not some innate or inevitable human condition waiting to be truly realised after religious mythology is worked through and removed. Quite the contrary, it has to be *ideologically* realised and advanced as a political space, a new myth of salvation without God, a sphere of sheer power – the power to privatise and marginalise the sacred. Disingenuously claiming to be neutral and inclusive, the emphasis on purely humanistic formulations becomes incompatible with orthodox Christian teaching built up over two millennia. Milbank shows that secular theories of politics, economics and the law assume the *inevitability of violence*.

Beyond enlightenment humanism, we have gone further into *anti*-humanist, *anti*-enlightenment territory, where Nietzsche, Foucault, Derrida, Bataille, Deleuze, Lacan *et al.* have gone, in their efforts to expose fully the underbelly of violence, disavowed by the Church and liberal humanism alike, full of their false benevolence and harmony. The anti-humanists both uncover power structures that control reality and yet espouse violence themselves quite openly in the cause of radical justice, as well as searching out a new transcendence, some "beyond," something sacred and worth dying for.

An unlikely debate has been occurring between *two* groups of "obscurantists" united insofar as they oppose secular humanism and its domination by scientism and materialism. Radical Orthodoxy (RO) is the site where orthodox Augustinian Christian theology meets radical postmodern philosophy.[18] For the last two decades, a group of Christian theologians have drawn upon pre-enlightenment thinking coming from the theology of Augustine, Gregory of Nyssa, Thomas Aquinas, Nicholas of Cusa, Meister Eckhart and others to develop a radical critique of modern secularism, understood by them as inherently nihilistic and based on hidden ontological violence. Modern liberal thought is re-interpreted through the lens of theological ontology. RO draws variously on the work of Karl Barth and his understanding of the paradoxical nature of divine truth, the Oxford movement, the Anglo-Catholic wing of an increasingly diverse Church of England and the earlier Cambridge Platonists. The latter believed that religion and reason are in harmony: reason is "the candle of the Lord," against the materialism of Hobbes and the narrow privacy of the Calvinist line to God. According to Reno, 'It is Augustine's vision of heavenly peace, made effective in the dynamic and binding power of divine purpose, that shapes RO's reflections, not Nietzsche's violence wrought by an omnipotent will-to-power'.[19]

The Neoplatonist understanding of the cosmos stressed its fundamental harmony: a hierarchy of differences to do with talents, wills, desires and so on, with God *present* at every point. Contrast this harmony as in "the body of Christ" to secular antagonism, present at every level in the endlessly contested hierarchy of power which has preoccupied us throughout the preceding chapters. Every group, every individual, every atom is fighting in the nil ethos of "no such thing as society" – the fragmented secular counterpart to the body of the Church. Everyone fights; everyone utters secular prayers for equality of the rhizomal type to eliminate difference, which only knows envy and resentment in the final analysis. The only ultimate allegiance is to self and to the in-group, with overall (violent) authority vested in the law and the nation state, which underpins via intense automated surveillance systems the weaker humanistic values of tolerance and trust that just about holds things together to give the appearance of peace for the time being, renamed security. Lock yourself in with passwords. Encrypt yourself.

Against such violent ontologies, RO thinking posits the Platonic-Augustinian notion of the "ontological primacy of the Good." Thus Evil does not exist in itself, but is understood as a lack of the Good, an absence of the Good. Evil is parasitical on the Good, a corruption of the Good. Commentators on the contemporary crisis have lost the ability and desire to recognise evil unequivocally for fear of causing offence; whose "evil" is it anyway? How can you be sure? Augustine believed that we have the perverse traits of preferring the false, believing it to be good and true, of preferring humanity to God, *our* creations to His.

Without the template of the Good our ability to see is compromised. Hence the constant complaint about a lack of vision. Plato understood the Good as analogous to the sun which alone makes the world visible. So, 'when the mind's eye rests on objects illuminated by truth and reality, it understands and comprehends them, and functions intelligently'. Without this truth giving light, coming from the Good beyond, the mind 'can only form opinions, its vision is confused and its beliefs shifting …'.[20] The 'Form of the Good' like the sun is situated beyond from whence it dispenses light to objects of thought, the Platonic Forms. Aquinas points out that the word God (*Theos*) comes from *theasti*, meaning to see. But we cannot stare directly at the sun! We see *only though a glass darkly* (1 Corinthians 13:12). Oedipus in despair about not seeing sticks the gold pins that hold Jocasta's dress into his own eyes. *Lear*'s Gloucester laments: 'I have no eyes and therefore want no way, I stumbled when I saw'.

Contrast this searing light with contemporary darkness: the *no anguish*, the *no loss* darkness, as we float freely in an indifferent realm of equal and relative opinions and theories. Instead of seers *á la* Plato, in the post-Christian world, transcendental vision is foreclosed. Only the blind can lead the blind, and, by extension, for instance, only gays can lead gays, only women can lead women, only children can lead children, only the abused can talk for the abused, only criminals can lead criminals (like terrorists who are allowed to control a section of the prison), only the Same can lead the Same, and so on. This is the best non-interference, non-judgemental practice that our elite classes not only insist on, but also legislate for. *Let them alone* is the cry that rings out into postmodernity. *Let them alone: they be blind leaders of the blind. And if the blind lead the blind, both shall fall into the ditch* (Matthew 15:14). *Abiding in the midst of ignorance, thinking themselves wise and learned, fools go aimlessly hither and thither, like blind led by the blind* (Katha Upanishad).

For Plotinus, interpreter of Plato, the first exteriority with regard to what he calls "the One" is the *intelligence* of the One, but only as multiplicity because of the distance that separates it from the One. However, we remain nostalgic, homesick out of love and piety for the ultimately unattainable One. Plotinus identified the "One" with the concept of Good and the principle of Beauty. However, Plotinus understood creation to be *ex deo*, paving the way ultimately for autonomous secular thinking with God confined to the far margins. Whereas the orthodox position is the more radical one of creation *ex nihilo*, which accords much more closely with the precarious, paradoxical, absurd and contingent viewpoint of this work – humming in the desert, and so on – haunted by nothing. All for nothing: creation suspended over nothingness. With the two groups of obscurantists, the philosophical *nihilo* meets and engages theological *nihilo*.

Rather than the *ex deo* God who created everything and then withdrew leaving us to get on with things in a godless universe, RO believes that God is present at every moment. The focus on the Neoplatonist account of "participation" is said to be at the heart of Aquinas's theology – 'All knowers know God implicitly in all they know'.[21] The metaphysics of participation extends back to Plato and Platonic Forms. Empirical reality only "borrows" existence from the Forms, ultimately the Form of the Good. RO adds an extra twist: creation is nothing until it participates in the gratuity of God's gift of being. The world participates in its transcendent source. There is no duality (natural and supernatural); creation has no autonomous existence, only an analogous relation to God. Creation does not stand alongside God, or indeed without God, but participates *in* God – the constantly arriving gift, the ceaseless giving of grace *ex nihilo*. Nothing exists until God breathes life into it. Renewal is ceaseless. I am nothing except by the grace of God.

With *this* transcendental orientation everything (secular) changes! The universe is generosity. Finite empirical reality however remains "not-all," un-totalised, indeterminate and aporetic and indeed nothing at all. Reality is insubstantial. RO understands finite reality as entirely dependent on God's divine donation, at one with Hopkins' assertion that 'The world is charged with the grandeur of God'. Reality has no "right to exist" *per se*, it only does so by the gratuity of God. Thinking in quantum terms, the universe is a void, but may be a positively charged void. Particular things appear when the balance of the void is disturbed. This perturbation is generosity.

While the choice between the orthodox Christian theology and the post-modern Žižekian realities is rationally undecidable, only Christianity according to

Milbank *et al.* allows differences to co-exist relatively peaceably and thus to flourish; that is there is no longer a need to fight violently and without end; the infinite can accommodate all. Being is plenitude. Being overflows. Being is larger than any real of antagonism, although humans are rarely big enough to see this wonderful plenitude.

Thus Creston Davis argues for staying close to what he welcomes as 'the world's unfolding openness in a manner that is both poetical and nuanced … [T]here is a real sense of playfulness in being's disclosure and enclosure of itself'.[22] Consider Milbank's assertion, against Heidegger and Lacan, 'the ontic must be seen as participating in ontological plenitude, just as every act of signification by the living linguistic animal can be seen as participating in an infinite reserve of the signified as well as of the signifier'.[23] And beyond the ontological deadlock of Sin/Law with which we have been preoccupied, *grace much more abounds*.

Milbank thinks through the political implications of RO. He has been dubbed Red Tory/Blue Labourite[24] who suggests 'the reception of grace and the giving of love as a social practice and economy', adding the very necessary and complicating caveat: 'Love and mercy are not exercised without measure, judgement, preferential discrimination, or due distribution'.[25] Milbank advocates a new politics of participation, against the excessive liberalism of both the Left and the Right. It is associationist, communitarian and linked to *objective* virtues and values. The city square, the *piazza*, represents the metaphysics and the politics of participation and plenitude. The graceful proportions of the buildings each with its history, the arcades, the shade cast by the trees, the cafes, restaurants, small businesses, the strolling families mingling, all generations together, the friends greeting each other, a shared charity, an entirely natural unforced mixing and meeting.

The de-sacralised a-theological alternative to the metaphysics of participation is biological life restricted to immanence, subordinated to death, scarcity and their narcissistic correlates – *my* life, not yours, *my* race-against-death strategies, *my* life at the expense of others, *my* safety, where life is reduced to a predictable, aggressively negotiated "given," as against the singularity of the "gift" wholly open to the gratuity of God. Catherine Pickstock points to 'the reduction of gift to contract … like the passing in the night of two "free" gifts that never acknowledge each other or discover a mutual appropriateness'.[26]

Perichoresis invokes the dance *not* the *agon*. *Perichoresis* is a Greek term used to describe the triune relationship between each person of the trinity – co-indwelling, co-inhering, and mutual interpenetration – 'God's self-joying and the human joy that arises[.] [T]o think that there is indeed first of all and finally such joy, even if it is for us now [in the Symbolic] in time almost totally concealed'. How could we miss this in the midst of our 'natural-historical darkness that has demonically concealed it from our view', continues Milbank. Thus, 'God in himself is relationship, and therefore is love conceived of as an infinite exchange – as Eros as well as Agape, and therefore in a very un-Lacanian fashion', continues Milbank, 'as the infinite transcendental possibility of a sexual relationship'.[27] He goes on to argue that such lightness of joy and dance, as opposed to conflict and agony, is also ultimately serious, in that it alone is the true source of justice and forgiveness, beyond the Law – justice beyond justice.[28]

The Good News, the Christian Event that emerges through the mysterious gift of grace, all but lost and buried, continues to appear via what Milbank calls the faithful 'relational weaving of witnesses through the course of time'.[29] Christianity survives via the recall through time by those who remain faithful to the original Christian Event, in the midst of the chaos and nullity of Badiou's mathematical many.

An example: the Eastern Orthodox Mass is musically sublime.[30] The Mass came from the northernmost monastery in Russia, Solovki, which the Soviet regime turned into a death camp for Orthodox priests. This place has seen generations of pilgrims. After the Revolution of 1917, Lenin's henchmen threw out the monks and the monastery was turned into a prison camp – the first and may be the worst. Unlike Auschwitz, it was intended primarily for labour rather than extermination, but the effect was not so different. Tens of thousands, the flower of a whole generation of believers, died there, ravaged by disease, starvation and the execution of anyone who stepped out of line. Bishops, clergy, political leaders, the intelligentsia perished here, anonymously.

Below is a poem written by one of the inmates.

> We are left to bloom where the King of Souls has sown us. If he has sown us in the field of sorrow, let us bloom in sorrow. If he has sown us in solitude, let us be in solitude, for the Creator sows even the most beautiful of flowers on inaccessible tracks between mountain paths. They have their value, even though nobody sees them. The anguish of the soul is unseen, but like blossoms it can be plucked and offered to the Saviour.

The focus on Catholic orthodoxy risks the accusation of being pusillanimous. Much of what has been outlined above is based on the *inevitability of conflict and violence*. After all, psychoanalysis *is* conflict; it is a conflict psychology; even the subject *qua* individual is divided. The metaphysics of participation in no way minimises conflict, but rather reveals its abject violating nature, through the Incarnation. Revealed also are the two aporias that haunt secular thinking. The *fragility* of the buffered self with its wish-fulfilling trust in reason. And the skating on the really thin ice of postmodern cool indifference which traces the nothing it constantly ionises.

Thus, there are two contradictory ways of ontologising the contradictory. First, the Protestant-Hegelian conflictual, antagonistic, dialectical way of eternal struggle, which stays closer to the modernist psychoanalytic experience of conflict: life versus death, sexuality versus self-preservation instincts, and so on, without direction. The Hegelian "whole" is just about kept together in spite of internal strife and antagonism. Violence is ubiquitous – the violence of negativity, leading to all manner of evil, to terror and mass immiseration, war machines and sacrificial violence. At best, there will be periods of mutual co-existence and peace as pacification. Liberal so-called stable democracies live with the illusion of pacification based on disavowed violence. Atomisation and social breakdown are constant dangers.

Second, the RO movement ontologises the contradictory in a paradoxical manner, reviving the lost divine vision of transcendence in which *opposites can coincide*, where the lion lies down with the lamb. Opposite poles co-exist in such a gracious expansive milieu that radical differences can exist without mutual destruction. *Come unto me, all ye that labour and are heavy laden and I will give you rest* (Matthew 11:18). The medieval paradox, *coincidentia oppositorum* associated with Nicolas de Cusa and others, has been made popular recently by Mircea Eliade and Jung, and is a Neoplatonic term.

As Oliver says, 'no discourse which seeks truth can count itself as wholly autonomous from issues of transcendent origin and purpose – that is issues of theology'.[31] Everything participates! Not that individual discourses lose their differences to theology, but quite the contrary, they now "participate" maybe without knowing it in a new transcendent way.

Milbank sees difference, often posited here as final and irredeemable, as paradoxical and analogical rather than dialectically agonistic. For purposes of illustration, Milbank imagines a misty morning travelling southwards towards the river Trent, close to his home. At first, it seems as if the images of vague shapes, roads, houses, churches, tend to merge into one pale mass in which it becomes difficult to maintain one's bearings. This is the univocal perspective[32] in the endlessly diffuse white light. However, the mist also challenges us to see, to pick out, distant objects more clearly. The outlines of distinct objects come into view; spires, houses, roofs, the river, different colours gain strange relief in the veiled sunlight, part of an emergent equivocal perspective.[33] Milbank acknowledges the dialectical tension here – the univocal sameness of the mistiness versus the equivocal pure difference of landscape objects that appear and disappear into opacity. The univocal, the same opacity of the mist and the equivocal differences of the spectral objects: 'it is the weaving of things in and out of the mist[,] the mist foreground/background [that] is the precarious setting for the gray jewels'. The monochrome world of white on the one hand, or sheerly different geometrical shapes on the other, each inadequate on its own; while acknowledging that the univocal and the equivocal are in dialectical tension, Milbank asserts rather their mutual *affirmation*. Rather than an impossible contradiction, our constant refrain, Milbank sees an 'outright impossible *coincidence of opposites* … the Catholic logic of *paradox* – of an "overwhelming glory" (*paradoxa*) which nonetheless saturates our everyday reality'.[34]

Nothing is ruled out in this analogical relationship. Nothing is negated. Milbank uses William Desmond's term – the metaxological.[35] Neither the one nor the many transcendentally rule, although at times there will be antagonistic relations where the "weaving" might be usurped for a time by one constituent or the other. The metaxological is shared and lies always "between." Thus, the ultimate beauty of the belonging together of the whole misty collage without reduction. The unity of the scene is achieved by the multiple differences belonging together, *without any equalisation, neutralisation or resolution*. Hierarchy is possible; difference is possible.

Every separation is a link, like a wall that separates two prisoners through which secret messages can be tapped; an absence can provide a link. Or like Robert Frost's

'Good fences make good neighbours'.[36] The mist over the river invites penetration of the veil for the objects concealed there. Milbank's criticism of the dialectical is that 'it finally pulls up the drawbridge of the between … to leave all behind forever in the surrounding marshlands of diversity'.[37]

The metaxu is beauty, glimpsed beyond and through appearances, through darkened glass, analogously and paradoxically. The imaginative faculty is attuned to the metaxological, by emptying and opening itself (kenosis) becoming nothing; a *donating* nullity, following Eckhart, who stresses being empty in order to be creative *from nothing*. As adults, inevitably deaf and blind to the metaxological, Milbank argues that, 'an explicit judgement [has] to be made in favour of the analogical … [being] prepared to concede an external reality exceeding what we can grasp …'.[38]

Simone Weil, French philosopher, social activist and Christian mystic, claimed that, 'The beautiful is the experimental proof that the incarnation is possible'.[39] The constituted world points to something *beyond* itself, establishing the essentially teleological character of all that exists. 'We must have faith that the universe is beautiful on all levels … The love of this beauty proceeds from God dwelling in our souls and goes out to God present in the universe'. Beauty also served a soteriological function for Weil, passing through and nourishing the soul. When she was 26 (in 1935), she was intensely moved by the beauty of villagers singing hymns during an outdoor service that she came across during a holiday in Portugal. Later, in Assisi in the spring of 1937, she experienced a religious ecstasy in the Basilica of Santa Maria degli Angeli – the same church in which Saint Francis of Assisi had prayed. She had another, more powerful, revelation a year later while reciting George Herbert's poem, *Love III*.[40]

Milbank's complaint about Žižek, Lacan *et al.* is that in 'this proximity to the chasm' – we *all* accept this void – they turn, 'images in the mirror [of divine logos] that is the world into free-standing images, so shattering the mirror, or pretending to deny that the world is *ontologically self-giving* … and reflecting back to us all the way down, even if we can never see into those depths'. We are therefore left with 'sterile and meaningless self-reference … self constituted in the very act of creation'.[41]

This was precisely Jacobi's point in his letter to Fichte in 1799:

> If the highest upon which I can reflect, what I can contemplate, is my empty and pure, naked and mere ego, with its autonomy and freedom: then rational self-contemplation, then rationality is for me a curse – I deplore my existence.

Kant's critique of traditional metaphysics had put God and the soul beyond any cognitive or imaginative reach. The noumenal ground of the self has no possible phenomenal presence. Jacobi objected because this break leads only to an impoverished egoism, allowing only nothing beyond the self. Pascal had made a similar critique of Descartes. According to Jacobi, therefore, the human subject has a simple choice: '*Nothingness or God*. Choosing Nothingness, he makes *himself* into a God'.[42] And the possibility still remains: 'Kant was not thwarting but abetting reason's self-destructive march towards the abyss'.[43] Therefore, Lacan was formally correct: *Kant avec Sade*.

Nietzsche spoke of a "good nihilism" and a "bad nihilism." The good version accepts the void, courageously anticipating the heroic and aristocratic Overman, self-determining, self-overcoming, anticipating, and believing in the donating plenitude of *self*-creation. The "bad" version fears the void, fears death, slipping into ennui, apathy and destruction, the pathetic "last man," who needs a crutch as he creeps hopelessly around, wasting life, devoid of any will to power and full of *ressentiment*.

To a Protestant-atheistic-postmodern-Lacanian mindset, we need the ultimate Nietzschean-Stoical courage proud to face life alone, *amor fati* in face of the void, whatever the risk of the backfire, reaction, *ressentiment* and mental illness. The RO position on the face of it seems less arduous, because it is connected and embedded and thus emboldened by the good. However, to *sustain* commitment to the other, to family, to a set of values, to the increasingly broken community and not least to faith in a persecutory world that rejects faith requires sustained courage. At the extreme it involves "detachment," loss of ego, kenosis, affliction, dying to life – in short, "the Cross" in anticipation of prodigality, donation and joy.

If we had Weil's unshakable conviction that, 'come what may, *the universe is full*',[44] would the paranoid machines finally stop their whirring in the presence of such numinous generosity? Would psychoanalysis just pass away with its pathetic Oedipal rivalries, conflicts, divisions and hatreds? Would self-hatred and *ressentiment* finally be halted with bitterness overwhelmed, neutralised, reversed – swept into the brimming tide of "becoming" as Nietzsche and Deleuze demanded? The anti-Oedipus complex would likewise be swept into oblivion along with its unavowed hatreds of the other, a receding symptom of the old world?

RO has its inevitable critics. Steven Shakespeare accuses RO of being as dogmatic as the secularism it opposes. He claims that by "romanticising" the Church, RO refuses dialogue with non-Christian sources, with an 'attack on all things autonomous'. Its targets are modernist secular philosophies that ground reality on purely immanent foundations, as well as postmodern thinking that eschews *any* grounding in favour of the play of appearances. Instead, RO believes its teachings to be the true continuation of Christ's incarnation.[45]

The proud metanarrative of postmodern secularism claims that a non-ideological, non-mythical space can be reasoned, from which *we* can gaze down upon and master reality within liberal democracies, arguably the faith of the faithless. Likewise, RO is postmodern asserting that "reality" is only redeemed through the orthodox narrative of participation in the being of God. There is no non-theological sphere. It seems to become a Romantic, Pagan or, at worst, a Fascist quest for a wholesome organic unity with the theological narrative *alone*. For example, 'The church exists as the witness to the reality of God's own story in which all created persons find themselves. The story of God in Christ does not out-narrate the stories of the world, but rather *enflames and enfolds them within the ardour of the Pentecostal Spirit of Triune Love*'.[46] Such fundamentalist knowing of Truth in the Real may be overpowering. Believing that the secular world has renounced God, RO wants nothing less than to redeem the world. Reno complains also that 'Milbank & Co. want to replace the presumptions of secularity with a Christian account of everything'.[47] Thus they replace the *particularity* and the *mediative* power of Christianity within the secular, with theory and ideal. Ironically, this is a *modernist* approach seeming to imply *total* transformation. In the background is the Neoplatonic *One*. Hyman affirms the RO diagnosis of the *violent* nihilism of postmodernity, *but not the cure* which goes about radically insisting 'that theology must become the ultimate metanarrative without remainder or reserve'.[48] This means theocracy! An accusation that Milbank rejects: 'For all the current talk of a theology that would reflect on practice, the truth is that *we remain uncertain as to where today to locate true Christian practice*. This would be, as it has always been, a repetition differently, but authentically, of what has always been done'.[49] However, Hyman argues rather lamely for "ambivalence" – a mix of the secular deconstructive and the theological, used in a "tactical" way. 'We do not *solely* utilise the tactics of critical theory in the manner of "secular" postmodernism, neither do we *solely* turn to the metanarrative of theology in the manner of RO'. 'Rather', continues Hyman, 'we recognise the necessity but insufficiency of each, and allow both to supplement and subvert each other'.[50]

Chesterton

Tactics, strategies, narratives, the language of politics will never be sufficient for the metaphysical. *Where two or three are gathered together in my name I am in the midst of them* (Matthew 18:20). No tactics, no strategies here, implying the logic of politics – getting it, possessing it, ultimately destroying it. *I am in the midst of them* means I am not "in" them – that way power, omnipotence, psychosis and nihilism lie – but "between" them. With Buber, *I-Thou* rather than an *I-It*, the I-Thou being a lost fraternity. Does not the RO teaching imply that the Gift is always already there giving itself gratuitously, but no one possesses it.[51] The Gift, the "donating affirmation" (Derrida above), more original than the origin, *is between us*.

Furthermore, the "Good News" of the Christian message is not limited to Christians. Oftentimes there is more joy among the non-Christians, the anti-Christians, atheists and Pagans. An irony not lost on Chesterton. Without need of academics and postmodernists, Christianity is thoroughly deconstructive; it deconstructs itself! Leaving aside those that come under Paul's radical judgement of the resounding gongs or a clanging cymbals, and turning to Chesterton's ironic stories, he points to St Francis of Assisi and asserts, 'his religion was not a thing like a theory but a thing like a love affair'.[52] At the beginning of *Orthodoxy*, Chesterton says, 'I did try to found a heresy of my own; and when I had put the last touches to it, I discovered it was orthodoxy'.[53] Chesterton is often the fool of his own story, combining the strange and the secure, wonder and welcome, happiness but not comfort, excitement and peril, defiance and humility, but above all a sense of freedom.

There must be some great ironist at work in Catholic metaphysics, suggests Chesterton, that holds commonplace and contradictory experiences yet transcendentally reframes them. Above all, Chesterton wants to communicate joy – part inheritor of some ancient tradition of happiness and pagan excitement. Plato or Shakespeare may be at breakfast tomorrow; he recalls that as a child, 'the whole world was to me a fairyland of wonderful fulfilments and it was like living in some Hebraic age, when prophesy after prophecy came true'.[54]

The Church thrives on opposites. In Chesterton's novel, *The Man Who Thought He Was Thursday*, the chief of police is also the chief anarchist who wants to destroy civilisation, and 'this equivocal being was meant for a serious description of the Deity'.[55] One of the anarchists in the story, a German philosopher of nihilism, had proved that the destructive principle in the universe was God, who needed 'a furious and incessant energy'. While the hero of the novel, Gabriel Syme (Thursday), declares with great emphasis, 'We see everything from behind. It is that we have only known the back of the world. We see everything from behind and it looks brutal'.[56] This has been largely the perspective displayed in the foregoing chapters.

Reinhold Niebuhr said the *only* doctrine of the Christian creed that is empirically demonstrable is that of original sin! Chesterton agrees. 'There are many who will smile at the saying; but it is profoundly true to say that the glad good news brought by the Gospel was the news of original sin'.[57] It goes back to the origin of religion, to do with the Law, with sexuality, with form as against formlessness (*jouissance*). Chesterton was once asked by a reporter what was wrong with the world. Chesterton skipped over all the usual suspects, corrupt politicians, greed, war, poverty, environmental degradation and so on, to say two words: *I am*! Man 'is at once a creator moving miraculous hands and fingers and a kind of cripple'.[58] The key point being, the hope for mankind lies in the fact that we have sinned and can be forgiven. No other religion juxtaposes sin with forgiveness, judgement with mercy.

Chesterton maintains that the Church is essentially a lion tamer making sure that no particular aspect of the truth gains an upper hand over any of the others, maintaining a strict Aristotelian balance. He refers to Christianity as 'a superhuman paradox whereby two opposite passions may blaze beside each other'.[59] Hence the symbolism of the Cross, with contradiction and paradox at its centre, the arms stretching out, reaching outwards to the other. Beyond theory and ideality, the contradiction of the Cross is incarnate, is existential. Here, we must introduce Weil's notion of "gravity," as the dead weight, part of the blind mechanism of the world, that makes everything fall, 'the force which above all others draws us from God', i.e. everything to do with power, the imaginary, etc., 'to bolster up from inside our tottering existence … apart from and opposed to God'.[60] The Cross represents a tearing apart – God's weeping. At the centre of the Cross, Weil imagines a nail: 'this nail has pierced cleanly through all creation, through the thickness of the screen separating the soul from God'.[61] At the centre of the Cross, always affliction.

Grossman also ponders contradictions of, say, the evil of the camp commandants and the beauty of the evening sun on mountain peaks. He declares, 'If the world were not so beautiful, the anguish of a dying man would not be so terrible, so incomparably more terrible than any other experience'.[62]

For Christianity the truth is *outside*, whereas for Buddhist spirituality its representation by an "O" or a circle or a zero signifies unity or recurrence *within*. Christianity looks outwards, Buddhism looks inwards, the outside being regarded as a veil, dream or illusion. Chesterton's joke was to see religious history as "noughts and crosses," where 'the cross … does really stand for the idea of breaking out of the circle … It does escape from the circular argument by which everything begins and ends in the mind'.[63] Buddhism is pantheism, immanence, quietude, introspection and ultimately indifference, whereas Christianity looks outwards to humanity, history and liberty. Chesterton notes that the Buddhist saint always has a sleek body with his eyes shut (looking inwards), while the Christian saint has his eyes wide open and alive, but with an emaciated body, having risked all. Against oriental peace and harmony, Chesterton stresses that 'The son of God came not with peace but with a sundering sword'.[64] Against the current spiritual and therapeutic notion of circular self-love, the sword separates, cuts off brother from brother to bring about the real possiblity of love – across the abyss of separation, difference and antagonism, where 'every man is hanging by a thread or clinging to a precipice'.[65]

The anti-Oedipal Buddhist-spiritualist, post-analytic vision is alternative-worldly, fatalistic and indifferent, while the Christian-European (analytic) vision risks engagement, perdition and existential ruin. It is a story with an unknown ending, at a crossroads, where courage and spirit are everything to drive the story on, to become free of symbolic Oedipal entanglements by engaging fully with them in order to lose attachment, eyes wide open.

Not so the various anti-Oedipal theorists, whom Chesterton would have identified as the "educated criminals" – 'the entirely lawless modern philosopher[s]'! These postmoderns, he believed, pose the greatest danger to mankind, unlike ordinary criminals who get punished for much lesser crimes. While Chesterton was adamant that modern law is unjustly protective of the rich, he could never (anti-Oedipally) abandon *all order* as such. Maybe Chesterton has elucidated the proper measure, the final analysis of the anti-Oedipus complex with which we have been wrestling throughout, involving the latent content of *this* dream (become nightmare) an often disavowed infinite regress of the death drive. Did not Foucault claim that after 'the death of man' the world would be a much better place? 'Man would soon be erased, like a face drawn in the sand at the edge of the sea'.[66]

'Thieves respect property. They merely wish the property to become their property', observes Chesterton, 'But philosophers dislike property as property; they wish to destroy all personal possession'. Likewise with bigamists, they essentially respect marriage, but anti-Oedipal philosophers attack the whole structure of society – marriage, the father and the family. He continues, 'Murderers respect human life … But philosophers hate life itself … the evil philosopher is not trying to alter things, but annihilate them'. With great prescience, Chesterton asserts, 'When they say that mankind shall be free at last, they mean that mankind shall commit suicide. When they talk of paradise without right or wrong, they mean the grave. They have two objects, to first destroy humanity and then themselves'.[67]

Chesterton re-injects passion and conflict into "participation;" no stroll in the square, but a radical call to arms against anti-Oedipal insanity, pursuing orthodoxy to its unorthodox limits. In a world that ordains transgression automatically, orthodoxy *is* radical. But limits for sure, illustrated by his fable of the walled island in the sea within which it is safe and free for the children to play and sing. When the wall is removed leaving only the cliffs' edge, the children are found huddling together for protection in the centre, no longer playing or singing.

Reason needs a wall. Reason unchecked goes to extremes. Reason and faith are intertwined. Reason is an act of faith – the belief that our thoughts might have some relation to a real reality *out there*, which has become a non-belief today. Reason without faith becomes irrational; faith without reason becomes fideistic, fanatical and fundamentalist. Faith and reason were once united in wisdom. Once religion is lost, reason and wisdom are not far behind. If thought goes on the rampage, if scepticism becomes unlimited, if humour and ridicule know no bounds, if scientific endeavour has no breaks, then all ends in destruction and madness, where the only thing permitted is *nothing*. Hence the fragility of contemporary secularism where thinking is already dangerously extreme, contemptuous and intolerant, having to do with enjoyment and power, bolstered by the pseudo fig-leaf faith of inclusivity and tolerance!

Analysis has its own limit, the navel of the dream, the unfathomable, unanalysable knot that cannot be untied or unravelled; the mycelium from which the mushroom of the dream wish emerges.[68] Derrida, in the same chapter of the "donating affirmation," points however to the *double* meaning of the word "analysis:" analysis which is archaeological and anagogical, which aims for the most elementary particles which cannot be further broken down; and the more radical version of analysis (*lysis* – destruction) which is 'the bearer of extreme death and the last word, just as the archaeological motif … is turned towards birth'.[69] Thus, there is not *one* psychoanalysis. The repetition compulsion is unlike the other forms of resistance to analysis. It is the resistance of resistance. As it is regressive, dissociative, asocial, unlinking, etc., we note that this *beyond* of the repetition compulsion is precisely the analytic *vocation*, that is, it does what analysis does – 'psychoanalytic theory, treatment, and institution represent the death drive or the repetition compulsion *at work*'.[70] This work of Derrida's makes Chesterton's point. Analytic thinking, in general, including schizoanalysis, can only go so far, scepticism can go so far in its archaeological quest, lest it becomes the bearer of insanity, of insane thinking, insane analysis, breaking every link, death bearing. It becomes the enabler of chaos and destruction. Analysis reaches a point in its work where it comes across what it itself resists, the stuff of which it itself is made. As we stumble upon the repetition compulsion in an analysis, we are alerted to go into reverse and try to provide a limit or a container. The container becomes the exception that supports the analysis *qua* healing, like the wall becomes the limit that supports the children's play.

As Chesterton explains, 'the whole secret of mysticism is this: that man can understand everything by the help of what he does not understand … [T]he mystic allows one thing to be mysterious, and everything else becomes lucid'. He recalls Plato, 'Like the sun at noonday, mysticism explains everything by the blaze of its own victorious invisibility'.[71]

For Chesterton, the insane man is someone who has lost everything but his reason. Without any breaks in thinking, thinking is all, he (It) cannot stop thinking. There is too much meaning for the psychotic; the whole world is mad meanings, many of them self-referential. As Chesterton says, 'it is reason used without root, reason in the void. The man who begins to think without the proper first principles goes mad'.[72]

Chesterton juxtaposes 1) the "inhuman" rigid guard of the outer ring (the fabled island wall) of Christianity with its authorities, as against the within, 'with its old human life dancing like children and drinking wine like men; for Christianity is the only frame for Pagan freedom'. Set against this, 2) modern philosophy, where the situation is reversed: 'it is its outer ring that is obviously artistic and emancipated; its despair is within'.[73]

Thus the entire might of the Catholic magisterium involving 'the Crusades, the hierarchies and the horrible persecutions were not organised, as is ignorantly said, for the suppression of reason [but rather for] the difficult defence of reason'.[74] The balance must be very carefully weighed,

> [A]n inch is everything when you are balancing. The Church could not afford to swerve a hair's breadth … if she was to continue her great and daring experiment of irregular equilibrium. …It was no flock of sheep the Christian shepherd was leading, but a herd of bulls and tigers, of terrible ideals and devouring doctrines, each of them strong enough to turn to a false religion and lay waste the world.[75]

Above all, the Christian thing is a narrative, it is personal. Unlike any other religion, the Christianity is a remarkable *human* story, pierced by the inhuman. Indeed, to take the title of one of Chesterton's chapters, 'The strangest story in the world',[76] a story riddled with paradox and complexity, but a story nevertheless containing the test, adventure, drama, ordeal, above all courage, and so on. A fighting story that takes on conflict and rails against the sub-suicidal morbidities that are the dead end point of much that we have been discussing above. Christianity is a monstrous story that carries its own excess and shirks absolutely nothing.

The monstrous element prevents the Christian thing becoming a spiritually consoling story of redemption and therapy. The key theme of the *Book of Job*, for instance, is the impossibility of understanding why God should allow good people to suffer. The God of the Old Testament, all powerful, all knowing and secretive, rejoices in the prostration of man before His divine will. The *Book of Job* asks: what is the purpose of God? Should we sacrifice our little lives for Him? Like us, Job assumes and expects the universe to justify itself and that God as all powerful is also good.

Job does not cry out for justice he cries out for *sense; does the universe make sense?* The subject questions the master. The clay questions the potter. He wants God to reveal himself as not insanely absurd. Job's urgent question is an ontological one concerning the meaning of meaning. Even after the calamities that befall him, Job does not charge God with unreason.

There were seven days and seven nights of suffering. Then, *Job broke silence and cursed the day of his birth* (Job 3:1–2). The cosmos is cursed. *Blind darkness swallows up the night* (Job 3:6). *May no star shine out in its twilight* (Job 3:9). *Why should the sufferer be born to see the light?* (Job 3:20). *Why should a man be born to wander blindly hedged in by God on every side?* (Job 3:23). Why? Why?

Chesterton calls this ancient yet perceptibly modern story a 'drama of scepticism', with God Himself as the arch-sceptic, not answering questions, not being at all reassuring but throwing down questions to his accusers in order to turn all their preconceptions upside down. To his accuser, He says: Now! You answer to Me! And like every sceptic-analyst, God asks Job who *he* is? *Who is this whose ignorant words cloud my design in darkness?* (Job 38:2). And Job like every analysand cannot answer! The Sceptic continues remorselessly: *Where were you when I laid the earth's foundations?* (Job 38:4). *Who watched over the sea when it burst its flood from the womb?* (Job 38:8). ...*Have you ever called up the dawn or shown the morning its place?* (Job 38:12). *Has the rain a father? Who sired the drops of dew? Whose womb gave birth to ice?* (Job 38:28, 29). Here God declares the radical otherness of the world and the arrogance of Job who presumes to know.

As Jehovah's litany of questions continues, Job is curiously enervated by the sceptical process, beginning to see in its absolute strangeness and poetry some obscure part of God's unknowable design. As Chesterton says in his introduction to the Book of Job, 'To startle man, God becomes for an instant a blasphemer; one might almost say that God becomes for an instant an atheist'. God insists the world is beyond human understanding. God is shocked and disbelieves his own creation. The lion, the raven, the goat, the wild ass, the ostrich, the crocodile, each described as a singularity, each monstrously original in turn. The whole is a sort of psalm or rhapsody to the sense of sublime wonder. Each is described from the perspective of *first* seeing, the absolute felt in the least thing: *when the morning stars sang together and all the sons of God shouted for joy* (Job 38:7).

The ontological question of meaning is met *not* with reason but with epic poetry which exalts rather than consoles. As Steiner says, God relies on 'the sheer absolute wondrousness that transcends thought, on the mysterium presented in its pure non-rational form … the well-nigh demonic and wholly incomprehensible character of the eternal creative power'.[77] Chesterton suggests that we glimpse in the metaphors that 'the secret of God is a bright and not a sad one'.[78]

The strength of Christianity shows uniquely in its willingness to be broken: Job is broken; God is broken. On the Mount of Olives, Chesterton visits the garden kept by the Franciscans on the site of Gethsemane, containing the gnarled slow-growing olive, said to represent the agony of Christ. Chesterton recalls that a child from one of the villages told him that it was the place where God said his prayers. Chesterton adds that 'he could not ask for a finer or more defiant statement of all that separates the Christian from the Moslem or the Jew'.[79] In all other religions, we pray to God, but in Christianity God prays to God.

In Gethsemane, the agony of Christianity is revealed. Christ is divided, no more so than at the Passion. As Chesterton fears to explain, 'the author of all things (in some remarkable way) went not only through agony, but also through doubt. It is written, "Thou shalt not tempt the Lord thy God." No; but the Lord thy God may tempt Himself; and it seems as if this is what happened in Gethsemane'. He went through an agony of doubt and darkness. This was the moment when the world shook and the sun was wiped out of heaven, not at the crucifixion, but the cry from the cross which confessed that 'God had forsaken God'. *My God my God why hast thou forsaken me*? (Matthew 27:46–47). Jesus is quoting Psalm 22:1, written about a millennium before; he was fulfilling the prophecy.

> *Be not far from me, for trouble is near; for there is none to help. Many bulls have surrounded me; Strong bulls of Bashan have encircled me. They open wide their mouth at me, as a ravening and a roaring lion. I am poured out like water, And all my bones are out of joint; My heart is like wax; It is melted within me. My strength is dried up like a potsherd, And my tongue cleaves to my jaws; And Thou dost lay me in the dust of death. For dogs have surrounded me; A band of evildoers has encompassed me; They pierced my hands and my feet. I can count all my bones. They look, they stare at me. They divide my garments among them, And for my clothing they cast lots.*
>
> (*Psalm 22:11–18*)

Chesterton challenges the atheists to find *their* god: 'They will find only one divinity who ever uttered their isolation; only one religion in which God seemed for an instant to be an atheist'.[80] God forsakes God. For Chesterton, Christianity is a revolutionary creed,

> ...a good man may have his back to the wall ... but that God should have his back to the wall is a boast for all insurgents forever. Christianity is the only religion on earth that has felt that omnipotence made God incomplete. Christianity alone has felt that God, to be wholly God, must have been a rebel as well as a king.[81]

Against the apparent peace of participation, our account sets God at the unfathomable epicentre of the violence of negativity and radical antagonism. Sunday, for example, the arch-rebel-God curses the police, curses the people in power, 'the fat smiling men in blue', not for their cruelty, not just because they are the law, but for being safe, for *never having been broken*. 'You are the seven angels of heaven, and you have had no troubles. I could forgive you everything, you that rule mankind, if I could feel for once that you had suffered for one hour a real agony such as I … "Have you," he cried in a dreadful voice, "Have you ever suffered?" … "Can ye drink of the cup that I drink of?"'[82]

Thus to the old questions: 1) Why does God permit suffering? 2) Where is God when we suffer? 3) Why is God powerless? The questions should be turned around: how would suffering be registered in all its anguish *without* reference to transcendence? Without God, there would be no suffering, that is, no means to *register* suffering, no *break* on suffering, no wrath of God. Without God, *there would be nothing but suffering.* After all, terror trainings and army trainings aim to bring about this *de*-meaning, desensitising effect, to make it possible to kill (the first killing is the most difficult), to engender indifference to suffering, to enable a pitiless universe, a mere field full of bodies, a pure biomass calculation that celebrates 'the job well done'. By 'drinking of that cup', by suffering that agony, by experiencing the absurd nihilism of the world, the God-forsaking-God of the afflicted, evil is revealed, the veil of the imaginary is removed. The truth is revealed – Christ's dereliction. As Weil has stressed, Christianity is finally not any consolation.

As we learnt from Girard, *only* Christianity takes suffering full on, declaring the innocence and powerlessness of the sacrificial victim. In the most radical way, by *becoming* the sacrificial victim via the incarnation, God became man, giving the lie to the rationally justifiable cycle of violence. Part of the pure machinics, the monstrous grinding of the deaf-blind necessity of the materialist universe *without God*, revealed in all its horror. The cosmos is cursed. Darkness swallows up the night. God permits his radical absence to be felt without consolation – *there is no God*!

Decadence or responsibility

The Czech philosopher, student of Husserl and Heidegger, Jan Patočka, returns us to our (psychoanalytic) quest to ground the subject *outside herself* non-indifferently within transcendence. Patočka refused to join the Communist party after WW2, and was therefore barred from academia and publishing except briefly during the Prague Spring in 1968. He did teach and his lectures were circulated in the so-called "Underground University." He joined Václav Havel and Jiří Hájek in the Charter 77 human-rights declaration. He was harassed, then arrested, and finally died of a heart attack during prolonged police interrogation in March 1977.

In his *Heretical Essays*,[83] Patočka develops a genealogy of European culture leading to the emergence of responsibility; his project being to account for 'the retreat of Europe from the centre of history' (96). He links this retreat with decadence. What has been defined here as anti-Oedipal, Patočka calls decadent: 'A society can be said to be decadent if it so functions as to encourage a decadent life, *a life addicted to what is inhuman by its very nature*' (97, emphasis added). Patočka defines decadence in the clearest manner, referring to life's intrinsic being, life as a whole (*Lebenswelt*), not specific behaviours or activities. A decadent life is disrupted at its "core" in such a way as to weaken or lose 'its grasp on the innermost nerve of its functioning' (97). He has in mind drug abuse, the revolt of the youth, suicidal disturbances and the destruction of all social taboos. Against decadence, Patočka speaks of fully taking on life's burden – responsibility rather than escape – leading to an authentic as opposed to an inauthentic existence.

His genealogy starts with the Sacred Real – the orgiastic, the demonic, the erotic, as against the profane world of the Symbolic. Patočka suggests that the subject *qua* subject emerges at the dawn of history, by *not* being lost in the Sacred, by not simply surrendering to it, but maintaining the tension between the Sacred and Profane. He speaks of an 'inner *mastering* of the sacred' and cites the emergence of epic and especially dramatic poetry, tragedy and philosophy as important correlates of this historical process, amounting to *rising above decadence*.

History is first and foremost a history of the soul and Socrates designated the *polis* as the proper place of history and the proper place of the care of the soul. The starting place is Plato's allegory of the cave, the womb of Earth Mother, source of the traditional mysteries and orgiastic cults. Plato's idea, recalled above, is to leave the cave and follow the pure "path of light," that is to subordinate the demonic to responsibility, towards the sun of "the Good." Hence the frequent celebration in Greek discourse of daybreak and first light.

Responsibility thus triumphs over the orgiastic and *incorporates* it at the same time. However, Patočka is clear, 'the orgiastic is not removed but is disciplined and made subservient' (106). Confrontation with the Sacred is also the facing of and vigil over death, the overcoming of death. Thus, as we have indicated above, the Neoplatonic philosopher, with the demonic confined to a subjugated realm (repressed), arrives as an inspired holy man – a thaumaturge, a medium, a holy fool, a Faust. In Simone Weil's Platonic conception, God seeks out man, in the forms of beauty, order, truth and justice which proceed from the Good. For Plato, perfection is One. The Roman Empire, made possible by the Platonic conception of the soul, brings a global dimension of Ideal Forms, 'raising the community out of the state of "nature"' (35), striving for truth and justice. Freedom is no longer defined in terms of equality, but in relation to the transcendent Good.

The "care for the soul" which is key, is the Greek bequest to Europe coming down to contemporary psychoanalysis. For Patočka (and for Freud), '[t]he care of the soul means that truth is … a lifelong enquiry, a self-controlling, self-unifying intellectual and vital practice' (82), governed, above all, by a "culture of insight."

Christianity represents a further development of the genealogy. Life is now seen as *a gift*, having the character of the Good, but *retaining* a relation, a link to the inaccessible, the sacred mystery. The Good in Christianity, however, is a self-forgetting Goodness and a self-denying love, ultimately a *mysterium tremendum*. No longer is the soul directed to the Good as ideal object, but to a *person*, who sees into the soul without being accessible to us. Transgression takes on a new meaning as sin, not against the Good as such but against divine love. As Patočka says in a Lacanian moment, 'The responsible human as such is *I*; it is an individual that is *not identical* with any role it could possibly assume' (107, emphasis added).

The soul within Christianity reveals 'not the truth of intuition [as in Greek metaphysical conception], but rather the truth of its own destiny, bound up with eternal responsibility from which there is no escape' (107). Open to the abyss of the divine – not the empty zero – Patočka understands the soul to be 'wholly incommensurate' with the eternal and is therefore always responsible *within* history; as he says, 'historical in all its being' (108), eschewing decadence. Patočka refers to this Christian development as 'an abyssal deepening of the soul', and he believes that 'Christianity remains thus far the greatest, unsurpassed but also *un-thought-through* human outreach that enabled humans to struggle against decadence' (108, emphasis added). The collapse of the Roman Empire and its oppressive slave culture enabled the birth of Europe with its "free" people, however exploited, modest and limited this autonomy was. This led to 'an awesome expansive power' from the Crusades to the imperialistic 'grasp for the wealth of the world' (110).

In a Heideggerian–Baudrillardian frame, Patočka understands modern capitalism with its 'cold "truth" of the coldest of cold monsters' (112) as a return to the orgiastic-Sacred, within an unspiritual, secular everydayness. Just as in revolutions, as Durkheim noted, where secular themes become sacred – Fatherland, Liberty, Reason – now also technology, which draws everything human into its orbit acquires a sacred mystique. Thus, 'a wild freedom takes hold of states, becoming "*total*." The same hand stages orgies and organises everydayness' (114). What Baudrillard called the 'technological realisation of the world', becomes for Patočka following Heidegger 'this gigantic Boredom which cannot be covered up'. He suggests that 'The most sophisticated inventions are boring if they do not lead to an exacerbation of the Mystery …' (114). Whereas for Baudrillard it is the loss of the Real, for Patočka it is the loss of Mystery and soul via the corresponding *total* identification of modern man since the Renaissance with his [virtual] role. We no longer seek 'to penetrate beyond and beneath every role but rather to play an *important* role' (115).

The loss of the soul, the fall into decadence, the loss of "inner grasp," the failure to overcome *ressentiment*, lay waste the gift of life, caught, as it were, in the slavery, fixation and rootlessness of the anti-Oedipus complex.

Consider by way of illustration those who have been "healed" in Oscar Wilde's short parable, 'The Doer of Good'.[84] The prose poem starts: It was nighttime. He was alone. He drew near to the city. He approached a wealthy palace of marble and entered the hall where there was feasting. He saw lying on a couch of sea-purple one whose hair was crowned with red roses and whose lips were red with wine. And he went behind him and touched him on the shoulder and said unto him, 'Why do you live like this?' And the young man turned around and recognised Him, and made an answer and said, 'But I was a leper once, and you healed me. How else should I live?' Later, in the street, he sees a beautiful couple and the eyes of the young man 'were bright with lust'. He followed swiftly and touched the hand of the young man and said to him, 'Why do you look at this woman in such wise'? And the young man turned around and recognised Him and said, 'But I was blind once, and you gave me sight. At what else should I look'? And he ran forward and touched the painted raiment of the woman and said to her, 'Is there no other way in which to walk save in the way of sin?' And the woman turned round and recognised Him, and laughed and said, 'But you forgave me my sins, and the way is a pleasant way'. Then he leaves the city and he sees on the roadside a man who is weeping. And the man looked up and recognised Him and made answer, 'But I was dead once and you raised me from the dead. What else should I but weep?'

Derrida has underlined the importance of Patočka's work which consolidates *three* interconnected histories – the history of the subject, the history of responsibility and the history of Europe. One can speak of religion only *after* the orgiastic-sacred has been *dépassé*, "outstripped," or "outmoded," not destroyed as such, but been made *subservient to responsibility*. Religion derives its meaning from 'a *passage* to responsibility'. Religion is nothing without responsibility. Yet, as Derrida emphasises, 'historical man does not want to *admit to* historicity, and first and foremost to the abyss that undermines his own historicity',[85] and that 'Christianity has perhaps not yet thought through the very essence of the self [in responsibility] whose arrival it nevertheless records' (6). Christianity is already ahead of itself.

Derrida repeats Patočka's genealogy with a psychoanalytic gloss. First, the break with the orgiastic-erotic, the demonic, the mystagogic, initiatory and esoteric. The *daimon*, as such, crosses the boundaries of the human-animal-divine, defined as "irresponsible" from this side of the genealogy being developed. From *within* the demonic there can be no question of responsibility. Plato breaks with the orgiastic mystery, by incorporating or repressing it, the secret of that history being carried forward into a thaumaturgical tradition. Thereafter, the *mysterium tremendum* of Christian responsibility. Plato's "conversion" towards the Good is a new mystery of the soul. One mystery is replaced by another, although the latter is undeclared and unacknowledged. Psychoanalytically speaking, the new version retains something of what it interrupts or represses.

For Derrida these conversions amount to 'a process of mourning, facing up to a loss, in the sense of keeping within oneself that whose death one must endure' (9). There are therefore *three* mysteries to be acknowledged – orgiastic, Platonic and Christian. The trajectory, depicted by Patočka and elaborated by Derrida, is a kind of extended mourning and as such Derrida will refer to 'the gift of death' [*se donner la mort*], which implies 'dying while assuming responsibility for one's death' (10), in the manner of Socrates, Christ and others, including Patočka himself. By 'keeping vigil', what Derrida has in mind is a 'subjectivising interiorisation, the movement of the soul's gathering of itself … to recall itself to itself … to keep itself in this gesture of *remembering*' (13). This vigil creates the psyche itself, as it 'assembles' and 'wakes' itself, in existence. 'The psyche as life, as breath of life, as *pneuma*, only appears out of this concerned anticipation of dying' (15). Assuming one's history in responsibility is precisely the psychoanalytic goal. Recall, that is witnessing on the edge of strangeness, meaninglessness and death, in the manner of a vigil, fully awake but anticipating death – is only fully possible in the light of the Good. As Levinas makes clear, 'Goodness gives to subjectivity its irreducible signification'.[86] To recall without responsibility to the Good risks sheer narcissistic indulgence, decadence and self-pity. While to recall while claiming nothing for oneself, in the light of the Good is mourning and sorrow which is at times intensely moving. Psychoanalysis is trivial and self-serving in the absence of this light which illuminates the wretched boredom of decadence, as well as joy and laughter in the effort of re-membering and gathering in the midst of grace. Without wakefulness, vigilance as well as playfulness and humour beyond self-seeking, psychoanalytic practice is decadent.

Patočka and Derrida stress that responsible freedom arising from overcoming the orgiastic slumber can go into reverse, can be undone, with the ever present danger of the sacred's irruption from its disciplined, repressed secrecy. As Derrida summarises, 'This genealogy has a [psychoanalytic] axiom, namely, that history never effaces what it buries; it always keeps within itself the secret of whatever it encrypts, the secret of its secret. This is a secret history of kept secrets' (21). Should we recognise that "contemporary" Christianity fails, or in Derrida's words, 'is incapable of reflecting on the Platonic thinking it represses, and at the same time it is incapable of reflecting on the orgiastic mystery that Platonic thinking incorporates' (24)? Just as there is a double secrecy infolded within Christianity, there may be corresponding double incapacity.

Responsibility implies *full* responsibility with the risk of apostasy, dissidence, or indeed regression, the return to irresponsibility and decadence. Psychoanalysis, by staying close to *jouissance* (the orgiastic sacred), underlines this risk and should make us hesitate here in our engagement with Christian doctrine. As Lacan reminds us, 'we take *that* path we miss the opening onto *jouissance*'.[87] Consequently, we have emphasised the paradoxical, contradictory nature of this complex doctrine to avoid simplistic and trite interpretations and fusions, or the (ab)use of Christianity to blame, coerce or censor the other. The Christian mystery is a terrifying mystery which represents a 'plumbing [of] the depths of this abyss of responsibility' (28). Therefore, Derrida following Patočka concludes that 'Christianity has not yet come to Christianity', by which he means that within European history and politics, and add Lacanian psychoanalysis, there has not yet come to fulfilment 'the new responsibility announced by the *mysterium tremendum*' (28).

There has not been the complete break with the Greek *polis* and the Roman *civitas*. And Derrida, with Patočka, wonders what that break might be like. No longer for them the imaginary register of the Platonic Good and the One, the shining new mythology of the soul, the soul rising on its eternal journey to the transcendent Good. But, quite the contrary: 'a supreme being, of God as one, holding me from within and within his gaze, defines everything regarding me, and so *rouses me to responsibility*' (31, emphasis added). The mystery returns as the ineffable *mysterium tremendum*, the radically inaccessible "wholly other," God beyond God. The soul that eternally intuits Platonic Ideas becomes a different and eternally precarious soul that faces death and responsibility, trembling in anguish and in hope between two eternities. Derrida asserts psychoanalytically that responsibility rests on 'a nucleus of irresponsibility' (20), the encrypted sacred, which nevertheless retains the power to deconstruct and destroy any firm notion of responsibility.

As we have indicated the decadence of modernity fosters the return of the orgiastic-sacred: 'The domination of technology encourages demonic irresponsibility' (35–6). Enslaved to gadgets and hedonism, the soul is quite lost to the myriad forms of the inhuman or post-human, the return of the thaumatological via the hubris of Platonic rationalism gone mad.

Goldman criticises this Derridian analysis, pointing to its Gnostic rather than specifically historical Christian perspective. He asserts, *á la* Girard, that, 'Rather than repressing the demonic, Christianity reveals the hidden truth of demonic violence'.[88] From his standpoint of generative anthropology, history begins with a revelatory "originary event:" Christianity reveals the scapegoat mechanism and our propensity for sacrificial violence. Thus, there is nothing "secret" or repressed about the demonic. As Goldman asserts, 'The figurality of the Cross is first and foremost the revelation of the scapegoat mechanism in the disfigured body of the victim'. The victim is a specific historical figure and he is *human*. Goldman points out that the Christian *mysterium tremendum* is first given in the Old Testament in Mosaic Law. The prophets demanded a radical interiorisation of the law in place of external rituals and sacrifice. *I will put my law in their inward parts, and write it in their hearts* (Jeremiah 31:33). Second, the Law is given in the Crucifixion as we come face to face with God. Goldman asserts that, 'We fear and tremble not because God is absolutely different, but precisely because he is identical to myself'. Christ deconstructs the scapegoat mechanism from within. Instead of opacity, secrecy and otherness, the Law could not be clearer. He stresses that 'Gnosticism, not Christianity, incorporates Platonism and the demonic'. Gnosticism, based on the denial of the historical Jesus, lacks the (appalling) doctrine of original sin and thus undermines human responsibility. It keeps things satisfyingly fluid and ungrounded, part of our postmodern generalised anti-Oedipul distrust directed towards any and every form of authority, especially Christian authority. Maybe Derrida's unexplicated notion of original sin is like Levinas's, in that any given situation of responsibility is effectively neutralised, made impossible, by the multiplicity of other demands that go unanswered. Every responsible act for *one* other is a betrayal of all others. Thus each responsible act for the one – a singularity – is the gift of death for the other; "absolute treachery" (68) no less.

As mentioned above, politics, the Law (Symbolic), peace (pacification) processes, top-down decision making and so on, may be good enough in the round but are treacherous and unjust to individuals, who oftentimes remain radically unresponded to, unheeded and marginalised. Derrida reminds us contented bourgeois, 'One simply keeps on denying [this] aporia and antinomy, tirelessly, and one treats as a nihilist, relativist, even post-structuralist, and worst still deconstructionist, all those who remain concerned in the face of such a display of good conscience' (85). Many of the "concerned" however seem to remain *unconcerned*: the mass of contented bourgeois who deny the aporia as well as those "concerned" who avow it, because they are confronted immediately with the Derridean "impossibility:" not *everyone* can be helped.

Goldman acknowledges that some of the worst collective violence has been carried out in the name of Christianity. 'The sacrificial is a constant temptation within human culture because of our inherent propensity to mimetic rivalry and conflict, and Christianity is by no means immune to the temptation of the sacrificial'. However, Goldman asserts that Derrida's anti-humanism is nostalgic for the Sacred and that more generally, 'academics have brought back the sacred with a vengeance. But as a result of iconoclasm, the sacred now takes the abstract form of absolute difference or alterity, and any attempt to understand or even discuss rationally the incommensurable is abandoned'. God is absent or leaves only a trace. Thus what Lacan was to desire-ethics, Derrida is to ethics: 'My first and last responsibility, my first and last desire, is that responsibility of responsibility that relates me to what no one else can do in my place' (44). No Catholic collectivity here, no common good, no *realisable* brotherhood; no Aristotelian virtue for sinful humanity accepting of imperfection, just ethical *me* and lots of ethical mes – with impossibility, with incommensurability, with aspiration for justice beyond justice, leading to nothing? Classically, Abraham alone on Mt Moriah about to sacrifice Isaac: the religious (singularity) beyond the universal; the suspension of the moral law for the sake of a higher law. Clearly, Derrida like Kierkegaard[89] points *beyond* the moral norm, the universal, and the admittedly *limited* human good that Goldman insists upon, towards the inhuman and the unspeakable, namely, the violent Sacred command to sacrifice Isaac, only rescinded at the last moment.

Notwithstanding, Abraham travels into exile, living in tents (Hebrews 11:9) within the context of the gift of God's grace. Thus he welcomes strangers, who *confessed themselves no more than strangers or passing travellers on earth* (Hebrews 11:13). His faith, their faith, points to their participation in the economy of grace, of generosity, of hospitality, indeed of responsibility. The deepest meaning of responsibility is our response-*ability* to the overflowing gratuity. The story of the hospitality of Abraham in Genesis 18 is exemplary. Three strangers appear at the entrance to the tent during the heat of the day. Abraham and Sarah offer hospitality to them, including foot washing, rest, and a sumptuous meal. Only later do Abraham and Sarah realise that they have given hospitality to God.

Derrida stresses the utter Otherness of ourselves to ourselves and the other, and the utter Otherness of God. Abraham's relation to God is analogous to my relation to every other. For Derrida, there must be no reassurance. He seeks to evoke the extremes of exile, uncertainty, estrangement, isolation, death, sacrifice, and so on; to evoke the Kantian absolute duty with no "good conscience," in a world which

> *allows* to die of hunger and disease tens of millions of children … participates in this incalculable sacrifice, it actually organizes it … this order is founded upon a bottomless chaos (the abyss or open mouth) is something that will necessarily be brought home one day to those [of *us*? All of us, including Derrida?] who just as necessarily forget the same. (86)

Ironically, Derrida's 'passage to responsibility' is simultaneously the passage to *im*-possibility and *ir*-responsibility. A Catharist vision opens up: the world as evil; being as evil; striving as evil. One cannot avoid the radical truth of his position. No incrementalist view of social progress is going to let us forget this apocalyptic discourse, the casualties of which are utterly transparent to us through the new *im*-media. Heidegger once quipped, 'Only a god can save us now'.[90] With absolutely no bridge between the cursed alleged totality of violent hegemony of present arrangements and the messianic *á venir*, we glimpse a perfectly pure space for the righteous gestural politics so typical of the postmodern. For Derrida, it puts to right the old accusation that "deconstruction" was apolitical.[91] For Derrida it is *hyper*-political with a full anti-Oedipal ethical vengeance.

There is an ironic twist. In 1981, when lecturing in Czechoslovakia, Derrida was suddenly arrested for smuggling drugs, planted in his case by a police officer who was himself later arrested. Derrida found himself briefly *without* the 'rule of law' that he had always enjoyed as a French citizen, while at the same time remorselessly attacking it. He was released only after the direct intervention of President François Mitterrand. Afterwards, when questioned about the irony of his situation, he claimed that the *two* levels – his anti-humanist rhetoric as against the reality of the hard fought for enlightenment-inspired human rights – do not intersect!

Similarly, for Levinas, there is no "outside" of ethics. Levinas suggests, counter-intuitively, that the unavoidable call of the other *qua* neighbour is our liberation! For Levinas, 'It is starting from the existence of the other that my existence can be posed as human',[92] that is, *not* in-human, *not* decadent. Everywhere in his writing, Levinas's philosophy contests the violent ontology of our sole aspiration to persevere in being – Spinoza's *conatus essendi*, an atomised self-striving, which psychoanalysis necessarily endorses. Instead, Levinas posits the originary "theological structure" of the psyche, 'a concave without a convex',[93] a turning inside-out, turning the other cheek, hyperbolic passivity, bursting of the skin and so on.

Against these postmodernist thinkers, Cunningham asserts, 'the hegemony of the nothing sucks all in, allowing (only) nothingness to escape'.[94] He points out that 'in the post-apocalyptic tone of the disaster [of being], the question is no longer "to be or not to be," but *to be without being*. In other words to *be* nothing: the nothing *as* something. Like Beckett, we cannot go on, but we do, we will, we must. Such is the positive discourse of nihilism'.[95] Cunningham speaks of nihilism's "univocity of nonbeing," the *one* Voice of the non-being that underlies everything and every being in-differently and pointlessly. Prophylactic suicide seems the best option. Pascal: the I is detestable. Simone Weil says, 'I regard the world as if I am not there'. To be nothing. To extinguish oneself. Sacrifice, as in Romans 12:1: *Therefore my brothers, I implore you by God's mercy to offer your very selves to him: a living sacrifice …* Kenosis. Levinas looks to the *other* humanity who will surrender life.

However for Levinas, there is the Good; there is plenitude of goodness beyond being. Levinas speaks of the good of the ordinary people in spite of enduring appalling conditions. The key reference is Vassily Grossman's *Life and Fate*, a *magnum opus* that bears witness to the end of totalitarian Europe. 'What remain[ed]', says

Levinas, 'is individual goodness, from man to man … Ethics without an ethical system'.[96] Goodness without thinking, without theory, without organisation; fragile before the power of evil. Goodness is recognised across cultures, because goodness precedes enculturation. The Good goes unnoticed, because it is *otherwise* than being. Derived ultimately from Plato (as above), but Levinas prefers Grossman's character Ikonnikov who says, 'There is neither God nor the Good, but there is goodness'.[97] Levinas adds, 'this is not a matter of rejoicing in a precious world-behind-the-scenes in which it would be convenient to install the God of religion comfortably'.[98] Levinas' whole oeuvre, like his contemporaries', is about separation from, and radical opposition to, any totalising ontology. Otherwise than being is so-to-speak *younger* than the cynical indifferent order of the world – wide awake, insomniacal, open, originary, giving.

As Levinas has it, 'From the Good to me, there is an assignation: a relation that survives the death of God'.[99] The Good is before being, 'the Good cannot become present or enter into a representation … it has chosen me before I have chosen it'.[100] Defenceless, one is affected by the other before one has any choice. 'Subjectivity is a subjection to the force of alterity, which calls for and demands goodness of it'.[101] This affection Levinas refers to as "anarchic trauma." The Good merely reabsorbs the sharp violent effects of this trauma.

For Levinas, the Good is not good because *we* choose it, desire it and it attracts *us*, but precisely the opposite. The Good is good because it *interrupts* ongoing desire and life, redirecting it towards responsibility for the neighbour. It breaks the decadent sacred spell (*jouissance*) to touch the forbidden Thing. However, the Good renounces any power. It is an an-archy that leaves us free. 'Anarchy cannot be sovereign, like an arche. It can only disturb the State'.[102]

The proximity of the other, closer to us than any neighbour – the traumatic, violent *im*-mediacy of this closer than close proximity – calls for control, the whole political apparatus of the State. But such controls 'must not be taken for an anonymous law of "human forces" governing an impersonal totality'.[103] A "fleeting trace" is left of the transcendent, which 'does not let itself be assembled'. Always, hints Levinas, 'the human plot is hatched in proximity'.[104]

Justice is key and justice should serve 'this priority of the other who remains the ethical measure of any politics. Once the State is created, it has its own proper (symbolic) reality. One must then be able to stop it when the anonymousness of the law suppresses "charity"'.[105] Here as elsewhere Levinas seems to moderate his radical position about the totality of being.

Levinas articulates a *secular* Judaism. By making infinity central, by removing God to just "a trace," Levinas has opened wide the void, implying human thought rests on nothing. The secular regime is supported by nothing, only the cold "*il y a*" and the destitute face of the other *qua* wretched stranger on the earth. A radically precarious and impossible ethics of alterity without limits stands in for religion, an ethics beyond religion. Judaism *à la* Levinas, emphasising universal responsibility, equality and justice due to all human beings, becomes the *sole* remaining moral conscience in a secular world, an ethics without content. Levinas asserts that the non-thematisable, unrepresentable monotheistic God should be evoked, should come to mind 'when I am called not to leave him [the other] alone'. 'The "otherwise than being" is the glory of God'.[106]

Three chapters collected into a slim volume, *Humanism and the Other*, acquire a special value here. Written before, during and after the '68 convulsions and mindful of the twentieth century horrors that preceded them; Levinas nails his *humanist* colours to the mast. Humanism is always insufficiently human and yet he strongly opposes the *anti*-humanism privileged by Levi-Strauss, Lacan, Foucault, Derrida *et al.*, and all the anti-Oedipals who pitilessly celebrated the death of the subject, the death of man, the death of God, the end of metaphysics, and so on. He criticises the "lofty literature" and the "lofty spirits" 'with no hold on the realities of violence and exploitation. All respect for the "human mystery" is therefore denounced as ignorance and oppression'. He speaks ominously of 'a mutation in the light of the world'.[107] He notes the chill nostalgia for the severe rigours of logical formalism and mathematical structures, which have no need of the subject. He is critical of Heidegger and the submergence of the human subject in the impersonal "truth of being." Absurdity, says Levinas, 'does not lie in nonsense, but in the isolation of countless significations, the absence of a sense that orients them ... Absurdity lies in the multiplicity within pure indifference'.[108] The anti-Oedipal echo here, resonating strongly throughout this present work, is strongest – absurdity – multiplicity – indifference. 'Referring to the climax of the German language in Hegel – the "Bacchic delirium when no limb escapes from drunkenness," Levinas declares that 'there needs to be a cell that is itself sober'.[109]

In Catholic teaching that "cell" is the family, the "home" of the Oedipus complex, the out-working of which, according to Freud, is fateful for psychoanalysis and society. Freud was always aware, unlike most post-Freudians, of the horrors that await what we have called the *anti*-Oedipus complex and its out-workings. Whatever the ambivalences, discontents and limitations of the former, they pale into insignificance in the deterritorialised God-forsaken lonely, isolated spaces of the latter.

Notes

1 Such ideological fervour maybe placed in better perspective if we view Žižek's claim in a specifically Irish Catholic context. During times of recession in Ireland, there have been reports of religious statues "moving," or statuesque figures "crying." These were said to be miracles utterly believed by believers. Events? Truths? Just as Mary is "seen" regularly by pilgrims at Knock shrine.
2 Žižek, S., 2009. In Davis, C., 2009: 236, emphasis added.
3 Freud, S., 1937b: 263.
4 Freud, S., 1923, 1922: 115; and Freud, S., 1911: 96.
5 It is nearly 20 years since Mikkel Borch-Jacobsen made the following observation in a discussion with Todd Dufresne: 'People who had come to Lacan because of his critique of the "subject-supposed-to-know" would turn into the most rigid, dogmatic, intolerant disciples; left radicals who had been attracted by Lacan's subversive aspects would

become ultra-conformist bureaucrats of the Lacanian school; free spirits would start reading the *Écrits* as if it was the Bible' (cited in Dufresne, T., 2000: 11–12).

6 See www.theguardian.com/commentisfree/2011/dec/18/christopher-hitchens-nick-cohen-tribute.

7 Derrida, J., 1998: 29.

8 Taylor, C., 2007: 25.

9 Ibid.: 253.

10 Ibid.: 243–4.

11 Ibid.: 142.

12 Ibid.: 309/.

13 Ibid.: 266.

14 Fukuyama, F., 1992.

15 See, for instance, Toft, M., Philpot, D., and Shah, T., 2011 and Westerlund, D., 1996. The separation of church and state has been increasingly questioned in recent decades by various religious movements and organisations. Christian, Muslim, Hindu, Buddhist and Sikh fundamentalists are seeking to overthrow established political, religious and social norms in their quest for a religiously based form of government. However, the conclusions of the Pew Research Centre's Forum on Religion and Public Life (September 2012) indicate the opposite trend. Analysing 197 countries and territories worldwide, they identify a sharp rise in the limits set on religious practice globally and a six per cent increase in restrictions in the last four years.

16 Lacan, J., 1964: 59.

17 Milbank, J., 1990.

18 See, for instance, Milbank, J., and Oliver, S., 2009.

19 Reno, R., 2000.

20 Plato, *The Republic*. Penguin Modern Classics, p. 273.

21 Aquinas cited in Cunningham, C., 2002: 179.

22 Davis, C. "Subtractive Liturgy," in Davis, C., Milbank, J., and Žižek, S., 2010: 148.

23 Ibid.: 73. This passage recalls our earlier discussion on the expansive generosity of languages in Chapter 7.

24 See, for instance, www.theguardian.com/politics/2008/may/22/2.

25 Milbank, J. in Davis, C., Milbank, J., and Žižek, S., 2010: 65–6.

26 Pickstock, C. in Milbank, J., and Oliver, S., 2009: 133.

27 Milbank, J. in Davis, C., 2009: 186.

28 One sees this possibility again and again in the psychoanalytic context. The subject is endlessly condemned by guilt and depression for real or imagined "crimes" for which there appears to be no possible atonement. Only an active and just forgiveness may break the deadlock. Something rigorous is required lest we be misunderstood as descending into sentimentality and banality: *I'm okay; you're okay*! (The title of a popular folk psychology book of the 1970s).

29 Milbank is following Badiou's 'latent Christian metaphysics', in Davis, C., Milbank, J., and Žižek, S., 2010: 226.

30 *The Sunday Service* broadcast on BBC Radio 4 on 20 January 2002.

31 Oliver, S. in Milbank, J., and Oliver, S., 2009: 19.

32 Univocal, one voice, sameness, same meaning, same sense. God and creation fall under *one* common concept of "being," with God having the most intense being at an infinite distance from us finite beings. Thus, God becomes irrelevant as he is unattainable at this infinite remove. The way is thus opened up for a secular atheistic space, according to RO theorists. All this begins with Duns Scotus. The univocal universe is flat and rhizomic.

33 Equivocal, pure difference, antithetical, dialectical. All is anarchic creativity and difference with no stability. The *relative* flux of history. Nothing is categorical.

34 Milbank, J. in Davis, C., 2009: 162, 163.

35 Simpson, C., and Caputo, J., 2012: 33–46.

36 From "Mending Wall," 1914.

37 Milbank, J. in Davis, C., 2009: 166.
38 Ibid.: 175.
39 Weil, S., 1947: 150.
40 Miles, S., 2005. An introduction to Weil, S., 1986: 28–9, 34–5.
41 Milbank, J. in Davis, C., 2009: 193, emphasis added.
42 Cited in Critchley, S., 2001: 27, emphasis added.
43 Ibid.: 29.
44 Weil, S., 1947: 18.
45 Shakespeare, S., 2000.
46 Comment by a contributor called Halden, italics added. www.inhabitatiodei.com/2007/07/03/outnarrating-nihilism/.
47 Reno, R., 2000.
48 Hyman, G., 2010.
49 Milbank, J., 1997: 1.
50 Hyman, G., 2010.
51 I have expanded on this theme here: Weatherill, R., 2011: 114–16.
52 Chesterton, G., 1924: 7.
53 Chesterton, G. K., 1908a: 3.
54 Ibid.: 115.
55 Ibid.: 210.
56 Ibid.: 191.
57 Chesterton, G., 1924: 18.
58 Chesterton, G., 1925: 20.
59 Chesterton, G. K., 1908a: 108–9.
60 Gustav Thebon, in the introduction to Weil, S., 1947: xxi–xxii.
61 Weil, S., 1951: 81.
62 Grossman, V., 1998: 142.
63 Chesterton, G., 1925: 88.
64 Chesterton, G. K., 1908a,: 97.
65 Ibid.: 100.
66 Foucault, M., 1966: 373.
67 Chesterton, G. K., 1908b: 44–7.
68 See Freud, S., 1905: 524.
69 Derrida, J., 1998: 20.
70 Ibid.: 24.
71 Chesterton, G. K., 1908a: 16.
72 Ibid.: 15.
73 Ibid.: 116–17.
74 Ibid.: 21.
75 Ibid.: 72–3.
76 Chesterton, G., 1925: 131ff.
77 Steiner, G., 2001: 48.
78 Chesterton, G., "Introduction to the Book of Job." www.chesterton.org/introduction-to-job/.
79 Chesterton, G., www.chesterton.org/meaning-of-crusade/.
80 Chesterton, G. K., 1908a: 102.
81 Ibid.: 101.
82 Chesterton, G. K., 1908b: 205–7.
83 Patočka, J., 1990. All numbers in parentheses refer to this text.
84 Wilde, O., 1948: 863–4.
85 Derrida, J., 1992: 4 Page numbers in parentheses from here on refer to this text.
86 Levinas, E., 1981: 18.
87 Lacan, J., 1959–1960: 186.
88 Goldman, P., 1998.

89 Kierkegaard, S., 1843.
90 Wolin, R., 1993: 107.
91 Foucault, Edward Said, Gayatri Spivak, among others have criticised the 'there is nothing outside the text' academic preoccupations of deconstruction. See Wolin, R., 2004: 229ff.
92 Levinas, E., 2001: 129.
93 Levinas, E., 1981: 49.
94 Cunningham, C., 2002: 250.
95 Ibid.: 242.
96 See Levinas, E., 2001: 80.
97 Ibid.: 89.
98 Ibid.: 249.
99 Levinas, E., 1981: 123.
100 Ibid.: 11.
101 Lingis, A., in Introduction to Levinas, E., 1981: xxvii.
102 Levinas, E., 1981: 194, note 6.
103 Ibid.: 161.
104 Ibid.: 162.
105 See, for instance, the interview with Salomon Malka in Levinas, E., 2001: 101.
106 Levinas, E., 1982: 109.
107 Levinas, E., 2006b: 58–9.
108 Ibid.: 24.
109 Ibid.: 48.

AFTERWORD

Pure poetry

The standard liberal-Left take on the ongoing European crisis is that there are two evils to be fought against, namely, the absolute power of the undemocratic centralised technocracy in Brussels,[1] part of globalised capitalism, and second, the emergence of neo-fascist identitarian groups in many countries, violently separatist, pro-Christian, pro-white, anti-immigrant, etc. Thus, so the argument goes, we should re-dedicate ourselves to radical emancipatory values – equality, molecular self-determination, social justice and so on; fight the fascist-racism of the old nationalist Right. The trouble here is of course that the "right-on" people are now in truth, post Deleuze and Guattari, the *conventional* people seemlessly aligned with global capital itself networking horizontally while claiming to be anti-capitalist. This drives radicals like Badiou further leftwards into an extreme of event-fullness: *mieux vaut un désastre qu'un désêtre.*[2] For Badiou, better even the Stalinist terror than the *non-being* of contemporary capitalism. What Badiou has in mind is that only totalitarianism *per se* will formally blast open a new political *space* free from capitalism. This is akin to Baudrillard's, 'revenge of the object'. He imagined the Real getting its revenge on the hyper-real, treating evil with evil. 'It is difficult to denounce a universe that has rid itself of the subject, salvation and transcendence'.[3]

All is machinic:

> I am in a large European airport. I am in departures with my luggage waiting for the flight to be called. I imagine a time lapse film, showing robotic figures moving, zig-zagging back and forth, stopping, checking, rushing on again at great speeds. These robotic atoms are part of a turbulent chaotic flow, like molecules or Brownian motion, that never stops. I am privileged to see just a few moments of a continuous never-ending process. What moves these people, including myself when my time comes, stopping and looking at numbers on a screen, then speeding off down corridors. They form long lines,

> then break up and form again. They go to outlets and come out again just as quickly. What makes them move as if purposefully in this Orwellian fashion? No, they are not subjects; they are consumers. Salvation has no meaning for them. It is terrifying and bizarre.

These little robots represent the 'non-being of contemporary capitalism'. Where is the resistance to these immense mimetic forces that seem unstoppable? But this global apocalyptic analysis never takes account of the "silent masses," the teeming millions who live in the shadow of these titanic powers from the extremes. They are the "*désêtre* beings" who provide for their families, sacrifice themselves for each other, their communities and their countries, who believe in and attempt to live out the common good, but have no power as such. They struggle with Oedipal conflicts which they want to overcome. Capitalism has taken nearly one billion of such people out of extreme poverty in 20 years.[4] However, the silent masses, the "innocent civilians," are the main casualities of the extremist mimetic power grids that openly threaten to immiserate whole continents, to create *un désastre* in their name!

Remember, for instance, the mothers in Primo Levi's If This Is a Man, who on the day before being taken by train to Auschwitz, 'stayed up to prepare the food for the journey with tender care, and washed their children and packed their luggage; and at dawn the barbed wire was full of children's washing hung out in the wind to dry'. Levi asks, 'Would you not do the same? If you and your child were to be killed tomorrow, would you not give (to) him … to eat today?'[5]

Throughout we have been tracing the latent creative criminality, revealing creative destructiveness behind all the revolutionary talk coming from the safe citadels of academia and with the power to influence governments, continents and so on, largely unopposed.

In the first chapter of Chesterton's *The Man Who Thought He was Thursday*,[6] he tells the story of two poets: Lucian Gregory, from the fashionable Saffron Park, who celebrates 'the art of lawlessness' and 'the lawlessness of art', and his visiting adversary Gabriel Syme, who announces that he himself is also a poet, but a poet of *respectability and law and order*! Only an anarchist can be a poet, opines Gregory – only a bomber is an artist, a lover of disorder, hater of convention. Gregory loves the brilliant flash of *jouissance*, the perfect clap of thunder. Otherwise poetry is about as exciting as the London Underground. He is laughing sardonically at this point. Quite so, declares Syme! The London underground *is* poetry; every time a train comes in, it has won a battle against chaos! When a man takes aim and hits his target, things working, that's pure poetry. Later they are on the street and Gregory points his stick at a lamp post lighting up a tree. That iron lamp post is your law and order and the tree is the pure anarchy, abundance and poetry, would you not agree? Maybe, says Syme, but you are only seeing the tree illuminated by the lamp. How might it be if you saw the lamp illuminated by the light of the tree?

A century later, nothing has changed. Now, the man who bombs a plane is the true poet of the blinding flash of *jouissance*, rather than the co-ordered teams of people, designers, scientists, engineers, crew, and so on, who have given themselves (by renouncing their drives) to aircraft construction and preparation right up to the time it takes its last flight. For Chesterton and Syme, this instance of the plane flying would be beyond a poem; it would be a *miracle*.

The awakening

While Europe is threatened with its own final unravelling, the Euro crisis, Right wing nationalism, the migrant crisis and so on, other poets are on the march globally to reconquer the spiritually disenchanted West through extreme warrior vengeance, the way having being cleared by those confident and triumphant anti-Oedipalist intellectuals who tell us there is nothing to fear from Islam, the religion of peace.

Not long after the Twin Towers' atrocity, people on the Left in Ireland and elsewhere were comforting themselves with the thought that 'America had it coming to them'. More recently, after the attacks in Paris, the Stoppers (Stop The War Coalition) tweeted that France had "reaped the whirlwind" of Western support for extremist violence in the Middle East. The tweet was quickly removed after complaints.

Several years ago, Yusuf al-Qaradawi, an Egyptian-born religious scholar who is based in Qatar and is considered a spiritual guide of the Muslim Brotherhood, was banned from France as well as Britain for, 'justify[ing] acts of terrorist violence'. Notwithstanding, in the late 1990s Mr Qaradawi established the so-called European Council for Fatwa and Research, based at the Islamic Cultural Centre of Ireland in Clonskeagh in South Dublin. A *fatwa* is a legal pronouncement in Islam, issued by a religious law specialist on a specific issue. Mr Qaradawi has visited Ireland several times because of his links with the council, and was due to attend a conference of Islamic scholars in Dublin in 2012, before he cancelled due to ill-health.[7] Thus Ireland permits an alternative, *pre-modern* legal system to set itself up as a rival system of Law to Irish and European Law. This goes completely unchallenged. While in the UK there are 85 sharia courts dispensing Islamic justice tolerated by councils up and down the country.[8]

Google *Mein Kampf* and you get 13 million hits and rising. In 1999, the Palestinian Authority gave its blessing to a translation into Arabic of Adolf Hitler's masterpiece. The translator, Luis al-Haj, writes approvingly: 'National Socialism did not die with the death of its herald. Rather, its seeds multiplied under each star'.[9] Bertolt Brecht was right: 'do not rejoice in his [Hitler's] defeat, you men. For though the world has stood up and stopped the bastard, the bitch that bore him is in heat again'.[10] *Mein Kampf* is a best seller across the Arab world. Thus the burgeoning Islamist Revolution is essentially Islamo-*fascist*.

It has often been said that Islamism is Marxism for the twenty-first century, as the radical Left has aligned itself with radical Islam.[11] What they have in common is a visceral hatred of the West, America, Israel[12] and capitalism.[13] What could the Left do after the disastrous and repeated failures of Communism, but hitch itself to the next global radical movement, while foreclosing on reactionary 'ethnic sensibilities', female genital mutilation, homophobic murders, oppression of women, etc.?

European intellectuals like Sartre and de Beauvoir at *Les Temps Modernes*, with the notable exception of Camus, encouraged anti-colonial nationalist terrorist movements in North Africa during the mid-twentieth century, which normalised terrorism as an exemplary liberation strategy, paving the way for Islamic terrorism later that century and into this one.

As the West was entering its cultural revolution, *Milestones*, the key text for political Islam, was published by Sayyid Qubt.[14] Widely regarded as the manifesto for violent political Islam against Nasser's secular Arab nationalism and written while Qubt was in prison, it engendered the great Arab 'awakening' in the 1970s, across the Islamic world. That decade ended with the Iranian Revolution and the ill-fated Russian invasion of Afghanistan.

According to Qubt, the secular West is in a state of *jahiliyyah* – a state of ignorance of divine guidance; specifically the ignorance that *preceded* the Prophet's time and that persists until today. The Arab awakening should have been a wake-up call to the West – *wake-up to the Real* of its own *jahiliyyah*! We prefer the sleep of *jouissance* – dreaming on to continue the quiet life of sleeping, just like the father of Freud's example: *Father. Don't you see I'm burning*?[15] The father slept a little longer then awoke, sleeping precisely to avoid the traumatic Real of *his* responsibility for his son's death.

By the twenty-first century, Islamic scholars widely argue that we are already at the *fourth* of the five stages in Islamic history outlined by the Prophet Muhammad. The first stage was the time of the prophet Muhammad himself and ended with his death. The second stage was the era of the righteous caliphate; the time of the four Caliphs who came after him. The third stage was the era of the benign kings and dynasties. The fourth stage is the one we are presently in, the era of the tyrannical nationalist rulers – Gaddafi, Ben Ali, Saddam Hussein, Mubarak, and so on, prior to the fifth stage of the righteous caliphate; an Islamic utopia on the path of the Prophet. Thus, the Iraq war, the Arab Spring, the fall of Gaddafi, the fight against Assad are all part of the predicted cataclysmic times of stage four. The Muslim Brotherhood have disseminated these prophesies widely to their people to encourage them in violent jihad – better times are coming. They have been predicted. Ironically, the liberals in Tahrir Square of the Arab Spring and the military interventions by the West in Iraq and Libya have succeeded in furthering stage four, the toppling of the tyrants. The manual for stage four – jihad *without mercy* – is entitled, *The Management of Savagery* by al-Qaeda strategist, Abu Bakr Naji. According to Naji: 'One who previously engaged in jihad knows that it is naught but violence, crudeness, terrorism, deterrence and massacring'.[16]

If we follow the groundbreaking *The Pursuit of the Millennium*,[17] a study of revolutionary millenarianism during the Middle Ages, we can recognise, that, according to Richard Landis,[18] we are living (again)[19] at an active cataclysmic End Times. The West is way behind the curve in its understanding here.[20] In liberal-secularist circles, almost any serious talk about Islamist attacks risks being immediately shut down as Islamophobic hate speech – if we understood their religion, if we weren't so racist, if we didn't provoke them, treat them as second-class citizens, if we weren't so paranoid, if we were kinder, and so on … Whereas, the true racism and Islamophobia is precisely the fear, refusal or phobia to confront Islamism.[21] Where now are the anti-war marches this time against Islamic atrocities? Where are the thousands in the streets in the world's capitals, millions worldwide angrily denouncing the murderous jihadis? Where are the placards, where are the speeches 'Not in my name', and so on?[22] As Oedipal "children," we can only find wrong in the "parents," the great, the powerful, the traditional. As *anti*-Oedipal "children" we *celebrate* the "parents'" destruction and the ruination of any order *per se* without shame or hesitation. Thus we tend to make, unconsciously or not, common cause with our enemies because we hate those old "white fathers" with such a bitter hate and now we have collaborators who will do the job properly.

The Islamo-fascist threat is 'extimate' (*extimité*). What is exterior is also interior and vice versa. The Islamist threat is not just "over there," but also intimate, inside us, outside and inside. Take the part-time ex-pat jihadists, like the East London cab driver; for just three months of the year he goes to Afghanistan to fight for the Taliban. Apparently, RAF spy planes operating over Afghanistan detected on occasion strong Yorkshire and Birmingham accents among the Taliban fighters.[23] Likewise, small sleepy villages in the nurturing leafy Home Counties of England spawn jihadis prepared to kill their infidel neighbours in the simplest of ways and with callous ease. In the heartlands of capitalism and extravagent consumption emerge radicalised killers with ferocious weapons in shopping malls, train stations, hotel lobbies, tourist destinations, on airplanes and so on, at first sporadically.

A generation ago, Ihab Hassan noted the antinomies of the postmodern age: 'Everywhere now we observe societies riven by the double and coeval process of planetisation [globalization, capitalism] and re-tribalisation, totalitarianism and terror, fanatic faith and radical disbelief'.[24] When Lacan was asked if religion will triumph, he said: 'Yes. It will triumph not only over psychoanalysis but over lots of other things too. We can't even begin to imagine how powerful religion is'.[25] Thus, Islamic *fundamentalism* is committed to destroying the worldless world of capitalism and hedonism. Fundamentalism and Western hedonism (drugs, sex, pornography, etc.) are structurally linked as an extreme antinomy – not so much the so-called "clash of civilisations" as a clash of barbarisms, if we are willing to concede that the radical disbelief and hedonism of the West is already a flaw – a fatal slippage of civilisation and civilised values – all the more so for *not* being understood as problematic, not being credible and thus ridiculed and enjoyed at every turn. The power to which Lacan refers is not to be confused with the old phallic power beloved of psychoanalysis, but an occult power – the power of belief, a sacred black power, what Freud had in mind with the death drive all the way to the current fanatical totalisations of Islamism. This sacred power, with its seeds multiplying under each star, opens up an intensely negative reactionary space, cellular black holes, great fractal zones of destruction. This now seems as a gift to some on the radical Left, the last chance to destroy the Great Satan capitalism as all else has failed. That this is quite clearly suicidal for the Left – they are *also* infidels – however much they cosy up. This unequal alliance is analogous to the Nazi officer's comment in Ernst Lubitsch's movie, *To Be or not to Be*, who jokes about the German concentration camps in occupied Poland: '*We* do the concentrating, and the Poles do the camping'.

It must now seem ironic that pagan fascism, the *return* of sacred violence, has outlasted the Communism and Socialism that it once sought to defeat. Its black seeds are flourishing again. Maybe this is how we must read Houellebecq's *Submission*,[26] in the manner of the Lacanian version of Freud's *Wo Es war, soll Ich werden*: where Europe was there shall Islam(ism) come to be. Freud's version would clearly have been the reverse: where Islam(ism) is, Europe (emphasising subjectivity, modernism, progress, freedom, etc.) should re-assert itself with massive force. This latter seems unlikely as radicals, as we have recounted throughout, celebrate the end of Europe's hegemonic enlightenment project along with its Judeo-Christian heritage.[27]

Simone Weil says that truth is more important than life itself.[28] To avoid this becoming just a cliché, add the assertion from Archmedes, 'Give me a fulcrum, and I will shake the world';[29] the function of *balance* is what is missing today, a place to stand with one's feet on the ground, to get one's bearings and so on. Without a fulcrum no leverage is possible. The fulcrum "holds" the contradictions: both poets Gregory and Syme are true.

If psychoanalysis is a search for truth, the truth about contingent "thrown-ness" (*Geworfenheit*) into a world that is overwhelming; it points to the central foreclosed truth-fulcrum, namely that of original sin and the struggle to get free from the Oedipus complex. The only freedom that is possible, singly or collectively, must take full cognisance of flawed human nature, the *division* in the Oedipal subject. This would bring gravity to bear on the impossibly ecstatic, endlessly celebratory, prideful narcissistic culture of gross inequality and indifference. The total visibility of the world of pleasure arouses so much impotent envious rage across the world, at the simulated perfection of the other, who is sometimes felt to be laughing – laughing with joy and punching the air – in the face of the suffering other *qua* "loser," whose felt emptiness and futility has never seemed so humiliatingly visible with nowhere to hide and often these days no support to call upon. Recall that envy of the other seeks to destroy the perceived good of the other *because it is good*. Envy is so contagious and destructive that Bion calls envy a cancer. Bion envisages the creation of "mental faeces," as 'the proliferation of fragmented envy'. As Bion says, 'The model for cancerous growth is … [the] splitting of envy, each "bit" then growing independently of every other "bit"',[30] recalling our discussion above of the "cells" and "seeds" of Islamic terror, growing in the indifference zone of the postmodern West.

Surely the networked totalitarianism of the imaginary on every screen, 'a culture devastated by frivolity',[31] condemns a few to rage-filled suicidal ideas and acts. Envy is a factor in Islamist revenge attacks in the West. Religious fanatical violence is thus used as a cover for the envious rage generated by the global ideal of incredible wealth and happiness, the undoubted success of the West, which *also condemns them to humiliating inferiority*. With *the* weapon of a *total* ideology which fuses humiliation, victimisation and religious fanatical righteous rage, new devastating spectaculars will happen in the pleasure centres of Western wealth and privilege across the globalised world, of which 9/11 was the prototype. The killing thing (*sic*) is that they see themselves as inferior, judging themselves, prior to any racist talk or action on our part. And our left-liberal "understanding" of their plight only fuels the flames, as it reminds them of their inferiority. This explains why most killing is Muslim on Muslim as all are consumed without differentiation. Envy is wildly indiscriminate.

If the mirror creates alienation, just how much more alienation is potentially created by the omnipresence of the social media, that calls up ever new bizarre and false ways to be seen, to be successful and to have endless pleasure. Psychoanalysis, beginning with Lacan in the late 1960s, has tried to keep up with the trends. Indeed, instead of maintaining its fulcrum with the Oedipus complex, it has sided with the deconstruction of all essentialism, all roots, all meaning. Left floating in a denatured world of impossible choice – you can be anything – prone to every unrooted emotion the first and foremost of which is envy. We have envy to fall back on if all else fails. Psychoanalysis needs to find a way back on *this* side of the mirror, on *this* side of the camera/video/screen, to bear witness to the unique stories of suffering and joy to be told, fleetingly, almost inaudibly, in secrecy, in hiding and in humility. These days, almost on the point of disappearance, the human *qua* human still has some time before the final seemingly unstoppable victory of the inhuman, the machinic and the sacred longed for in *Anti-Oedipus*.

Notes

1 Symbolised by the Euro currency. The Euro is 'a crime against humanity', according to the Italian Right's Matteo Salvini. See www.telegraph.co.uk/business/2016/05/11/italy-must-chose-between-the-euro-and-its-own-economic-survival/.

2 Cited in Žižek, S., 2014: 145.

3 Baudrillard, J., 2001b: 46.

4 www.economist.com/news/leaders/21578665-nearly-1-billion-people-have-been-taken-out-extreme-poverty-20-years-world-should-aim.

5 Levi, P., 1959: 21.

6 Chesterton, G. K., 1908a: 1–13.

7 MacCormaic, R., 2012.

8 www.dailymail.co.uk/news/article-3358625/Inside-Britain-s-Sharia-courts-EIGHTY-FIVE-Islamic-courts-dispensing-justice-UK-special-investigation-really-goes-doors-shock-core.html.

9 https://futiledemocracy.wordpress.com/2015/10/23/hitlers-mufti-the-middle-eastern-nazi-inheritance/.

10 Cited by Cohen, N., 2016.

11 Horowitz, D., 2004.

12 Herf, J., 2016 documents the Left's involvement with anti-Zionism and anti-Semitism in the Soviet Union and East Germany, exploiting opportunities for diplomacy with the Arab states, up until the collapse of communism in 1989.

13 See Wolin, R., 2004: 278ff.

14 Qubt, S., 1964.

15 Freud, S., 1900: 510.

16 More can be found at www.aljazeera.com/indepth/opinion/2015/07/isil-management-savagery-150705060914471.html. As one respondent says: How much longer are we going to let this go on before we get serious about ISIL?

17 Cohn, N., 1957.

18 Follow Landis and a discussion that informs this section here: *What is IS*? BBC Radio 4, 9 January 2016. www.bbc.co.uk/programmes/b06sdlmb#play.
19 Earlier "End Times" movements were the Anabaptists in 1530s (passive cataclysmic), Taiping in China, Communism, Fascism in Europe – secular and active cataclysmic. These movements in search of utopia – secular and religious – brought about the deaths of millions of people.
20 This is why the second Iraq war was such a disaster in the aftermath of the invasion. There was no post-invasion planning because Bush and Blair seemed to believe that once democracy was in place in Iraq, all would be well! This just goes to show the West's utter failure to understand the mad fanatical intensity and complexity of the global threat posed by the Islamists from the Arab and Islamic world.
21 As Trevor Phillips, former head of the Equality and Human Rights Commission who coined the term "Islamophobia" in 1997, has made clear that multiculturalism has failed and that 'Muslims are creating nations within nations', and that a significant minority support violent jihad. (Channel 4 documentary: *What Muslims really think*, 11 April 2016).
22 As Bayan Rahman, the Kurdish ambassador to London, said to Nick Cohen in 2013: 'Everyone wants to remember Fallujah and no one wants to remember Halabja'. www.theguardian.com/commentisfree/2013/mar/03/10-years-right-invaded-iraq.
23 See The Guardian, 24 November 2010 "The Taliban troop with an East London cab driver in its ranks."
24 Hassan, I., 1991, cited in Jenks, C., 1992: 204.
25 Lacan, J., 1974 p: 64.
26 Houellebecq, M., 2015.
27 For those left-liberals who might say, 'Well what would be so bad about an Islamic Europe in the future?' we should point to an interesting series of photographs of the graduates of Cairo University from 1959, where the women graduates are all wearing Western clothes, to the most recent photo in 2004, where all the women are wearing head scarves. According to Nonie Darwish, 'These photos represent the gradual but steady Islamic radicalization invading the Middle East and the rest of the world in the last three decades'. www.frontpagemag.com/fpm/48901/how-veil-conquered-cairo-university-jamie-glazov.
28 Weil, S., 1951: 139.
29 Weil, S., 1951: 47.
30 Bion, W., 1970: 128.
31 Vargas Llosa, M., 2012: 164.

REFERENCES

Alliez, E., 2004. "Anti-Oedipus Thirty Years on." Trans. Toscano, A. *Radical Philosophy*, RP 124, 6–12. Available at: www.radicalphilosophy.com/commentary/anti-oedipus- %E2%80%93-thirty-years-on.

Amis, M., 1997. *Night Train*. London: Random House.

Amis, M., 2002. *Koba the Dread*. London: Jonathan Cape.

Amis, M., 2012. *Lionel Asbo: State of England*. London: Jonathan Cape.

Antliff, M., 2011. "Bad Anarchism: Aestheticised Mythmaking and The Legacy of George Sorel." *Anarchist Developments in Cultural Studies Art and Anarchy*, 155–87. Available at: www.anarchist-developments.org/index.php/adcs_journal/article/.../53.

Arnold, M., 1869. *Culture and Anarchy: An Essay in Political and Social Criticism*. London: Smith, Elder and Co.

Badiou, A., 1997. *Saint Paul: The Foundation of Universalism*. Stanford: Stanford University Press.

Badiou, A., 2003. *Saint Paul: The Foundation of Universalism (Cultural Memory in the Present)*. Trans. Brassier, R. Stanford: Stanford University Press.

Badiou, A., 2006a. *Logiques des mondes*. Paris: Seuil.

Badiou, A., 2006b. *Polemics*. Trans. Corcoran, S. London and New York: Verso.

Badiou, A., 2007. *Century*. Trans. Toscano, A. Cambridge, MA: Polity Press.

Badiou, A., and Burchill, L., 1999. *Deleuze: The Clamor of Being*. Minneapolis: University of Minnesota Press.

Balint, M., 1968. *The Basic Fault. Therapeutic Aspects of Regression*. London: Tavistock, 1979.

Ballard, J. G., 1973. *Crash*. New York: HarperCollins.

Barish, E., 2014. *The Double Life of Paul de Man*. New York: W.W. Norton.

Bataille, G., 1962. *Eroticism*. Paris: Éditions de Minuit. Trans. Dalwood, M. London: Marion Boyars Ltd., 1987.

Baudrillard, J., 1976. *Symbolic Exchange and Death*. Paris: Éditions Gallimard. Trans. Hamilton Grant, I. London: Sage, 1993.

Baudrillard, J., 1977. *Forget Foucault*. Paris: Éditions Galilée. Trans. Beilchman, P., Hildreth, L., and Polizzotti, M. LA: Semiotext(e), 2007.

Baudrillard, J., 1979. *Seduction.* Paris: Éditions Galilée. Trans. Singer, B. Montreal: New World Perspectives, 1990.

Baudrillard, J., 1990. *The Transpirition of Evil.* Paris: Éditions Galilée. Trans. Benedict, J. London and New York: Verso, 1993

Baudrillard, J., 1995. *The Perfect Crime.* Paris: Éditions Galilée. Trans. Turner, C. London and New York: Verso, 1996.

Baudrillard, J., 1999. *Impossible Exchange.* Paris: Éditions Galilée. Trans. Turner, C. London and New York: Verso, 2001.

Baudrillard, J., 2000, [2003] *Passwords.* Paris: Éditions Feyard. Trans. Turner, C. London and New York: Verso.

Baudrillard, J., 2001a. *Cool Memories IV: 1995–2000.* Paris: Éditions Galilée. Trans. Turner, C. London and New York: Verso, 2003.

Baudrillard, J., 2001b. *Fragments.* Paris: Éditions Albin Michel. Trans. Turner, C. London and New York: Routledge, 2004.

Baudrillard, J., 2004. *The Intelligence of Evil or the Lucidity of the Pact.* Paris: Éditions Galilée. Trans. Turner, C. New York and Oxford: Berg.

Baudrillard, J., 2005. *Cool Memories V.* Paris: Éditions Galilée. Trans. Turner, C. Cambridge: Polity Press, 2006.

Baudrillard, J., and Noailles, E., 2005. *Exiles from Dialogue.* Paris: Éditions Galilée. Trans. Turner, C. Cambridge: Polity, 2007.

Bauman, Z., 2000. *Liquid Modernity.* Cambridge: Polity Press.

Berlant, L., 2011. *Cruel Optimism.* Durham, NC: Duke University Press.

Bettelheim, B., 1983. *Freud and Man's Soul.* London: Hogarth.

Bion, W., 1957. "Differentiation of the psychotic from the non-psychotic personalities," in Bion, W. *Second Thoughts. Selected Papers on Psycho-Analysis.* London: Maresfield, 1967.

Bion, W., 1958. "On hallucination," in Bion, W. *Second Thoughts. Selected Papers on Psycho-Analysis.* London: Maresfield, 1967.

Bion, W., 1963. *The Grid.* London: Maresfield.

Bion, W., 1970. *Attention and Interpretation.* London: Maresfield.

Boyers, R., 1971. *Laing and Anti-Psychiatry.* Harmondsworth: Penguin Books.

Bragg, M., 2011. *The Book of Books. The Radical Impact of the King James Bible 1611–2011.* London: Hodder and Stoughton.

Bristow, J., and Wilson, A. (Eds) 1993. *Activating Theory: Lesbian, Gay, Bisexual Politics.* London: Lawrence & Wishart.

Brousse, M.-H. (Ed.) 2009. *Ordinary Psychosis. Psychoanalytic Notebooks,* No. 19. London: The New Lacanian School of Psychoanalysis.

Bruchner, P., 2006. *The Tyranny of Guilt. An Essay on Western Masochism.* Trans. Tendall, S. Princeton and Oxford: Princeton University Press, 2010.

Burgoyne, B., and Sullivan, M., 1997. *The Klein-Lacan Dialogues.* London: Rebus Press.

Butler, J., 2000. *Antigone's Claim: Kinship Between Life and Death.* The Wellek Library lectures. New York: Columbia University Press.

Capuder, A., 2004. "Vino in most." *Demokracija,* No. 50, year IX, Ljubljana. Trans. Žižek, S. Available at: www.lacan.com/essays/?page_id=2#_ftn1.

Caputo, J., 2015. *Truth. Philosophy in Transit.* London and New York: Penguin.

Carr, N., 2010. *The Shallows: How the Internet is Changing the Way We Think, Read and Remember.* London: Atlantic Books.

Caruth, C., 2001. "An Interview with Jean Laplanche." Available at: http://pmc.iath.virginia.edu/text-only/issue.101/11.2caruth.txt.

Casey, P., 2009. "The Psycho-Social Benefits of Religious Practice." Dublin: The Iona Institute. Available at: www.ionainstitute.ie/pdfs/Religious_practice.pdf.

Castenet, H., 2015. "Amongst men: three clinical cases." *Lacunae. APPI International Journal for Lacanian Psychoanalysis*, Issue 11, 41–62.

Chang, J., and Halliday, J., 2005. *Mao. The Unknown Story*. London: Jonathan Cape.

Chesterton, G. K., 1908a. *The Man Who Thought He Was Thursday. A Nightmare*. London: Penguin Red Classic, 2007.

Chesterton, G. K., 1908b. *Orthodoxy*. Looe, UK: The House of Stratus, 2008.

Chesterton, G., 1924. *St. Francis of Assisi*. Mineola, NY: Dover Publications, 2008.

Chesterton, G., 1925. *The Everlasting Man*. London: Hodder and Stoughton; Eastford, CT: Martino Publishing, 2010.

Chorost, M., 2005. *Rebuilt: How Becoming Part Computer Made Me More Human*. Chicago: Houghton Mifflin Harcourt.

Chorost, M., 2011. *World Wide Mind: The Coming Integration of Human Machines and the Internet*. New York and London: Free Press.

Cioran, E., 1995. *Tears and Saints*. Trans. Zarifopal-Johnston, I. Chicago and London: University of Chicago Press.

Cixous, H., 1981. "The Laugh of the Medusa," in Marks, E., and de Courtivron, I. (Eds). *New French Feminisms*. New York: Schocken.

Clarke, A. C., 1992. "The nine billion names of God," in Clarke A. C. *Of Time and the Stars*. London: Penguin.

Cohen, N., 2007. *What's Left. How Liberals Lost their Way*. London: Fourth Estate.

Cohen, N., 2016. "Anti-Semites made me a Jew." *The Observer*. 6 April. Available at: https://nickcohen.net/2016/04/06/anti-semites-made-me-a-jew/.

Cohn, N., 1957. *The Pursuit of the Millennium: Revolutionary Millenarians and Mystical Anarchists of the Middle Ages,* Revised and Expanded Edition. London and New York: Oxford University Press.

Cooper, D., 1971. *The Death of the Family*. London: Allen Lane.

Courtois, S., 1997. *Le Livre Noir du Communisme: Crimes, Terreur, Répression*. Paris: Éditions Robert Laffont.

Crews, F., 1993. "The Unknown Freud," In The Memory Wars: Freud's Legacy in Dispute. London: Granta Books, 1995.

Critchley, S., 2001. *Continental Philosophy. A Very Short Introduction*. Oxford: Oxford University Press.

Critchley, S., 2012. *Faith of the Faithless. Experiments in Political Theology.* London and New York: Verso.

Cronin, M., 2016. "From vivid faces to frozen masks? Remembering to forget in late modern Ireland." *Lacunae* 12: 21–36.

Cudden, J., 1977. *A Dictionary of Literary Terms and Literary Theory.* London: Deutsch.

Cunningham, C., 2002. *The Genealogy of Nihilism*. London and New York: Routledge.

Damasio, A., 2000. *The Feeling of What Happens. Body, Emotion and the Making of Consciousness.* London: Vintage.

Davis, C. (Ed.) 2009. *The Monstrosity of Christ. Paradox or Dialectic*. Cambridge, MA: MIT Press Books.

Davis, C., Milbank, J., and Žižek, S., 2010. *Paul's New Moment. Continental Philosophy and the Future of Christian Theology.* Michigan: Brazon Press.

Dean, T., 2000. *Beyond Sexuality.* Chicago: Chicago University Press.

de Chardin, P., 1956. *Man's Place in Nature*. Trans. Hague, R. London: Fontana Religious, 1971.

Deleuze, G., 1962. *Nietzsche and Philosophy*. Trans. Tomlinson, H. London: Continuum, 1983.

Deleuze, G., and Guattari, F., 1972. *Anti-Oedipus. Capitalism and Schizophrenia*. Trans. Hurley, R., Seem, M., and Lane, H. London and New York: Continuum, 2004.

Deleuze, G., and Guattari, F., 1980. *A Thousand Plateaus. Capitalism and Schizophrenia.* Trans. Massumi, B. London and New York: Continuum, 2004.

Derbyshire, J., 2013. "Heidegger in France: Nazism and Philosophy." *Prospect Magazine.* Available at: www.prospectmagazine.co.uk/blogs/jonathan-derbyshire/heidegger-in-france-nazism-and-philosophy.

Derrida, J., 1992. *The Gift of Death.* Trans. Wills, D. Chicago and London: University of Chicago Press.

Derrida, J., 1997. *Adieu To Emmanuel Levinas.* Trans. Brault, P.-A., and Nass, M. Stanford: Stanford University Press.

Derrida, J., 1998. *Resistances of Psychoanalysis.* Trans. Kamuf, P., Brault, P.-A., and Nass, M. Stanford: Stanford University Press.

Di Cesare, D., 2015. "Heidegger – 'Jews Self-destructed'" Trans. Watson, D. Available at: www.corriere.it/english/15_febbraio_09/heidegger-jews-self-destructed-47cd3930-b03b-11e4-8615-d0fd07eabd28.shtml.

Dufresne, T., 2000. *Tales from the Freudian Crypt.* Stanford: Stanford University Press.

Durkheim, E., 1897. *On Suicide.* Trans. Buss, R. London: Penguin Modern Classics.

Ehrenreich, B., 2009. *Smile or Die. How Positive Thinking Fooled America and the World.* London: Granta Publications.

Enzensberger, H. M., 1995. *Civil Wars: From LA to Bosnia.* New York: The New York Press.

Ettinger, B. L., 2006. "Matrixial Trans-Subjectivity." *Theory Culture Society* 23, 218–22.

Ettinger, B. L., 2012. "RED SCAR IN THE SKY. Ashes of *I & Non-I* – (No)body's Roses." Work in progress presented in Dublin, March 2012.

Faulks, S., 2007. *Engleby.* London: Hutchinson.

Fen, S.-N., 1986. "The May 7 Cadre Schools in the People's Republic of China: 1968–1976." *Administration & Society,* 18, 1: 29–43.

Ferenczi, S., 1933. "Confusion of tongues between adults and the child (the language of tenderness and of passion)", in Borossa, J. (Ed.). *Sándor Ferenczi: Selected Writings.* Harmondsworth: Penguin Books, 1999, 293–303.

Ferguson, N., 2006. *The War of the World. History's Age of Hatred.* London and New York: Allen Lane.

Fink, B., 1997. *A Clinical Introduction to Lacanian Psychoanalysis. Theory and Practice.* Cambridge, MA: Harvard University Press.

Fletcher, J., 2007. "Seduction and the Vicissitudes of Translation: the Work of Jean Laplanche." *Psychoanalytic Quarterly,* 76: 1241–91.

Fonagy, P., 1999. "Memory and therapeutic action." *International Journal of Psycho-Analysis,* 80, 215–23.

Fonagy, P., 2001. "The Talking Cure in the Cross Fire of Empiricism – The Struggle for hearts and mind of psychoanalytic clinicians." *Psychoanalytic Dialogues,* 11, 647–58.

Foucault, M., 1966. *The Order of Things: An Archaeology of the Human Sciences.* New York and London: Routledge, 1989.

Freud, A., 1936. *The Ego and the Mechanisms of Defence.* London: Hogarth.

Freud, S., 1894. "The Neuro-Psychoses of Defence." *Standard edition (SE) 3*: 43–70.

Freud, S., 1900. *The Interpretation of Dreams. SE 4*: 5.

Freud. S., 1905. *"The Three Essays on the Theory of Sexuality." SE* 7: 125–249.

Freud, S., 1909. "Notes upon a case of obsessional neurosis." *SE 10*: 151–318.

Freud, S., 1911. "The handling of dream-interpretation in psycho-analysis." *SE 12*: 85–96.

Freud, S., 1912. "Recommendations to physicians practising psychoanalysis." *SE 12*: 109–20.

Freud, S., 1913 (1912–13). *Totem and Taboo. SE 13*: xi–164.

Freud, S., 1914a. "The Moses of Michelangelo." *SE 13*: 211–40.

Freud, S., 1914b. "On narcissism: an introduction." *SE 14*: 67–104.

Freud, S., 1916–1917. "Lecture 18. Fixation to traumas – the unconscious." *Introductory Lectures on Psycho-Analysis, SE 16*: 273–85.

Freud, S., 1917. "A Difficulty in the Path of Psychoanalysis." *SE 17*: 135–44.

Freud, S., 1923, 1922. "Remarks on the theory and practice of dream interpretation." SE 19: 109–24.

Freud, S., 1924. "The dissolution of the Oedipus complex." *SE 19*: 173–82.

Freud, S., 1927a. *The Future of an Illusion. SE 21*: 3–58.

Freud, S., 1927b. Fetishism. *SE 21*: 149–58.

Freud, S., 1930 (1929) *Civilisation and its Discontents. SE 21*: 59–148.

Freud, S., 1933 [1932]. Lecture 31. "The dissection of the psychical personality." *New Introductory Lectures on Psycho-Analysis, SE 22*: 57–80.

Freud, S., 1937a. "Analysis, terminable and interminable." *SE 23*: 209–54.

Freud, S., 1937b. "Constructions in analysis." *SE 23*: 255–70.

Freud, S., 1939 (1934–38). "Moses and Monotheism." *SE 23*: 3–140.

Freud, S., 1940 (1938) "An Outline of Psycho-analysis." *SE 23*: 141–208.

Freud, S., 1950 [1892–1899] "Extracts from the Fleiss Papers." *Letter SE 1*: 175–282.

Friel, B., 1980. *Translations.* London: Faber and Faber.

Fukuyama, F., 1992. *The End of History and the Last Man.* New York: Avon Books Inc.

Gallagher, C., 2002. "The new tyranny of knowledge: Seminar XVII (1969–1970) – background and overview." *The Letter*, No. 24: 1–24.

Gauthier, D., and Forsyth, C., 1999. "Bareback sex, bug chasing, and the gift of death." *Deviant Behavior*, 20: 85–100.

Girard, R., 1972. *Violence and the Sacred.* Paris: Éditions Bernard Grasset. Trans. Gregory, P. London: Continuum, 2005.

Girard, R., 1978. *Things Hidden Since the Foundation of the World.* Paris: Éditions Grasset & Fasquelle. Trans. Bann, S., and Metteer, M. Stanford: Stanford University Press.

Girard, R., 2010. *Battling to the End: Conversations with Benîot Chantre.* Paris: Éditions Carnet Nord. Trans. Baker, M. East Lansing, MI: Michigan State University Press.

Goldberg, J., 2007. *Liberal Fascism.* London and New York: Penguin.

Goldman, P., 1998. "Christian mystery and responsibility gnosticism in Derrida's *The Gift of Death*." *Anthropoetics*, IV, No. 1 (Spring/Summer 1998). Available at: www.anthropoetics.ucla.edu/ap0401/pg_DERR.htm.

Goldner, L., 1998. "The Nazis and Deconstruction: Jean-Pierre Faye's Demolition ofDerrida." Available at: http://breaktheirhaughtypower.org/the-nazis-and-deconstruction-jean-pierre-fayes-demolition-of-derrida/.

Graves, R., 1960 [1955]. *The Greek Myths.* Harmondsworth: Penguin Books.

Gray, J., 2002. *Straw Dogs. Thoughts on Humans and Other Animals.* London: Granta.

Grossman, V., 1980. *Life and Fate.* Levier: Éditions L'Age d'Homme. Trans. Chandler, R. London: Harville Press, 1995.

Grossman, V., 1998. *An Armenian Sketchbook.* Trans. Chandler, R., and Chandler, E. London: MacLehose Press, 2013.

Grunbaum, A., 1984. *The Foundations of Psychoanalysis: A Philosophical Critique.* Berkeley: University of California Press.

Haddon, M., 2004. *The Curious Incident of the Dog in the Night-Time.* London: Vintage.

Hamilton, H., 2004. *The Speckled People.* London: Fourth Estate.

Hanaghan, J., 1957. *Society, Evolution and Revelation.* Dublin: The Runa Press.

Hand, S. (Ed.) 1989. *The Levinas Reader.* Oxford: Blackwell.

Hanisch, C., 1969. "The Personal is Political," in Firestone, S., and Koedt, A. (Eds). 1970. *Notes from the Second Year: Women's Liberation. Major Writings of the Radical Feminists.* New York: Radical Feminism. Available at: www.carolhanisch.org/CHwritings/PIP.html.

Hassan, I., 1991, cited in Jenks, C., 1992. The Post-Modern Reader. New York: St. Martin's Press; London: Academy Editions.

Heidegger, M., 1927. *Being and Time*. Trans. MacQuarrie, J., and Robinson, E. New York: Harper & Row.

Heidegger, M., 1929. "What is Metaphysics," in Heidegger, M., 1978. *Basic Writings*. Farrell Krell, D. (Ed.). London: Routledge, 2000, 89–110.

Heidegger, M., 1929–1930. *The Fundamental Concepts of Metaphysics. World, Finitude, Solitude*. Trans. McNeill, W., and Walker, N. Bloomington and Indianapolis: Indiana University Press.

Heidegger, M., 1947. "Letter on Humanism," in Heidegger, M., 1978, *Basic Writings*. Farrell Krell, D. (Ed.). London: Routledge, 2000, 213–66.

Heidegger, M., 1959. *On the Way to Language*. Trans. Hertz, P. New York: Harper & Row, 1971.

Heidegger, M., 1978. *Basic Writings*. Farrell Krell, D. (Ed.). London: Routledge, 2000.

Henri-Levi, B., and Houellebecq, M., 2008. *Public Enemies*. Trans. Wynne, F., and Frendo, M. London: Atlantic Books.

Herf, J., 2016. *Undeclared Wars with Israel: East Germany and the West German Far Left, 1967–1989*. Cambridge: Cambridge University Press.

Hitchens, C., 2002. *Orwell's Victory*. London: Allen Lane.

Hitchens, P., 2010. *The Rage against God*. London and New York: Continuum.

Horowitz, D., 2004. *Unholy Alliance: Radical Islam and the American Left*. Washington: Regnery Publishing Inc.

Houellebecq, M., 2015. *Submission*. Trans. Stein, L. London: Penguin Random House.

Hyman, G., 2010. "Radical Orthodoxy, Ethics and Ambivalence." Available at: www.jcrt.org/archives/03.2/hyman.shtml#_edn36.

James, W., 1902. *The Varieties of Religious Experience: A Study of Human Nature*. New York: Modern Library, 2002.

Jameson, F., 1985. "Post-Modernism and Consumer Society," in *Postmodern Culture*. Foster, H. (Ed.). London and Sidney: Pluto Press.

Jameson, F., 1991. *Postmodernism or the Cultural Logic of Late Capitalism*. London: Verso.

Jenks, C., 1996. *Childhood*. London: Routledge.

Joseph, B., 1985. "Transference: The Total Situation." *Int. J. Psycho-Anal.*, 66: 447–54.

Kafka, F., 1925. *The Trial*. Trans. Mitchell, B. New York: Schocken Books.

Kiberd, D., 1995. *Inventing Ireland. The Literature of the Modern Nation*. London: Jonathan Cape.

Kierkegaard, S., 1843. *Fear and Trembling*. Trans. Hannay, A. London: Penguin Classics, 1985.

Klein, M., 1946. "Notes on Some Schizoid Mechanisms," in *Melanie Klein: Envy and Gratitude & Other Works*. New York: Delta, 1975, 1–24.

Kohon, G., 1999. "The Greening of Psychoanalysis: André Green in dialogues with Gregorio Kohon," in *The Dead Mother: The work of André Green*. Kohon, G. (Ed.). The New Library of Psycho-Analysis. London: Routledge, 9–58.

Kohut, H., 1977. *The Restoration of the Self*. New York: International Universities Press.

Kopping, W., 2008. *The Third Jihad: Radical Islam's Vision For America*. A film produced by Werth, E., and Shore, R. Clarion fund. Available at: www.clarionproject.org.

Kundera, M., 1984. *The Unbearable Lightness of Being*. Trans. Heim, M. H. London: Harper & Row.

Kundera, M., 1991. *Immortality*. Trans. Kussi, P. London: Faber and Faber.

Lacan, J., 1938. *The Family Complexes in the Formation of the Individual*. Trans. Gallagher, C. Private circulation only.

Lacan, J., 1950. "A theoretical introduction to the functions of psychoanalysis in criminology," in Lacan, J., 1970. *Ecrits. The First Complete Edition in English*. Trans. Fink, B. London and New York: W.W. Norton, 2002, 102–50.

Lacan, J., 1953. "The Function and Field of Speech and Language in Psychoanalysis," in Lacan, J., 1970. *Ecrits. The First Complete Edition in English*. Trans. Fink, B. London and New York: W.W. Norton, 2002, 197–268.

Lacan, J., 1954–1955. *Seminar 2. The Ego in Freud's Theory and in the Technique of Psychoanalysis*. Miller, J.-A. (Ed.). Trans. Tomaselli, S. New York and Cambridge: Cambridge University Press, 1988.

Lacan, J., 1955–1956. *Seminar 3. The Psychoses*. Miller, J.-A. (Ed.). Trans. Grigg, R. New York and London: W.W. Norton, 1993.

Lacan, J., 1957. "The Instance of the Letter in the Unconscious," in Lacan, J., 1970. *Ecrits. The First Complete Edition in English*. Trans. Fink, B. London and New York: W.W. Norton, 2002, 412–41.

Lacan, J., 1958–1959. *Seminar 6. Desire and its Interpretation*. Trans. Gallagher, C. Dublin. Available at: www.lacaninireland.com/web/wp-content/uploads/2010/06/THE-SEMINAR-OF-JACQUES-LACAN-VI.pdf.

Lacan, J., 1959–1960. *Seminar 7. The Ethics of Psychoanalysis*. Paris: Seuil, 1986. Trans. Porter, D. London: Routledge, 1992.

Lacan, J., 1960. "The Subversion of the Subject and the Dialectic of Desire in the Freudian Unconscious," in Lacan, J., 1970. *Ecrits. The First Complete Edition in English*. Trans. Fink, B. London and New York: W.W. Norton, 2002, 793–828.

Lacan, J., 1964. *The Four Fundamental Concepts of Psycho-Analysis, Seminar XI*, J.-A. Miller (Ed.). Trans. Sheridan, A.. London: Hogarth Press, 1977.

Lacan, J., 1966–1967. *Seminar 14. The Logic of Phantasy*. Trans. Gallager, C. from unedited French manuscripts for private use. Dublin. Available at: www.lacaninireland.com/web/wp-content/uploads/2010/06/THE-SEMINAR-OF-JACQUES-LACAN-XIV.pdf.

Lacan, J., 1968. *Speech and Language in Psychoanalysis*. Trans. Wilden, A. Baltimore and London: John Hopkins University Press.

Lacan, J., 1968–1969. *Le Séminaire, Livre XVI: D'un Autre à l'autre*. Paris: Seuil. Miller, J.-A. (Ed.), 224.

Lacan, J., 1969–1970. *Seminar 17. The Other Side of Psychoanalysis*. Trans. Grigg, R. New York: W.W. Norton, 2005.

Lacan, J., 1970. *Ecrits. The First Complete Edition in English*. Trans. Fink, B. London and New York: W.W. Norton, 2002.

Lacan, J., 1970–1971. *Seminar 18: On a Discourse that might not be a Semblance*. Available at: www.lacaninireland.com/web/wp-content/uploads/2010/06/Book-18-On-a-discourse-that-might-not-be-a-semblance.pdf.

Lacan, J., 1972–1973. *Seminar 20. Encore: On Feminine Sexuality, the Limits of Love and Knowledge*. Ed. Fink, B. London: W.W. Norton, 1998.

Lacan, J., 1974. *The Triumph of Religion: preceded by Discourse to Catholics*. Trans: Fink, B. Cambridge: Polity Press, 2013.

Lacan, J., 1975–1976. *Le séminaire de Jacques Lacan: Livre 23, Le sinthome*. Paris: Seuil.

Lacan, J., 1977. *Écrits: A Selection*. Trans. Sheridan, A. London: Tavistock Publications, 1977.

Lacan, J., 2013. *On the Names-of-the-Father*. Trans. Fink, B. Cambridge and Malden, MA: Polity Press.

Laplanche, J., 1989. *New Foundations for Psychoanalysis*. Trans. Macey, D. Oxford: Blackwell.

Laplanche, J., 1997. "The theory of seduction and the problem of the other." *International Journal of Psycho-Analysis*, 78.

Laplanche, J., 1999. "The so-called 'death drive': a sexual drive," in Weatherill, R., 1998. *The Sovereignty of Death*. London: Rebus, 40–59.

Laplanche, J., and Pontalis, B., 1974. *The Language of Psychoanalysis*. London: Hogarth.

Leibniz, G.W., 1714. *The Principles of Nature and Grace, Based on Reason*. Available at: www.earlymoderntexts.com/assets/pdfs/leibniz1714a.pdf. Copyright ©2010–2015. All rights reserved Jonathan Bennett.

Levi, P., 1959. *If This is a Man? The Truce*. Trans. Woolf, S. New York: Orion, 1960; London: Sphere Books, Penguin, 1979.

Levinas, E., 1947. *Time and the Other.* Trans. Cohen, R. Pittsburgh: Duquesne University Press, 1987.

Levinas, E., 1961. *Totality and Infinity*. Trans. Linguis, A. Pittsburgh: Duquesne University Press, 1969.

Levinas, E., 1981. *Otherwise Than Being Or Beyond Essence.* Trans. Lingis, A. Pittsburgh: Duquesne University Press, 1988.

Levinas, E., 1982. *Ethics and Infinity. Conversations with Philip Nemo.* Trans. Cohen, R. Pittsburgh: Duquesne University Press, 1985.

Levinas, E., 2001. *Is It Righteous To Be? Interviews with Emmanuel Levinas.* Robbins, J. (Ed.). Stanford: Stanford University Press.

Levinas, E., 2006a. "Emmanuel Levinas in conversation with Bracha L. Ettinger. What would Eurydice say?" in *Athena: Philosophical Studies. Nr 2.* Lithuania: Vilnius, 137–54.

Levinas, E., 2006b. *Humanism and the Other.* Trans. Poller, N. Urbana and Chicago: University of Illinois Press.

Löwith, K., 1933. "Heidegger's Existentialism. Political Implications." Trans. Wolin, R. Available at: www.lacan.com/symptom/?p=55.

Lyotard, J.-F., 1993. *Postmodern Fables*. Paris: Éditions Galilée. Trans. Van Den Abbeele, G. Minneapolis: University of Minnesota Press.

McCarthy, P., 2002. "The reverse of psychoanalysis – how far? A commentary on discourse, knowledge and enjoyment'. *The Letter*, 24, 111–25.

McCarthy, J., 2006. *The Road*. London: Picador.

Maccormaic, R., 2012. "Cleric with Dublin links not welcome 'on French soil'." *The Irish Times*. 7 May. Available at: www.irishtimes.com/news/cleric-with-dublin-links-not-welcome-on-french-soil-1.489465.

Macey, D., 1988. *Lacan in Contexts*. London and New York: Verso.

MacFarquhar, R., and Schoenhals, M., 2006. *Mao's Last Revolution*. Cambridge, MA: Harvard University Press.

McIntosh, M., 1993. "Queer theory and the war of the sexes," in Bristow, J., and Wilson, A. (Eds). 1993. *Activating Theory: Lesbian, Gay, Bisexual Politics*. London: Lawrence & Wishart.

MacIntyre, A., 1982. *After Virtue*. London: Duckworth.

MacLelland, B., 1907. *Prosperity Through Thought Force*. New York: Elizabeth Towne.

McNerney, A., 2004. *The Gift of Cancer: A Call to Awakening*. Baltimore: Resonant Publishing.

Mailer, N., 1968. *Miami and the Siege of Chicago: An Informal History of the Republican and Democratic Conventions of 1968*. London: Weidenfeld and Nicolson.

Malkowsky, E., 2007. *The Spiritual Technology of Ancient Egypt: Sacred Science and the Mystery of Consciousness.* Rochester, Vermont: Inner Traditions.com.

Marchant, O., 2007. "Acting and the Act," in *The Truth of Žižek*. Bowman, P., and Stamp, R. (Eds). London: Continuum.

Marcuse, H., 1969. *The Dialectics of Liberation*. London: Pelican.

Masoni, S., Maio, A., Trimarchi, G., de Punzio, C., and Fioretti, P., 1994. "The Couvade Syndrome." *Journal of Psychosomatic Obstetrics and Gynaecology*, 15(3), 125–31.

Massumi, B., 2002. "Navigating Movements," in *Hope*, Zournazi, M. (Ed.). New York: Routledge, 224.

Matson, J., 2012. "Vestiges of Violence: Towering Gamma-Ray Jets Point to Past Outbursts from Milky Way's Black Hole." *Scientific American*, July, 2012.

Mayer, C., Borch-Jacobsen, M., Cottraux, M. J., and Pleux, D., 2005. *Le livre noir de la psychanalyse: Vivre, penser et aller mieux sans Freud*. Paris: Éditions Les Arénes.
Mehlman, J., 2006. *Genealogies of the Text: Literature, Psychoanalysis, and Politics in Modern France*. Cambridge: Cambridge University Press.
Milbank, J., 1990. *Theology and Social Theory: Beyond Secular Reason*. Oxford: Blackwell.
Milbank, J., 1997. *The Word Made Strange*. Oxford: Blackwell.
Milbank, J., and Oliver, S. (Eds) 2009. *The Radical Orthodoxy Reader.* London and New York: Routledge.
Miles, S., 2005. *Simone Weil. An Anthology*. London: Penguin Modern Classics.
Miller, J.-A., 2003. "Religion, Psychoanalysis." Trans. Fulks, B. *Lacanian Ink. 23*. Available at: www.lacan.com/frameXXIII2.htm.
Miller, J.-A., 2006. *L'Anti-Livre Noir de la Psychoanalyse.* Paris: Seuil.
Miller, J.-A., 2008. "Extimity," in *The Symptom*, No. 9. Available at: www.lacan.com/symptom/?p=36.
Monod, J., 1969. *From Biology to Ethics*. San Diego, California: Salk Institute for Biological Studies.
Morelli, M., and Morelli, E., 1997. *The Lonergan Reader.* Toronto: University of Toronto Press.
Nafisi, A., 2003. *Reading Lolita in Tehran*. London: Fourth Estate.
Nietzsche, F., 1882. *The Gay Science*. Trans. Kaufmann, W. New York: Vintage, 1974.
Nietzsche, F., 1883–1891. *Thus Spoke Zarathustra*. Trans. Hollingdale, R. Harmondsworth: Penguin, 1961.
Nietzsche, F., 1888. "Notes," in *The Portable Nietzsche*. 1954. Trans. Kaufmann, W. London and New York: Viking Penguin.
Nietzsche, F., 1967. *On The Genealogy of Morals and Ecce Homo*. Trans. Kaufmann, W., and Hollindale, R. New York: Vintage.
Olds, J., 1956. "Pleasure centers in the brain." *Scientific American*, No. 195, 105–16.
Orwell, G., 1938. *Homage to Catalonia*. London: Penguin, 1962.
Panek, R., 2011. *The 4 Percent Universe: Dark Matter, Dark Energy, and the Race to Discover the Rest of Reality*. Boston: Houghton Mifflin Harcourt.
Pascal, B., 1670. *Pensées*. Harmondsworth: Penguin, 1966.
Patočka, J., 1990. *Heretical Essays in the Philosophy of History*. Trans. Kohák, E. Chicago and La Salle. Illinois: Open Court, 1996.
Paz, O., 1986. "The ghosts of religion," in *The Listener,* 115, 17 April, 18–20.
Phillips, M., 2006. *Londonistan*. New York: Encounter Books.
Polt, R., 2015. "7 New translated excerpts on Heidegger's anti-Semitism." Available at: www.critical-theory.com/7-new-translated-excerpts-on-heideggers-anti-semitism/2/.
Qubt, S., 1964. *Milestones.* New Delhi: Islamic Book Service, 2006.
Raban, J., 2006. *Surveillance*. London: Picador.
Reiff, P., 1959. *Freud: The Mind of a Moralist*. London: Victor Gollancz.
Reno, R., 2000. "The Radical Orthodoxy Project," in *First Things.* Available at: www.firstthings.com/article/2000/02/the-radical-orthodoxy-project.
Riviere, J., 1929. "Womanliness as Masquerade." *International Journal of Psychoanalysis*, 10, 303–13.
Robinson, A., 2005. 'The Political Theory of Constitutive Lack: A Critique'. Available at: http://muse.jhu.edu/demo/theory_and_event/v008/8.1robinson.html#authbio.
Rosenfeld, H., 1987. *Impasse and Interpretation*. London: Tavistock.
Roudinesco, E., 1993. *Jacques Lacan*. Trans. Bray, B. New York: Colombia University Press.
Roudinesco, E., 2008. *Philosophy in Turbulent Times*. New York: Columbia University Press.
Rowland, T., 2011. "Gospel and culture after Vatican II: John Paul II and Benedict XVI." *Religion and Ethics*. Available at: www.abc.net.au/religion/articles/2012/10/13/3610041.htm.

Sagan, D., and Margulis, L., 1986. *Origins of Sex: Three Billion Years of Genetic Recombination*. Bio-Origin Series. New Haven:Yale University Press.

Saviano, R., 2006. *Gomorrah. Italy's other Mafia*.Trans. Jewiss,V. London: Macmillan.

Sebald, W.G., 2002. *On the Natural History of Destruction*. Trans. Bell, A. London: Hamish Hamilton.

Segal, H., 1986."The paranoid-schizoid position," in *Introduction to the Work of Melanie Klein*. London: Hogarth, 24–38.

Shakespeare, S., 2000."The New Romantics.A Critique of RO." *Theology*, 103, 163–77.

Simpson, C., and Caputo, J., 2012. *The William Desmond Reader*. New York: State University of New York Press.

Sloterdijk, P., 1947. *Rage and Time.A Psychopolitical Investigation*.Trans.Wenning, M. New York: Columbia University Press.

Sloterdijk, P., with Heinrichs, H.-J., 2001. *Neither Sun Nor Death*. Trans. Corcoran, S. Los Angeles: Semiotext(e).

Spence, J., 2001. Adapted from, "Introduction to the Cultural Revolution," in *The Search for Modern China*. Available at: http://iis-db.stanford.edu/docs/115/CRintro.pdf.

Stavrakakis, Y., 2007. The Lacanian Left: Essays on Psychoanalysis, Theory, Politics. New York: SUNY Press.

Steigler, B., 2008. *Taking Care of Youth and the Generations*. Trans. Barker, S. Stanford: Stanford University Press.

Steigler, B., 2010. *For a New Critique of Political Economy*. Cambridge: Polity Press.

Steiner, G., 1975. *After Babel. Aspects of Language and Translation*. Oxford: Oxford University Press.

Steiner, G., 1978. *Heidegger*. London: Fontana.

Steiner, G., 1989. *Real Presences*. London: Faber and Faber, 1991.

Steiner, G., 1998. *Language and Silence: Essays on Language, Literature and the Inhuman*. New Haven and London: Yale University Press.

Steiner, G., 2001. *Grammers of Creation*. New Haven and London: Yale University Press.

Taylor, C., 2007. *The Secular Age*. Cambridge, MA and London: The Belknap Press of Harvard University Press.

Taylor, J., 2001. *The Race for Consciousness*. Cambridge, MA: MIT Press.

Thompson, D., 2008. *Counterknowledge: How We Surrendered to Conspiracy Theories, Quack Medicine, Bogus Science and Fake History*. London: Atlantic Books.

Thompson, D., 2012. *The Fix: How Addiction Is Invading Our Lives and Taking Over Your World*. London: Collins.

Tillich, P., 1949. *The Shaking of the Foundations*. London: Pelican Books, 1962.

Toft, M., Philpot, D., and Shah, T., 2011. *God's Century: Resurgent Religion and Global Politics*. New York and London: W.W. Norton.

Vargas Llosa, M., 2012. *Notes on the Death of Culture. Essays on Spectacle and Society*. Trans. King, J. London: Faber and Faber, 2015.

Vattimo, G., 2004. *Nihilism and Emancipation: Ethics, Politics and Law*. Trans. McCuaig, W. New York: Columbia University Press.

Verhaeghe, P., 1999. "The collapse of the function of the father and its effect in gender roles." *Journal for the Psychoanalysis of Culture & Society*, 4(1), 18–31.

Verhaeghe, P., and Declercq, F., 2002. "Lacan's analytical goal: '*Le Sinthome*' or the feminine way." In: Thurston, L. (Ed.). *Essays on the Final Lacan. Re-inventing the Symptom*. New York: The Other Press, 59–83.

Vincent Peale, N., 1952. *The Power of Positive Thinking*. New York: Fawcett Crest.

Virilio, P., 2000a. *Art and Fear*. Trans. Rose, J. London and New York: Continuum.

Virilio, P., 2000b. *The Information Bomb*. London: Verso.

Virilio, P., 2001. *Virilio Live. Selected Interviews*. Armitage, J. (Ed.). London: Sage Publications.

Virilio, P., 2005. *The Original Accident.* Trans. Rose, J. London: Polity Press.
Voruz, V., and Wolf, B. (Eds) 2007. *The Later Lacan. An Introduction.* New York: The State University of New York Press.
Weatherill, R., 1994. *Cultural Collapse.* London: Free Association Books.
Weatherill, R., 1998. *The Sovereignty of Death.* London: Rebus.
Weatherill, R. (Ed.) 1999. *The Death Drive: New Life for a Dead Subject.* London: Rebus.
Weatherill, R., 2004. *Our Last Great Illusion.* Exeter: Imprint Academic.
Weatherill, R., 2011. *Forgetting Freud? Is Psychoanalysis in Retreat?* San Francisco: Academica Press.
Weatherill, R., 2016. "Turning right. Part one." *Lacunae. APPI International Journal for Lacanian Psychoanalysis,* 12, 115–24.
Weber, M., 1905 (1930). *The Protestant Ethic and the Spirit of Capitalism.* London and New York: Routledge, 1992.
Webster, R., 1995. *Why Freud Was Wrong: Sin, Science, and Psychoanalysis.* London: HarperCollins.
Weil, S., 1947. *Gravity and Grace.* Trans. Crawford, E., and von de Ruhr, M. London and New York: Routledge, 2002.
Weil, S., 1951. *Waiting for God.* New York and London: Harper, 2009.
Weil, S., 1986. *An Anthology.* London: Penguin, 2005.
Westerlund, D. (Ed.) 1996. *Questioning the Secular State: Worldwide Resurgence of Religion in Politics.* London: C. Hurst & Co.
Wilde, O., 1948. *Complete Works of Oscar Wilde.* London and Glasgow: Collins.
Wilson, J., 2014. "Counting on Billionaires," in *Jacobin, Reason in Revolt.* Available at: www.jacobinmag.com/2015/03/george-soros-philanthrocapitalism-millennium-villages/.
Winnicott, D., 1960. "Ego Distortion in Terms of the True and False Self," in Winnicott, D. *The Maturational Processes and the Facilitating Environment.* London: Hogarth, 140–52.
Winnicott, D., 1971. "Transitional Phenomena and Transitional Space," in Winnicott, D. *Playing and Reality.* London: Hogarth, 1–25.
Wolin, R., 1993. *The Heidegger Controversy: a Critical Reader.* Cambridge: MIT Press.
Wolin, R., 2004. *The Seduction of Unreason. The Intellectual Romance with Fascism from Nietzsche to Postmodernism.* Princetown and Oxford: Princetown University Press.
Wolin, R., 2012. *The Wind from the East. French Intellectuals, the Cultural Revolution, and the Legacy of the 1960s.* Princetown and Oxford: Princetown University Press.
Wolin, R., 2014. Heidegger cited in, "National Socialism, world Jewry, and the history of being: Heidegger's black notebooks." Available at: http://jewishreviewofbooks.com/articles/993/national-socialism-world-jewry-and-the-history-of-being-heideggers-black-notebooks/.
Wright, E., 2000. *Postmodern Encounters. Lacan and Postfeminism.* London: Icon Books.
Zafiropoulos, M., 2010. *Lacan and Levi-Strauss or The Return to Freud (1951–1957).* London: Karnac.
Žižek, S., 2000. *The Fragile Absolute.* London and New York: Verso.
Žižek, S., 2001. *On Belief.* London: Routledge.
Žižek, S., 2002. *Welcome to the Desert of the Real.* London and New York: Verso.
Žižek, S., 2004 *Iraq: The Borrowed Kettle.* London and New York: Verso.
Žižek, S., 2006 *The Parallax View.* Cambridge, MA: MIT Press.
Žižek, S., 2008. *Organs Without Bodies. Gilles Deleuze.* Available at: www.lacan.com/zizsalsation.html.
Žižek, S., 2009. *Violence.* London: Profile Books.
Žižek, S., 2014. *Trouble in Paradise. From the End of History to the End of Capitalism.* London and New York: Penguin Books, 2015.
Zola, E., 1885. *Germinal.* Trans. Tancock, L. London: Penguin, 1994.
Zupančič, A., 2000. *Ethics of the Real: Kant and Lacan.* London and New York: Verso.

INDEX

For Product Safety Concerns and Information please contact our EU representative GPSR@taylorandfrancis.com
Taylor & Francis Verlag GmbH, Kaufingerstraße 24, 80331 München, Germany

www.ingramcontent.com/pod-product-compliance
Lightning Source LLC
LaVergne TN
LVHW021123300926
849160LV00010B/834

* 9 7 8 1 1 3 8 6 9 2 3 5 0 *